75

# REFLECTIONS
# OF EDEN

# REFLECTIONS OF EDEN

## My Years with the Orangutans of Borneo

Biruté M. F. Galdikas

LITTLE, BROWN AND COMPANY

BOSTON     NEW YORK     TORONTO     LONDON

To *Pak* Bohap,
Binti, Fred, and Jane
and
to Cara, Carl, and Cindy

First Edition

Excerpt from "Little Gidding" in *Four Quartets,* Copyright 1943 by T. S. Eliot and renewed 1971 by
Esme Valerie Eliot, reprinted by permission of Harcourt Brace & Company.

*Library of Congress Cataloging-in-Publication Data*

Galdikas, Biruté Marija Filomena.
    Reflections of Eden: my years with the orangutans of Borneo /
Biruté M.F. Galdikas. — 1st ed.
        p.    cm.
    ISBN 0-316-30181-7
    1. Galdikas, Biruté Marija Filomena. 2. Orangutan — Behavior —
Research — Borneo. 3. Primatologists — Biography. 4. Women
primatologists — Biography. I. Title.
QL31.G34A3 1995
599.8'092 — dc20
[B]                                                93.22948


10  9  8  7  6  5  4  3  2  1

MV-NY
*Published simultaneously in Canada*
*by Little, Brown & Company (Canada) Limited*

Printed in the United States of America

# CONTENTS

# AUTHOR'S NOTE

WHILE I WAS WORKING on this book, my editor in New York called me at my home in Borneo, in the village of Pasir Panjang. An elderly man, a Dayak from the interior of Kalimantan, came into the room. Hearing me speak and seeing no one else, he assumed that I was addressing him and sat down to talk. This man had never left Borneo, and probably had never seen a telephone before. How could I explain that I was talking to someone halfway around the world, someone who was sitting at a desk with a computer in an office on the twentieth floor, about a book that would be read primarily by people who had seen orangutans only in zoos, and the rain forest only on their TV screens?

This man grew up in a Borneo that no longer exists, a Borneo of seemingly endless tropical rain forests, abundant wildlife, and isolated villages, where people lived much as their forebears had, hunting and planting crops on fields slashed out of the forest, practicing an ancient religion. This was the Borneo I found when I arrived in 1971. At that time there were almost no scheduled flights to and from Borneo, no roads, no electricity, no regular mail or magazines, no telephones or television, no hotel or water taxis on the river, no national park. A few people in some of the coastal towns were somewhat in touch with world events. But much of Borneo was still isolated and pristine.

I had come to Borneo to study orangutans, the last arboreal great ape on this planet. When I went into the field, virtually nothing was known about the life of orangutans in the wild. Several researchers had conducted one- or two-year field studies. But the terrain in Borneo and Sumatra is difficult, and orangutans, living high in the forest canopy, are elusive. These researchers had not been able to habituate the red apes or to follow the same individuals for any length of time. Science had "snapshots," but little information on orang-utan life histories or orangutan social organization.

My first years in the field were years of discovery, when merely finding a wild orangutan was exciting, when following an orangutan for a week or more was a triumph, when almost everything I learned about orangutans was new. The boundaries — and the purpose — of the Tanjung Puting Reserve were ill-defined. (Only in 1982 was Tanjung Puting upgraded to national park sta-tus.) Local people, including high-level government officials, openly kept wild-born orangutans as pets.

When I sat down to write this book, I tried to re-create Borneo and the forests as they were then. I introduce the orangutans, wild and ex-captive, who introduced me to the orangutans' world, each a unique individual at a different stage in life. I describe the people who have influenced and helped me over the years — Louis Leakey, Jane Goodall, and Dian Fossey, my first husband, Rod Brindamour, and Mr. and Mrs. Binti, Dr. Soedjarwo, my husband, *Pak* Bohap, and many other Indonesians. I relive the joys and sorrows of rescuing wildborn captive orangutans and returning them to the wild. I talk about what I have learned about orangutans, and what orangutans have taught me about human nature.

Today, in 1994, the situation facing wild orangutans and the issues facing those of us who study and seek to protect great apes are far more complicated than when I set out for Borneo. As a result of poaching and habitat destruction, all of the great apes are endangered. Indeed, some would say that all pri-mates — including monkeys, apes, and humans — are imperiled. Understand-ing is the first step to action. I hope my book will help people understand orangutans and their tropical rain forest world, a world which is in grave dan-ger of vanishing forever.

# REFLECTIONS OF EDEN

# 1
# AKMAD

And the end of all our exploring
Will be to arrive where we started
And know the place for the first time.

— *T. S. Eliot*

AKMAD AND I were alone by the edge of the great forest of Borneo, the second largest continuous stretch of tropical rain forest in the world. Akmad had just given birth, and her gentle, elongated orangutan face with its delicately etched features looked tired. The light of the late afternoon sun shone eerily through Akmad's long auburn hair, silhouetting her form in an incandescent halo.

I wanted to photograph the tiny, wrinkled, nude face of Akmad's newborn infant. I moved forward on my knees and elbows and focused on the baby's elfin face pressed to her mother's bosom. Moving my hand gently, I shifted the little infant. Her bright orange hair, newly dry from the fluids of birth, was soft and fluffy and contrasted with the deep, almost mahogany red of her mother's longer, coarser coat. Despite my touch, the infant rested quietly in her mother's arms. Akmad's liquid brown eyes remained expressionless. She seemed unaware of my hand on her newborn. Her arm brushed carelessly across my leg as she reached for a pineapple, almost as if I didn't exist. The magical soft light, peculiar to dusk in Borneo, etched the scene in gold, a moment transfixed in time.

Other orangutans began to emerge from the trees and descend to the iron-wood causeway that runs from Camp Leakey, my research base deep in the forest, to the Sekonyer Kanan River six hundred feet away. Mr. Achyar, the camp feeder, appeared pushing a cart of food. In his forties and very slight, like a shadow, he walked with the slow, deliberate gait typical of older Indonesians. His Green Bay Packers T-shirt, faded from the equatorial sun and countless sudsy beatings in the name of cleanliness, was a reminder that the outside world intruded even here in Borneo.

Mr. Achyar stooped low as he passed by us, twisting sideways politely, his right arm and shoulder bent forward in a pose reminiscent of a figure on an ancient Egyptian mural. His bow reflected the courtesy typical of traditional Dayaks. Paradoxically, these most gentle and courteous of any people were once fierce headhunters, the "wild men of Borneo."

The spell continued as Mr. Achyar began chanting. He called the orang-utans in a singsong voice, like a supplicant in an ancient ritual, the names of ex-captive orangutans like the names of spirits. His voice rose over the trees, "Pola, Kusasi, Hani, Kuspati, Siswoyo."

Mr. Achyar had been feeding the mature ex-captive orangutans at Camp Leakey for seven years. Of all my Dayak assistants, he was the one most trusted by the orangutans. Many Indonesians called him a *pawong,* a person who has the power to call wild animals to him. He had no children of his own and had developed a special relationship with the orangutans, referring to them as his children. His devotion to them was obvious as he moved among them in a careful, solicitous way, making certain each received an equal share of rice, bananas, and pineapple. Although Mr. Achyar was slim and slightly stooped, in this particular orangutan hierarchy he was the dominant male. Gigantic wild male orangutans who occasionally came to camp, attracted by orangutan fe-males, deferred to him.

Dusk ends suddenly in the tropics, and I felt hurried. I twirled the focusing mechanism on my Nikon, clicking rapidly. I wanted to record this moment, to celebrate this as yet unnamed female infant on the day of her birth.

To take a clearer picture, I moved back from Akmad and her baby and crouched nine or ten feet away. A piece of dry fern had caught in the infant's hair, obscuring her face. Mr. Achyar was nearby cutting pineapples into quar-ters. He was closer to Akmad than I. Speaking in the hushed voice that the moment dictated, I asked him to take the fern from the infant's hair. Nestled on her mother's side, the baby was dozing peacefully, her miniature fingers clenched tightly around strands of her mother's hair.

Mr. Achyar gently approached Akmad and slowly reached over to remove the fern. Akmad seemed oblivious to his approach. My fingers closed around the lens, preparing for another shot. The golden light still held.

Never, not in a millennium, could Mr. Achyar or I have anticipated Akmad's reaction to his simple gesture. His fingers never touched the infant's head. Without warning, Akmad recoiled. Baring her teeth, she exploded. Her hair went erect, tripling her size, and she lunged at Mr. Achyar, her fangs glistening, the soft expression on her face gone. Not large for an adult female orangutan, Akmad weighed about seventy pounds. Yet leveraged, taut muscles provide even female orangutans with the strength of perhaps five men. An orangutan female's teeth can rip off a person's scalp or arm. Had Mr. Achyar not been so agile, he would have been badly mangled. However, he leaped back in one motion. Akmad did not pursue her attack. Her point made, she simply sat down and picked up the pineapple she had been eating. Her face was once again expressionless.

Shocked, Mr. Achyar stared at Akmad as if his own child had turned on him. "Not once, not ever before," he gasped in bewilderment. "I have never been attacked by an orangutan before. They are all my children and my friends." He sighed, "Akmad is the gentlest of them all. I never expected her to attack me."

I moved over to Akmad and gazed at the infant nestled against her. Without hesitating, I reached out and pulled the fern from her infant's hair. Akmad did not even blink to acknowledge me. Her eyes were focused elsewhere, somewhere in the distance. She was back in the universe orangutans inhabit.

Emboldened, I carefully moved the infant into a better position for a photograph in the fading light. As I gently tugged at her, the infant squealed. Akmad's opaque, inner-directed gaze did not change. I glanced at Mr. Achyar, who was watching me intently. The wonder on his face was palpable. I, too, was amazed. Up to that moment I had never imagined the degree to which Akmad accepted me.

When I arrived in Kalimantan, or Indonesian Borneo, fifteen years earlier in 1971, my goal was to study wild orangutans in their natural habitat. But almost immediately I became involved in the rescue and rehabilitation of wildborn orangutans who had been captured by humans — to keep as pets or to sell to zoos, circuses, and laboratories. I have always felt strongly that saving orangutans is as important as studying them. By working to return captive orangutans to the wild, I was trying to eliminate the captive orangutan trade

in the area and so protect the wild orangutans. My work rescuing and rehabilitating ex-captive, wildborn orangutans has always been distinct from my main
work, studying wild orangutans. Over the years these separate endeavors
sometimes rivaled and sometimes reinforced one another but never became
blurred.

Akmad was one of the first of many ex-captives I rescued from captivity
and returned to the forest. Although she had been independent for some years,
she occasionally left the trees and came to camp for the feeding we provided
daily.

I had not realized until that moment how much I identified with Akmad and
how deeply our lives were linked. Akmad started her life as a wild orangutan
and now had returned to the forest. But part of her passage through life was
totally different from the experience of orangutans who spend their entire lives
in the great forest of Borneo. Akmad had been kidnapped by humans in her
youth. When we rescued her, she had elected to live in my camp for a time,
as my adopted orangutan "daughter." But gradually she had returned to the
forest and the freedom that were her natural rights.

Like Akmad, I, too, followed a life path that differed radically from those
of my family, my childhood companions, and my university friends and acquaintances. I left the experiences and culture of my youth to live as an adult
in Kalimantan. Yet my life in Kalimantan gave me a deeper understanding of
the life and youth I left behind. Like Akmad, I had been touched by two
worlds, that of humans and that of orangutans. I gained experience in the
forest, learned from the orangutans and from the Dayaks, who are the aboriginal people of Borneo, and then, like the T. S. Eliot poem, came back to where
I started. I rediscovered the woods where I played as a child in Canada, the
forests of my Lithuanian forebears, and ultimately the tropical rain forests
where our ancestors evolved — our Garden of Eden.

The choices that had been forced on Akmad paralleled the paths that I had
chosen consciously and voluntarily. Akmad and I were kindred spirits.

I first saw "Akmad" only a month after I arrived in Borneo, at the door of
our hut, clinging to the arm of our assistant, Mr. Hamzah. As he brought
her in, Mr. Hamzah lifted his arm and unrolled her like a paper towel
spilling onto the floor. She stood up, still holding on to his arm above her.
Her long face was serene, the fluid brown of her eyes veiled by thick

lashes. My first thought was, "Why, she looks just like a Parisienne! A lady from Paris!"

The weeks that followed confirmed this initial impression; Akmad was a lady. She had a gentle way about her. She never ran, she always walked. She never grabbed, she always reached. Even her squeal had a daintiness that the vocalizations of other orangutans lacked.

How human she appeared, like an orange gnome, with her intelligent, quietly inquisitive face. Like all orangutans, Akmad was covered with dark orange hair. Although coarser and thicker than ours, the distribution is similar. Her face, her palms, and the soles of her feet were hairless, while her small naked ears, almost identical in shape to human ears, protruded from the hair on her head. When Akmad stood up, however, her long arms dangled to her knees while her legs were proportionately shorter than ours and slightly bowed. What distinguished Akmad's body most from a human shape was her rotund belly that made her look perpetually pregnant, although at the time she was far too young to bear offspring. Had Akmad been an infant, her eyes and mouth would have been encircled by patches of whitish skin. Akmad's face was already dark, although not as black as it would become once she reached adulthood.

The look on Akmad's face was aware but self-contained. Whatever emotions she might have been feeling, her soft brown eyes revealed nothing. Orangutans, in general, are even-tempered and serene compared to their volatile African cousins, chimpanzees. Even among members of her own tranquil species, Akmad stood out as being exceptionally calm. We named her after an official of the Indonesian Institute of Sciences, Ms. Sjamsiah Akmad, who had been kind and helpful when we first arrived in Jakarta.

At this time Akmad was about six years old, the orangutan equivalent of a young girl. Her sweetness was all the more impressive given her history, for she had been kidnapped under what must have been brutal circumstances.

Several weeks after we arrived in Borneo, we heard from local people that nearby loggers had captured a young orangutan and were holding her in a rough cage at their camp just outside the Tanjung Puting Reserve, where we were based. Killing, capturing, or selling a wild orangutan was illegal in Indonesia, but the law was rarely enforced. I was determined to change this.

My husband in those early years was Rod Brindamour (known locally as "Mr. Rod"). A take-charge kind of person, Rod always seemed to display the self-assurance and determination essential to official transactions. While I went to the forest to observe wild orangutans, Rod set out with Mr. Hamzah and a young official from the Forestry Department to confiscate the orphaned orangutan, much as a North American social worker might remove a child from a home where she was being neglected or abused.

In Indonesia there is a phrase *"negara hukum,"* meaning that Indonesia is a "country of laws." It is also a country where power, position, and connections command respect. At this time, Forestry Department officials were empowered to enforce forestry laws directly, without assistance from the police. Many of these laws, such as those protecting orangutans, stemmed from Dutch colonial days; they were not grounded in local norms and customs. But the head of the Forestry Department in Kalimantan, Mr. Widajat, had taken us under his wing and made it clear that he expected his officers to be helpful to us. Any Indonesian under his command would feel compelled to assist us, regardless of personal attitude.

Mr. Hamzah and Rod arrived at the logging camp, the reluctant local forestry officer in tow. Even at this late stage, the official queried doubtfully, "Are you sure that I must confiscate this orangutan?"

Without hesitation Rod declared, "You must."

The officer summoned up his most official manner and announced, "It is against the law to keep an orangutan without special permission." Akmad was released into Rod's custody.

Rod did not learn the exact circumstances under which Akmad had been orphaned, but the only way to capture a wild orangutan is to kill a mother and abduct her infant or juvenile. Akmad's mother must have been killed by the loggers. Firearms are under tight control in Indonesia, available only to the army and police, but the guards at the logging camp probably had guns to protect the cut timber and to provide fresh meat. Most often the guards hunted deer and wild pigs. But the logging operations had cut wide paths through the forest, forcing orangutans into the open where they became "fair game."

An equally unpleasant possibility was that Akmad's mother had been murdered for the express purpose of acquiring a young orangutan for sale abroad. To local entrepreneurs, baby orangutans meant easy cash. They could buy an orangutan from loggers or from Dayak hunters for a hundred dollars (several months' wages in Borneo at the time), then sell the prize to a sea captain or sailor with connections abroad for two or three times that amount. The infant orangutan would then be crated, stowed below deck, and often kept for days without food or water until the ship was outside Indonesian waters. For every five baby orangutans smuggled out of the country, at least three died en route. But the potential profit made the risks worthwhile. In Hong Kong or Singapore, an orangutan sold for five thousand dollars or more. The ape trade was an open secret in those days. Asian zoos were still buying wild orangutans, as were private collectors in both Asia and the West.

There are no photographic records of an orangutan kidnapping. But missionaries who work in the interior of Borneo have seen and described what happens. Once a mother-infant pair is spotted, the rest apparently is very easy. When a mother orangutan is threatened, her infant or juvenile invariably rushes to her side and clings tightly to her body. This slows the mother down, making her an easy target. Spotting a group of humans, Akmad's mother probably vocalized and dropped branches on them in a display of fear. Hearing her kiss-squeaks and hoots, Akmad rushed to her mother. One or two well-placed shots, and the mother would have crashed to the ground, clutching for branches, screaming as she fell. If the shots hadn't killed her, the fall might have. Rather than fleeing, Akmad would have clung to her dead mother's body until she was pried loose. She might have tried to bite her attackers, but at twenty or twenty-five pounds she could not have put up much resistance. The final horror, as reported by missionaries, might have been when Akmad, secured with a rope or chain, watched as her mother was skinned, gutted, and prepared for consumption. In some cases the mother's flesh is cut up and laid out to dry, for "orangutan jerky," and the infant is kept and fattened up for a stew.

On her first night with us, I lured Akmad into the jackfruit trees in front of our thatch-roofed hut. Without much fuss, Akmad climbed into the trees, made a nest, and fell asleep. Although she easily could have fled, she chose to stay. When I began fixing breakfast the next morning, she climbed down and joined me.

This was not always my experience with ex-captives her age; some escaped at the first opportunity. Although no longer an infant, Akmad attached herself to me, the only woman in camp. She sometimes clung to my side, insisted that I share my cups of sweetened tea with her, and followed me wherever I went. Akmad had only one ambition: to be my foster child.

Of all the orangutans who later joined our household, she was the most ladylike. Our hut, made entirely of materials from the forest, was ideal for orangutans; nowadays it would be called "orangutan-friendly." Other ex-captives would sit in the rafters, looking down like brooding buzzards. Akmad always had a benign expression. Other ex-captives tore at the bark walls and ripped apart the nipa-frond roof, as if the hut were just another piece of the forest. Not Akmad. When the other orangutans took a tin cup of milk into the rafters, they would simply drop the cup when they were finished, as if dropping the skin or pits of fruit to the forest floor. Akmad, however, would neatly balance the cup on a cross beam. A collection of cups would accumulate in the rafters until Rod climbed up to retrieve them.

Most mornings Rod and I would leave Camp Leakey shortly after dawn, and walk the length of the *ladang,* or abandoned dry-rice field, that stretched as a tongue of solid ground through the deep swamp on either side and into the great forest beyond. In the forest, I would search for wild orangutans, walking as many as ten miles a day, while Rod cut trails. It was difficult and grueling work. I frequently arrived home at Camp Leakey exhausted, discouraged, drenched in sweat, and convinced that the wild orangutans had all moved out of the study area simply to spite me. What a pleasure it was to find Akmad waiting. Most afternoons she shared my standard meal of rice, sardines, and sweetened tea.

Several months after Akmad arrived, we decided to relocate our living quarters. I wanted to spend more time in the forest and less time traveling back and forth. I had hoped to take Akmad with us, but she was not in camp the day we moved. Reluctantly, we left without her.

At last I began locating wild orangutans more or less regularly, and felt confident enough to move back to Camp Leakey. Three months had passed. The only trace of Akmad was a bright red cocoa can bearing the trademark of a nun with a flying headdress. As if representing Akmad's reaction to my unexplained disappearance, the can was embellished with orangutan canine marks and tossed on my mattress under the light pink mosquito net that hung from the rafters.

As the months slipped by, I worried about Akmad and wondered what had happened to her. She was old enough to survive on her own, but she had seemed too dependent, almost too "domestic," for life in the forest. I feared the worst. Then, one morning, a familiar orangutan face peered out of the trees by our hut. By this time our separation totaled six months. Akmad's face had thinned, her cheekbones stood out, and her eyes dominated her face.

I quickly mixed up some full-cream milk-powder (which was the only kind available in Kalimantan at that time) and water and handed her the cup. She hungrily drained the cup, then handed it back to me for more. She drank three full cups before she finally put it gently on the table where I was sitting. That she came back indicated that she still needed a mother figure. But Akmad had survived a full six months in the forest, as a wild orangutan!

Gradually Akmad began spending less time in camp and more time on her own. But she never gave up her place in camp. Shy and docile most of the time, she greeted each new female ex-captive we acquired with a nip (or worse), as if to inform her who was boss. Even now, more than twenty years later, Akmad remains the dominant female in Camp Leakey. This small, quiet female — the type who modestly drops her eyes to the ground when others walk by — holds sway over all the other ex-captive females. Perhaps her lack of bluster contributes to the respect which the others have for her. Or perhaps it is the simple fact that she was the first, the "nest-mother" so to speak, and all later females acknowledge this.

My relationship with Akmad grew less intense as she grew older and appeared in camp less frequently. At one point she was gone for a whole year. On the rare occasion when she did visit camp she always hurried back to the forest to make her nest before dark. Then the nightmares started.

One calm, pitch-black tropical night, an orangutan swung onto our house screaming in terror. I couldn't imagine what was going on. Infant orangutans often squealed during the night. But adult orangutans are adapted to very old rhythms; they go to sleep at nightfall and rise with the sun. As a rule, they sleep quite soundly during the night. They sometimes snore.

Rod wakened with a start. "What on earth is that?" he shouted. He grabbed a cattle prod. Dr. William Lemmon, a clinical psychologist who had established a colony of captive chimpanzees in Oklahoma, had insisted that a cattle prod was essential equipment for anyone who worked with adult great apes. This expert had showered us with dire warnings about how adult chimpanzees, suddenly, without warning, become aggressive and dangerous. He was concerned that we understand the "real" truth about what happens when great apes turn adult. He was so convincing that we actually brought a cattle prod to Borneo and, for a time, kept it at the ready.

Jumping from our bed, Rod opened the front door and thrust the cattle prod into the damp darkness. Suddenly he gasped, "Oh, my God, it's Akmad!"

He withdrew the prod, opened the door farther, and Akmad rushed in, still screaming. She climbed to the top of our store room, settled onto its flat ceiling, and promptly fell asleep. Rod, too, fell back to sleep almost instantly. But like most mothers, I lay awake puzzling over her behavior. She must have been in the grip of some terrifying nightmare, so terrifying that when she awakened in her nest alone, she needed me, her adopted mother. What thoughts, what frightening memories, whirled behind her tranquil eyes and sweet expression I could only guess.

The next morning Akmad slipped out the front door when I opened it for her at dawn. As noisily as she had arrived, she departed silently.

A few weeks later, a shrieking Akmad materialized a second time in the middle of the night. It had been almost six years since Akmad had attempted to sleep in our bed. Now she became clingy — as clingy as she had been when we first rescued her from the logging camp. She would come and sit on my lap and hold on to me for dear life. I didn't know whether to be flattered or frightened, wondering what was causing her terror.

This clingy stage ended as abruptly as it had begun, about six months later. Akmad stopped coming to camp simply to be held. When she saw me she would walk by with barely a glimmer of recognition. I began to suspect that her nightmares were related to her maturation. By now Akmad was thirteen or fourteen years old and frequently returned from her wilderness travels in the company of subadult males. She was probably beginning to mate, though two years would pass before she became pregnant. Like humans, female orangutans go through a period of adolescent sterility. Perhaps, like some humans, she was ambivalent about coming of age.

At about age fifteen, Akmad found a mate and became pregnant. She gave birth when she was about sixteen. Before her first infant, "Arnold," was born, a large four-year-old female we named "Carey" came to camp. Recently orphaned and apparently lonely, Carey tried to get a human to adopt her. By now I had my own son, Binti, and could not be a surrogate to a clinging, demanding orphan orangutan. No other person in camp volunteered for the job.

Rejected by humans, Carey tried orangutans. Her first target was "Sobiarso," a fluffy, engaging adolescent who captivated visitors with her energy and charm. Following one of the "I'm-a-poor-orphan" advances, I saw the usually very sweet Sobiarso smash Carey onto the boards of the causeway, then run away to escape further advances. Carey looked ruffled but unhurt by this fierce rejection. I also saw Carey attempt to cling to a subadult male. He pried her off his body as if she were a disgusting parasite.

Finally Carey turned to Akmad. Despite a period of initial rejection (I once counted as Akmad peeled Carey off her body seventy times in a mere thirty minutes), Carey persisted. In a resigned fashion, perhaps with as much anguish and doubt as I had felt toward my orphaned orangutan babies, Akmad finally accepted the young female. Orangutans learn by imitation, just as we humans do. Akmad was mothered by a stranger of another species; now she became a mother to a stranger of her own species.

Once Carey sensed Akmad's good nature (and her no doubt abundant maternal hormones), the die was cast. For the rest of her pregnancy, Akmad carried Carey everywhere, even allowing her to suckle. An orangutan pregnancy lasts eight months, and Carey had been suckling for several months by the time Arnold was born. Akmad gave birth in a nest on a low-lying branch in a tree near the edge of camp. I climbed as high as I could into a nearby tree to watch. Akmad seemed tired after the birth and stayed in the nest for a long time. Usually the mother consumes the placenta, but in this case Carey, not Akmad, devoured the afterbirth. Carey's face and hands were smeared with Arnold's life blood. In my mind, this became symbolic of their whole relationship.

I began to worry about how Akmad would cope. Ordinarily, an orangutan does not give birth until her previous offspring is large enough to be independent. As I discovered after many years of research, the average birth span for wild orangutans is almost eight years. Nobody has reported twin orangutan infants in the wild. Nor has anyone reported a wild female adopting another female's infant. I wondered what price Akmad would pay for taking care of two babies.

I don't think I have ever seen a more harried mother — human or orangutan — than Akmad. She would come into camp, the usually neat-looking hair framing her forehead in disarray, pouches under her eyes, and her normally benign expression strained. My eyes would shoot down to her breasts, where Carey and Arnold both sucked fiercely, their bodies swinging below her nipples as she walked. Both infants grew and thrived; it was Akmad who carried the burden. Often I would watch her climbing ever so slowly to the forest canopy 150 feet up, one infant on her shoulder and the other clinging to her side.

As Arnold grew, he seemed remarkably independent for his age. Infant orangutans rarely leave their mother's body for the first year of their life, and usually stay within touching distance for another year after that. Even at five years they do not let their mother out of their sight. But at age three, Arnold sometimes lagged far behind as Akmad moved on the ground in the seasonally dried-up swamps near camp. Perhaps he was imitating his older stepsister,

Carey, or perhaps his mother carried him less often to avoid having to lug Carey as well. One thing was certain: Arnold was the one who paid the price of the adoption, not Carey.

When Arnold was a little over four years old, he vanished. The day after he disappeared, Akmad came to camp to feed in the late afternoon. I was watching her when she suddenly dropped her bananas. She climbed into the tallest tree overlooking the bridge and began a series of actions that, in the orangutan lexicon, expressed severe annoyance and distress. She started with kiss-squeaks of irritation, followed by a series of low, prolonged grunts. Her eyes fixed on something in the distance with an almost maniacal stare. Then she started breaking branches. With enormous anger she hurled them toward the distant object. This display went on for over an hour. Not once did Akmad allow her eyes to stray from that single point of concentration.

I walked around trying to see what was upsetting Akmad so much. In the distance a crested serpent eagle sat with a snake in its talons. But this was not an uncommon sight in Kalimantan, and the bird was behind Akmad, not in front of her. I was mystified. Ex-captive orangutans were slowly congregating toward the end of the bridge where Mr. Achyar was dispensing the day's meal, rice and bananas. The other orangutans were busy eating; everything seemed normal. I kept looking for the object of Akmad's violent display. All I could see was a glimpse of a large forest pig in the distance.

Close up, Bornean wild pigs are an odd sight. A dirty pale white, they can stand three and a half feet at the shoulder. The end of their long snout is cloaked with a line of rough bristles, which give these animals the name "bearded pig," and their tusks curve upward cruelly over their top lip. The pigs' day vision is not very good, and their beady little eyes peep out almost grotesquely from the layers of lard and gristle that cover their skull.

Visitors often exclaim about the size of the bearded pigs, claiming they look almost like rhinoceroses. Indeed, the last known Sumatran rhinoceros in the province of Kalimantan Tengah (Central Indonesian Borneo) was shot by a Dayak hunter who thought he was tracking a wild pig. Only after he had downed the animal with a homemade shotgun and run to examine the carcass did he realize that he had killed a rhinoceros. The Sumatran rhinoceros is the smallest of its kind, standing four feet at the shoulder.

In the Bornean rain forest, pigs are primarily fruit eaters, congregating under trees whose ripened fruit has dropped to the ground. On occasion, however, they kill small prey, including ducks, chickens, and even tethered goats. I had heard stories of local people being sheared in half by the pig's razor-sharp tusks. But pigs often appeared around our camp, and most of the time, neither humans nor orangutans paid them much heed.

Akmad abruptly moved off into the treetops near camp. She had eaten nothing. Gradually the other orangutans left, one by one. The bridge, minutes earlier the scene of frenzied activity, once again became an oasis of calm. Only the sound of cracking branches betrayed the presence of orangutans building night nests nearby. Mr. Achyar walked toward me, silently pushing the cart with the remains of the evening meal.

"Mr. Achyar," I said, breaking the silence, "what happened to Arnold?" I paused, studying his face. "Do you know what happened to Arnold?"

Mr. Achyar answered sadly, "I believe he was eaten by the pig, *Ibu.*" He used the term of respect for women in Indonesia.

"Are you sure?" I asked, not wanting to believe his words.

"I am sure," he replied, his face hardened by an inner pain I was feeling as well. "I didn't see it, but why else would Arnold be gone?" Mr. Achyar paused.

"I am sure," he repeated. "*Permissi, Ibu,*" he said slowly, and then he picked up the handles of the cart and continued moving down the bridge toward camp.

I was left alone with my thoughts and the darkening sky. Mr. Achyar was right; nothing else could explain Akmad's uncharacteristic behavior. I knew. I remembered the last time I had seen Arnold, way behind Carey and Akmad, in a vulnerable position on the ground with no large trees nearby. A bearded pig, with his enormous jaws and massive teeth, could have swallowed Arnold (who had weighed less than twenty pounds) almost whole.

Carey's persistent demands on Akmad had led, indirectly, to Arnold's death. I couldn't blame Carey; she had only sought a mother to replace the one killed by humans when she herself was captured. But nonetheless Arnold was dead, sacrificed to Akmad's intense efforts to rear her own offspring plus an unrelated foster child. Having nurtured so many orphaned infant orangutans myself, I understood Akmad's behavior. There is something so compelling, so insistent, about their demands that it is difficult *not* to sacrifice one's comfort and personal life in their behalf. How many times had I given them my food, let them come between me and my husband, almost crowding us off our mattress? Ultimately, Arnold was the victim of the illegal trade in wild orangutans that produced Carey and other orphans like her. I told myself that I had chosen to take part in their rescue, but perhaps I had merely succumbed to my maternal instincts. Were Akmad and I so different? That evening, as on many occasions, I thought not.

❖

Now Akmad had given birth again, and I was photographing her newborn infant. Akmad was free; she had an infant who was free. In a moment of absolute clarity I realized the intensity of the bond that I had forged with Akmad. She had singled me out for this unique historic honor: I was a female of another species, but as her bonded mother I had been granted the privilege of sharing her newborn infant. I was probably the first human being in history who was truly an orangutan infant's grandmother.

The light shifted, putting an end to my musing. The otherworldly glow that illuminated the causeway and gave the line of forest trees in the distance an almost surreal beauty vanished. Akmad's eyes went upward. The machinelike rhythm of the evening cicadas and the fading light were signals as old as time. Slowly she scanned the distant forest. It was time to nest. Without even a glance in my direction, she ambled away.

It had taken me more than a decade of living with orangutans, day by day in their great forest home, to understand finally that orangutans are not just simpler versions of ourselves. All those years that orangutans had walked by me, seemingly oblivious, I had despaired of ever reaching them. For a split second, Akmad had allowed me a clear glimpse of her universe. And yet, without knowing it, I already had been allowed into that world years before. What I had taken as indifference and rejection was the orangutan expression of acceptance. I had measured orangutans by human standards of sociability, and had misunderstood. In that moment everything I had been through — the heat, the mud, the humidity, the torrential rains, the fire ants, the leeches, the cobras, pythons, and pit vipers, the fevers, the deaths, the frustrations — became insignificant. I knew that my journey, my personal odyssey into the uncharted depths of the rain forest and the orangutan mind, started years earlier, had truly begun.

Orangutans reflect, to some degree, the innocence we humans left behind in Eden, before our social organization, bipedalism, and toolmaking gave us "dominion over" the planet. Thus, understanding orangutans gives us a clouded, partial glimpse into what we were before we became fully human. Such a partial glimpse is the best we can hope for until time machines are invented that will actually take us back to face our ancestors in the flesh, to smell their sweat and to hear their voices.

I had understood orangutans intuitively without realizing that I understood them. Now, that intuition crystalized. By giving Akmad her freedom and encouraging her independence, I had forged the deepest possible bond, that of a female and her adult daughter. Reintegrating ex-captives into the wild orangutan population had been my ultimate goal. I wanted them to forget the time they had spent in captivity, the period when they depended on humans. But being human, I could not avoid a twinge of loss when they disappeared into the forest. It was a feeling not unlike that mothers feel when a child leaves for college: success and relief, mixed with nostalgia. Yet the distance was so much greater. In returning to the forest, the ex-captive orangutans were crossing back over the line that has divided our two species for millennia. Their life with us would become a remembered dream, I imagined, sometimes joyful and sometimes terrifying. Irrationally, I had joined the mothers who complain, "They never call, they never write." But now I saw that Akmad remembered, in her own, and very special, orangutan way.

I continued sitting on the causeway long after darkness fell, thinking about what name I should give Akmad's newborn. The name had to begin with "A"; this was to keep members of Akmad's and other family groups easily identifiable. I thought of my human family back in North America, so far from the forests of Southeast Asia. I thought of my sister. Her beautiful, kind face appeared before me: in her gentleness she was much like Akmad. I didn't have the time to write to her as often as I would like, but I thought of her often. Aldona. . . . I named the tiny orangutan infant "Aldona."

A year passed before I had close contact with Akmad again. I was sitting on the bridge, the same bridge where I had photographed her newborn infant. It was feeding time. Unexpectedly Akmad materialized from the forest. She came straight over to me, sat down, and leaned into me as she ate. She stayed there, leaning lightly against my side, for more than fifteen minutes. When she finished eating her dark brown eyes flickered over my face, as if I held only momentary interest for her. Then she stood up, adjusted her infant with my sister's name, Aldona, on her head as though the one-year-old were an oversize Easter bonnet, and moved away.

The buzz of the evening cicadas evaporated into the humidity as Akmad slowly made her nest in the nearby canopy. I felt blessed. Twice that year Akmad had acknowledged, however briefly, the relationship we had shared more than fifteen years earlier. Now I understood how for orangutans, honed by countless generations of living mostly alone in the canopy of the dank, dark forest, volumes could reside in a glance. Orangutans do not need to endlessly test and reaffirm their relationships, as chimpanzees, gorillas, and especially humans do. It had taken me fifteen years to understand that for orangutans, a bond once forged is forever.

# 2

# NATURAL SELECTION

We wonder, ever wonder, why we find us here!

— *Thomas Hardy*

Humanity has in the course of time had to endure
from the hands of science two great outrages upon
its naive self-love. The first was when it realized that
our earth was not the center of the universe, but only a
speck in a world-system of a magnitude hardly conceivable. . . .
The second was when biological research robbed man
of his particular privilege of having been
specially created, and relegated him to a
descent from the animal world.

— *Sigmund Freud*

---

As FAR BACK as I can remember, I have been fascinated with human origins. I continually asked: How do humans fit into the universe? Who were our ancestors? Where and how did they live? When did they live? Where does humankind stand in relation to the whole? Where do we stand in relation to our nearest living relatives, the great apes? As a child, I thought about the question that has puzzled us all. Why do humans exist in the first place?

It was this question, this wish to understand human origins, that led me to study the orangutans in the dense jungles of Central Borneo. From my reading, I understood that our earliest ancestors left the tropical rain forests to forge their hominid destiny on the plains and the savannas of our planet. But it was what our ancestors left behind that interested me. What they left in the relics of those ancient tropical rain forests, in our original Eden, were the great apes: chimpanzees, gorillas, and orangutans.

Even today as I write, deep within the forests of Borneo and Sumatra, living in the shadow and the shade of the canopy are these creatures, the orang-utans. They are our relatives; they are our kin. The kin who never left the Garden of Eden and thus never lost their innocence, kin who never made complex tools, never used fire, and never went to war. These are kin who seek no masters, kin who do not need to be redeemed, kin who approximate the ancestors who are no longer on this earth, and kin who indicate the direction that we are going. My laboratory is the living one that has existed for millennia.

The great eighteenth-century Swedish naturalist Carolus Linnaeus created the system of biological classification we still use today. Linnaeus grouped plants and animals according to their resemblances, and arranged these groups in a hierarchy. He named our species *Homo sapiens,* or "wise person," and placed us in the order Primates, which means "first," along with monkeys and apes. Linnaeus recognized the similarity between apes and humans. "It is remarkable that the smartest ape differs so little from the wisest person," he wrote. But to Linnaeus, "similar" did not mean "related" in terms of ancestry or lineage. He put humans in one family, Hominidae (which today includes ourselves and our immediate ancestors, the hominids), and the apes into another family, Pongidae (which today includes orangutans, chimpanzees, bonobos or pygmy chimpanzees, and gorillas).

Linnaeus was a strict creationist. His Great Chain of Being was a fixed set: he believed that God had breathed life separately into each individual species. Nevertheless, Linnaeus identified the pattern of relationships among living things, and recognized the specific relationship between apes and humans. He organized and explained the "what." But it was Charles Darwin who explained the "how."

An indifferent divinity student but an ardent naturalist, Charles Darwin left Cambridge at age twenty-two to join the survey voyage on HMS *Beagle.* The voyage lasted five years and circled the globe. At every stop Darwin traveled inland, taking notes on local geology and collecting fossils and specimens to send back to England. He waded along coral reefs, stood on the rims of volcanos, and saw glaciers crashing into the sea. But nothing impressed him more than the Amazon jungle, which he described as "temples filled with the varied productions of the God of Nature, . . . the glories of another world."

Darwin returned to England convinced that plants and animals were the product of gradual, or evolutionary, change. He began a series of notebooks filled with often cryptic, rambling thoughts on "transmutation." An essay on population by the Reverend Thomas Malthus led him to the mechanism of evolution. Each generation of plants or animals has the potential to produce more offspring than can possibly survive. Individuals must compete for food, living space, and mates. Each generation also includes variations that make some individuals better adapted to their environment, and therefore better competitors, than others. These individuals produce more surviving offspring; their offspring inherit the adaptive trait and produce more offspring themselves; and so adaptive characteristics are incorporated into succeeding generations and the population evolves. Simple but brilliant! Humans had been practicing artificial selection for centuries, selectively breeding plants and animals for specific qualities. Yet the idea of *natural* selection had been overlooked.

Darwin did not rush to publish. To the contrary: in 1840 he wrote a brief sketch of his theory, placed it in a sealed envelope, and attached detailed instructions for its publication after his death. Over the next twenty years, Darwin lived the life of a country squire, earning a reputation as one of the leading naturalists of his generation. But except for hints to a few very close friends, he kept natural selection — his "dreadful secret" — to himself. The idea that human beings are related to all living things, not the product of special divine creation, was heresy.

Indeed, Darwin might never have published if not for a letter from a young naturalist, Alfred Russel Wallace. Wallace had just completed a trip through the Malay Archipelago, including a long stay in Borneo, and was on his way to New Guinea when he came down with a high fever, possibly malaria or dengue. The idea of evolution by natural selection occurred to him as he lay in a feverish delirium. He dashed off an essay to Darwin, his mentor. The older man was devastated: after years of waiting for the right moment, he was about to be scooped. A joint paper was read at the next meeting of the Linnean Society.

The paper attracted little notice. But it prompted Darwin to complete his book, *On the Origin of Species by Means of Natural Selection,* which was published in 1859. The initial printing (1,250 copies) sold out the first day. His book was not a suspenseful, heart-wrenching Dickensian novel, but a dry, scientific tome, and Darwin was stunned to hear that commuters were snatching up copies at stalls outside Waterloo Station. The idea of evolution was especially popular among socialists and other "rabble-rousers." If species could change, they reasoned, then so could the social and political system. Nothing was preordained. In explaining and documenting evolution by natural selection, Darwin became not only a heretic, but also a traitor to his social class. He told one friend that he felt like he was "confessing a murder." In no time, biologists, theologians, pamphleteers, and even politicians were taking sides. Plans to award Darwin a knighthood were quietly canceled.

A reluctant revolutionary, Darwin avoided using the word "evolution" and did not apply his theory to humankind in *Origin*. He alluded to our species in a single, muted sentence, buried near the end: "Light will be thrown on the origin of man and his history." Ten years passed before he addressed the subject of human evolution. Ultimately, Darwin concluded that human beings, as well as our closest living relatives, the great apes, originated in Africa.

To scientists who study primates today, the connection between humans and apes is clear. We study primates in large part for the insights they give us into human nature and human origins. Although not living fossils, the primates still on earth provide clues about where we come from and who our ancestors were. Simply stated, the path led from an ancestral primate to prosimians, monkeys, and apes, and to early humans.

All primates have certain traits in common, traits they inherited from a common, arboreal progenitor. Their hands and feet (except in humans) are adapted for climbing and grasping, with five fingers and toes, and nails instead of claws. Their eyes look forward rather than sideways, and their sight is better than their sense of smell. Whereas other animals explore by poking their noses into things or tearing them with their teeth, primates reach, touch, and look. Primates also have relatively large brains for animals their size; they bear only one or two offspring at a time (not litters) and spend a long time rearing each one; and they live in permanent groups with individuals of both sexes and all ages — though these traits are not universal.

Prosimians (or "pre-monkeys") tend to be small, nocturnal creatures who cling to branches vertically and move by leaping, like tree-living rabbits. With their flat heads, frozen, expressionless faces, mobile ears, pointed snouts, and wet noses (like a dog's), prosimians are the least recognizable of our relatives. Yet two characteristics reveal their primate pedigree: their relatively large brains and their grasping fingers.

Today prosimians are found in both Africa and Asia. The world's prosimian capital is the island of Madagascar, off the southeastern coast of Africa. Here, free from competition with monkeys and apes, the Malagasy lemurs spread and diversified, filling a wide range of ecological niches.

Monkeys are true quadrupeds who move on all fours, whether leaping and jumping in the trees or running on the ground. Like cats, dogs, and most other mammals, monkeys have a deep, narrow chest. The head is thrust forward on a spinal column that is long and flexible and ends in a tail. Monkeys are social animals par excellence. Most species live in troops that include members of both sexes and all ages, organized by a system of status and rank. Troop members function as a unit, sleeping, traveling, and eating together.

Today monkeys live in a broad equatorial belt that stretches from southern Mexico to Central and South America, tropical Africa (except Madagascar), and Asia. Baboons and macaques have the broadest geographical range of any primate other than humans, and also occupy the widest range of habitats. Baboons live in semiarid environments on the edge of the Sahara, while macaques have adapted to remote islands in northern Japan, prospering in the wintry snows. Whereas the number of great apes shrinks daily, some monkey populations are increasing. Because of crop-raiding, a few monkey species are classified by some governments as "pests."

The terms "monkey" and "ape" are often used interchangeably, but in fact, apes are much more closely related to humans than they are to monkeys. This kinship can be seen in the ape's broad, flat chest, mobile shoulders, and long arms and fingers. Like humans, apes do not have tails.

Apes are divided into two main groups. The small-bodied gibbons and slightly larger siamangs are called "lesser apes" because of their size (about twenty pounds at maturity). Gibbons are the aerialists of the ape family. Their elongated arms allow them to hang from branches and swing from tree to tree, a form of locomotion called brachiation. In many ways, gibbons mimic birds. Living high in the treetops, gibbons form lifelong monogamous pairs who jealously guard their territory from others of their species. Also like birds, gibbons produce haunting, hooting songs that rise and fall in crescendos of graduated halftones, like soaring symphonies.

Today, gibbons are densely packed into the tropical rain forests of Southeast Asia, and penetrate into China. With nine species and millions of individuals, they are the most successful of the apes.

Great apes are called "great" because of their size: they are the largest primates. The African great apes, chimpanzees and gorillas, are covered with short, coarse, black hair. Although the African apes have the broad shoulders and long arms of brachiators and are adept at climbing, they are equally at home on the ground. Quadrupedal knuckle-walkers, they hold their wrists stiffly as they walk on all fours with the weight of the front part of their bodies falling on the knuckles, somewhat like football linebackers in a scrimmage. Occasionally, they walk bipedally for short distances.

Chimpanzees are found primarily in tropical rain forests, although some populations have adapted to woodland and even savanna habitats. They usually live in loose communities of thirty or more. Members of this community do not travel or forage as a unit, but they do treat outsiders with suspicion and often hostility. Highly vocal, chimpanzees use series of loud hoots and screams to advertise their presence, maintain contact, announce a bonanza of ripe fruit, and warn off outsiders. The strong bonds between a mother chimpanzee and her offspring persist after the young have reached maturity, and may span generations. When in estrus, chimpanzee females typically mate with a number of males. Fatherhood is unknown among chimps, although older brothers may act quite "paternal." Chimpanzee males and females are quite similar in appearance, standing about four feet tall and weighing about a hundred pounds.

The chimpanzees consist of two closely related forms, the so-called common chimpanzee and the smaller, more upright, pink-lipped, pygmy chimpanzee or bonobo. Chimpanzees once occupied a wide, continuous band across equatorial Africa. Today they are found only in isolated pockets of forest, crisscrossed by the boundaries of twenty-one nations. Bonobos are confined to one rain forest in Zaire.

The gorilla is the largest primate, the greatest of the great apes. Adult males weigh four hundred pounds or more; gorilla females weigh half as much. Adult males develop a large bony ridge on the top of the skull, to support their huge jaws and chewing muscles, and a saddle of silver-gray hair across their backs, from which the term "silverback" arises. Gorillas usually live in families composed of a dominant male silverback, several adult females, and their young. Not surprisingly, given their massive bulk, gorillas spend much of their time on the ground, eating and resting. Less excitable and vocal than chimpanzees, virtually the only time gorillas stand at full height and vocalize loudly is when they are threatened. Males then perform their famous chest-thumping charge.

There are two subspecies of gorillas. The mountain gorilla, today numbering perhaps six hundred individuals, is found only in a corner of the Virunga volcanoes where Uganda, Rwanda, and Zaire meet. The lowland gorilla ranges throughout Zaire and is also found in Cameroon, Congo, Gabon, and Angola. It is doubtful that there are more than thirty thousand lowland gorillas left in the world.

Orangutans are the sole surviving great apes of Asia. The fossil evidence suggests that orangutans originated in Africa but then dispersed to Asia, always remaining in tropical rain forest. Although orangutans once ranged throughout Southeast Asia and into China, today they number fewer than thirty thousand and are found only on the islands of Borneo and Sumatra.

Unlike the African apes, orangutans are covered in sparse orange hair, which varies in hue from dark brown to light blond. Orangutans are primarily arboreal; they are the largest tree-living primate. They spend most of their time in the canopy of the forest, holding on with their powerful arms, which are almost twice as long as their legs. The original quadrumanous or "four-handed" ape, orangutans' hips and legs are as flexible as their shoulders and arms, and both their hands and feet are long and hooklike.

Mature male orangutans may weigh over three hundred pounds, twice the size of females. Captive adult males, who are easier than wild males to measure, have exhibited eight-foot arm spans and have stood almost six feet tall when upright. Adult males also are distinguished by large, encircling parabolic cheekpads, which frame their faces, and dangling throatpouches, which function as resonators for the booming long calls that alert others to their presence. Orangutans are semisolitary apes, who spend most of their time traveling and eating alone (or in the case of females, with dependent offspring). At maturity males begin to roam; females may establish home ranges that overlap with their mother's range.

Although the details of the hominoid (human/ape) lineage are still mired in puzzles and controversy, the general outline of this family tree is clear. All the great apes share a common ancestor with humans, as demonstrated by their similar body structure, similar behaviors, and similar DNA. The genetic clock and other evidence suggest that orangutans branched off from our common family tree between ten and fourteen million years ago, and gorillas, eight to ten million years ago. Humans and chimpanzees became distinct lines about five million years ago, while bonobos and chimpanzees probably diverged from each other less than a million years ago.

Chimpanzees are "blood relatives," who share almost 99 percent of our genetic material. Once blood groups are matched, humans could receive a transfusion from a chimpanzee (but not a gorilla or an orangutan). Indeed, some scientists believe that assigning humans and chimpanzees to different families is artificial. Humans, argues UCLA physiologist Jared Diamond and others, are the third chimpanzee.

Ever since Darwin, people have sought the "missing link," the intermediate form between apes and humans that would complete the evolutionary sequence. But few accepted Africa as the cradle of humanity. One who did was Raymond Dart, a young British-born anatomist who immigrated to South Africa. Dart agreed with Darwin that fossils of our ancestors would be found not in lush tropical forest but in open savanna, where the struggle to survive would have provided an evolutionary push. In 1924, Dart's convictions were rewarded: a woman student sent him a box of stones from the Taung caves that contained a small fossilized face and skull mold. Dart was convinced it was the remains of a hominid (humanlike) juvenile. When he announced his discovery in the prestigious British journal *Nature,* Dart was met with near-universal skepticism. The scientific world was not willing to grant such a small-brained creature a role in human evolution. One of Dart's few supporters was Robert Broom, an itinerant physician who supplemented his income collecting specimens for museums. Together Dart and Broom uncovered several examples of the small, or gracile, form of *Australopithecus africanus* ("southern ape of Africa"), which later became the leading candidate for hominid ancestor. They also found specimens of the robust form of australopithecines, now relegated to the sidelines of human evolution.

Not long after Dart discovered the "Taung child," another paleoanthropologist began looking for our ancestors farther north in Africa. The son of English missionaries, born and raised in Kenya among members of the Kikuyu tribe, Louis Leakey sought an environment that would match Darwin's predictions, and found it at Olduvai Gorge in Tanzania. Within minutes of arriving at Olduvai, Leakey discovered an ancient stone hand ax. These simple tools seemed to be everywhere. Leakey reasoned that if stone tools littered the Olduvai landscape, then the remains of the hominids who made them must be there, too, waiting to be found.

Olduvai Gorge is part of the great African Rift Valley that runs more than a thousand miles and divides East Africa from the rest of the continent. A river once flowed through this valley, wearing away a gorge three hundred feet deep. Walking to the bottom of Olduvai is like flipping through the pages of the book of time. The geological layers of the gorge correspond to the pages. As you descend, the layers go from modern soils at the top to layers almost two million years old at the bottom. These are the pages of time Louis Leakey spent a lifetime reading.

For twenty-eight years straight, Louis and his second wife, Mary, made the grueling eight-hundred-mile journey from their home in the suburbs of Nairobi along mud tracks across seemingly endless savanna to Olduvai Gorge. It was one of the most persistent — and unrewarding — efforts in the history of paleoanthropology. Over the years the Leakeys collected what they believed to be the earliest stone tools made by hominids, but they found not even a scrap of fossilized hominid bone. Searching for fossils in the heat of the African sun becomes more difficult when compounded by the light of the African sun. In that homogenizing brilliance, nuance, color, and shade disappear, and bones and stones become as one, bleached white by the scorching equatorial sun. Olduvai Gorge steadfastly refused to yield its secrets until finally, in 1959, the Leakeys' persistence paid off.

Louis lay sweating in his tent with a fever. Mary went to the gorge with her dalmatians, whom she kept to hold lions at bay. As Mary walked slowly along the hillside of the lowest layer of the gorge, she spotted the top of a skull recently uncovered by erosion. Mary ran back to the tent shouting, "I've got him! I've got him!" When he grasped what she was saying, Louis jumped from his bed, fever forgotten, and raced to the site.

The hominid fossil turned out to be a magnificent specimen of an extremely robust australopithecine, which the Leakeys named *Zinjanthropus boisei*. Zinj turned out to be the first of many hominid fossils uncovered by the Leakey family. Olduvai Gorge had one distinct advantage over the limestone caves in South Africa where other australopithecines had been found. The layers of the canyon were interspersed with volcanic ash, which could be dated with great precision. When the data came back from the laboratory, Leakey was ecstatic. The sample of ash above Zinj was 1.75 million years old, meaning that Zinj himself was probably 2 million years old.

In a display of public relations genius, Leakey immediately proclaimed Zinj "the oldest man." Coupling his personal charisma with the scientific weight of the National Geographic Society in Washington, D.C., Leakey became a media star in the Marshall McLuhan mold. People called him "the Darwin of human evolution." He was probably the first scientist who smiled and told jokes as he pronounced the importance of his findings, the first scientist who spoke in sound bites for radio and the new medium of television.

The son of conservative Anglican missionaries who gave up their comfortable lives in middle-class England to bring Christianity to Africans was spending his life working in Africa to bring the reality of human evolution back to the Western world.

A restless, energetic man, Leakey continued to seek. He later repudiated Zinj as the toolmaker in favor of a new ancestor, *Homo habilis* (or "handy man"), based on a discovery made by his son Jonathan. In part because Leakey had been so successful promoting Zinj, few researchers accepted this new candidate. Thanks to the tenacity of anatomist Phillip Tobias and later discoveries by Louis, Mary, their son Richard, and others, *Homo habilis* has withstood the test of time.

The longer Leakey labored at Olduvai, the more convinced he became that stones and bones were not enough. He wanted to superimpose the current over the ancient, the living flesh over the decayed bone. He believed that studying the great apes, our closest living relatives, would provide insight into how the ancient hominids might have lived. At that time, this was not the conventional view.

In the 1950s, most anthropologists still looked at technologically primitive people as prototypes of early humans. Leakey disagreed. To compare ancient prehumans to modern hunters and gatherers such as the Congo pygmies or the Kalahari bush people (the !Kung San) was misleading. These people are biologically modern human beings, exactly like us. Moreover, they live in environments very different from those where early hominids lived.

The great apes, even though they have been slowly evolving over the millennia, are not very different from their ancestors in anatomy, behavior, and ecological niche. Human beings, in contrast, have departed radically from their ancestors, in anatomy as well as adaptations. Thus, the modern great apes resemble our own ancestors more than we ourselves do. But in the 1950s, very little was known about the great apes.

In 1927, Robert Yerkes had gathered all the material then available on great apes in the wild and published a book entitled simply *The Great Apes*. Yerkes was astounded to learn that the only information came from travelers, explorers, missionaries, and the occasional incidental comment by a naturalist. The result was a scattered collection of anecdotes, like the pieces of an unassembled jigsaw puzzle.

Alfred Russel Wallace's descriptions of the orangutans of Borneo were among the best. An astute observer, Wallace recorded orangutan behavior in uncanny detail. Orangutans, he claimed, were solitary fruit-eaters. So enamored were they of the fruit durian, that they would sit in durian trees, stuffing themselves with its succulent, odiferous flesh, even at night by the light of the moon.

Wallace's most vivid images, however, were of orangutans dying. He described methodically lobbing shots into mortally wounded orangutans to make them lose their grip on the branches and fall to the ground a little faster. Sometimes, he related, it took hours to kill them. Wallace slaughtered orangutans by the dozens, ruthlessly and efficiently, clinically describing their dying agony.

Wallace was not alone. The Victorian naturalist was not unlike the Victorian husband who kissed his wife on the cheek after dinner, then ordered a cab and drove off to a brothel. Victorian naturalists recorded lovely descriptions, then slaughtered their subjects. The desire for taxonomic trophies far out-weighed matters of conscience. Collecting, like hunting, was considered an appropriate hobby for gentlemen, and the violence ensured that few women would participate. The "gentleman collector" was a familiar figure in nineteenth-century Europe, represented by Charles Darwin and other self-taught scientists of independent means.

Vivid (and harrowing) as these early accounts were, no one had attempted a systematic, scientific study of apes in the wild. Yerkes persuaded several colleagues to launch field studies of chimpanzees and gorillas, but none even got close to the animals. The first successful study of a wild ape took place in Asia. In the 1930s, Clarence Ray Carpenter studied white-handed gibbons in Thailand, identifying such crucial features of gibbon adaptation as territoriality and monogamy. Unfortunately, the tradition of the gentleman collector was still strong, and all the gibbons Carpenter studied were afterward shot for their skins and skeletons and to examine stomach contents. Almost thirty years would pass before another field study, in a different mold, would be launched.

While traveling in Tanzania, Louis Leakey had noticed chimpanzees scampering up sparsely wooded hillsides that rose directly from Lake Tanganyika. It was a perfect spot to study apes in the wild. Leakey needed to find someone willing to live in an isolated, hot, uncomfortable place with none of the Western comforts; someone with the dedication and patience to spend months, even years, doing long-term, on-site research. Penetrating the world of chimpanzees, he knew, would be as difficult as locating the ancient inhabitants of Olduvai Gorge.

Leakey found that person in Jane Goodall, a young British woman who had come to Africa simply because she loved animals. Leakey hired Jane as his secretary and invited her to Olduvai for a season of excavation before asking her if she would be interested in studying chimpanzees at the Gombe Stream reserve. She readily agreed. Shortly thereafter, in 1960, Jane, accompanied by her mother, Vanne, began her long-term study of chimpanzees.

Scientists laughed when Louis picked his secretary to study chimpanzees. Making matters worse, Jane was attractive and photogenic. Newspaper articles ran headlines like "Blonde prefers chimps to men." No one thought she would last — except, of course, Leakey.

With her quiet dignity and British poise, Jane Goodall yielded nothing to her critics. Within a year of arriving at Gombe she accomplished more than anyone had before her. She gained the trust of wild chimpanzees, habituating them so that she could observe them up close. She identified individuals and families. She saw behavior that no one else had seen. One by one, she challenged the prevailing definitions of humankind. According to one definition, the primary difference between apes and early humans was that our ancestors hunted. "Man" was, in Robert Ardrey's phrase, "the killer ape." Jane saw chimpanzees not only hunt, but hunt in apparently cooperative groups and share the meat. Another definition focused on humans as toolmakers. Jane saw chimpanzees make tools and watched offspring learn the simple technology from their mothers. When she wrote to Leakey of her discoveries, he crowed like a proud father. Anthropologists, he pronounced, would have to change the definition of human, change the definition of tool, or accept chimpanzees as human!

Not since Linnaeus and Darwin had basic assumptions about the uniqueness of humankind received such a blow. Chimpanzees were all too human: they even engaged in rudimentary warfare and cannibalism.

Over the years, Goodall's research became an icon of modern science. Through her *National Geographic* articles, books, television specials produced with her first husband, photographer Hugo van Lawick, and lecture tours, Jane turned the daily flow of activities among a group of wild chimpanzees into a family saga for the public. "Flo" and "Fifi" became part of the American family. Long before *Dynasty* and *Dallas,* a generation of North Americans grew up with "Mike," "Melissa," and "David Greybeard." Flo was probably the only wild animal who ever received an obituary in the *London Times.* Lecture audiences literally wept as Jane in her eloquent way described the deaths of Flo and Flo's son, "Flint."

In 1959–1960, George Schaller spent many months studying the mountain gorillas of the Virunga Volcanoes. Observing the gorillas from a distance, Schaller succeeded in sketching the broad outlines of their lifestyle, reported in two eloquent books. But then Schaller moved on to other species, eventually studying animals as diverse as the lions of the Serengeti and the giant pandas of China. Leakey wanted to find someone who would follow in Jane Goodall's footsteps, study the gorillas close-up for an extended period, and provide more intimate portraits and detailed data.

At about the same time, thirty-one-year-old Dian Fossey, an American occupational therapist who worked with handicapped children, fulfilled a lifelong dream: a safari to East Africa to see wild animals. In Africa, Dian toured the Serengeti, visited Olduvai Gorge, where she met Louis and Mary briefly, and then went to see the mountain gorillas Schaller had studied. Enchanted by the shy but curious apes, Dian later said that she knew at once that she would return. Back in the States, she wrote an article about the gorillas that caught Leakey's eye. When they met again at a lecture in Kentucky, Leakey asked Dian to be his "gorilla girl" (her words).

Leakey told Dian that if she were serious about studying wild gorillas, she should have her appendix removed before she went into the field. Six weeks after Dian had the operation she received a letter from Leakey saying that he was only testing her determination. Dian described the incident as her introduction to Leakey's "unique sense of humor." (Leakey later made the same request of me; I didn't take him seriously.)

In 1966, with funding arranged by Leakey, Dian returned to Africa to study the mountain gorillas. Only six months after she arrived, civil war broke out in the Congo and she was forced to flee. She refused to give up, however, and set up a new base camp in Rwanda, on the other side of the Virungas. Ten months passed before she was able to get close to the gorillas, but over time she became a welcome visitor, perhaps even an adopted member, of several gorilla families. By the early seventies Dian had written two *National Geographic* articles and was well on her way to providing the kind of "inside information" on mountain gorillas that Jane Goodall had collected on chimpanzees.

Dian's joy and humility in the company of the gorillas, captured on film and in the book she later wrote, served as a bridge between humans and apes, the urbanized West and the forests of central Africa. Almost single-handedly, over eighteen years, Dian converted the public image of the gorilla from monstrous King Kong to peaceful vegetarian. The giant four-hundred-pound silverbacks so feared by early explorers turned out to be family-oriented patriarchs, patient fathers and protective mates. The gorillas were not always gentle; Dian documented fierce male combat for females and even occasional infanticide. The emerging portrait was one of complex, intelligent apes under heavy assault from hunting and from escalating demands on their habitat. Increasingly, Dian became a crusader for the gorillas she was studying, a crusade that brought her into conflict with poachers, farmers, and cattle herders. In the end it may have led to her own death. Her greatest achievement was saving the mountain gorillas from extinction.

Fossey's success encouraged Leakey tremendously. Now that chimpanzees and gorillas were being studied, the next great ape in line was the orangutan.

Orangutans had always been an enigma. Although data on the African apes were pouring in during the 1960s, virtually nothing was known about orang-utans. What was known, from nineteenth-century naturalists, only intensified the mystery. Wallace and others reported that the giant red apes deep in the forests of Borneo and northern Sumatra lived solitary lives, rarely meeting with others of their kind. Sociability is one of the trademarks of the primate order; why were orangutans different?

As recently as the 1960s, few scientists had even seen an orangutan in the wild. Clarence Ray Carpenter had produced a brief report on orangutans in Sumatra. George Schaller, on the way home from his study of mountain goril-las, spent several weeks trying to study the elusive orangutan in the jungles of northern Borneo but saw little more than vacant nests. Two Japanese primatol-ogists, K. Yoshiba and later T. Okano, went to the same area. One never encountered a single orangutan; the other saw a single female once. Barbara Harrisson observed wild orangutans informally, but her main work was with orphaned ex-captive orangutans.

In the mid–1960s, R. K. Davenport left his research post at the Yerkes Re-gional Primate Research Center in Atlanta, Georgia, to study orangutans in the Malaysian state of Sabah. Davenport's eleven-month study produced ninety-two hours of observations. Perhaps more than anything else, Davenport documented the inevitable difficulties and hardships of attempting to study orangutans in their natural habitat. An accomplished observer of apes in captiv-ity, Davenport never returned to the field.

From nineteenth-century accounts, and from reports of more recent expe-ditions, the wild orangutan emerged as reclusive, wary, and shy. People warned Louis Leakey that his quest to find a researcher to study orangutans was futile. Anthropologist Sherwood Washburn told Leakey point blank, "It simply can't be done." Washburn knew; he had been on Carpenter's expedition before World War II.

Academia was left with an image of the great red apes roaming through the vast expanses of Borneo and Sumatra's unbroken rain forest, looking for fruit in the top of the canopy. Orangutans were here today, gone tomorrow, remaining almost invisible to the observer peering up from the forest floor. Over time, the elusive orangutan had attained an almost mystical status as an animal that could not be studied.

# 3
# LOS ANGELES

This is the story of how we begin to remember.

— *Paul Simon*

Los Angeles has indeed become
the metropolis its shameless boosters predicted.

— *Joseph Giovanini*

---

I WAS BORN to study orangutans. My cultural outlook and perspective come from the great northern forests of the land of my forebears, Lithuania, as well as my own country, Canada. Today I live most of the year in the tropical rain forests of Indonesia, the home of orangutans. Although these forests are separated by great distances, I feel it was inevitable that I, a Balt, would feel an affinity for those "people of the forest," the orangutans. I was born to study orangutans because they, like me, are of the great forest.

I recall stories my parents told of the hills, swamps, and woods of their native Lithuania. I see the gray concrete of the two Canadian cities, Toronto and Vancouver, where I grew up and was first educated. I visualize the tropical rain forests where I have studied orangutans for more than twenty years. Although I spent the first seventeen years of my life in Canada, it was in the United States, in California, in the city of angels, Los Angeles, that I completed my education and began preparing for my lifelong study of the great apes. In Los Angeles I would meet Louis Leakey, and, in a way, my life would begin.

Louis Leakey was a man of many interests, who believed in learning by doing. As part of his study of African culture, he learned to practice many traditional arts. One of his favorites was the African children's game cat's cradle. Leakey frequently entertained family and friends with his mastery of the game. With a deft movement of the string, Louis would create a geometric figure, the "cradle." With another deft movement, he could transform a simple figure into something incredibly complex, filling time and space. Still another twist, and these same intersections would unravel.

A cat's cradle is fluid. The patterns are always changing, always in motion. It was when I watched Louis's flying hands that I began to feel that people and events in our lives are part of a larger, ever shifting plan: patterns waiting to evolve on strings in some colossal cat's cradle, being played somewhere by some superhominoid.

Louis Leakey's study of early humans, Jane Goodall's study of chimpanzees, Dian Fossey's study of mountain gorillas, and my study of orangutans were inextricably and inevitably connected. The invisible loop in the cat's cradle that drew me into this pattern closed in Los Angeles. Although I didn't realize it at the time, for me, the first step toward studying orangutans in Borneo was getting to California.

Someone looking at my life from an Eastern perspective might see this cat's cradle as a web of mystical connections that were ordained by fate or by the gods. A Western economist or sociologist might attribute my meeting Leakey in Los Angeles to the inexorable pull of market forces, forces that are the result of individuals making rational economic decisions, yet beyond the control of individuals. Like countless Canadians before them, my family was drawn to California by the dream of prosperity.

Toward the end of his active career as a paleoanthropologist, Louis Leakey, too, felt himself drawn to California. It is a gathering place for the most restless, wandering people in North America, those who have hit the wet wall of the Pacific and can go no farther. To the pioneering types who crossed prairies and mountains, it was the promised land. There is an ease that comes from living in an almost perfect climate for humans, where the sun always shines and the weather does not shift from one extreme to another with the seasons. California has the same climate that nurtured the ancient civilizations of Egypt, Babylon, Greece, and Rome.

The combination of restlessness and ease contributes to the vitality of California, the easy eccentricity and tolerance of various points of view. Highly conservative California spawned President Ronald Reagan. Counterculture California boasts cities like San Francisco. For me, the essence of California was captured in a scene I witnessed on a cable car: an older woman in a mink coat, gloves, and hat sitting beside a young, long-haired man sporting beads, cowboy boots, and a purse.

Louis Leakey, adventurer and iconoclast, found a second home in California. Among the newly wealthy business people who had made their fortunes in oil and computers, and academics who thrived outside the Ivy League, he found a certain type of soul mate and supporter. Leakey admired their entrepreneurial spirit. They, in turn, seemed to intuitively understand Leakey's greatness, to understand how difficult it might be to wrest the secrets of human evolution from the hard, white, sun-bleached African soil. A small group of southern Californians established the L. S. B. Leakey Foundation in Los Angeles in 1968 to support his quest for understanding human origins. Leakey found many of his angels in the city of angels.

When poor health limited his ability to conduct fieldwork and he began devoting more time to lecture tours and fund-raising, Leakey gravitated to California more and more. He had a room permanently reserved for him in the home of his ever-gracious friends and supporters Joan and Arnold Travis. The Travises lived in Westwood, a well-to-do section of Los Angeles that nestles against the UCLA campus. At one point, there was talk of creating an endowed chair for Leakey at UCLA. But his conditions were too stringent. Although a superb teacher who interacted easily and well with young people, he really did not want to be tied down to teaching for more than a few days at a time. Kenya was his homeland; Los Angeles, his home away from home.

My story begins in the nineteenth century in my parents' homeland. My ancestors were born in Lithuania, one of the republics of the Soviet Union and now once again an independent nation. Tucked away in northern Europe on the Baltic Sea, Lithuania is a lowland of peat bogs and gently rolling hills once covered by thick forest. Those dense gloomy forests, which insulated and isolated the Baltic people for centuries, surely had a hand in shaping their character. Balts are quiet, stubborn, tough, resilient, phlegmatic people who have withstood the onslaught of history. Lithuanians today still speak a language that was already old when Sanskrit and classical Greek were living tongues. As I write these words, Lithuania and the other Baltic states, Latvia and Estonia, are undergoing major transitions that speak of the strength of these ancient peoples, my ancestors, who refused to let their language and culture be destroyed.

My great-great-grandparents were born during the first Russian occupation of Lithuania, which lasted from 1795 to 1918. Free farmers, they lived in the county of Utena in eastern Lithuania. Their farm, named "Krunkiskis," stood apart from the village, on the edge of a forest.

Throughout the Russian occupation, young men were forcibly recruited into the army to serve a twenty-five-year term in the far regions of the vast Russian empire. Many young men left Russia, sneaking across the border into Germany in the hope of sailing to America. Among those young emigrants was my future grandfather Dominikas Slapsys, who arrived in 1907, passing through Ellis Island. He went to America to join family members who had left Lithuania in the nineteenth century. On a return visit to Lithuania, Dominikas was introduced to Maria Sirutyte, a beautiful girl with sky blue eyes and long golden hair. After Dominikas returned to New York, where he worked at a rail depot, he and Maria wrote to each other and soon became engaged. My grandmother came to America in 1914 on the last passenger ship to cross the Atlantic before World War I. They were married in 1916. Their first child, a daughter named Bronice, was born in Brooklyn.

Bronice is my oldest aunt, and the first member of my family to be born an American citizen. She would be a crucial part of the pattern of invisible strings that ultimately drew me to Los Angeles. The year Bronice was born, World War I ended and Lithuania declared its independence from the Russian empire. Now the Slapsys family could fulfill their dream: to return to Lithuania, use the money they had saved to improve their farm, and live peacefully forever after. My pregnant grandmother, with two-year-old Bronice, went first; my grandfather followed a year later.

My grandmother described seeing her husband's farm again from an overlooking hill: it was rustic and tranquil, a "fairyland in the sunlight." The house and other buildings sat in an orchard of cherry trees; on the south and west flank of the outbuildings huge oaks, birches, and maples stood guard like sentinels. Beyond lay green fields, and beyond the fields, the even darker green forest. My grandmother wanted to stay forever.

My aunt Eugenie was born at the farm in the summer of 1920 and my mother, Filomena, in 1925. Everything went well until the exceptionally cold winter of 1928–1929. During a great flu epidemic, everyone in the family became ill, the hired people as well. Forced to run the farm by himself, my grandfather in a weakened state took sick. Of all the people on the farm who were sick, my grandfather was the only one who died in the epidemic. He was forty-eight.

My grandmother was left a widow with three young daughters. She had many suitors but never married again, and managed the farm by herself. My mother remembers her sunny days growing up in old Krunkiskis, "walking in the fields picking flowers and berries in the summer and mushrooms in the fall." Saturday evenings, especially in summer, her sisters would invite the youth from nearby villages for dances in the courtyard. They danced swift polkas and Viennese waltzes to the music of harmonicas, accordions, and violins, the music echoing in the tops of the centuries-old oaks. My mother says, "I wish I had the talent to preserve the beauty of my ancestors' birthplace on canvas, so that my children and grandchildren would be able to see what I carry in my heart to the smallest detail."

But the fairy tale did not last. At the beginning of World War II, in a secret pact signed in 1939, Nazi Germany and the Soviet Union divided up Europe. Along with the other Baltic states, Lithuania was occupied by the Soviet army on June 15, 1940. Tiny Lithuania with three and a half million people could not withstand the onslaught of the Soviet army, which numbered in the millions.

With the help of collaborators, the Soviet regime compiled secret lists of people to be killed or deported. A peddler who traveled from village to village by horse and buggy told my grandmother that he had seen her name on a list of the people to be deported to Siberia. A widow with three daughters was hardly a threat to the Soviets, but because she had lived in the United States for six years, my grandmother was known as "the American." She also had a prosperous farm that was coveted.

My mother's family had to flee. Compared to others, they were fortunate. Aunt Eugenie had just married a minor member of the Baltic German nobility, and the Germans and Russians were allies. Using Eugenie's husband's documents, they were able to board a train to Berlin legally, but were allowed to take only one suitcase each. Still, that was a bargain. My mother's family was spared the fate of hundreds of thousands of other Lithuanians who were stuffed into cattle cars nailed shut without food or water and carted to labor camps in Siberia.

For most Lithuanians the most terrible days were in June 1941, under the Soviet occupation, just before the German attack on Russia when the Nazis came into Lithuania. For Lithuanians of Jewish, Gypsy, or Tartar heritage the horror was only beginning. The friendly peddler who had warned my mother's family to flee probably perished in the Holocaust.

When Germany was finally defeated, the Soviet army moved back into Lithuania and eastern Europe. My grandmother's dream of living forever on the farm came to an end. She now longed to return to America. As the Soviets closed in on Berlin, the family fled westward, stopping along the way to work on German farms. Their goal was to reach the American-occupied sector of Germany.

After the capitulation of the Third Reich on May 8, 1945, all foreign refugees, including my mother's family, were sent to refugee camps by the Allied forces. My parents met at a dance at a camp near Standal. Filomena thought the tall, muscular Antanas Galdikas was handsome. Antanas had fled Lithuania alone. His relatives were convinced that their country would soon become independent again and saw no need to leave their homes and possessions. But Antanas saw the size of the Soviet army and knew that the Soviets had come to stay.

My mother's family, accompanied by Antanas, left the refugee camp and traveled westward. My parents were married in June 1945, in the little German town of Obisfelde. But the Soviet army was closing in and, early the next morning, my family and about twenty other refugees who had attended the wedding celebration moved on. They traveled by foot, dragging handcarts laden with their belongings. Sometimes German farmers would drive them to the next village in horse-drawn wagons. Eventually, they reached the American zone, where I was born the following year.

The whole family wanted to go to the United States, but the Americans were choosy. Emigration to the U.S. was the longest, slowest route out of the refugee camps. Rather than wait, my grandmother and Aunt Eugenie's family went to Australia. My grandmother never saw America again. Aunt Bronice did not have to wait. Even though she had left America at the age of two and did not speak any English, she was an American citizen. She simply produced her Brooklyn, New York, birth certificate. The invisible lines that pulled me toward Louis Leakey were operating, for my aunt eventually settled in Los Angeles.

My father soon emigrated to Canada to work in the gold and copper mines in the town of Rouyan-Noranda in the province of Quebec. My mother and I followed him three months later. After a year and a half in Quebec, we moved to Toronto. My brother Vytas Anthony was born in Quebec. My sister, Aldona, and my brother Al were born in Toronto, where my parents bought their first house.

My parents became part of a growing Baltic community in Toronto. They were active members of their Catholic Lithuanian parish and Canadian Lithuanian organizations. I went to Lithuanian elementary school on Saturday mornings until I graduated in grade eight. In its own conservative way, the Lithuanian community throughout North America revolved around the church, and was supportive of its members.

Perhaps because of the tumultuous events that displaced them from their homeland, my Baltic family displayed a fierce determination and commitment to education. My parents stated clearly that because we were "New Canadians" and had no family connections in Canada, the only way that we children could get ahead was through education. I was the oldest child, and my mother believed that my education came before all else. When a mathematics teacher told me that the highest degree was a Ph.D., that became my goal, although my mother leaned toward an M.D. as being more practical.

At bedtime when I was a child, my mother would read gripping, sometimes gory, stories from the Old Testament, and improvise tales about the rise of Western civilization from the Egyptians, Babylonians, Greeks, and Etruscans to the Romans. At an early age, I became a devotee of ancient cultures and later read all that I could about the Aztecs, Incas, and ancient Chinese.

On weekends my family picnicked in parks and yards near downtown Toronto, or went hiking, camping, and fishing in the vast forests of northern Ontario. Like other people with strong ties to the land, Balts believe that humans can achieve harmony with themselves only if they are in touch with nature.

Because of my mother's tales and my parents' fondness for nature, I became that unlikely combination of bookworm and nature lover. One of the biggest events of my early childhood was a trip to the public library with my first grade class. I went back on my own the next day and took out my first library book — about a jungle explorer in a bright yellow safari suit and his unruly, banana-eating monkey, "Curious George." By age six, I was using the streetcars of Toronto on my own, and I got to know the city quite well. In grade two, I had decided on my life's work: I wanted to be an explorer.

For a while my parents owned a large, rambling, three-story house. Behind it stood seven oak trees whose tall, straight boles shot up into the sky. Respect for the spirits of trees was central to the ancient Baltic religions, which were related to Druidism. Gigantic oaks were said to house human souls. I felt that the oaks in our back yard connected me to the great forests of my parents' homeland. Many years later these trees would be replaced in my life by the trees in the tropical rain forests of Borneo.

I spent whole days roaming High Park, which was only two blocks from our house. Today the park has been landscaped and tamed with flower beds and park benches. But I remember it as a vast, wild place where one could follow little streams under trailing willows and find huge land turtles and nesting mallard ducks. Sometimes High Park seemed so virginal and wild that a file of feather-bedecked Huron natives slipping silently past on their way to some rendezvous with French fur traders at a nearby fort would not have seemed out of place. In my imagination, I was exploring untouched wilderness.

If I couldn't be an explorer, my alternate ambition was to be a ballerina. As a child, I took ballet lessons for several years. To become a ballerina, that epitome of feminine perfection, could only be achieved by arduous exercise and tremendous hard work. The delicate satin ballet slippers with the ribbons tied gracefully around the dancer's ankles frequently conceal feet rubbed raw and bloody. The strict mental and physical discipline that ultimately led through sweat and pain to the beauty and lightness of the dance probably helped sustain me in future years when I went to Indonesia.

I liked to dance, but I decided I did not want to become a ballerina. Even so, I was in awe of my ballet teacher, known only as "Madame." An ancient Russian, she had started dancing when the Czars still ruled. Despite her lined, heavily powdered face, with bleached orange braids piled high on her head, she had the figure of a twenty-year-old. The picture of Madame with her swirling skirts, glorious fox furs, suede coats, and high-heeled, knee-high black Cossack boots, is still clear in my mind.

Madame failed to make me a ballerina, but I doubt that this was ever her intention. Madame succeeded in a more important way, by giving me insight through her example and her words. Despite a revolution that shook the world, despite world wars, exile, even despite increasing age, Madame continued to dance and continued to be what obviously really mattered to her most, a dancer. The last time I saw Madame she was dressed in an ethnic Ukrainian costume on a CBC television show, still dancing. I remember her face, with its concentrated look of vitality, surrounded by swirling, colored ribbons. The model that she provided was a lasting one. Like my mother, she showed me how a woman can be empowered by the purity of her convictions. She showed me that patience and perseverance were qualities for all time.

We left Toronto when one of my parents' real estate transactions collapsed in a sluggish economy. They lost everything. My father found a job in the uranium mines of Elliot Lake in northern Ontario. At Elliot Lake High School I had serious homework for the first time. Studies and part-time jobs replaced my childhood dancing, forays, and explorations.

It was during high school that I became interested in orangutans. I was a voracious reader, and photographs and brief descriptions of the red apes of Asia occasionally turned up in textbooks or magazines. Orangutans appealed to me because I thought they must resemble our own ancestors who stood at the beginning of prehistory.

Los Angeles continued its pull. As my parents coped with financial ups and downs, the image of my aunt and uncle's easy prosperity in the California sunshine and the reputation of Los Angeles as an open-handed employer stayed in my parents' minds. They computed their wages as if they were paid at California rates and realized how much better off the family could be. In the late 1950s, my parents began investigating moving to Los Angeles. My father drove to visit my aunt Bronice in our new two-tone-green Studebaker Lark, and came back even more impressed than before with the city's vitality. Later my mother, who did not drive, went by bus. She brought back glossy, brightly colored postcards portraying glamorous, wide boulevards lined with tall palms bending against brilliant blue skies. Compared to the gloomy scene of a dark, damp Toronto on a wintry afternoon, Los Angeles looked like paradise.

But it took three years to reach California. Although my parents were Canadian citizens, their land of birth put them in the Lithuanian category. The quota for Lithuanian immigrants stood at a hundred people per year. If you had a relative who was an American citizen, however, you moved to the front of the line of visa applicants at the American embassy. Aunt Bronice provided the loop in the cat's cradle. While waiting we moved to Vancouver, which by my parents reckoning was the closest point in Canada to Los Angeles.

Shortly after my seventeenth birthday, I enrolled at the University of British Columbia. By today's standards, UBC was old-fashioned in the extreme. My staid academic adviser, in his British tweed jacket with the inevitable elbow patches, recommended calculus, physical chemistry, physics, and medieval church history. The professors, who occasionally wore their caps and gowns to class, sometimes seemed to be lecturing to themselves and not to the students.

I won a British Columbia government scholarship for the following year, but I never used it. Barely had I finished my final exams when I boarded a Greyhound bus to join my father in Los Angeles. A new pattern was taking shape in the cat's cradle.

Los Angeles was bursting with vitality. Even on the first day, when I descended from the bus at the Greyhound terminal in downtown Los Angeles, I could feel the ferment and excitement in the air. I was met by my father and an old chum from his childhood village whom he had encountered after thirty years on an earlier trip to Los Angeles. Leaving the bus terminal downtown, I sat in the back seat of our car as my father drove along the Hollywood Freeway. I was amazed to discover that Los Angeles looked exactly like the postcards. Even the slender palm trees were bending appropriately in the California wind.

Our first home in California was a white bungalow surrounded by avocado trees whose heavy branches, laden with fruit, dipped almost to the ground. I worked full time for six months, taking night courses at Los Angeles City College. When I had saved enough money to pay my nonresident tuition fees, I entered the University of California at Los Angeles.

UCLA in 1965 was a world apart from UBC. I felt I had not only changed countries, but also decades and universes. A vibrant, energetic place, UCLA teemed with excitement. It exuded potential. Women students wore jeans; faculty were approachable and lectured in their shirt sleeves. There were even a few women on the faculty.

A Canadian friend and I once impulsively walked into an unfamiliar professor's office to ask him for academic advice, and he spent twenty minutes explaining courses in the zoology department. At this university, he told me, I could take courses in animal behavior and ecology, anthropology and archeology, and even gypsy folklore or ancient Mesopotamian civilizations. Taking anthropology as a major seemed like a sin. I liked it too much. I didn't want to waste my tuition money to pay for something I enjoyed so much.

I took a variety of undergraduate courses at UCLA, ranging from invertebrate marine biology to industrial psychology. I raced from class to class, studied with my friends, spent hours in the library, went to film festivals and rock concerts, carpooled, and went to the beach. My university life became regulated and predictable.

Then a strange, mystical incident occurred. I had just turned nineteen. I was sitting in the back row of one of the huge auditoriums that are standard for some undergraduate psychology classes. (Psychology was the most popular major at UCLA.) There were more than two hundred students in the class. The lecturer mentioned, in passing, something about "the young British woman living with chimpanzees."

As I sat at the back of the lecture hall, I heard a sound from far away, a crystal-clear chime in the distance. The sound lingered briefly, and was gone. I know this sort of experience is supposed to happen only in the movies, but it happened to me. Even today I remember the professor's face, his posture, his expression, and where he was standing at the instant of the distant chime.

At the moment the distant chime sounded, I knew he was talking about me. I wasn't British and I wasn't interested in chimpanzees. But something within me stirred. I am reminded of a line by theoretical physicist Stephen Hawking that opens a novel by Margaret Atwood: "If we can remember the past, why can't we remember the future?" At that precise moment, I remembered the future. I remembered the future with such clarity that the moment remains in my mind as if it were engraved on glass.

Two years passed before I learned, in graduate school in anthropology, that the British woman's name was Jane Goodall.

Around this time, a photograph of a Sumatran subadult male orangutan with a wispy beard and intelligent eyes caught my attention. I may have seen it first in *LIFE* magazine, *National Geographic,* or a textbook; I know it was reproduced repeatedly. I was fascinated by his humanlike appearance and demeanor. This particular photograph emphasized the relative flatness of his face, and the white surrounding the brown irises of his eyes. It was only his large teeth and jutting, prognathic jaws which gave him away as being pongid. Although orangutans do look somewhat like humans, the photograph was uncanny in highlighting the affinity between ape and human. It clarified the origin of the word "orangutan" in two Malay words, *orang* and *hutan,* meaning "person of the forest."

I saw other photographs of orangutan infants with haloes of red hair standing erect as though their fingers were plugged into electric sockets. They looked like little Einsteins, sticking out their tongues at the camera. As I studied the photographs and read the few enigmatic tidbits of information, I felt drawn to the orangutans as though I had known them before.

I dreamed of going to the great forests of the Far East to study orangutans. I became obsessed with the idea. I wrote letters to the newly independent nation of Malaysia, which had incorporated the states of Sarawak and Sabah in the northern part of Borneo. I haunted UCLA professors' offices. I wrote to Tom Harrisson, the head of the museum in Sarawak, after I read that his wife, Barbara, had kept orangutans. But neither the Malaysians nor Tom Harrisson replied, and the professors had no useful advice to give me.

The invisible loop on the string in the cat's cradle that drew me to Los Angeles brought Rod Brindamour there as well. Rod lived near Vancouver, but I met him in Los Angeles.

That meeting with Rod, more than twenty-five years ago, is still fresh in my mind. I was driving home from UCLA in the green Studebaker, which was now mine, when I passed a young man in a black leather jacket standing on a corner. He caught my eye and smiled. The impact was visceral. I veered over, running up onto the sidewalk and almost hitting him. Only then did I notice my younger brother standing beside him. They had been introduced by a mutual friend that day and were looking for a store on Sunset Boulevard.

With Rod it was instant and mutual love and respect. He was very easy to like, relaxed, unpretentious, and jovial. Philosophically, both of us were utterly opposed to marriage. I believed that marriage was a scheme by which men enslaved women; Rod believed that marriage was how women preyed on men. United in our opposition to marriage, within days we became engaged.

Like me, Rod was Canadian. He had grown up in the mountains three miles outside Hope, British Columbia, and had spent two summers logging while in high school. He loved science and, in his early teens, he had hoped to get a scholarship to go to college. But now his sole ambition was to travel. We were a perfect pair: the studious, serious, nineteen-year-old UCLA senior with glasses and the seventeen-year-old motorcyclist with his blue Harley-Davidson Sportster. I planned to go to the wilds of Borneo and Sumatra, and Rod wanted to see the world. Somewhere along the line I guess I should have told him that I wasn't coming back.

In 1966, I received my B.A. *summa cum laude,* in psychology, and went on to graduate school in the Department of Anthropology, specializing in archaeology. In graduate school, I took advantage of every opportunity to join weekend excavations, not so much because I was interested in North American prehistory, but for the field experience. I also spent a semester at the University of Arizona field school, working at the Grasshopper field site in the middle of the Fort Apache reservation.

When I arrived in Arizona, I was assigned a "pit partner." Judy Amesbury and I spent the next few months excavating a burial ground on a small slope, meticulously pushing aside the dirt from the bones with dentist's tools and trowels. As we worked, we chatted. Judy told me that she had once written to Louis and Mary Leakey about working at Olduvai and that they had encouraged her to come.

"You mean the Leakeys actually replied?" I said to Judy. "Famous scientists actually write back?"

"Oh, yes," she said. "They do indeed. The Leakeys actually did reply."

Judy regretted that she had not been able to raise the money to go. This was the first time that I had met a fellow student who had actually had firsthand communication with a famous scientist. My only direct experience with a world-famous scientist was during my first semester at UCLA when Francis Crick, the codiscoverer of the double-helix model of the DNA molecule, stepped on my foot in a crush of people after a lecture.

At UCLA I was reading voraciously about the recent advances in molecular biology, in which Francis Crick had participated; recent primate studies on baboons, chimpanzees, and langurs; and reports on fossil hominids that were coming from Africa.

My vision of studying orangutans became stronger with time. My obsession with the rare red ape increased. I spoke to some of my professors at UCLA about a wild orangutan study, but they were quietly discouraging. A few said bluntly that such a study simply couldn't be done.

If I couldn't get academic support for a study of wild orangutans, I decided, I would finish my doctorate, save my money, and go to the forests of Southeast Asia independently. It was simply what I felt I must do, a personal quest. Rod and I talked about it endlessly; he was as enthusiastic as I was. As I completed work for my master's degree, I envisioned that it would take me at least another ten years to reach the great rain forests of tropical Asia where the orangutans have their home. It never occurred to me that the oblique route that led my parents from Lithuania to Toronto, to Vancouver, and then to Los Angeles would ultimately be the straightest path to Borneo. Although I didn't know it, the orangutans were waiting for me right there — in the city of angels.

# 4
# LOUIS

I will support anyone who knows what they want to do
and will go out and do it.

— *Louis Leakey*

You can't do it. It's crazy. It's insane.
Leakey will just have to find himself
some other young woman to study orangutans.

— *American anthropology professor*

I N MARCH 1969, Louis Leakey lectured at UCLA. Leakey was billed as
the famous anthropologist from East Africa with a flair for discovering hominid
fossils. Dr. Rainer Berger, a professor of anthropology and geophysics at
UCLA and a friend of Leakey's, scheduled him to speak to my archaeological-
dating-techniques class. When it became apparent that our small classroom
would be swamped, Berger changed the lecture site to a larger hall.

Louis Leakey was a charismatic speaker. He was stout, with a typically long,
narrow Anglo-Saxon face that had widened over the years. He had bright eyes
a tiny bit too close together, and a short mane of white hair. Leakey was in his
sixties, and his health was deteriorating. He was missing most of his teeth and
couldn't walk without a cane. These problems made him neither shy nor
inhibited. The twinkle in Leakey's dark eyes exuded the good cheer of
Santa Claus. He seemed barely able to suppress his incessant laugh, and
words tumbled from his mouth so quickly that they almost tripped over
each other.

Across the whole room Leakey projected an image of incredible vitality, a
vitality that belied his fragile condition. I recognized him as someone who had
survived through sheer force of will. Leakey had an uncanny ability to stir

people up; he would have made a great politician, a rabble-rouser. So sure of himself and so sure that what he believed in was important, Louis Leakey seemed almost evangelical.

What I remember most of that lecture was the enthusiasm of the crowd. Leakey talked about Olduvai Gorge and finding the fossil hominid "Zinj" after many years of searching. He also set forth a strange theory, that the "domestication" of Neanderthal hominids had somehow changed their genetic structure so that they could mate with biologically modern humans. Even with my limited knowledge of genetics, I found the Neanderthal discussion bizarre. But who knows, maybe Leakey was in some way right.

He showed the audience drawings of "lions" and "dogs" from the Miocene. Pointing out how easy it was to recognize the ancestors of these familiar creatures, he claimed that we could as clearly recognize the ancestors of humans. Leakey argued that the gracile two-million-year-old South African australopithecines then being touted as early humans did not fit the bill. They simply did not look the part. Rather, he insisted, they represented a collateral branch of the hominid line, a branch that was doomed to extinction. It was this iconoclastic view, among others, that made him very controversial among his peers.

I recall one of my professors, James Sackett, saying that as the son of missionary parents, Leakey "looked for modern humans behind every ancient burning bush." Professor Sackett concluded that Leakey was an eccentric genius. Perhaps Leakey was never completely socialized to either the world of the Kikuyu, with whom he grew up, or that of the British. He fell into the crack between the two worlds. When Leakey left Africa to go to school in England at about age sixteen, British classmates thought him eccentric. For example, Louis walked in the Kikuyu way, one foot in front of the other, as if walking on the narrow paths of an African village. His humor was African. He laughed at things his classmates did not consider funny. Yet his Kikuyu-British upbringing gave him a unique strength. The opinions of other scientists never mattered to Leakey, the solitary African lion. I suspect that he cared more about the opinions of the Kikuyu, who had made him a tribal elder.

At UCLA that day, Leakey caught fire during the question and answer period. Someone asked him about the relevance of primate studies for understanding hominid evolution. "Imperative!" Louis declared. Living primates provided the models from which we could put flesh on the fossil bones of long-extinct hominid forms.

"In fact," he gloated, "I have just received a telegram from Dian saying that the mountain gorillas are becoming so habituated to her presence that one is even untying her shoelaces."

Leakey patted his shirt pocket to indicate that the telegram was right there. He was a master showperson. Envious colleagues called him the "abominable showman"!

When Leakey began talking about primate studies, I felt as if he had read my mind and knew I was there. Immediately after the lecture, I rushed up to him and told him that I wanted to study orangutans. He looked totally disinterested, but I persisted. I knew that he was the one who held the key. I told him that I already had written to the Malaysian government and to various researchers, and that I was taking field classes in archaeology. I also mentioned writing to Tom Harrisson. At the mention of Harrisson's name Leakey looked startled. I later discovered that Leakey knew Tom and Barbara Harrisson well.

For the first time Leakey really looked at me. It was as though he suddenly recognized me. No longer laughing, he scrutinized my face intensely. Professor Berger seemed eager to take Leakey away. One or two students were examining some stone tools placed in front of the podium. Someone snapped our picture. Our relationship, though brand new, had instantly become easy and familiar. I felt that my dream of an orangutan study was within reach.

In a single heartbeat, all the invisible strings linking Lithuania, Toronto, and Nairobi to Los Angeles intersected. Louis Leakey, Rod, the Leakey Foundation, Barbara Harrisson, Jane Goodall, Dian Fossey, and I were all linked together. Leakey had been looking for someone to study orangutans. He was already expecting me when I walked into his life.

I left the lecture hall in a daze. On my way out I muttered to a fellow graduate student that I was going to study orangutans. She looked very skeptical. When I returned to the office I shared with other teaching assistants, I ran into Reiner Protsch, an older student from Germany who worked in Dr. Berger's radiocarbon lab, where he had met Leakey on Louis's previous trip to Los Angeles. I told Reiner that I had just spoken to Leakey. I explained that my dream of studying orangutans was closer to reality.

Reiner was delighted. He soon embarrassed me by booming out to everyone that Leakey had chosen me to study wild orangutans. I was doubly embarrassed because the other students in the office looked at Reiner as though he had lost his mind and I would be studying little green men on Mars.

When I got home that afternoon, my normally calm and sedate mother was very excited. Someone had just called on behalf of Louis Leakey. I was to see him the next day at a home near UCLA where he was staying. My mother recognized the Leakey name and assumed that the appointment must be important. I was amazed — and relieved. Given the skepticism in my office at UCLA, I was grateful that I didn't have to take the initiative. My feeling that Leakey took my goal of studying orangutans seriously was vindicated.

The next morning, promptly at ten o'clock, I arrived at Joan and Arnold Travis's home in Westwood. Leakey gave me some "intelligence" tests, the kind you might find in a popular magazine as brain teasers. He later told me that he liked testing people, just to learn about them.

Louis spread out a deck of cards face down on the coffee table. "Which ones are red and which ones are black?" he asked.

I quickly dismissed a trick deck, since all the designs on the back of the cards were identical. I replied, "I don't know which are which, but half of the cards are slightly bent and half are not."

Louis had, indeed, bent the backs of the black cards almost imperceptibly. Beaming, he told me that both Jane Goodall and Dian Fossey had easily passed this test, but all the men had failed.

At this first meeting, Leakey expounded his views on the differences between men and women. I was to hear these views time and again. He staunchly believed that women made better observers than men. Women were more perceptive, he claimed, and better able to see details that at the time might seem unimportant. (Studies indicate that this may be true, at least for North Americans.) Women were also more patient. Finally, he claimed, women did not excite aggressive tendencies in male primates the way men did, however unintentionally. Men, he conceded, made better camp managers.

Leakey told me that he would begin making inquiries about a research site and funding. In the meantime, I was to keep in touch. He wanted me to be ready to leave for the field that September. I told him that I wanted to finish my master's degree and become a doctoral candidate first, and suggested January. With a shrug he said that was okay, but then cautioned, "I'm not promising you anything." He also said that he had not decided whether or not I was "his candidate" for orangutans. But I knew I was. The next time we met, Leakey leaned over, patted my hand in a fatherly fashion, and admitted that he had made up his mind in the lecture hall at UCLA.

"When I first met you I knew that you were going to be the one," he confided, "the one I would support to the fullest extent for a long-term orang-utan study."

Leakey's support was critical. As a mere graduate student, with no experience in primate field research, hoping to do the impossible, to study the wild orangutan that had eluded well-known, seasoned field researchers, it was unlikely that anyone would fund me. Being Louis's candidate put me into a whole different category.

Naively, I thought that Leakey's support would produce instantaneous results. In my mind, I almost began packing. But this speedy departure was not to be. I was twenty-two years old when I met Louis Leakey. I would be twenty-five when I finally went to Borneo. If I had the tiniest shred of impatience, I lost it during the years of waiting.

January 1970 came and went. When Louis heard that I was engaged, he was delighted. Even before meeting Rod, Louis decided that my husband should accompany me as project photographer and camp manager. Rod and I began to wait together, counting the days. When you are young and eager, a year or two can stretch to eternity. In the meantime, Rod and I got married. Twice. When we discovered that our Mexican marriage might not be valid in California, we married again in Los Angeles.

We were pioneers in that modern phenomenon, the commuter marriage, driving back and forth from Vancouver to Los Angeles. While we waited, Rod went back to school in Canada, graduated from high school, and started college. I finished all my requirements for the Ph.D. except the dissertation. Then I started marking time. Through an ad in the UCLA student newspaper, *The Daily Bruin,* I became a house sitter for Norman and Frances Lear. Although best known as the producer of the groundbreaking TV sitcom *All in the Family* and the editor of the sophisticated *Lear's* magazine, respectively, the now-divorced Norman and Frances are also dedicated philanthropists. I have remained friends with them over the years. I wrote poetry. I read, I walked, I window-shopped, my impatience fueled by idleness. I really felt suited for nothing. I wanted only to go to Borneo or Sumatra.

I heard through the academic grapevine that the government of Malaysia, where I initially wanted to go, had banned foreign scientists from the forests of Sabah. Fortunately, orangutans are also found in Indonesia. I decided I would go to Sumatra, which is part of Indonesia. Clarence Ray Carpenter had briefly visited Sumatra and had seen orangutans there after his pioneering gibbon study in Thailand before World War II. I sent the Indonesian government my application for a scientific study and waited.

On top of my sleeplessness and constant anxiety about when I would begin my study, it became awkward to see friends and acquaintances. I could see written on their faces, "Haven't you gone yet? Perhaps you're not really going." In an elevator at UCLA one day an acquaintance looked as though he had seen a ghost when I entered.

"What? When did you come back?" he asked. I had to admit that I hadn't gone.

Another friend saw me standing next to two suitcases (not mine) by a door. He rushed over, shook my hand, and, taking the suitcases, ushered me out the door wishing me fond farewells. He had assumed that the suitcases were mine and that I was finally leaving for Indonesia! I began to feel like the woman in *Twilight Zone* who, while traveling, calls home to find out that her parents are in mourning because she died in an automobile accident days earlier. There was a strange unreality of being in limbo, supposedly in the rain forests of Southeast Asia but not yet there.

One bright spot was the time I spent at the Los Angeles zoo studying the six immature orangutans housed there. When I first arrived, several of the orangutans were playing with their own feces. On subsequent visits, I did everything I could to enliven their drab existence, surreptitiously feeding them milk, raisins, coffee, and fruits and bringing them small pieces of brightly colored cloth. The primary keeper for the orangutans, a heavyset, muscular ex-marine with tattoos on his arms, approved. The feces eating and smearing soon stopped.

One day I gave one of the young female orangutans a nylon stocking, which she promptly put over her head and face in apparent imitation of a bank robber. It was a hilarious sight and attracted a huge crowd of laughing, pointing zoo-goers, perhaps a hundred people. Another keeper came to check on what the fuss was all about. He was appalled. The orangutan juvenile was now basking in all the attention and strutting bipedally from one side of her cage to the other with the nylon "mask" over her head. "How did that orangutan get a stocking?" asked the keeper. I just looked sheepish and didn't answer. Unable to retrieve the stocking from the orangutan juvenile, he soon left, muttering to himself.

When Rod visited from Canada, I introduced them. Like most people,

Rod had never seen an orangutan except in black-and-white textbook photographs. He soon became as enthralled with those gentle, silly creatures as I was. I wished that I could take these delightful orange delinquents back to the forests of tropical Asia.

Louis Leakey visited Los Angeles regularly and we met frequently. Rod and I were willing to leave for Indonesia with nothing but our tickets and our personal savings. Louis, however, insisted that we have at least five thousand dollars beyond the price of airfare. Although he periodically complained about North American researchers who squandered precious research funds by staying at luxury hotels and importing bottled drinking water while doing fieldwork, he did not want us to be stranded penniless in the middle of a forest.

Sometimes I felt as though, even with Leakey's help, the orangutan project would never get started. Early on, he had suggested that I keep bonobos in mind as an alternative. At one point, with neither funding nor government permissions, the situation looked bleak. During a visit to Los Angeles, Leakey turned to me with an air of finality and said, "Well, I guess it's going to be the pygmy chimpanzees."

My heart sank. Very carefully, I explained to him that I had worked so hard and waited so long to study orangutans that I could wait a little longer. Leakey never mentioned the pygmy chimpanzees again. I have often wondered how our lives, Rod's and mine, would have changed had I enthusiastically gone along with Louis's suggestion that we go to Zaire and study bonobos.

Shortly afterward, permission for an orangutan study arrived from the Indonesian government. I was overjoyed. But a few of the anthropology department's faculty at UCLA were not encouraging. They saw me as one of "Leakey's foibles." These doubters tended to be young, temporary, and untenured. It was as though they resented my choosing Leakey and Leakey's choosing me.

At the time, Leakey was preoccupied with Calico, a site in southern California. Leakey was convinced that the site held concrete evidence that human beings were present in the New World as early as fifty thousand or even one hundred thousand years ago. At that point, the only unequivocal evidence of human habitation in the Americas was about twelve thousand years old. In his forthright fashion, Leakey invited the world's leading paleoanthropologists to Calico for a conference. He also invited me to attend. I felt very much out of place with my miniskirt among all the graying, predominantly male, luminaries, but it was a chance to see Leakey in action.

He was everywhere, holding up a "tool" here, touching a colleague there, using his vast persuasive powers to the utmost. But weight of the evidence was against him. One could see the experts clustered in small groups, muttering among themselves, shaking their heads. In the end everyone agreed that nature, not the hand of early humans, was responsible for Leakey's "tools."

The conference received wide media attention in southern California. After it was over, Louis received a call from Ruth Simpson, a cosponsor of the Calico project. A radio station had just reported Louis as saying that North American archaeologists wouldn't recognize a hominid fossil unless it bit them. Louis had said no such thing, he told her, and Simpson wanted the radio station to make an immediate on-air retraction and apology. Louis wouldn't hear of it. He was delighted, roaring with laughter. He wished that he *had* thought up the line.

But after the conference, Louis didn't mention Calico very often. He was the kind of person who took his losses in stride and moved on. Leakey did not commit the Concorde fallacy of "throwing good money after bad."

While marking time, I made two trips to former Yugoslavia to work on joint American-Yugoslav archaeological ventures. I was shocked by the level of misunderstanding and hostility between the American and British students on one side, and the Yugoslavs on the other. Once the hostility erupted into physical violence. It started when the Yugoslavs reacted to American criticism of Yugoslav archaeological techniques by refusing to let the American academics into the team van, which had been purchased with American dollars. Furious American Ph.D.'s punched the Yugoslav driver, dragged him from the vehicle, and took over the van to drive themselves to the site. Like most cases of cultural misunderstanding, the first mistake was compounded by others. This incident caused the Yugoslav archaeologists to be even more stubborn in refusing to listen to American archaeological theory.

Even though I sympathized with their scientific ideals and methodology, I thought the fault lay with the Americans, at least at first. They had forgotten that they were guests in another country. The American archaeologists refused to make allowances for the fact that everything, even archaeology, was done differently in Yugoslavia. I was flabbergasted that American researchers with graduate degrees in anthropology could be so ethnocentric. It was a lesson I tried to remember in Indonesia.

Jane Goodall had become one of my heroes. By now she had been studying wild chimpanzees at Gombe National Park in Tanzania for more than ten years. In the process, she had discovered that these close relatives made tools, ate meat, and even practiced something akin to rudimentary warfare, thus bringing them closer to humankind behaviorally and ecologically than ever before imagined.

One fall, on my way back to North America from Yugoslavia, I spent two weeks in London, visiting Louis Leakey at the Goodall family flat in Earl's Court Mansions. In addition to Leakey, Jane, her mother, Vanne Goodall, Jane's then husband, Hugo van Lawick, and their small son, Hugo, nicknamed "Grub," were all present. Dian Fossey also stopped by for a few days. Vanne and Jane seemed quite different in temperament. While Jane tended to be quiet and reserved, Vanne was a spunky, outgoing person who always had a twinkle in her eye.

I didn't sleep at the flat, but arrived every morning by underground and stayed until after dinner, trying to make myself useful. I spent much time with Grub, who was three or four years old. At that time small children didn't particularly interest me, but even then I realized that Grub was special. He was one of the sweetest and most perceptive children I have ever met. Vanne told me a story that typified Grub. One day, just before I arrived, he had bought a bag of candy. After paying for it, he opened the bag and offered some to the cashier. She burst into tears, saying, "I have worked at this cash register for twenty years, and this is the first time a customer has offered me anything. And a child yet!"

At the Goodall flat, I often answered the phone. I could barely resist a smile when someone rang up haughtily asking for "the baron," meaning Hugo van Lawick, who held that title. The first time it happened, I had no idea who or what the caller wanted.

Louis and I spent hours poring over supply lists, planning logistics, and discussing funding. Leakey was optimistic; he had just made contact with a wealthy Hollywood filmmaker who had agreed to underwrite an orangutan study in exchange for movie rights. Louis thought it was a good idea. Hugo van Lawick's films on the Gombe chimpanzees already had assumed classic status. I was somewhat dubious, given the wild orangutan's shy and reclusive nature. However, I went along. Once Louis became enthusiastic about something, it was difficult to dissuade him.

Jane Goodall initially seemed rather cool, and I was totally in awe of her. However, once we started talking about chimpanzees, I saw the warmth behind her reserved British exterior. I came to appreciate Jane's wonderful, wry sense of humor. At times, her humor could become quite raucous. At dinner one night someone asked, "How do chimpanzees express dominance? submission?" Without a word, Jane sprang up from the candlelit dining room table, swung her behind into Hugo's startled face and said, "That's how!"

Louis roared in approval.

Jane Goodall also impressed me as a woman who had her priorities very much in order. Grub and chimpanzees came first. When her mother-in-law, a very pleasant, genteel woman, asked if Jane and Hugo would accompany her to a society wedding at a castle in Luxembourg, Jane grimaced. She wore a red ski parka over a fancy dress to a publicity dinner for her book *In the Shadow of Man,* which was just being published.

Louis Leakey frequently cooked dinner. One afternoon he couldn't get back to the flat in time and called to make sure that dinner would get cooked. "How he frets," said Vanne, shaking her head and smiling. "He thinks we simply can't get along without him."

I was impressed by the warm relationship shared by Jane, her mother, her sister, Judy, and Louis Leakey, who played the role of a doting, cherished uncle. I considered it a great privilege to have been admitted, at least temporarily, into the family circle. Hugo van Lawick, in contrast, seemed distant, aloof, and preoccupied, although he was generous with his photographic advice. He was always elegant and poised. Hugo is somewhat short, but I remember his opening doors for Dian Fossey, who at six feet plus seemed to tower over him, with the born assurance of a true aristocrat.

Dian was in London for several days. When she arrived she brought a stuffed toy gorilla for Grub, which left him unimpressed (after all, he was used to live chimpanzees). Jane and Dian had met once before, when Dian visited Gombe for a few days before beginning her own study in the Virunga Volcanoes. Jane told me that she had puzzled over Dian on first meeting. But Dian's warmth soon won her over.

Because of his frailty, Louis's doctors were adamant about his taking naps every day. Louis's concession to the nap was to lie on his bed as he continued talking on the phone nonstop or carried on conversations with people around his bedside. He hadn't seen Dian for some time and wanted to hear the latest news of the gorillas directly from her. As soon as she appeared at the Goodall flat, Louis called her to his side. But Dian fixed her warm and gracious gaze on Jane. In a voice flowing with a Southern lilt of honey Dian said, "Right now there's only one person in this whole world I want to talk to."

Jane smiled but looked slightly abashed, almost to the point of blushing, at such open hero worship. They talked for some time and then Dian went to attend to Louis, but the incident stayed in my mind. Later that evening, Jane told me that when she first met George Schaller, who had studied mountain gorillas, she had "followed him around like a puppy dog." Schaller had actually been successful in getting close to the gorillas; at that time Jane couldn't get within a quarter mile of a wild chimpanzee.

Dian came to dinner several times. I felt very pleased to be included, but never having seen an ape in the wild, I felt somewhat uncertain of my right to be there. When Dian asked my opinion on whether or not she should station observers on the other mountains over which the gorillas ranged in order to help protect them, I was quite surprised. I suggested that if she was comfortable with it, then she should do it.

At that time, I was in awe of both Jane and Dian. On first acquaintance, Dian reminded me of the Snow Queen of Narnia, in the C. S. Lewis series — the "White Witch" whose magic ensured that it was always winter in Narnia, but never Christmas. Dian was charming when she was talking to me or wanted something from me, even my advice, but totally cold and oblivious to my presence otherwise. I had never met a person who switched so quickly from intense regard to near disdain. Over the years I came to realize that this was not uncommon among people who lead busy lives and are preoccupied with their work.

I remember an incident one evening after dinner. Dian had finished her after-dinner drink. There were only four of us in the room, Louis, Dian, Jane, and me. We were still nursing our drinks, especially me, since I didn't drink very much. Dian seemed oblivious to the fact that her glass was empty. But Louis noticed. He was like a considerate father. I saw him look at each of us in turn. Finally, he took Dian's glass from her hand and, without rising from his seat, motioned to me. As I rose, Louis handed me the glass, saying, "Dian needs another drink."

Dian protested vigorously that she didn't need me to get her another drink. Seemingly oblivious to my standing there with the empty glass in my hand, Louis and Dian argued about whether or not she needed another drink and whether or not I should get it.

Finally, without a word, I went to the kitchen, where Hugo van Lawick was sitting alone with a moody expression on his face and a drink in his hand. I asked where the drinks were kept. He looked surprised to see me in the kitchen.

I said, "It's for Dian."

He looked even more surprised. He helped me find the bottles of spirits and the ice. I poured the drink and went back to the sitting room. I handed the glass to Dian. She suddenly noticed me, and a brilliant, warm smile flooded her face as she said, "Oh, Biruté, you really didn't have to go and get me a drink."

For the first time, I found myself liking Dian without reservation. Her gratitude was totally genuine. For a split second, I glimpsed the real Dian. I realized that she had to ration herself and her emotions or she would give all of herself away.

I still think back on my time at Earl's Court Mansions. Viewed in passing, Louis Leakey, Jane Goodall, Vanne Goodall, Hugo van Lawick, and Dian Fossey were seemingly ordinary people, but I think it was that very "ordinariness," revealed in their day to day existence, that made them so extraordinary. There was a modesty about them and a carefulness that indicated their high moral sense of obligation to the world and to the animals that had made them academic celebrities. They were easygoing, calm people, who appreciated each day together and who had not lost touch with reality and the common civilities of life.

Indeed, they were "ordinary" to the point of eccentricity. They wore old, comfortable, primly ironed, colorless clothes, slept on mattresses on floors, sat on tattered, lumpy sofas while centuries-old oil paintings of horses and English country scenes and still lifes hung undusted on their walls. They insisted that certain rituals be followed precisely: the high teas, the brandies and sherries, the lace tablecloths, and the dinners by candlelight. But after dinner they washed their own dishes. They laundered their own clothes and carried their own suitcases.

I was confused by this lifestyle. In my youthful naivete, I never would have thought that such an eminent figure as Louis Leakey would sleep on a mattress on the floor in a London flat. When I confided this to a Canadian acquaintance who had been going to school in England for many years, he seemed bemused.

My Canadian informant explained that what I had seen as idiosyncratic behavior was actually cultural, typical of British gentry. He told me about working for charity with a duchess and other titled people who lived in what by North American upper-middle-class standards would be squalor in their London flats, far removed from their country estates, which were their real homes. He spoke of shabby woolens worn by major aristocracy until holes appeared, of rubber galoshes being standard footwear, and of the almost ostentatious mending of old linens. Our conversation placed much of my London experience in perspective.

On my way back to Los Angeles, I also spent a few days at Cornell University in Ithaca, New York, with Barbara Harrisson, whom many considered to be the world's leading authority on orangutans at that time. Louis had introduced me to Barbara. He felt it very important that I spend time with her, because she had lived for many years in Sarawak, a former British colony in northern Borneo. From her, I received invaluable advice on the absolute necessity for hospitality and generosity in the Far East, and a cotton sarong. A sarong has many uses, Barbara explained. It serves as a skirt, a sleeping bag, a scarf, a bathrobe, and a small, personal tent.

A slim, striking woman in her late forties, Barbara was in the midst of a divorce. It was, she felt, an unusual case. Her husband, Tom Harrisson, who was in his fifties, was leaving her for an older woman. The woman, reputedly in her sixties, was said to be a diamond heiress. I was struck both by Barbara's dignity and by the fact that she was divorcing a man she obviously loved and admired. She did not blame Tom for leaving her to seek a better life, nor did she blame the other woman for wanting Tom. The idea that someone might divorce a person whom they still loved was new to me. I never forgot the conversation.

I had assumed that meeting Louis would put my orangutan mission on fast forward. I was wrong. I waited and waited, and wrote letters to Louis reminding him that I was waiting. Disappointments piled up. The Hollywood filmmaker withdrew his offer. Two and a half years passed. The strain of not knowing when we would depart took its toll on Rod as well as me.

Finally, my first grant came from the Wilkie Brothers Foundation of Des Plains, Illinois, as a result of Louis's earnest pleading on my behalf. I was in good company. Leighton and Robert Wilkie had not only provided seed money for Jane Goodall and Dian Fossey, but also had supported Raymond Dart, whose earlier discovery of the first South African australopithecine had opened up a new chapter in our understanding of hominid evolution.

The next grant came from the Jane and Justin Dart Foundation, again after an urgent call from Leakey. Years later, while staying with then widowed Jane Dart in Pebble Beach, near Monterey, California, I discovered that Louis's call to ask for money for my orangutan project was not the only such request he made of the Darts.

Justin Dart, a crusty industrialist, had no particular interest in human evolution. In fact, he had refused Louis's invitation to visit Olduvai. "No!" Dart told Louis. "What would I do there?"

Expressing similar sentiments, he later refused to join the board of the newly established Leakey Foundation, although his wife, Jane, did. Nonetheless, Louis would call Justin — usually at four o'clock in the morning — demanding that thousands of dollars be sent to some particular project or place before ten o'clock that same morning. Justin usually complied. The two feisty, stubborn men admired one another, each recognizing a similar kind of greatness in the other.

Louis once said to me of Justin, "Now there's a man!"

And Jane Dart said to me years later, "It takes one to know one."

Then the National Geographic Society provided a grant. On September 1, 1971, thirty months after I first met Louis Leakey, Rod and I finally began the journey to Southeast Asia. Our first stop was the National Geographic Society headquarters in Washington, D.C., where Mary Griswold Smith and Bob Gilka loaned Rod photographic equipment and provided extensive advice, moral support, and many rolls of film.

Leonard Carmichael was then head of the Science and Explorations Committee of the society. He took my measure, questioning me in depth about orangutans, tropical rain forest ecology, and even Finno-Ugric languages. I will always remember the story he told about being mugged on the streets of Washington, D.C. Tall, dignified Carmichael had brushed the mugger aside, saying, "I'm sorry but you must have the wrong man." The mugger was so surprised that he let Carmichael pass.

From Washington, Rod and I flew to London and then on to Africa. We stopped in East Africa for several weeks, staying at the Leakey family residence in Langata, a suburb of Nairobi, Kenya. Nairobi surprised me. I had expected a lush, tropical city, but Nairobi was arid and even cold because of its elevation.

Louis virtually adopted us. While we were in Africa, he paid many of our expenses from his own pocket. He drove us to Fort Ternan — a site where he and his associates had discovered important Miocene fossil hominoids — and other places of interest. Louis was determined that we see as much as possible of Africa in the short time that we were going to be there.

At Fort Ternan I caught a glimpse of the Leakey stubbornness that had served him so well over the years. He was almost seventy and recovering from hundreds of wild bee stings that might have felled a lesser man. No one could dissuade him from walking up the steep hillside in the heat of the equatorial sun to inspect the excavations firsthand.

Rod and I also visited Olduvai Gorge, where Mary Leakey was still working. It was the only time that I ever saw Louis genuinely angry. Rod is a private pilot, and we had rented a small plane in Nairobi to fly out to Olduvai. Louis wanted us to take Mary a case of Scotch, but in line with flying regulations Rod refused to carry more than one bottle of whiskey across the Tanzanian border. Louis was furious, but Rod, who took his flight regulations very seriously, wouldn't budge. Besides, we knew that Mary was due back in Nairobi within the week.

In the end Louis reluctantly agreed to send Mary only one bottle, but we were very touched by his desire to provide her with what she wanted and possibly also needed. I remember thinking at the time about the silly rumor that had gone around UCLA a few years earlier that Louis and Mary were getting a divorce. People joked that Mary was getting custody of Olduvai. How inappropriate it now seemed. Louis was enormously proud of her work at Olduvai Gorge.

Nonetheless, there were problems. After almost single-handedly polishing off the bottle of Scotch at Olduvai that same evening, Mary, short-haired, stout, and cantankerous, told us that there were times when she was "ashamed to be a Leakey," presumably referring to some of Louis's unorthodox theories and projects, such as Calico. Mary also told us in no uncertain terms what she thought of primatologists in general, especially the female ones whose studies were launched by her husband. Dian she dismissed as "simply mad." Her dislike of Jane Goodall seemed totally unwarranted, apparently based on Jane's good looks and the extensive attention her work had attracted throughout the world.

As the evening wore on, however, Mary warmed up. She literally fluttered her eyes at the good-looking young, blond, six-foot-two geologist who was also visiting from the University of California. She proposed collecting wildflowers with him on the edge of a nearby dormant volcano. She shared stories and joked with us. At the end of the evening, she turned to us and said, "You're not like the others" (meaning primatologists, no doubt).

The next day Mary drove us to our plane and stayed on the field with her dalmatians until we took off, waving from below.

Louis arranged for us to visit Gombe National Park. It was awesome to contemplate Jane Goodall's enormous achievements firsthand. The wild chimpanzees were so habituated that they didn't pay the slightest attention to human observers. One afternoon Rod and I followed a mother and infant, "Passion" and "Pom," out of camp. They climbed straight up a rugged mountainside as we struggled behind them. At one point they encountered another adult female and her juvenile offspring. Passion barely glanced in the female's direction, but Pom ran over to the juvenile and promptly was bitten. She ran back to her mother squealing, but Passion didn't even glance at her daughter or the other chimpanzees.

I was surprised by how small the wild chimpanzees were in comparison with captive chimpanzees I had seen at the Los Angeles zoo. The baboons, however, were decidedly larger and more aggressive than I had remembered them at the zoo. One day, alone, I passed uncomfortably through the center of a large troop, with adult males yawning ostentatiously and exposing formidable fanglike canines. I just kept walking, looking neither left nor right. By the time I reached the small clearing where the wild chimpanzees were fed, the baboon troop had almost magically melted away.

A professor from Stanford University where Jane held a visiting appointment, Paul Ehrlich, arrived at Gombe with his wife, Ann, at the same time we did. He was the author of a recent best-selling book, *The Population Bomb,* that everybody was talking about. Dr. Ehrlich asked me and Rod what we were doing. When I told him we were on our way to study wild orangutans, he asked what kind of preparations we had made and if anybody in Indonesia knew we were coming.

Although we were in touch with a number of Indonesian officials, nobody was going to meet us at the airport in Jakarta. Without thinking I said, "Nobody is waiting for us." A look of total skepticism passed over his face; he turned away and never spoke to us again the whole time we were there. I guess he thought we were orangutan day-trippers.

Gombe was especially beautiful. There were parts of it that truly seemed to be paradise on earth — green and lush, with colorful flowers and a dazzling waterfall. I regretted having to leave after only a week. Jane had to return to London, so for a few days we meandered through the valleys on our own. But time was pressing for us as well; we had to return to Nairobi. We also wanted to go to Karisoke in the Virunga Volcanoes to see mountain gorillas. Unfortunately, Dian was not in camp, and we decided with Louis that we could not wait for her to return. We had to move on to Indonesia. Although I deeply regretted not seeing the mountain gorillas, we thought it bad manners to go to a researcher's camp in her absence.

Mary was due back in Nairobi. Before her arrival Louis took us aside and mentioned that it might be difficult, as Mary would not be enthusiastic about our presence in her home. He indicated that he would appreciate our tolerance and help in keeping her "happy."

At our first dinner together, Louis sat down with Rod and me. Mary sat accompanied by her entourage of two students, who were, however, not staying at the house. After dinner, with a flourish Louis brought out a large box of chocolates bedecked with a red satin ribbon and bow. He handed it to Mary, saying, "From an anonymous admirer."

It was clear the chocolates were from Louis. Mary didn't acknowledge the candy verbally but accepted the box. She opened it, took a chocolate for herself, and passed the box to Louis and then to the two students. Finally she set it down on the table near her. She and the two students started nibbling. Louis looked at her. There was a long silence. At last Louis said, "Perhaps Rod and Biruté would also like some chocolate."

Some unidentifiable sound came from Mary's throat, and she gruffly shoved the box across the table in our direction. Rod and I each took a chocolate, thanked her, and passed the box back to her. Rod and I were flabbergasted. Louis didn't look surprised at all. It was apparent that he, the most gracious of men, was used to such behavior.

Mary, in some deeply personal way, resented the attention Louis gave to primate studies. She thought they were useless. I later realized that it wasn't primate studies Mary resented so much as the fact that Louis had adopted us and "squandered" his personal resources and energy on us to the extent that it even interfered with his health. He referred to Jane as his "fairy foster daughter," and made similar comments about Dian.

Leakey's "primates," as he called us, were competing with Mary and her offspring for Louis's attention, time, energy, and resources. While she was laboring at Olduvai under extremely primitive conditions, Louis was gallivanting around the world, being wined and dined as a celebrity and raising funds for great ape and archaeological studies. No wonder she disliked us!

A number of years later, after Rod and I had been in the field for some time, and after Louis's death, my mother met Mary Leakey in southern California. Upon being introduced, my mother warmly thanked Mary Leakey for the help and support that her late husband, Louis, had given me. Mary Leakey looked at her coldly and said, "Don't thank me. I had nothing to do with it," then turned on her heel and walked away. I told my mother not to take Mary's rebuff personally.

During the three weeks that Rod and I were in Africa, Louis was also helping a curly-haired Beverly Hills, California, student of approximately my age, Elizabeth Meyeroff, to launch a study of a relatively untouched traditional African tribe. Elizabeth visited the Leakey home in Langata only when Mary was not around. Mary's scathing remarks about the innocent Elizabeth reflected a groundless, almost indecent jealousy. Since Rod and I spent virtually twenty-four hours a day with Louis, we knew Louis's schedule and his frailty. We knew that there was absolutely nothing improper in his mentorship of Elizabeth.

In her bright, sunny, southern California way, Elizabeth bubbled with enthusiasm and joy; her unrestrained love for Africa sparked something in Louis. It was actually quite touching. Louis was enchanted by her, as by a favorite daughter. Sweet and seemingly uncomplicated, she was the apple of his eye.

Rod watched Elizabeth with amused skepticism. One day he said to me, "Look at the fashionable way she dresses, at her short skirts and jewelry. How does Louis ever expect her to study some remote African tribe?"

I was annoyed that Rod, of all people, would make such a superficial appraisal, making the same mistake about women and research that everyone else did. Elizabeth's appearance had nothing to do with her ability and her determination to conduct serious research.

"She's for real," I said. "Don't you realize that people could just as easily dismiss me in the same way? Look at Paul Ehrlich. He did to me exactly what you are doing to Elizabeth." Rod thought about it and admitted that I could be right, but he still wasn't convinced.

Elizabeth occasionally accompanied us on outings. One afternoon the four of us were out on the savanna enjoying a picnic. Louis had cut up a very ripe pineapple, which we were all slurping down. Elizabeth, always a hearty eater, had most of it, and her fingers were sticky with pineapple juice. I was closest to Louis, and he glanced at me and said, "Could you get Elizabeth a towel from the car? She needs a towel."

It was true, she did, urgently. I was about to rise but then stopped myself. Louis was looking at me intently. Normally, I would have leaped to my feet, especially since I liked Elizabeth.

Instead I said, "Elizabeth can get her own towel." Louis continued to stare at me. I stared back. Elizabeth quickly got up and came over to where Louis was sitting.

"I didn't do anything wrong," she said. "Why is Biruté angry with me?" She was almost cringing.

Then Louis laughed. "She's not angry," he said, putting his hand on her shoulder, the only time that I ever saw him touch her. "But she should be." He laughed again, but nobody else joined in. Elizabeth went for her own towel.

It was the only time that I ever directly defied Louis, and he was pleased as punch. Was it another test? I wondered. That evening after supper, Rod turned to me, looking very pleased, and said, "You stood up to him. Louis really respects you now."

"He always did," I replied. I was surprised at how proud Rod was that I stood up for myself.

A minor incident perhaps, but there had been a principle at stake, one that Louis himself quickly recognized and acknowledged. It was similar to Dian's ignoring Louis's requests to come to his bedside in London because she wanted to see Jane first. The Kikuyu in Louis appreciated predictability and order, in which everyone knows his or her place.

Louis did not follow conventional social rules about who should wait on whom (in those days, the wife on the husband), however. Mobility was a problem for him. He could only walk with the benefit of his walker or with the help of a sturdy cane. Once he sat down, it was an effort to get up. I think that's why he liked to drive so much. Driving allowed him the full freedom of mobility just like everyone else in the driver's seat, without any concession to his frailty. I noticed that whenever Rod and I were in the room with Louis and Louis needed something, he invariably asked Rod. Rod, who idolized Louis, would immediately leap up to get the great man his glasses, his book, or his drink.

How correctly Louis had judged Elizabeth was verified long after Louis's death. Elizabeth finished her Ph.D. thesis, married a man who worked with the same tribe, and as far as I know, to this day continues to study this African group. Louis would not be surprised.

I savored those final days in Nairobi with Louis. It was said that Louis couldn't get along with other men, but Rod and Louis got along famously. Rod and I used to joke that it was because Rod was shorter than Louis. Still, there was no mistaking the fact that Louis Leakey particularly liked women. What most people missed was the fact that it didn't make the slightest difference whether the woman was a slim twenty-year-old with waist-long hair in a cotton mini-dress or a sturdy sixty-five-year-old in combat boots. Externals didn't matter.

I always felt that Louis Leakey viewed women as a separate species. I suspect that growing up among the Kikuyu, he did not have intimate contact with girls or women. When he went to England as a student and suddenly discovered the female species, he became fascinated by these formerly forbidden creatures. And this fascination was reflected in his lifelong passion for women. He really loved them — but it was "women" in the collective more than the particular. North Americans tend to equate love with sex. But certainly during the time I knew him, Louis was platonic in his ardor. In the tradition of medieval court-iers, for whom the grandest passions were never consummated, Louis wrote love poems (which he tried to have published) about passionate romance that went no further than an embrace or a mere touch. His imagination went be-yond mere sex.

Louis craved female attention and warmth. He seemed most at ease in the presence of adoring females. He clearly loved Mary; she was the principal person in his life. But cigar-smoking, blunt-talking Mary in her khaki trousers spent most of her time at Olduvai. Louis once told me that when he and Mary traveled to Angola in colonial days, before World War II, they were always addressed as "Dr. and Mr." and not "Dr. and Mrs." Mary did not act like a typical wife. Also I realized that he and Mary had only sons, not daughters. (There was a daughter from his first marriage, but she was in England and apparently estranged from Louis's African life.) So Louis "adopted" adoring women like Elizabeth. It was less complicated to keep refilling the "daugh-ter" slot.

Jane, Dian, and I became his daughters, too, but on a different level. Like Mary, we did not worship him. We saw his frailties and his foibles. We stood up to him on occasion. We sometimes disagreed with him. But we still loved him. In this, Jane, Dian, and I became each other's siblings. Like true siblings, we did not choose each other, but were fated to be tied together, often referred to as the "trimates."

The last time I saw Louis was the day we left Africa. Although he was very weak and died soon thereafter, Louis remained spiritually triumphant. He stood leaning on his cane, smiling proudly and broadly, waving vigorously from the doorway of the museum where he had his office. I remember Dian saying that she saw his cane from the air glinting down below in the sun as she was leaving Nairobi. For me, in my mind's eye, Louis's broad smile had the same effect. I still saw it as the plane took off from Nairobi. My heart went out to him. I owed him so much. For me, the journey was just beginning. For him, it was about to end.

# 5
# KALIMANTAN

. . . the indifferent immensity of the natural world.

— *Sir Henry Morton Stanley*

But what about the snakes?

— *Filomena Galdikas*

---

T HE PLANE touched down in Jakarta, the capital of Indonesia, land of seventeen thousand islands, home of the great orange apes. I stumbled out of the air conditioned plane into the heavy heat and trudged with my hand luggage toward the terminal. It was dusk. The airport building seemed to be under construction. Inside, fluorescent lamps cast a dim, greenish glow over the entire scene, compounding my feeling of unreality. Passengers, porters, and customs officials jostled each other in a medley of noise and confusion. Random shouts punctuated the din. The air was scented with clove-flavored cigarettes. This slightly sweet, spicy smell would become the distinctive fragrance of Indonesia for me.

Trancelike, I wandered through the crowd, searching for the conveyor belt that held our green backpacks. Beside me, Rod was silent, seemingly in a daze. After picking up our luggage, we slowly snaked our way through the immigration, disease control, and customs checks. The various officials seemed curiously uninterested in our reason for being in Indonesia, stamping our passports with a tired air as if the heat weighed on their shoulders.

The scene outside was chaotic. Dozens of taxis were stalled at awkward angles, their drivers all honking and shouting to attract emerging travelers.

Trying to find a metered taxi was futile, so we bargained furiously to bring the price of the taxi ride down to less than the cost of a plane ticket.

By the time we arrived at our hotel, it was pitch black and raining hard. After checking into our room, we ate our first meal in Indonesia at midnight in a deserted coffee shop. The rain was so loud that it drowned out conversation.

The next morning, my first impression of Jakarta was of one huge bazaar, jammed with shops, stalls, stands, pushcarts, and roadside markets with piles of wares. The main roads overflowed with an improbable assortment of ancient trucks and buses, pedicabs, and three-wheeled motorcycle cabs, all of which served as public transportation. The shifting smells, sounds, and colors seemed like an illustration from the 1001 tales of Scheherazade. But Jakarta is also a modern capital, with enormous statues and monuments towering overhead, giving the city an imperial air. Neighborhoods with tree-lined boulevards and walled white villas crowd against gleaming skyscrapers and sprawling shanty-towns.

My most vivid and lasting impression was of the people. Everyone in Indonesia smiled. No matter where I looked, no matter what happened, no matter how inappropriate, people seemed to smile. At first, the incessant smiling made me uneasy; it seemed pathological. In time, however, as I became used to it, I found it wonderfully comforting. How nice to be surrounded by people whose first reaction to any problem is to smile.

Finding our way through the streets was bewildering. Neither Rod nor I spoke Indonesian. We had mastered numbers, having heard that bargaining was an essential skill, but little more. When we located our first government office, we were relieved to find that many Indonesian government officials spoke English. The officials we talked to at the Institute of Sciences — Ms. Sjamsiah Akmad, Dr. Bachtiar Rifai, and Mr. Napitapulu — seemed to be accustomed to dealing with foreigners, and gave us detailed, step-by-step instructions as to the various offices we had to visit.

Once cleared by the police, immigration, and other agencies, our next step was to report to the Forestry Department in the city of Bogor, forty miles south of Jakarta. Founded five hundred years ago and built around a huge, lush, botanical garden, Bogor was the old Dutch colonial administrative capital. Today it is a center for scientific studies and administration. It is also the thunderstorm capital of Indonesia, perhaps even of the world. Two days out of three, storms sweep in from the mountains during the late afternoon.

Our first meeting in Bogor was with Mr. Walman Sinaga, the head of

P.P.A., Indonesia's Nature Conservation and Wildlife Management Agency, a branch of the Forestry Department. Mr. Sinaga reported to the director general of the Indonesian Forestry Department, Dr. Soedjarwo, who was said to be immensely powerful. Mr. Sinaga was a tough but jovial Batak from northern Sumatra, who had fought in the guerilla war that led to Indonesia's independence from the Dutch. By local standards, Mr. Sinaga was a large man. His bluff and hearty manner made us feel instantly welcome. Louis Leakey had written to him, and Mr. Sinaga was eagerly awaiting our arrival. He immediately invited us to stay in his home, where we were treated most graciously. Mr. Sinaga's strong support paved my way in Indonesia.

We had all the permits we needed to establish a field site. The question now was where it should be. Our various letters specified only that we were going to study orangutans. Before I left North America, I had made up my mind to go to Sumatra. The few studies of orangutans published so far had all been done on the island of Borneo. Little was known about the Sumatran subspecies. But Mr. Sinaga already had decided to send me to Tanjung Puting Reserve in the province of Kalimantan Tengah, or Central Indonesian Borneo.

In the face of my resistance, Mr. Sinaga outlined his arguments. Dutch scientists had just begun an orangutan study in northern Sumatra, and P.P.A. has a strong presence there. The orangutans of Kalimantan Tengah were virtually unknown. In living memory, no foreigner had visited the Tanjung Puting Reserve. Proudly, Mr. Sinaga announced that we would be the first Western visitors to the area, and that I would be the first scientist to conduct field research in Kalimantan Tengah.

Mr. Sinaga went on to explain that there was no conservation officer in the entire province. The closest P.P.A. official was hundreds of miles away. Mr. Sinaga was very blunt. Regular forestry officers were stationed in the province. But their primary job was to supervise cutting the forest; conservation came second. The Forestry Department received more money from selling concessions to logging companies than from protecting the forests.

Mr. Sinaga himself was a dedicated conservationist and a master at walking the tightrope between forestry and conservation. He achieved this balancing act in part by sending his children and other relatives to serve in distant P.P.A. offices. The Bataks are one of the few Indonesian ethnic groups who use surnames. I was later told that there were Sinagas in P.P.A. offices throughout the country. In Southeast Asia in general, this was an expected practice. After all, it made sense to surround yourself with people whom you liked and could

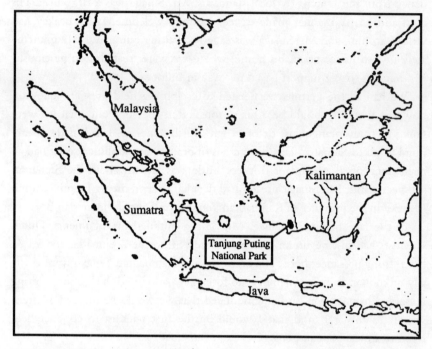

Location of Tanjung Puting Reserve (now a national park), the site of Camp Leakey.

trust, and who did you like better or trust more than your own family? But Mr. Sinaga had no officials in Kalimantan Tengah. We would serve as Mr. Sinaga's "eyes and ears," reporting directly to him.

Mr. Sinaga saved his strongest argument for last. "By the way," he added, "a P.P.A. team found orangutans in Tanjung Puting just three months ago." The recent, documented presence of orangutans was the clincher. Without further discussion, I agreed.

Mr. Sinaga seemed to like me and to understand my mission to explore the world of wild orangutans. He sincerely wanted me to succeed. At that first meeting, he mentioned his correspondence with Louis Leakey several times, as if he had made a promise to Leakey.

"But," said Mr. Sinaga, "you must get one thing straight. I will do everything in my power to help you. But I want no criticism."

Mr. Sinaga made it clear that if we disagreed with how things were done, we should not criticize him or his agency in public, but speak directly to him. He would welcome constructive proposals, but only if presented privately and discreetly. "You are my guests," he stated emphatically. "Polite guests in someone's home do not criticize their host." He stopped and looked at us thoughtfully before he continued. "Westerners have an unfortunate tendency to criticize, criticize, criticize." I recalled my field experience in Yugoslavia.

Once I agreed to go to Kalimantan Tengah, Mr. Sinaga called Mr. Soegito, a trusted lieutenant, into his office. Slight and somewhat stooped, Mr. Soegito seemed shy and unassuming. Whereas Mr. Sinaga was a typically hearty, outspoken Batak, Mr. Soegito personified Javanese deference and reserve. While Mr. Sinaga, Rod, and I talked, Mr. Soegito did not say a word. I would learn later that this silence masked considerable energy, endless patience, and an intimate knowledge of local officialdom and protocol.

Mr. Soegito would escort us to Tanjung Puting, making all the arrangements for our trip. First, however, he had to fulfill previous commitments in Bogor. We would have to wait.

I felt trapped in a time warp again, so close to Borneo, but still waiting. The wild orangutans were only one island away, but with every passing day, I sensed that they were slipping away. In lieu of observing live orangutans, I was reduced to studying the collection of orangutan skeletons and skins in the natural history museum in Bogor. I was afraid to fall asleep at night, afraid that the dream would end and I would wake up back in Los Angeles.

To pass the time, Rod and I shopped for supplies in local markets. One day, out of curiosity, we bought a durian, which I had read was a favorite fruit among orangutans. A durian is a large, almost volleyball-sized fruit covered with sharp spikes, like the head of a medieval mace. In its heavy armor, durian resembles a dinosaur. When ripe, the seams open and the fruit spills out in sections, revealing creamy-textured yellow flesh surrounding large hard seeds. The common description of durian — "It tastes like heaven and smells like hell" — is only half true. To me, eating durian was like sleeping with a skunk on my pillow. The odor was so overwhelming that by the time we opened the fruit I had a headache. We hurriedly gave the rest to the cook. Durian is an acquired taste; only much later would I recognize it as the king of fruits.

As the days of enforced waiting dragged by, I began to grasp the traditional Indonesian concept of time. Expressing impatience or trying to hurry things along was useless. The Javanese believe that time is infinite. Time never runs out. Since there is always enough of it, time has little meaning. With the exception of Indonesia's professional military, Indonesians refuse to live under the tyranny of the clock. This does not mean that they are always late. It means that they are unpredictable. Indonesia is the only place where I have ever known a regularly scheduled airplane flight to leave two hours early! When asked to attend a function at a certain time, Indonesians politely inquire, "Military time or rubber time?"

After two interminable weeks, we left Bogor and flew across the Java Sea to the island of Borneo. In 1971, Borneo was still a backwater. When we inquired at the Indonesian Embassy in Washington, D.C., before we left North America, we found that no one at the embassy had ever been to Borneo. No one could tell us whether the practice of head-hunting still existed on the island. All our information came from books written by turn-of-the-century explorers and adventurers. It was like going to Arizona with only nineteenth-century newspaper accounts of Apache raids as background. But in some ways, these early accounts were still accurate. In the interior of Borneo, time had stood still. Men in loincloths still hunted with blowguns; women with dangling earlobes still carried babies in beaded backpacks. Although head-hunting had apparently disappeared, bone-cleansing ceremonies — in which an ancestor's bones are exhumed, purified, and, after much dancing, drinking, and reciting, reburied — were still common.

Borneo is the third-largest island on this planet, after Greenland and New Guinea. With nearly 290,000 square miles, it is five times the size of England

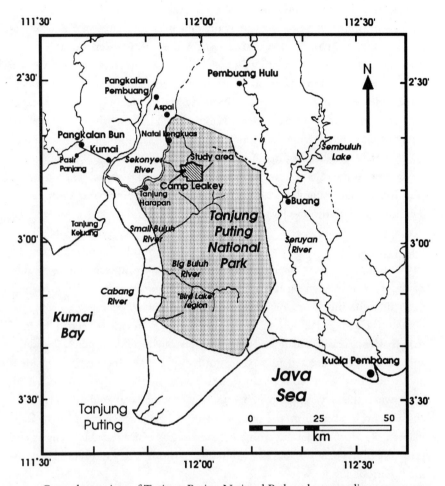

General overview of Tanjung Puting National Park and surrounding areas.

and Wales and almost qualifies as a minicontinent. Borneo and Sumatra, the only other island on which orangutans are still found, are both geologically part of the Malay Archipelago, the string of islands that stretches across the equator between the continents of Asia and Australia.

The northern third of Borneo is divided into the states of Sarawak and Sabah, which are part of modern Malaysia, and the tiny, independent, oil-rich sultanate of Brunei Darussalam. (The name "Borneo" is an Anglicized version of "Brunei.") The remainder of the island is part of Indonesia. "Kalimantan" is the Indonesian name for Borneo. Nobody knows precisely what this stands for. Whereas some speculate that "Kalimantan" means "river of gems" or "river of diamonds," which are found in abundance in some areas, others suggest that it means "land of many rivers." Kalimantan is divided into four provinces (East, South, Central, and West). Tanjung Puting Reserve, where I would launch my wild orangutan study, is located in Central Kalimantan, on a large peninsula jutting into the Java Sea.

Our plane landed in Banjarmasin, the capital of South Kalimantan. An old city of houses on stilts, floating markets, and crisscrossing canals and streams, Banjarmasin is located on the banks of the winding Martapura River, which flows into the much broader Barito river. The next day we took a longboat upriver to Palangka Raya, the provincial capital of Kalimantan Tengah. In contrast to Banjarmasin, Palangka Raya is a new town, with concrete buildings and paved roads, created in 1957 by order of former Indonesian President Soekarno (usually spelled "Sukarno" in the Western press). Kalimantan Tengah is known as the Dayak province, because the province was established by Dayaks who broke away from the predominantly Melayu province of South Kalimantan. The provincial government bureaucracy of Kalimantan Tengah was primarily in the hands of Dayaks, although many officials of the central government stationed there were Javanese.

After a brief meeting with the Dayak governor, Mr. Sylvanus, we were introduced to the head of forestry for the province, Mr. Widajat. A tall, square-faced Javanese, Mr. Widajat beamed a good deal, but clearly took his position and responsibilities quite seriously.

During our first meeting, Mr. Widajat brought out maps of Tanjung Puting Reserve. At P.P.A. headquarters in Bogor, Mr. Sinaga had told us that the reserve was approximately three hundred thousand hectares (more than eleven hundred square miles, or about the size of Yosemite National Park in the United States today). On Mr. Widajat's maps, the reserve had been reduced to a postage stamp. Less than a third (ninety thousand hectares) was left. Making matters worse, Mr. Widajat pointed to places where various logging concessions had been granted within the reserve. I was shocked. I turned to Mr. Soegito, who was sitting by silently.

"What about this?" I gasped in disbelief.

Mr. Soegito's expression did not change. "We'll discuss it later," he murmured.

I could not restrain myself. I turned to Mr. Widajat and said, "But Mr. Sinaga told us that the reserve was over three hundred thousand hectares."

Mr. Widajat smiled pleasantly at me. "Oh," he replied, "Sinaga just wishes it were so."

Total innocent that I was, I assumed there must be some mistake. Immediately after the meeting I questioned Mr. Soegito again. He seemed unconcerned. "I will mention this to Mr. Sinaga when I return to Bogor," was his only response to my vehement protests. It was the first of many lessons that things were not always as they seemed in Indonesia. To a Westerner the idea that a national reserve could be one size on one map and two-thirds smaller on another, literally losing ground as one moved from central to provincial headquarters, was unthinkable. That Mr. Soegito, a high-ranking forestry official, seemed so nonchalant about this was equally incomprehensible. But it appeared that, for the moment, there was nothing to be done.

Talking to Mr. Widajat and other officials, I began to learn about the history of national parks and how conservation is organized in Indonesia. The basic system was established under the Dutch, who created two types of reserves. In a nature reserve, nothing could be touched, not even a leaf or a small stone. But the Dutch had established only a few nature reserves, all on the island of Java. All other conservation areas, including Tanjung Puting, were game reserves. In a game reserve, the animals could not be touched, but this protection did not extend to the habitat itself. It was legal to cut down trees for timber or for slash-and-burn horticulture within the reserve. Robbed of their habitat by logging and burning, animals cannot survive. In any case, protection and preservation were moot issues.

At the time we arrived, the laws protecting wildlife were not being enforced. Tanjung Puting had been established specifically as a reserve for rhinoceroses, orangutans, and proboscis monkeys. But the rhinoceroses that once roamed Tanjung Puting were already extinct, sacrificed to the overseas market for their horns, particularly in China and Singapore where powdered rhino horn is considered an aphrodisiac and also is used to treat fevers. All that remained of the rhinoceros's once common presence in the reserve were a few dried-up wallows where wild pigs now congregated. The orangutans and proboscis monkeys remaining in the reserve were highly endangered. Some of the reserve's other primates (agile gibbons, red leaf-eating monkeys, tarsiers, and slow lorises), as well as the endemic Borneo golden muntjac or "barking deer," Malayan sun bears, and a few vestige herds of wild banteng cattle had protected status but still were hunted. No one knew how many of these animals remained, let alone such rarely encountered animals as the reclusive, nocturnal, clouded leopard. Even conservation officials seemed to take wildlife for granted.

Despite his stance on the reserve, Mr. Widajat was an excellent host and I found myself liking him. He threw a lavish party for thirty or more in our honor. After a sumptuous buffet (but no alcoholic drink, because Mr. Widajat was a devout Muslim), we all settled down to a comfortable evening, some sitting cross-legged on finely woven reed mats, others reclining on plush sofas. Suddenly, Mr. Widajat stood up and vigorously burst into song. Several other provincial officials did the same. Then the entire party turned expectantly to Rod and me.

Singing is not a strong suit for either of us. We protested, but Mr. Widajat and Mr. Soegito jovially insisted that it was the custom. Finally, after much consultation, Rod and I stood and croaked out a few verses of "Jingle Bells." Our feeble musical performance was greeted with stunned silence. A few of the guests even stopped smiling.

It was in Palangka Raya that we first encountered captive orangutans. Western visitors were relatively rare in those days, and word of our interest in orangutans circulated quickly. Most people seemed puzzled that anyone would travel a great distance merely to see an ape, but they tried to be helpful, telling stories of their own experiences and pointing out houses where orangutans were kept as pets. Although I saw only a few, I got the impression that captive orangutans were common. The sight of an orangutan infant confined to a small, filthy cage in someone's yard horrified me.

"Mr. Soegito," I demanded of our Forestry Department guide, "isn't it against the law to keep captive orangutans?"

"Yes, it is," answered Mr. Soegito agreeably.

"Why isn't the Forestry Department doing something? Why isn't P.P.A. confiscating captive orangutans?"

Mr. Soegito did not reply immediately, but looked at me as if I were unbelievably naive.

"Why don't they confiscate captive orangutans?" he repeated. With a shrug, he finally answered, "Perhaps they will. Someday."

While I fumed, Mr. Soegito gazed down benevolently on the captive orangutans, exchanging pleasantries with their owners. I felt a bit like Alice in Wonderland, where nothing was as it seemed.

One of the first captives I met was a young female named "Cempaka." Owned by a retired forestry officer and his wife, Cempaka was clearly a substitute child for the wife, whose children had grown up and left home. The orangutan slept under a mosquito net with the wife at night, was carried and hugged like a baby much of the day, and took her meals with the owner. During the Muslim holy month of Ramadan, Cempaka observed the dawn to dusk fast along with other family members. When the wife was busy with other chores, however, Cempaka had to be caged. She was not housebroken, and could be quite destructive of household goods.

Cempaka was locked up when we arrived. I asked to see her outside of the cage, and the owners kindly agreed. It took the husband almost fifteen minutes to untie, unwire, and unlock the cage. The tangle of contraptions to prevent Cempaka from escaping looked like something contrived at a convention of mad inventors. It was pure Rube Goldberg: all that was missing were the bells, whistles, and wheels. The owner explained that ordinary locks and chains were like child's play to the orangutan.

No sooner had the husband released her than Cempaka climbed to the top of the tallest coconut tree in the yard and refused to come down. With my few words of Indonesian I tried to suggest that Cempaka needed to be with her own species in the wild. The owners appeared uncomprehending. I didn't know whether it was my Indonesian, or the idea that wild animals have needs of their own, that the couple couldn't understand.

Dusk came, but still Cempaka could not be coaxed or intimidated back into her cage. I can still see her black silhouette clinging to the tree trunk, ignoring the insistent demands of the owner's husband and a growing band of neighbors below, as we drove away.

When we met Cempaka, we had no idea of the extent of the problem. We later learned that many orangutan "owners" were otherwise respectable people, who were not only members of the upper-middle class, but also government officials. Apparently owning an ape was a status symbol in Kalimantan. The one high official in Palangka Raya who did not keep a wild animal as a pet was the governor himself. The governor was a Dayak. Although he held an engineering degree, Governor Sylvanus had been born in a longhouse in the interior and had grown up in the forest. To him, orangutans would have seemed commonplace, perhaps even a symbol of the more technologically primitive life he had left behind.

Before we left Palangka Raya, Mr. Widajat added another member to our group, Mr. Heurybut, a forestry officer who had recently surveyed parts of the Tanjung Puting Reserve to assess their logging potential. Mr. Heurybut also was an artist. He had sculpted the bas-reliefs, full of trees and animals, for the exterior walls of Mr. Widajat's office. Though we had talked little, I felt instant empathy with Mr. Heurybut through his art.

Bidding goodbye to Mr. Widajat, we flew from Palangka Raya to Pangkalan Bun, the closest town with an airport to the reserve at Tanjung Puting. Whereas Palangka Raya is in the interior of Kalimantan Tengah, Pangkalan Bun is located on the Arut River, near the southern coast. In those days, Pangkalan Bun was a small, sleepy town of about ten thousand, with one main street and no sidewalks, reminiscent of the old Wild West. The streets were dusty in the dry season and muddy during the rainy season. The few stores in town carried only sardines, canned pigs' feet from mainland China, and packaged noodles. A small selection of local produce was sold from stalls in a daily market near the river. In the entire town there were only six or seven jeeps, some ancient trucks, and a few motorcycles.

We were met at the airport by a delegation of local forestry officials, arrayed in formation on the airfield as the plane taxied in. They were obviously impressed by Mr. Soegito's high status. They shook our hands and took our luggage as we stepped off the plane, then rushed us to the quarters for visiting dignitaries.

Before settling in, we paid a courtesy call on the *Bupati*. The office of *Bupati* is an ancient one, predating colonial rule. Originally the *Bupatis* acted as officials for the reigning sultan; today they are regents for the provincial governor. All Indonesia is divided into districts called *kabupatens*. Within his district, the *Bupati* exercises considerable authority. In areas rarely visited by foreigners twenty years ago, all visitors were expected to report to the *Bupati*, state their business, and gain his approval. Whether scientist or tourist, outsiders could be expelled by the *Bupati*, no explanation given or required.

At the time we arrived, the *Bupati* was a former major in the Indonesian army, from the small island of Madura. The Madurans are seafarers who are known throughout Indonesia for their hospitality, their sense of honor, their clan loyalty, and their feuds. People say if you start a fight with one Maduran, you end by fighting thirty. Major Rafii, now *Bupati*, was the first official we had met who did not speak any English. Although the interview was brief and he seemed unclear about our goals, he welcomed us. We had observed the correct protocol.

Our way cleared, we returned to our room in the official guest house. It was a spacious room with peeling, whitewashed walls, large windows, and curtains too small and flimsy to keep curious passersby from peering in. Part of the room jutted out over the Arut River, which links Pangkalan Bun to the Java Sea. Through numerous holes in the wooden floors we could look down into the current below. To go to the toilet we had to step outside to a stall built directly over the river. The river was also the communal bathtub. I watched in disbelief as people unconcernedly brushed their teeth and bathed a few meters from outhouses, while human feces floated by.

This (to us) unsanitary condition notwithstanding, Indonesians are probably the cleanest people in the world; they take baths two or three times a day. Bathing is almost a national hobby. In contrast, during the few days I was in Pangkalan Bun, I remained unwashed. There were no private facilities for bathing. Knowing that the river was filthy and that huge crowds would gather for the spectacle of a Western woman trying to bathe, I decided not to take a bath at all.

During our stay in Pangkalan Bun, we were visited by the local Roman Catholic priest, a German. He and his sister, a nun, were the only resident Europeans in the whole area. Since he did not speak English very well and we spoke no German, we conversed in an odd mixture of English and Indonesian.

Clearly he had a pressing message to convey to us. After much consultation with dictionaries, we decoded one phrase: "red onions." He was genuinely worried that we would go into the forest unprepared and starve. Many people who are not familiar with the rain forest imagine a tropical paradise, where the trees are loaded with pineapples, bananas, papayas, and other fruits just waiting to be picked. But although the forests look lush, there actually is very little to eat in any one place. This is why the tropics have been called a "counterfeit paradise." The priest wanted to explain that red onions and a few spices could turn plain white rice, the bread and potatoes of Asia and the only food readily available, into a tasty meal of fried rice.

Meanwhile, the head of forestry in Pangkalan Bun added another officer,

Mr. Yusuran, to our growing escort. The Forestry Department also insisted on making all the arrangements for our trip to Tanjung Puting. I was eager to begin the last lap of the journey to the great forests where the wild orangutan live. But yet again we were told to wait. No reason was given.

A few days later all our supplies were loaded onto the Forestry Department jeep and our group — now five people — drove to Kumai. Although only ten miles from Pangkalan Bun, the dirt road had turned to mud and the drive took five hours.

Distance cannot be measured in miles in Borneo. Because there is so little dry land, most travel is by boat, not by foot or wheeled vehicle. Rivers are Borneo's highways. Located on two different rivers, Pangkalan Bun and Kumai might as well be on separate continents. The two towns face in different directions. When you leave Pangkalan Bun by river, you face into the interior and begin the long journey into the heart of Borneo, where the Dayaks live. Kumai faces outward to the sea. A community of fishermen and shipbuilders perched on the coast, Kumai has little in common with inland communities or culture.

Pangkalan Bun and Kumai were worlds apart in other ways. Because Pangkalan Bun is the seat of local government, the *kabupaten* capital, its population included officials from Java, Madura, Sulawesi, and other Indonesian islands, Dayaks from the interior of Borneo, Chinese merchants, and coastal Malays or Melayu. Walking through town, one might hear conversations in a dozen native dialects as well as the Indonesian language. Muslims, Catholics, Protestants, Hindus, Buddhists, and animists mingled freely. In contrast, Kumai in those days was ethnically and religiously homogeneous, its population entirely Melayu and exclusively Muslim. The Melayu are a distinct ethnic group, who probably originated on the Malay Peninsula and now also live in villages on the sea coasts of Borneo. Their forebears were strongly influenced by the Arab travelers who brought Islam to Indonesia in the fourteenth century, and the Melayu remain orthodox Muslims today.

In Pangkalan Bun people may have stared at us, but in Kumai, crowds gathered. We were probably the first Westerners to walk the streets of Kumai since colonial times.

In Kumai, yet another man joined our group. He was not directly introduced to us, but was simply pointed out as our cook (Mr. Hamzah, we later learned). We were never asked if we would like a cook or any other assistants. It was simply assumed that we wanted companions. No one goes anywhere alone in Indonesia. The idea of traveling solo is as foreign as walking (not driving) to the supermarket would be in Los Angeles. And so at each place we stopped, another person was added to our party: Mr. Heurybut, a forestry officer, in Palangka Raya; Mr. Yusuran, also a forestry officer, in Pangkalan Bun; and last, Mr. Hamzah, our cook, in Kumai.

Finally we loaded our belongings, our supplies, and our growing entourage onto two small speedboats. After all the years of planning, dreaming, and waiting in North America, and the slow, hot, humid weeks in Indonesia, our departure from Kumai seemed almost sudden.

We followed the wide, brackish Kumai River south, downstream toward the Java Sea, then turned left into the mouth of the Sekonyer River, shrouded in nipa palms. A black-water river, the Sekonyer is the color of diluted Coca-Cola. About ten miles upstream the solid walls of nipa palms, which require salty water, give way to the tall trees and tangled vines of primary tropical rain forest.

A mile past the nipa palms, at a place called Tanjung Harapan, stood the Sekonyer Village. At the time, this small village of several hundred Melayu stood inside the Tanjung Puting Reserve. The village consisted of a collection of small huts, built on stilts to keep out the damp and the snakes and to protect inhabitants from frequent floods and, in times past, from head-hunting raids.

Fifteen miles past the village, the river divides. The left branch, the Sekonyer Kiri, leads northwest toward camps and villages where local people would later pan for gold. At the time, there were only small settlements of slash-and-burn horticulturalists and wild-rubber tappers. The right branch, the Sekonyer Kanan, enters the reserve, narrowing perceptibly as it winds northeast. Although the river is deep, the vegetation on either side is so close that it almost obscures the water. If the local people did not keep the Sekonyer Kanan open, the river would be choked by its own vegetation. The place where I would establish my base camp is approximately five miles upstream.

The driver of our speedboat that day raced up the river, taking the twists and turns of the Sekonyer at death-defying speeds. Occasionally, the side of the boat dipped into the river and water poured in. I was convinced that the Orangutan Research and Conservation Project would end up on the bottom of the Sekonyer River. There were no life vests on board, and I imagined us all, generously flavored with red onions, becoming hearty morsels for a crocodile feast.

At the fork of the Sekonyer Kanan and Sekonyer Kiri Rivers we transferred to two small dugout canoes, which materialized at the side of the river. In our canoe, a silent Melayu steered while Rod and I took turns paddling. It was raining steadily. For much of the trip I sat hunched over in the middle of the boat, drenched, trying to cover Rod and myself with a useless umbrella. Silently, we glided past ominous, dark, apparently endless forest. I saw no animal or bird life in the gray rain. Even the occasional huts on the riverbank seemed deserted. The forest was absolutely still, a seemingly impenetrable fortress of vegetation.

Then, suddenly, around a bend, the river opened up into a wide lake with tall, single trees rising majestically out of the mists, almost as if the trees were floating above the water. We passed into a second lake and a third; then our little dugout veered to the side, through the river-edge swamp to a landing place. We had arrived at my study site, the place I would name "Camp Leakey."

There stood a small, bark-walled, nipa-thatched hut, similar to those we had passed in the rain. The hut had been built by hand-loggers and then abandoned about a year earlier. It was in such bad condition that some weeks later Rod admitted he had fully expected me to take one look and insist that we return to Kumai. How wrong Rod was. After hours on the river in the rain, the hut offered welcome relief. Most important, I had finally arrived in the great forest, home of the wild orangutans. Besides, I told myself, the hut was only going to be temporary; we would soon build a solid, wood shelter.

Hurrying out of the rain, we carried our belongings inside. On that first evening, we heard the voices of unseen Melayu in a temporary settlement about a mile away. Fragments of their sad-toned, almost wailing, song floated across the lake, mingling with the whine of cicadas and endowing the night with a mystical quality as the sun took its downward plunge. Working in the dark, the men cooked rice and fried sardines — flavored with red onions. But I was too exhilarated and too tired to eat. I fell asleep on an old worn reed mat on the floor of the hut, lulled by the rain and the knowledge that I had reached my destination.

Beyond the hut, stretching for what seemed to be forever, was the tropical rain forest, a relic of the ancient forests from which humankind had emerged so long ago, and where orangutans still make their home. It was November 6, 1971.

Mr. Soegito later told me that a male orangutan long-called in the distance, persistently and repeatedly, that night.

The next day we began settling into the small, primitive hut. This "temporary" shelter would be our home for several years. Constructed of peeling, chocolate-brown bark, with only one small window, the hut was perpetually gloomy. A hall stretched along one side; the other side was divided into a large room with open rafters and a smaller storeroom, or *gudang,* with a ceiling of wooden boards. We eventually put a mattress on the ceiling of the *gudang,* creating a loft bed of sorts.

My first week at Tanjung Puting felt like a jail sentence. For years I had dreamed of wandering the forest by myself, "alone with nature," searching for wild orangutans. Instead I was confined to a tiny, airless hut with five men. I had no privacy except after sundown, when oil lamps made from small sardine cans left most of the hut in darkness and I could retreat into the shadows.

My Indonesian escorts would not let me go anywhere by myself, or even with Rod. Nor were they eager to venture out with me. They explained that the adjacent forest, which shimmered, mysterious yet inviting, was swamp, or *rawa.* The way they spoke about the swamp, *rawa* sounded like the most feared word in the Indonesian language.

Our first morning, Mr. Soegito and the forestry officers led us across an open field to dry-ground forest, almost a mile away. I remember scrambling over huge fallen logs, desperately trying to keep up. All the men seemed to be in superb physical condition, including Rod, as if they did this every day of their lives. Louis Leakey had proudly told people that I was practicing on trapezes and trampolines for the tall tropical rain forest. During my first week, I wished it were true. In reality, I had just been walking long distances — this was before the rage for jogging in North America — and taking an occasional modern-dance class. Even before we reached the forest I was drenched with sweat.

Most of that week, however, we hardly ever left the hut. We had arrived during the wet season. It usually rained all day, but if it didn't rain in the morning, it was sure to in the afternoon. Our Indonesian companions seemed to be in horror of the rain. It would take me years to understand this seemingly irrational fear. My companions also seemed to be terrified of the leeches, which came with the rain. I can remember Mr. Heurybut, the young forestry official from Palangka Raya, using a handkerchief to pick one off his trouser leg, with a look of total disgust. Mr. Soegito, who had been so meek and obliging before, now declared that we *must* return from whatever excursion we began by eleven o'clock in the morning, to avoid the dreaded rain.

Since it didn't get dark until almost seven o'clock in the evening, this meant that we had to spend another eight hours in the confines of the hut, or nearby, each day. In the afternoons the atmosphere in the tiny hut was claustrophobic. I could not move in any direction without bumping into someone. There was no furniture. After several days of sitting on the damp floor, Rod and I slung our Singapore army-surplus hammocks from the pole supports of the hut. We were relatively comfortable, but horribly bored. The only reading material I had allowed myself were two *National Geographic* magazines, with cover stories by Jane Goodall and Dian Fossey on their work with the African apes, plus a book on the snakes of Malaysia, which I had bought secondhand in Singapore. We waited for the inevitable rains, lit our antimosquito coils, tried to dry our wet clothing, ate our rice and sardines, and then went to bed.

Our four Indonesian friends were unfailingly cheerful, despite the cramped quarters. They talked, took long naps, washed their clothes, and talked some more, in Indonesian. Whenever they caught my eye, they smiled, but smiling back was becoming more and more of an effort for me.

One day I found myself alone with Mr. Heurybut. As if he had been waiting for this opportunity, Mr. Heurybut immediately sat down, leaned toward me with a look of concern sparked with curiosity, and asked in English, "Aren't you afraid?"

"Of what?" I asked, annoyed by his presumption.

"Of studying wild orangutans all by yourself," he replied.

"No, why should I be?" I inquired.

"You are a young woman. It could be dangerous." He seemed very intent. "You know," he continued, "orangutans sometimes take women up into trees and rape them!"

I didn't know what to say. There was a long moment of silence. "What nonsense these people believe," I thought to myself. "How preposterous."

Finally, trying to be diplomatic, I replied, "Well, maybe so, but I am not afraid."

Mr. Heurybut looked skeptical, but said no more. He went outside, leaving me to contemplate something that wasn't in the primatology textbooks. When I later recounted the exchange to Rod, we both chuckled at the naivete of local beliefs. How could Mr. Heurybut, a college graduate, actually think that orangutan males raped women! It was too ridiculous for words.

Toward the end of the week, on a rare sunny morning, Mr. Soegito and I were resting after a trek into the forest. We sat under a jackfruit tree beside the camp. There were so many questions I wanted to ask, beginning with the issue of captive orangutans. But at this point, I didn't speak Indonesian and Mr. Soegito's English seemed limited. I knew that he rarely volunteered information, and was not sure how to open a discussion. But I didn't have to. Mr. Soegito glanced up into the foliage of the jackfruit tree and said, "Just think.

Someday there will be captive orangutans in this very tree. And you will release them."

That is all he said. Then he fell silent. I was stunned; it was totally out of
character. Mr. Soegito had been given a job to do: take this North American
couple to Kalimantan Tengah, introduce them to the right officials, show them
the ropes, and deposit them safely in the forests of Tanjung Puting. This quiet,
agreeable man was not one to initiate confrontations. He understood the
difficulties of wildlife conservation in Indonesia, yet he seemed to comprehend
my need to do something.

That statement, "Someday there will be captive orangutans in this very tree.
And you will release them," gave me permission to start the captive orangutan
rehabilitation program at Tanjung Puting. With his words, Mr. Soegito was
proffering his support, while still covering his tracks in case something went
wrong. Perhaps he thought I could accomplish more than a local person because, as an outsider, I wasn't involved in local political or economic struggles.
Also, I would be more visible. Or perhaps he sensed my deep conviction and
my Western desire to take action.

I already had seen wild orangutans, briefly. Mr. Heurybut, Mr. Yusuran,
Rod, and I were near the fork of the Sekonyer Kanan and Sekonyer Kiri rivers,
paddling a small dugout canoe. Suddenly I glimpsed a spot of red quickly
moving away from the river, followed by a smaller fluff of orange. It was a
mother orangutan and her juvenile offspring. They climbed as high as they
could into the canopy, squeaking and hooting as they showered us with
branches. I wanted to get out of the canoe for a better look, but the orangutans
started moving away. Mr. Heurybut forbid me to leave the boat. I agreed reluctantly, but he was probably right. Without trails or supplies, it was impossible
to pursue fleeing orangutans into the shoulder-deep swamps.

I was exhilarated. Difficult as they might be to follow and observe, I had
actually seen the elusive red apes. Already I had disproved the skeptical UCLA
professors who predicted that I might never even find my subject. I knew the
orangutans were there, as they had been for centuries, even millennia.

His mission of taking us to the orangutans accomplished, Mr. Soegito was
ready to return to Bogor. Bouraq Airlines, a private company established only
months earlier, flew a DC–3 into Pangkalan Bun every Saturday morning, but
exactly when the plane would arrive and depart were unpredictable. Good
manners required that everyone accompany Mr. Soegito to the airport. That
Friday we arose before dawn to take the forestry boat, which had arrived the

night before, to Kumai. We spent the night in Kumai. The next morning, we were joined by the local forestry officer, and all traveled by jeep to Pangkalan Bun. At the airport we sat on a hard, backless wooden bench, struggling to make polite conversation. Hours passed, but the plane didn't come.

Mr. Soegito finally turned to us and said, "There is no need for you to wait with me; please feel free to go back to Tanjung Puting." We protested, but he insisted. Much later we discovered that poor Mr. Soegito sat on the hard wooden bench every day for a week. The plane did not arrive until the following Saturday morning. Mr. Soegito's waiting was characteristic of traditional Indonesian patience.

We said good-bye to Mr. Heurybut in Pangkalan Bun and drove back to Kumai with Mr. Hamzah and Mr. Yusuran. When we boarded the boat to return to Tanjung Puting late that afternoon, we were surprised to learn that Mr. Yusuran was returning with us. No one had told us that the forestry office in Pangkalan Bun had posted Mr. Yusuran to the Tanjung Puting Reserve, with instructions to assist us in any way he could.

The trip was slow, and we did not arrive until the next morning. The captain stayed for a cup of tea, then boarded his boat and headed back to Kumai. At last I was alone (more or less). As the Forestry Department boat pulled away, my journey into the great forest began in earnest.

What I remember most clearly from my early days in the great forest of Tanjung Puting is the rain and the dampness. Camp Leakey stood only a few feet above the swamps in a dry-ground forest clearing. Water was everywhere. We could never walk out of Camp Leakey. To "walk" to Kumai would have meant crossing two rivers, the Sekonyer and the Kumai, the second as wide as the Mississippi.

In the nineteenth century, Henry David Thoreau had described Walden Pond as "remarkable for its depth and purity." He marveled that "a single glass of water held up to the light is as colorless as an equal amount of air. The bottom [of the pond] can easily be discerned at the depth of twenty-five or thirty feet." The Sekonyer River that flows past Camp Leakey is also about thirty feet deep, but stands in dark contrast to Walden Pond. Unlike the crystal water described by Thoreau, a glass of Sekonyer River water looks like weak tea. In fact, the tannins that flavor tea are also a prominent part of the organic acid soup that makes up the Sekonyer River.

The Sekonyer is a small black-water river, the largest and best known example of which is the Rio Negro in South America. It is said that when the Rio Negro meets the Amazon, the two streams of water, one black, one yellow, flow together without mingling for tens of miles before finally blending into brown. The Sekonyer flows into the mouth of the Kumai River, where the black waters melt imperceptibly into the brown, turbid waters of Kumai Bay. Yet Sekonyer water itself is not muddy. If solidified, it would be as transparent as unclouded Baltic amber, the fossilized sap that the ancient Greeks and Romans valued above gold and revered as the sweat of the sun. The irony is that while amber from the depths of the icy Baltic is warm to the touch, the dark amber waters of the Sekonyer, flowing under the equatorial sun, are icy cold. I was chilled swimming in what appeared to be the "sweat of the sun."

The forest immediately adjacent to the camp clearing was tropical peat swamp. In a peat swamp forest, falling leaves and vegetation become compacted. Because certain bacteria are missing from the soil, the vegetation does not rot or compost, but builds up, sometimes to a depth of more than sixty feet. Gradually, the weighted, soggy vegetation coalesces into peat, which after millions of years becomes coal. Under certain conditions, the coal may later turn to diamonds. Peat swamp forests are the ultimate source of the gems mined in South Kalimantan, and may be the reason for the island's Indonesian name, "River of Diamonds." There is no truly solid ground in a tropical peat swamp forest. Between giant trees with exposed roots, water sits on the surface in dank pools, only slowly seeping downward, carrying with it the organic matter that accounts for the phenomenon of black rivers.

Often in the days and months ahead I would wade up to my armpits in the acidic, tea-colored swamp water, craning my neck to catch even a glimpse of the wild orangutans who traveled in the canopy created by the massive hundred-foot trees. Although we were near the equator, I shivered from the coldness of the swamp water, my fingers and toes numb, my skin shriveled from constant immersion, my body raw from allergic reactions to the tannins and toxins of the water. Shaded from the sun, in perpetual gloom, the opaque waters of the tropical peat swamp forest merged into deep pools that felt like black ice.

The dry-ground forest in the distance was a somewhat different environment. Tropical heath forest, as this is called, stands on very thin, porous soils. The infertility of the soil produces a forest of relatively spindly trees with open spaces and a discontinuous, broken canopy. When the trees are cut down, the driving rains wash away most of the nutrients and the exposed earth turns to sand, supporting little more than razor grass and ferns. It is a habitat fit mostly for snakes. Tropical heath forest is the dry-ground sister of tropical peat forest, and the two are often found together.

The forests of Tanjung Puting were not the forests of my imagination. My naive vision of a tropical rain forest was compiled from old Hollywood movies, Sir Arthur Conan Doyle's *Lost World,* nineteenth-century travelers' tales, book illustrations, and the artificial tropics created in botanical gardens and arboretums. My imaginary forest was a jungle alive with colorful blossoms, gigantic butterflies, raucous birds, pythons coiled on every branch, teeming wildlife, and enormous trees that seemed to buttress the sky. Now I realize that my fantasy forest was a patchwork of images, like the children's books I read in my youth, where Asian gibbons and South American toucans cavorted with African lions and giraffes.

I also expected to find areas of parkland cathedral forest. I had read about these majestic forests in Alfred Russel Wallace's description of his exploration of Sarawak, on the opposite side of Borneo, in the nineteenth century. And I had seen cathedral-like forests with ordered columns of magnificent trees during a visit to the redwood forests of northern California. The term "cathedral forest" is used as a metaphor, to suggest that great woods are like great medieval churches. But I have often felt that this is backward, that the stone cathedrals are a re-creation of the forests where our distant ancestors once lived. This is why they strike a chord deep within us. The soaring ceilings of a medieval cathedral, the cool, damp air, the dark punctuated by beams of brilliant light colored by stained glass windows mimic our ancient home, our Garden of Eden.

I knew from reading that much of Borneo is mountainous. The island is famous for its steep, heavily wooded mountains and ridges, deep ravines, and roaring rivers with treacherous rapids. This difficult terrain is one of the reasons why the island's native Dayak peoples and natural habitat remained unspoiled for so long. But Tanjung Puting is on the coast. The terrain is flat and, to the untrained eye, featureless. Its low-lying, swampy forests are more intimate, and because of their modest aspect became infinitely precious to me. I treasured the Tanjung Puting forests the way one might favor an ugly child over the attractive one, because one knows the ugly child is more vulnerable and more in need of care and protection.

Tropical heath forest is not that different, at least superficially, from some forests in the northern hemisphere. A drab, monochrome green punctuated by occasional brown, the Tanjung Puting forest at first seems relatively mundane. The understory is a tangle of seedlings, saplings, and small vines. The 100- to 150-foot-high canopy, with emergent trees surging to 180 feet, is tall compared to many other forests. Nonetheless, it pales next to the world's grandest, such as the California redwood forests and those in northern Borneo, where trees soar to 300 feet, almost out of sight.

On first encounter, I found that the trees of Tanjung Puting looked bewilderingly alike. Only when I spent time looking at the minutia did I see the contrast to temperate forests. While the details of the temperate forest infinitely repeat themselves, the tropical rain forest is endlessly varied. In northern forests, trees are found in groves or stands of the same species. In equatorial rain forests, species are scattered over wide distances; neighboring trees are rarely of the same species. A team of American and Brazilian scientists recently surveyed a two-and-a-half-acre plot of coastal rain forest in Brazil. In that one small plot they found an astounding 450 different species of trees, thirteen of which had not been identified before. The same size plot of temperate forest might contain ten tree species.

The scale of the tropics is small. Except for the trees, vines, and epiphytes, much in the tropical rain forest seems miniaturized. The Malayan sun bears weigh only one hundred pounds. The Javan tiger is nowhere near as robust as its Siberian kin. The Sumatran rhinoceros once found in Tanjung Puting is dwarfed by its African cousins on the savanna. Even the golden-skinned Melayu I met in the forest collecting wild rubber were slight and rarely over five feet tall.

The tropical rain forests are not characterized so much by giant gavials (crocodilians) and enormous elephants as by ants, beetles, and cockroaches and more ants, beetles, and cockroaches, as well as legions of other insects and spiders, multitudes of invertebrates, and numerous amphibians, reptiles, and bats, most of them cleverly camouflaged.

Scientists and naturalists once estimated that there were two to three million species of animals in the world. More recent work in the canopy of the Amazon rain forest indicates that these figures grossly underestimate the actual number of species found on the planet. Using an insecticide fogging device, biologist Terry Erwin and his colleagues found that virtually every tree that they tested in the rain forest yielded new species of insects. A single species of tree was home to 163 different species of beetles, along with many other inhabitants. He estimated that there must be at least fifteen to thirty million species of insects in the world, an order of magnitude far greater than the previous estimate. If Erwin's figures are accurate, more than 90 percent of all land animal species on this planet live in tropical forests.

To the untrained eye, much of this diversity, and its beauty, are hidden. The forests in Tanjung Puting are beautiful like one or two women I have known: initially, they seem plain, but then they turn their heads, the light hits their face at a certain angle, and suddenly they are transformed. I am transfixed by the sheer translucence of their beauty. Then, as the light shifts again, I am at a loss to explain why they appeared beautiful before. Thus it is with the drab, dry-ground forests of Tanjung Puting. The shifting light patterns transform the dark monotony of dull green dripping with gray rain into a spectrum of bright verdant shades and emerald hues pulsating with radiance and sunshine. The light is so variable that a year's worth of seasons can be compressed into a few hours.

Even more profound than this elusive beauty is the music of the forest. It varies from hour to hour, but the underlying symphony, so pervasive that it permeates the fabric of one's being, is the whine of the cicadas. Multifarious cicada voices, some ebbing, some flowing in crescendo, overpower other sounds. The noise of the cicadas echoes in the inner ear, penetrates the bones, and reverberates in the marrow. Sometimes like the roar of traffic or a jet taking off, sometimes like a thousand violins all tuning up at once, sometimes a mere hum, it is always there. In the forests of Kalimantan one can never be physically free of the sound of the cicadas.

But the most distinctive sensation of the rain forest is the oppressive humidity, which weighs down the frail human frame like a ball and chain. The dampness permeates everything, a palpable physical presence that one can taste on the tongue and a mildewed, musky odor that fills the nostrils. The heavy invisible gauze of humidity wraps itself so tightly that, enveloped inside its transparent folds, one fights suffocation.

Even today, I am still enchanted by the forest. It is here, in this evolutionary hothouse, that so many varieties of life have emerged. Every time I enter the forest, I feel I am no longer in Kansas, but in the Land of Oz, where wondrous delights are waiting to be discovered and savored. No matter which way I look, I always discover something new. Sometimes it is just the way a drop of water glistens at the end of a wet leaf or the way a spider's web becomes bejeweled with dew. Sometimes it is the sight of an insect that incongruously camouflages itself as a snowflake. Other times it is the raucous noise of pied hornbills in the distance sounding like garrulous old men coughing, wheezing, and quarreling. Or it could be the fleeting scent of some hidden blossom, or even the way a sudden breeze, seemingly arising out of nowhere, feels against the cheek.

Physically, the tropical rain forests are one of the most complex ecosystems that ever evolved on this planet. Nourished by the unyielding heat and high rainfall that prevail at the equator, these forests have been the crucible of evolution, spawning increasingly specialized forms of life inhabiting ever more narrow niches. Millions of species, many rare, are packed into the three-dimensional, dripping, dank world of the rain forest. The background hum of the cicadas reminds me, as I walk through the forest searching for orangutans, the largest arboreal mammal on this planet, that most of these species are insects, most undescribed and unknown to modern science.

Competing for limited resources, the countless plants and animals of the tropical rain forest are finely adapted to a maze of highly specialized ecological niches. In Borneo and Sumatra, there are certain species of fig trees that can be pollinated only by a certain species of wasp; neither would survive to propagate without the other. Thousands of orchids have evolved different shapes and smells to attract particular insects, which in turn have evolved specialized anatomy to tap a particular orchid's nectar. In the rain forest there are plants that devour insects, predatory insects that look like innocent flowers, edible butterflies and caterpillars that protect themselves from birds by disguising themselves as poisonous species. The sheer diversity of life, the evolutionary ingenuity, found in the rain forest overwhelms the human observer. Nowhere else is the invisible hand of natural selection or the interdependency of the earth's flora and fauna more visible.

As I sit, my back leaning against a damp, moss-covered tree trunk, my eyes sweeping the canopy above, my ears straining to catch the crack of a distant branch that betrays an orangutan moving in the treetops, I think about how we humans search for God. The tropical rain forest is the most complex thing an ordinary human can experience on this planet. A walk in the rain forest is a walk into the mind of God.

# 6
# BETH

Gentle cousin of the forest-green . . .

— *John Keats*

*Homo sylvestris,* orang-outang:
Thinks, believes that the earth was made for it,
and that sometime it will be master again.

— *Carolus Linnaeus*

---

I HAD BEEN in Kalimantan for nearly two months. Since my first sight of wild orangutans two days after I arrived in Tanjung Puting, I had spent day after day searching. With my notebook, binoculars, machete, and a bottle of cold coffee, I tramped the forest from daybreak until early evening. Although teeming with birds and insects, the area around Camp Leakey seemed devoid of primates. I saw numerous night nests in the trees, mute testimony to the presence of orangutans, but the apes themselves eluded me.

Twice more while paddling on the Sekonyer River I caught glimpses of wild orangutans. But as soon as my dugout approached, they fled into the river-edge swamp. On the rare occasions that I spotted orangutans in the forest, they were almost hidden in the heights of the canopy. A few minutes' observation and the orangutans were gone. Once I lost them, I could not seem to locate them again. I had decided in advance to follow Jane Goodall's practice of giving orangutans names, and using names that began with the same letter for individuals whom I knew to be related. So far the only wild orangutan I could recognize was "Alice," whose large black face and prominent cheekbones were very distinctive. I had seen Alice, with her offspring "Andy," about three times, and then only for a few minutes before she vanished. Days passed without even the shadow of an orangutan.

In the late afternoons, I would stumble back to camp through the now boiling *ladang,* the abandoned dry-rice field, now overgrown with elephant grass and ferns, next to camp — tired, thirsty, and disheartened.

Before I arrived in Borneo, I had heard about fifteen-foot-long, human-eating crocodiles; poisonous cobras, vipers, and kraits; pythons as thick as a person's thigh; sun bears with unpredictable tempers; bearded pigs whose razor-sharp tusks could shear a human being in half; and mysterious clouded leopards that pounced out of nowhere.

The Indonesians I met in my first months in Tanjung Puting embellished this list of dangers. A Melayu admonished, "Don't sit on hollow logs," explaining that hollow logs sometimes house cobra nests. Mr. Yusuran, the forestry officer who returned with us to camp, repeatedly warned, "Don't sit on *any* logs in the forest!" When I asked why, he mumbled something about logs that burned. I told myself that he must have heard a garbled version of the Biblical story of Moses and the burning bush and, to my regret, I ignored his advice.

The wild-rubber tappers who passed through camp were most adamant about the "*ut ut,*" a long-legged, humanlike creature that cuts off your head while you sleep. The only way you could recognize an *ut ut* was when it sat down, for its knees were higher than its head. "Don't ever sleep in the forest," they warned me, "especially when you are alone." When I appeared skeptical, they would swear that they had seen the *ut ut* and repeat their warning.

Like many Indonesians, the Melayu do not draw a sharp distinction between the natural and the supernatural; one blends seamlessly into the other. The word *orangutan* comes from the Malay for "person of the forest," and some Melayu take it literally. According to one story, orangutans are descended from human beings who were deprived of language and banished to the forests for blasphemy. Similarly, the Melayu believe the *ut ut* are living creatures, elusive but real, just like the rarely seen orangutans and leopards.

As a Westerner and a scientist, I considered the *ut ut* a piece of fiction, on a par with the abominable snowman. But I later learned that the story might have some basis in history. Many of the Dayak people of the interior are called "*Ut* (or *Ot*) *Danum.*" Traditionally, when the Dayak went on head-hunting raids they traveled far from home and collected their gory trophies from strangers, presumably to avoid retaliation. To the Melayu, marauding, muscular Dayaks with their elaborate tattoos, long hair, strange dress, and unfamiliar tongues may have seemed like forest creatures, only distantly related to human beings. Certainly, the fear of head-hunting had been real.

The true hazards of the rain forest were not natural or supernatural killers but little nagging things like viruses, parasites, insects, and plant toxins. The leeches were so abundant that we lost track of how many we took off our bodies during the course of any one day. Bloated with our blood, leeches fell out of our socks, dropped off our necks, and squirmed out of our underwear.

Borneo leeches are not like the bulbous water leeches made famous by Humphrey Bogart in the movie *The African Queen*. The leeches of the dry-ground forests look like harmless inchworms until they fill up with blood. They are the same brown as the forest floor litter, but have a yellow giveaway stripe down their back. Blending into their surroundings, the leeches stand absolutely rigid, frozen in hunger. But as soon as someone walks by, they begin frantically waving their suckered end as if trying to smell the victim's scent. I wondered how they located their prey. The answer was, through heat sensors.

One night while Rod and I were eating supper on the floor, a leech maneuvred itself onto our single candle. We amused ourselves for a half hour watching the leech go up the candle as fast as it could, then, when the flame got too hot, quickly turn around and descend, only to turn back when it was halfway down the candle, irresistibly drawn to the heat, advancing and retreating mindlessly.

Most of the time, leeches are not amusing. In order to feed, they first bite through the skin with three tiny razor-sharp teeth, reminiscent of the Mercedes Benz logo, then produce an anticoagulant that allows them to suckle directly on warm mammalian blood. The bite gushes blood even after the leech falls off, sometimes for an hour. Often I didn't know I was bitten until I felt the warm flow of blood. Leeches are implicated in the spread of only one obscure blood disease. The real danger is that leech bites tend to fester, creating open, weeping sores that refuse to heal. The sores ooze for months and leave permanent scars.

These small draculas of the rain forest are distantly related to earthworms: I suspected that if you cut one in half, you might produce two new leeches. I cut all the leeches I could into thirds.

My blood would also nourish countless generations of mosquitoes, sand flies, and elephant flies. Tiny red ticks, looking like chili powder sprinkled on the skin, bore their heads into the armpits, the backs of the knees, and the groin, causing spasms akin to electrical shock every time the ticks were touched. Large wolf spiders and hairy, black, tarantula-looking creatures scuttled through our hut, and smaller black spiders with red hourglass markings wove their webs below our eaves. Fire ants by the tens of thousands, in vast armies, invaded our hammocks at night, causing us to bolt like screaming horses trapped in a burning barn. The truth of the statement that tiny insects and their allies make up the bulk of the animal species on this planet became vividly apparent in the rain forest.

As much as I itched and oozed, I think I suffered even more from impatience, frustration, and, underlying these, fear of failure. Trudging through the forest alone, hour after hour, day after day, with no one to talk to and — worse — nothing to report, I couldn't help brooding.

I often recalled a conversation I had before we left North America, with a couple who had just returned from a remote outpost in New Guinea, where the husband had been collecting data for his Ph.D. thesis. Over coffee in their apartment near UCLA, they described difficulties they had encountered in the field, complete with gleaming color slides of the funerals of three villagers who died of snake bites while they were there. I could feel my anxiety building.

"Did you ever think you would fail?" I asked him.

"No," he replied.

"I wonder if I will fail," I mused. "Orangutans are notoriously difficult to study."

"You won't fail." he said solemnly.

"Why are you so certain?" I inquired.

"Because," he replied, "you want to come back." And he added, "You can only do that if you succeed."

After two months in the field I understood what he meant. I could not go home, even to visit, empty-handed. The glimpse of a retreating orangutan's back or the sight of a dry, abandoned orangutan nest merely strengthened my determination. I didn't know whether wild orangutans were there, all around me like hidden figures in a drawing, or whether my initial, brief sightings were a fluke and the orangutans had moved on to other areas. All I knew was, I had to find them. I owed it to myself to persevere. I also owed it to my mentor, Louis Leakey.

I recalled the time in Nairobi when Louis leaned across the table toward me and, with eyes twinkling, said, "The whole world may be against you. The whole world may say that you are wrong. But I will always support you." Louis's eyes sparkled even more as he repeated, "I will always support you, because *I* will know that you are right."

Then he had laughed uproariously, as if at some private joke. Louis's conviction that I would succeed came from a lifetime of experience. He had dedicated his life to searching for fossils at Olduvai, and to battling the odds. It had taken Louis and Mary more than a quarter-century to find a fossil hominid at Olduvai.

Louis once told me, "I give you ten years to contact an orangutan." I could hardly quit now. But two months had passed and I had not made any headway.

To study orangutans, I had to find them first. Large and mostly silent, orangutans are relatively slow, solitary animals. They do not travel in big, noisy groups like chimpanzees, or in large families like gorillas. Spotting one orangutan did not mean that others were nearby. Traveling one hundred feet up in the dense tropical rain forest canopy, orangutans are masters of hide-and-seek — now you see me, now you don't.

At first I simply could not understand how a large, lumbering, two- to three-hundred-pound male orangutan covered with bright red hair could virtually melt into the dark shadows of the canopy. I finally deduced that in the shade, the sparse hair of the orangutan almost disappeared from view because no light caught its tips. All one could see was the orangutan's dark skin. Only in the sunlight would the hair catch the light, causing it to blaze as though the orangutan were on fire.

Hidden high in the crowns of trees, amid heavy foliage, an orangutan becomes a shapeless black shadow. To perfect my spotting technique, I had to learn the search images. I needed to look for shadows that were black and amorphous, and not for the shape and color of large, bright orangutans.

Mainly, I had to listen. When an orangutan moved through the trees, branches crashing and breaking heralded the great ape's approach better than a trumpet. With no predators (other than humans), orangutans do not seem to worry about betraying their presence. As long as the orangutan kept moving, I could find him or her from several hundred feet away. But if the orangutan stopped, the only clue might be the distant snap of a branch, a rustle of leaves shaking, or the regular sound of fruit stones dropping through the trees. I sat and listened for the second snap or rustle, barely daring to breathe. Sometimes I would sit in silence for an hour or two before giving up and moving on.

I would walk, stop, and listen. The forest is eternally in shade. Visibility is poor. There are many saplings, seedlings, and pole trees (thin, spindly trees that would serve as poles if cut), but their growth is limited by the shadows of the tall, old trees that loom overhead. Only when an old tree dies or is uprooted by the wind does a bit of golden sunshine burst through the gloom. When I found a clearing, I would sit and soak up the rays, but within minutes it would become unbearably hot, and I would quickly move on. Even in the shade the sweat poured from my body until I thought surely no more could come. People marvel at how thin I was then. It was a thinness born of flesh turning to water and flowing out of my pores.

When we arrived at Tanjung Puting, there was only one trail through the forest, a footpath used by the men who tapped the wild rubber known as *"jelutung."* This watery, white latex, which the Melayu men carried from the forest on their backs, eventually found its way to North America as chewing gum. Rod and our assistants began cutting a crisscrossing network of small trails through the unmarked jungle of the study area. Although it was possible to walk through trackless forest using a compass to find one's way, trails would make it much easier to follow the orangutans . . . if only I could find them.

Christmas Eve began like any other day. Rising before dawn, Rod and I left Camp Leakey and crossed the *ladang.* When we reached the forest, Rod set off to cut trails while I prepared to search for wild orangutans.

I was checking my watch and entering the date in my notebook when I heard the telltale sound of branches snapping. I whirled around. The leaves of a large tree just off the trail were shaking. I spied an orangutan female with an infant on her shoulder rapidly climbing up the trunk. She must have seen me first, because she began moving away, high in the trees. But I was on dry ground, not in the swamp or on the river, which meant I could follow her. I let out an involuntary gulp of joy, called Rod, and we immediately began following her together.

"Beth," as we named her, showed her displeasure at our presence by dropping branches, hooting, and kiss-squeaking, but she did not flee, as other wild orangutans had. Rather she stopped a short distance away and began to eat something unidentifiable high in the tree. Beth was a medium-sized female orangutan, weighing perhaps seventy or eighty pounds. Like Alice, who inhabited the same area, she had high, wide cheekbones, but with a distinctive furrow under one eye. Her face was placid, almost expressionless. Her infant, whom we named "Bert," was a small ball of orange fuzz on her shoulders; she herself was dark red. After staring at us intently for more than a minute, Beth began to construct a small day nest, bending and twisting branches into a circular platform and covering it with a cushion of leafy twigs. Sitting in her nest, Beth continued to vocalize and shake branches at us. Occasionally she stopped to bend a new branch into her nest. Then, less than fifteen minutes later, she left the day nest and moved slowly on through the trees, continuing to kiss-squeak.

Only after three hours did Beth finally settle down in a large tree and begin to eat. I watched as she held a piece of bark in her hands and gnawed methodically, as though she were eating corn on the cob. The ends of other branches in the tree had been stripped, indicating that she or another orangutan had been there before. Beth fed at five different trees that day, combining fruit and bark. Her infant, Bert, rode on her shoulders, his arms wrapped around her neck like a scarf, never leaving her body. His big round eyes stared down at us unblinking. I would learn that this blank stare was typical of wild infant orangutans. Their eyes seem glazed, almost as if they were "stoned"; there is no hint of recognition or even curiosity.

During the ten hours we followed Beth that day, I recorded the beginning and end of each bout of activity. Noting the time, I wrote down everything she ate, what the fruit or bark looked like, how she had extracted or prepared this food, how high she was in the trees, how far she traveled between various fruit trees and vines, and her interactions with her infant son, filling nearly thirty pages of my notebook. I also collected and examined for identification the bits of bark and fruit remains Beth dropped.

That first day, Beth traveled less than half a mile. Nonetheless, I was exhausted. The intense concentration was enormously wearying. My neck ached from continuously looking up into the treetops. But I didn't dare take my eyes off her for fear I would miss something important.

Clearly, our presence annoyed Beth, but she did not let us interrupt her routine. Finally she constructed a night nest in the top of a tree and went to sleep. It was still early enough to get back to Camp Leakey before the sun went down. I was overjoyed: for the first time I had followed a wild orangutan for an entire day.

This was what I had come to Borneo to do. The cat's cradle, linking my work to Jane Goodall's study of chimpanzees, Dian Fossey's study of gorillas, and Louis Leakey's vision of a living picture of human evolution, was coming into focus.

That evening over dinner in our small hut at Camp Leakey, Rod and I kept asking ourselves, would she still be there in the morning? Tired as I was, I could hardly sleep. The excitement was mounting. This was by far my longest follow. But would Beth slip away in the night?

The next morning I returned to Beth's nest at dawn and sat below, waiting. The sun came out; the gibbons finished their morning calls; birds sang and chirped. Beth's nest, however, was ominously still. Ignoring me, a pygmy squirrel, as small as a chipmunk, clawed at the crevices in the bark of a large tree a few feet away. The squirrel was so close that I wondered if the animal were nearsighted. By now the sun was shining brightly, the morning mist had lifted, and the sky was a brilliant lapis lazuli blue. I began to get fidgety. Not a leaf or a branch quivered up above in the nest. I was convinced that Beth had fooled me into thinking she was asleep, then left her nest as soon as we were gone or slipped away in the predawn hours.

Then the nest tree started shaking. There was a flurry of branches moving and cracking; twigs and leaves tumbled down everywhere. Finally Beth emerged with the infant Bert around her neck. Only then did I remember that it was Christmas Day. Beth's emergence from her nest that morning was a Christmas present, the best Christmas present I have ever received. Unaware that it was a holiday or of my elation, Beth sat on an adjacent branch and urinated at length.

All Christmas Day, Beth continued her regimen of eating, moving, and eating again. I watched infant Bert suckling. Experimentally, perhaps copying his mother, Bert dropped a bit of bark on me. Then I watched in fascination as, sitting on Beth's thigh, the infant started sucking his thumb, exactly like a human child. He sucked his thumb briefly, and then moved to his mother's other side, tucking himself under her right arm. A few seconds after he shifted positions, Beth got up from her seat on a large branch and moved to the other side of the tree. It was as if Bert shifting positions had been Beth's signal to move. The mother and infant seemed to be in perfect harmony, silently communicating their needs and wishes to one another.

Beth resumed eating. Still on his mother's body, Bert reached out with his right hand and jiggled a twig that was hanging in front of him, much as a human baby might play with a mobile. Bert continued to play with the twig for several moments while his mother concentrated on extracting the seeds from large prickly pods with her teeth and tongue. These prickly pods are known locally as *sindur*. *Sindur* trees are members of the legume family, the same plant family to which cultivated beans and peas belong.

Some weeks earlier I had briefly watched an adult male orangutan eating in the same tree. Looking at Beth, I recalled his enormous size; Beth was barely half as big. They almost could have been members of different species. Like gorillas, orangutans are sexually dimorphic. We humans are more like chimpanzees: the degree of difference between males and females is relatively slight. Indeed, one of the most famous performing chimpanzees in the United States, "Mr. Jiggs," who is dressed in a tuxedo and given a cigar for his night-club act, is a female. Like chimps, humans need different clothes, hairstyles, and ornaments, and even cultivate different postures and walks, to differentiate easily between the sexes. Not so for orangutans. An adult male orangutan could never be a transvestite. His humongous size and fat-padded cheeks would give him away every time, no matter how much makeup and jewelry he wore. As I mused, Beth concentrated on the *sindur* pods.

And so the day passed, with Beth eating in one tree for an hour or so, moving to another, eating, nursing infant Bert, resting, and moving on. Aside from the fact that Beth added young leaves to her diet that day, "nothing happened." This solitary foraging, at a relaxed, leisurely pace, is characteristic of orangutans. Compared to humans, chimpanzees, and most other primates, orangutans seem to operate in slow motion. Their movements are usually pro-longed and deliberate, as if they had all the time in the world. Years later, Jane Goodall commented that it took me two years to observe as much orangutan social activity as she observed with chimpanzees in two hours!

The third day was a repeat of the first and second. At one point, Beth sat very still, not moving a muscle, while Bert suckled. She watched me intently for six or seven minutes. But her stare seemed more curious than hostile, and she was not dropping branches or vocalizing as much as before.

On the fourth day Beth moved into the inland swamps. The swamp forest began gradually, with small pools of fetid, standing water. Superficially, the swamp forest did not look very different from the dry-ground forest where Beth had spent the past three days. But there is no level ground in the swamp. Bits of earth covered with trees, roots, and tangled vegetation alternate with small pools of black water. Walking was difficult. I would either be stepping up onto a root or a piece of ground, or stepping down into the dark swamp water. After an hour on this uneven terrain, I had sea legs. For Beth, however, the swamp forest was no different from the dry-ground forest. Moving slowly through the canopy, she reached for branches from adjacent trees, used her weight and smaller trees to pole-vault from one large tree to another, and climbed carefully but confidently along the tangled network of vines and tree limbs that formed her aerial pathways. All the great apes are agile climbers, but only orangutans are truly arboreal. With hip joints as flexible as their shoulders, and four long, hooklike hands, they are as finely adapted for hanging and swinging in the treetops as humans are for walking on dry ground. In the swamp, this arboreality was clearly an advantage.

Not once during the days I followed her did Beth descend to the ground, even to drink. The foods she preferred were high in the trees, and it was the height of the rainy season, so that the young leaves and pulpy fruits were dripping wet, providing all the liquid she needed.

After a hundred feet or so into the swamp, the ankle-deep water gave way to thigh-deep pools. Beth began eating nasty-smelling acornlike fruits, which produced a heavy brown syrup that dripped from her mouth onto her arm. She put her upper arm to her mouth and licked the fruit drippings from her hair. It began to rain. Hurriedly, I shoved my notebook and binoculars under my shirt. Raindrops pelted my face, making it difficult to keep my eyes open when I looked up. Unconcerned, Beth continued to eat, the broken velvety shells of the greenish fruit splashing in the swamp puddles. Soon the sound of the splashing was camouflaged by the pounding rain.

On the fifth day Beth stayed primarily in the swamp, eating the foul acornlike fruit, and the rain continued unabated. By the end of that day I was utterly weary. I had been making observations and taking notes nonstop each day for up to twelve hours straight. I was worn down from the constant wetness. It became torture to get into the damp clothes of the previous day's follow. My body was covered with mosquito and gnat bites, unhealed sores, and unidentified rashes. My feet and ankles were bloody from recent leech wounds. Yet despite this assortment of physical torments, I was overjoyed.

I had proved to myself that it was possible to follow wild orangutans for days at a time. I recalled an article I had read in graduate school by a researcher who had spent almost two years in the jungles of West Africa. He had glimpsed the large monkeys he was trying to study for less than one hundred hours. At least I would be spared that fate. After five days of following Beth I already had logged fifty hours of observation. Just as important, by the fifth day Beth seemed slightly less disturbed by my presence. She seemed to be getting used to me! Habituation — getting subjects accustomed to your presence so that they go about their activities as though you were not there — is an essential part of fieldwork.

At the time, finding and following Beth seemed like a small miracle. Only later would I begin to understand why she tolerated my presence. Adult male orangutans roam over vast distances in pursuit of food and females. Female orangutans frequently limit their foraging to a home range of ten to twelve square kilometers (roughly five square miles). Beth's range turned out to be the area between Camp Leakey and the Sekonyer River on one side, and the dry-ground forest on the other. We had settled in her home range. For all I knew, she might have been observing me for weeks before she revealed her presence.

Furthermore, the old *jelutung* footpath ran through her territory. She probably had seen Melayu rubber-tappers traveling back and forth. The Melayu do not hunt monkeys or apes for meat; their Muslim religion is strict about dietary prohibitions. Nor do the Melayu use blowguns, as Dayak hunters do. With their dogs, machetes, and spears, however, the Melayu are dangerous to orangutans on the ground. Given the opportunity, many Melayu will kill a mother and seize the infant to keep or to sell for profit. But in the forest swamps, the Melayu are not a serious threat. Perhaps Beth gave me the benefit of the doubt.

The afternoon of the fifth day of observing Beth and Bert, I felt a burning sensation on my buttocks. I assumed it was an insect bite, and thought little of it. But the next morning, the burning was so intense that I could hardly move. I took a closer look at the "insect bite" with a mirror and gasped. A large black area on my behind looked as though it had been burned to a crisp, like the skin of an overtoasted marshmallow. I couldn't sit down, nor was I comfortable standing, so I had to lie on my stomach. I remembered sitting on a wet log for hours in the swamp the previous day. The log was probably oozing sap that burned my bottom. Too late, I recalled the forestry officer, Mr. Yusuran, emphatically warning me about logs.

It took me a full week on my stomach to recover. I had plenty of time to assess my five days with Beth and Bert. When I left for the field, the prevailing wisdom held that orangutans were solitary creatures who got together only to mate. The idea of a "solitary ape" ran counter to everything we knew about the higher primates. Although there are occasional loners among the lower primates (some lemurs and the lorises), the great majority of monkeys and apes live in year-round groups or communities. In fact, persistent sociality is one of the distinguishing features of the more advanced members of the primate order. Beth seemed to confirm the anomalous, asocial orangutan pattern. She fit the orangutan stereotype. During the whole time I followed Beth and her infant, they had been totally and utterly alone.

Most people in the world equate solitude with loneliness and deprivation.

Around this time, Rod and our two assistants went to Kumai, leaving me alone for five days. A group of Melayu women paddled to camp, carrying their babies in bright batik cloth slings. The women had come by canoe from the Sekonyer Village at Tanjung Harapan to collect reeds for making mats. Unaccompanied by men, they cut down pole trees and constructed a temporary camp on the edge of the shallow lake nearby. They were shocked to see me alone.

"Aren't you afraid?" they asked.

"No. Afraid of what?" I asked.

"Of being alone," they answered. The idea had never occurred to me; in fact, I was enjoying the time to myself.

"If I were alone, I would cry," said one woman, rubbing her eyes in a realistic rendition of weeping. *"Takut"* (afraid) and *"menangis"* (crying) became two of the first words I learned by heart in Indonesian, after the feared *"rawa"* (swamp).

As the slim, delicate Melayu woman dramatically rubbed her eyes, I vividly recalled a large-boned, heavyset Serbian woman making exactly the same motions and saying exactly the same words, "I would cry if I were alone," to a group of incredulous American archaeologists in former Yugoslavia. These two scenes, juxtaposed from different continents and cultures, brought home to me how rare it is for a woman to be alone anywhere in the world. Remembering the claustrophobia I felt when my tiny hut at Camp Leakey was brimming with people, I felt sorry for these women who were never alone. Yet as I watched them depart, bright and smiling, carrying their babies and their machetes, I wondered. Their identities grounded in their families, their independence tied to women's tasks performed in female groups, the Melayu women had their own reality, no less powerful than mine.

In equating peace and tranquility with solitude, I had more in common with Beth and with orangutans than with these women or most other traditional peoples. Of all the higher primates in the reserve that night, perhaps only Beth, her fellow orangutans, and I were content to be alone. I wondered if this was part of what had attracted me to the rain forests and the orangutans.

Later I would see lone orangutans move past each other in the trees with barely a glance, almost like two New Yorkers rushing past each other on a crowded street, except that the orangutans' aerial sidewalks were not overcrowded and they had no obvious schedules to keep. Though nearby, the orangutans wouldn't even feed in the same tree. Many years would pass before I understood, with the help of my orangutan "daughter" Akmad and other orangutans, the significance of their brief glances as they went their separate ways. Orangutans can be quite social, but they also seem to be perfectly at ease being alone. They can form lasting relationships, but they do not need constant social reassurance, nor do they fear being alone and lonely.

I spent the next weeks typing my notes on Beth and writing letters. One of my first letters was a triumphant account to Louis Leakey of my five-day follow. I heard that just as he had crowed about Jane's and Dian's letters and telegrams, he now told everyone about mine.

My scorched behind healed, I went back to searching for wild orangutans while Rod continued to cut trails and map the study area. Although I saw an occasional orangutan, and even Beth and Bert, once again I was unable to make more than fleeting observations.

Rod and I decided to build two additional camps, deeper in the forest, to give me better coverage of the study area. We named them Camp Wilkie and Camp Dart, in honor of my patrons. The new encampments were even more primitive than Camp Leakey. Although flimsy, at least the hut at Camp Leakey had walls. Each of the smaller camps consisted of a simple platform with a thatched roof. Because they were open on all sides, Camp Wilkie and Camp Dart allowed us to merge with the rhythms of nature, to be part of the rain forest, to hear its sounds and to feel the crush of humidity that presaged a downpour.

Camp Wilkie was about a mile and a half from Camp Leakey, across the open field or *ladang,* inside the dry-ground forest. Camp Dart was three miles in the opposite direction, on a tributary of the Sekonyer Kanan River, to provide easier access to the deep swamps. We later decided to abandon Camp Dart, because it was too far from Camp Leakey to carry in supplies. But I continued to use Camp Wilkie for many years.

As the weeks passed, I became increasingly frustrated. Five months had elapsed since we arrived. Our spartan lifestyle, the swamps, the sores, and the frequent fevers were beginning to take their toll. Rod and I were perpetually tired, wet, and hungry.

In North America, you don't think about your body very much because most of the time, you are comfortable. In Borneo you become extremely conscious of your body. Most of the time you are either sweating from the heat or shivering from the rain. You are covered with rashes and sores, plagued by itches and fevers. Your feet become blistered and raw, you twist your ankle. Your body becomes an impediment, a physical weight on your will. It slows you down. Young as I was then, I couldn't search for wild orangutans as much as I wanted, simply because my energy was depleted.

Rod and I lived on a meager, monotonous diet of plain white rice and tinned sardines. To keep going we drank endless cups of tea and coffee saturated with sugar. A trip to the nearest market town, Pangkalan Bun, was a major expedition, requiring two or three days' traveling. We went only every few months. Even then, there wasn't much to buy. With no refrigeration in town or in camp, we went without fresh vegetables, fresh fruit, real milk, and meat of any kind. Rod and I probably lost twenty-five pounds each in the first few months. Looking back, I believe we were tired all the time because we were half starved. I craved ice cream, pizza, and Mexican food so much that it was obsessive. I longed for black bread, herring, and boiled potatoes, our family's traditional Baltic fare during my youth in Canada. I lusted wickedly for steak, medium rare, the juices still red (even though I generally avoided red meat).

Determined to stretch the little money we had as far as it would go, Rod and I shared five sets of clothing between us: khaki jungle shirts, blue jeans, and one pair of khaki pants for "special" occasions. There was no open space around camp to hang a clothesline; in any case, it rained every day. We tried to dry our clothes over an open fire in the evening, without much success. One night the clothes caught fire and we lost the leg of one of our precious pairs of jeans. Rod fashioned a new leg out of a white sheet. Meanwhile, each morning we had to force ourselves into the previous day's still damp clothes.

The idea of a hot bath or shower was like a remembered dream. Even bathing in the river was a rare luxury: to get there we had to cross six hundred feet of swamp. Most days we washed with a bucket and a scooper, or simply soaped and rinsed in the rain. And then, as often as not, we got into a set of clean but damp clothes.

When I visited her in Ithaca, New York, before we left, Barbara Harrisson, who had spent many years in northern Borneo, warned me about "mysterious fevers." Some of these fevers were probably malaria, carried by mosquitoes. The mosquitoes were everywhere, swarming out of the swamps into our camp. Their constant buzzing was like white noise in the background; we could never get away from them. Antimosquito incense coils became one of our major purchases. Other fevers had no apparent cause, but simply came and went. Even more mysterious were the rashes. I recognized heat rashes from my first summer in Los Angeles. But we also developed unidentifiable eruptions and sores, whether from allergies, diseases, or parasites, we had no idea. We simply treated them topically with antibiotic creams containing cortisone.

Searching the forest for orangutans gave new meaning to the title of the movie *The Sky Above, The Mud Below,* set in New Guinea. I was in swamp water all day, every day, dragging myself from one pool of slimy mud to the next. I had to constantly watch my feet to keep from tripping, falling, slipping, or sliding. The slick, moss-covered logs were treacherous. More than once I reached for a branch to haul myself out of the muck, only to discover, at the last second, a stout, beautifully green, poisonous viper coiled around the limb. I would fall back, shuddering in surprise. At the same time I had to keep my eyes on the treetops, searching for orangutans, watching for rain so that I could hastily stow my notebook under my clothes. After I began finding and following orangutans more regularly, it "rained" branches, fruit peels, and bark — and urine as well. My feet in the mud below, my eyes shaded from the deluge from above, I had to take notes as meticulously as if I were sitting in a gleaming high-tech lab, wearing a spotless white coat.

To save money, we had only one flashlight between us, which Rod always carried. But most days we went separate ways. If I spotted an orangutan, I would tie a white handkerchief around a tree before I left the trail so Rod could find me. This system worked well most of the time: in the forest gloom the handkerchief stood out like a beacon. But on many days we lost track of one another. After months of stumbling home by myself in the dark over roots and vines, I decided that buying a second flashlight would not ruin us financially. The blackness of the forest combined with the dankness of the air felt claustrophobic, like pushing my way through curtains of black velvet. People often ask if I was afraid. On one level the answer is, of course; but on another level, I couldn't afford to be. I imagine that the terror of being alone in the forest after dark without a flashlight is like the fear of drowning while swimming: if you give in, you may never surface. So you keep going.

I had expected to be far from "civilization," yet the reality of our isolation was total. Deep swamps hemmed us in on all sides. Our only link with the outside was the river, and our only means of transportation at that point was an ironwood dugout canoe. By canoe, the trip to Kumai took at least twenty hours. (Even after we acquired a small motorboat, the river was frequently choked with weeds, making the journey to the outside just as long and arduous.) Since we didn't have a two-way radio or other means of communication, the river was our lifeline. Yet it was also like an imprisoning moat, cutting us off from the world beyond.

Our Indonesian assistants were unfailingly courteous and hardworking. But the demands of my study, combined with the language gap, ruled out easy friendship. Neither Mr. Hamzah nor Mr. Yusuran spoke much English, and I was too exhausted at night to study Indonesian. Rod, however, spent a good deal of time talking with Mr. Yusuran, and Rod's Indonesian was improving rapidly. Rod was the kind of person who would find himself a gang of male buddies wherever he went, even here in the Borneo rain forest. When Mr. Hamzah and Mr. Yusuran moved into another hut nearby, Rod would often wander over there to practice his Indonesian. I envied his easy access to the male camaraderie of our two assistants.

As a young female and their "boss," I knew that it would be inappropriate for me to do the same. Women do not befriend unrelated men in a predominantly Muslim society, even in a tolerant one such as Indonesia. Nor does a supervisor socialize familiarly with assistants. Certain formalities must be observed. It is considered impolite to address someone outside the family simply by their name, without the addition of Mr. or Mrs. (or in Indonesian, *Pak* or *Ibu*). While most people called me "Mrs. Biruté," Mr. Yusuran's boss in the Forestry Department insisted on calling me "Madame Rodney," causing me to stifle giggles.

At that time, the only Westerners in Pangkalan Bun were Christian missionaries. Much has been written about how missionaries destroy local cultures. But in Kalimantan most people saw missionaries as good, kind, altruistic men and women who were doing God's work by healing the sick and helping the weak. Missionaries were respected, even revered. The almost exaggerated respect I received in those days, especially from older people, was in part a reflection of the goodwill the missionaries had created. Strangers sometimes addressed me as "Sister," the title for a nun or a nurse. This formality was flattering but also isolating. Aside from Rod, I had no one with whom I could talk freely.

Some of the stress hit home, literally, one day when Rod and I split up to follow two female orangutans. I was straining to keep a red blur in focus through my binoculars when I heard Rod behind me. I turned to see his face smeared, his eyes brimming with disgust. He had been hit, directly in the eye, by an orangutan turd that exploded all over his face. Had we been on a short vacation, or had we a group of colleagues at camp to share the story with, he might have laughed it off. But our defenses were too worn down. Rod could not hide his humiliation. He took the hit personally and never followed that orangutan again for more than a very short time. I couldn't say that I blamed him.

For me, the worst part was not knowing how long it would take me to start observing orangutans on a regular basis. Bookstores and libraries are full of successful field reports. You don't read about the researchers who quit after months in the field, or spend years collecting data that proves useless and never write their dissertations, or even die in the field. As a graduate student, however, I knew about the untold tales of failure. I was told that more than 50 percent of the anthropology graduate students at UCLA who had attempted fieldwork never completed their degrees. I tried to take things one day at a time. I knew I would be successful, but I also knew it would not be easy.

By now, my original excitement at following Beth was fading. At the time, I thought that I had made a critical breakthrough, that the door to the orangutan's world had opened. Now I realized that I had only peeped in through a keyhole. Louis Leakey's time limit of ten years to contact wild orangutans began to feel less like a vote of confidence and more like an ominous prediction. He had given me ten years, but I had given myself a lifetime. I began to think I might need a lifetime.

# 7
# CARA

IN LATE FEBRUARY Rod and I were living in the forest at Camp Wilkie. I had begun to locate orangutans more regularly. But I had not been able to repeat my extended follow of Beth; nor had I seen anything more than glimpses of such routine behavior as eating and sleeping. Until Cara.

It was the end of a particularly disappointing week. For five days I had not seen or heard a single orangutan. Aside from a few pigs, the white flash of a barking deer's tail, and one or two scampering squirrels, I hadn't seen any animal activity whatsoever. The forest seemed lifeless. Of course, most of the life in the jungle takes place a hundred feet up in the canopy, the last frontier on earth, rivaled in its mystery only by the dark floor of the deepest ocean. And many mammals in the tropics are nocturnal, active at night, or crepuscular, active at dawn or twilight. Only orangutans continued moving through the canopy at noon in their never-ending quest for food. Their smaller, lighter primate cousins, such as gibbons and red leaf-eating monkeys, snoozed or rested in the heat of the day.

I was on the edge of the swamp, about a half hour's walk from Camp Wilkie, girding myself for a sixth day of searching the seemingly empty forest, when I heard loud cracking in the branches and spied a large orange body in the trees beside the trail.

This was my first meeting with the orangutan I named "Cara." Cara made a very loud, passionate kiss-sound to register her annoyance, but she did not move higher up into the canopy. She stayed put, in the banitan tree where she was eating. Her large juvenile son, whom I judged to be at least eight years old and whom I named "Carl," was several trees away. Carl had a big round tummy and a self-satisfied expression. At first he did not see me, but moments later he began to vocalize and throw branches. During this expression of juvenile outrage, I observed that his mother had unusually white, swollen genitalia. I remembered having read that swollen genitalia indicates pregnancy among orangutans.

Carl had moved several trees ahead of Cara. When she did not respond to his display by catching up, he hurried back to her and sat by her side. Cara was eating banitan nuts. Extracting a bit of nut from her mouth with his hand, Carl began chewing contentedly.

Banitan turned out to be a favorite of Tanjung Puting orangutans. It grows in the swamps or swamp-edge habitats. Banitan is a round green fruit encasing two pits so hard that a machete sometimes can't open them. Inside each pit is a tiny bit of meat that reminds me of slightly rotten coconut. Orangutans spend up to eight hours at a time crushing these nuts with their teeth to obtain the meager contents. Infants and juveniles, lacking the enormous jaws of their mothers, usually cannot open the nuts, so instead snatch bits and pieces from their mothers' mouths.

This time Cara shared. As Cara and Carl sat chewing banitan, a subadult male appeared lower in the trees. Although larger than Cara, he lacked the fat cheekpads and loose throatpouch that characterize fully adult males. He paid no attention to me, but climbed up the trunk beneath Cara. As he approached her from below, Cara urinated; I could see drops of fluid glistening in his hair. Undeterred, he put his arms around her back and gently nuzzled her genitalia. Cara moved a few feet away, out of the male's grasp. Then, to my amazement, Carl came over and clung to the subadult male's side, as if he expected to be carried. Getting no response, Carl moved away.

Now the subadult male saw me and froze. He was silent and motionless for four minutes, staring down fixedly, as if mesmerized by the sight of a thin, white primate below. Then, with the orangutan equivalent of a shrug, he, too, started eating banitan. I initially called him "Mute," because of his uncharacteristic silence, but this didn't seem a respectable enough name. I decided on "Howard." As Howard picked the banitan, peeled the skins, put the nuts in his mouth, and cracked them, he continued to peer down curiously, as if he did not know what to make of me.

After several minutes Carl approached Howard again, and put his hand over the older male's mouth. I couldn't see his facial expression, but he seemed to be asking for a piece of nut. Howard apparently refused, but Carl did not seem bothered by his unwillingness to share. Soon the two males started play-fighting, wrestling and hitting at each other.

I thought to myself, "Orangutans are great apes, after all!" It had taken me months of searching and observation to see social interaction. A casual student of wild monkeys would probably have seen equivalent behavior in only a few hours.

Howard stayed with Cara and Carl for the rest of that day and nested near them that evening. I was beginning to appreciate the orangutan's skills as an engineer. The ease with which orangutans build nests belies the complexity of the structure. First, the orangutans must select a sturdy support — a strong limb or, less frequently, the tops of two trees brought together or the crotch of a large tree. Next they bend and twist the smaller branches of the limb at ninety-degree angles, folding them into a springy, circular platform, like a box spring. This rarely takes more than three or four minutes. But they spend up to a half-hour picking loose, leafy branches, and piling them on top of one another to form a mattress almost a foot thick. The end result is a bouncy arrangement, quite comfortable but, for the orangutans, small. They have to curl up inside or either drape their limbs over the edges or hang them over nearby branches. Young orangutans exhibit a natural tendency to bend branches over and under their bodies, but building nests is not instinctive (as in birds). Juveniles practice for years, starting with play nests, and only later graduate to the real thing.

Somewhat to my surprise, Cara, Carl, and Howard were still together when I returned the next morning. Rod came with me, hoping to take some photographs. The day began peacefully, with the three orangutans leisurely moving and feeding.

Abruptly, the morning's calm was shattered. Not far away, a snag crashed to the ground. Snags are dead, branchless trees. A strong wind — or a strong orangutan — can send them smashing to the forest floor. This crash was immediately followed by the tremendous long call of an adult male. A long call consists of a series of low grumbles that peak into loud bellowing, then subside into more grumbles and sighs. Sometimes a long call can be heard one or two miles away. The sound seemed to hang over the forest even after the call ended.

Howard moved one tree in the caller's direction and uttered several low hoots, staring intently into the distance. Squeaking, Carl raced to his mother and clung to her, suckling her breast. Only Cara failed to react. She continued to sit with both arms above her head, holding on to a branch, totally relaxed, a blank, Mona Lisa expression on her face. She did not so much as glance in the caller's direction. I had the feeling she knew exactly who he was.

Less then twenty minutes later, we found out. The earth seemed to shake, branches cracked, and snags toppled as the gigantic male moved toward us. Howard didn't hesitate; he disappeared. Cara and Carl followed, though I was too intent on seeing the approaching caller to notice. The orange titan was about ninety feet away when we spotted him high in the canopy. On seeing us, he stopped cold and veered off in the trees. Rod was able to take exactly one photograph. We saw him for only a few seconds before he vanished, soundlessly. The sudden, silent disappearance of this ostentatious colossus was an example of the uncanny ability of these large animals to appear and disappear. No wonder some of the local Melayu claimed that adult male orangutans were not animals. The Melayu said they were actually ghosts.

We were left alone in the forest; it was still early and the cacophony of morning sounds had not yet stilled. There was no sign that only a minute earlier the branches overhead had been alive with orangutans.

I followed Cara off and on for the next several weeks. She was as different from Beth as she could be. Cara was anything but solitary, slow, and shy. Whereas Beth had been mild and timid, Cara was brash and self-assured. When Beth first saw me, she shot up into the branches of the tallest available tree; Cara stayed where she was. Beth and her infant son, Bert, spent most of their days in seclusion; Cara was rarely alone. Beth accepted my presence passively, though she stayed high in the trees; Cara tried to get rid of me, in one unforgettable scene.

I was following Cara in the dry-ground forest. I had clambered over an enormous log, almost four feet in diameter, only to discover another, even wider log on the other side. Trapped between the two, I was struggling to heave my whole body over the second log. I felt like a fish stranded on a sandbar, trying to wriggle itself back into the ocean.

Suddenly I heard a crack straight above me. I looked up and to my horror, I saw that Cara was trying to push a huge snag in my direction. I was trapped between the two enormous logs. My first thought was to dive under the angle between them, but there was no hollow space where I could hide. I was caught, and Cara knew it. She had been watching silently but intently as I worked my way into the trap.

Cara sat above me in the sunshine, against a sapphire-blue sky, peering down. I had underestimated her, and now I was going to pay. The huge snag cracked. It is impossible to know what a wild orangutan is thinking, but humans and orangutans are closely enough related for a human to guess. Cara wanted to kill me. She stared straight into my eyes as she repeatedly pushed the snag in my direction. Her eyes had an air of deep concentration, as if she had determined to be rid of the pale intruder once and for all.

The snag cracked again but refused to fall. It was too wet; Cara was unable to snap it. Adult male orangutans, I later discovered, get a snag rocking back and forth, loosening it before they give the final heave-ho that sends it crashing to the ground with pinpoint accuracy. But Cara was half the size of a male orangutan and seemed to lack experience in manipulating snags. She didn't understand the physics of the situation. When she finally gave up and returned to her perch, I had the distinct impression that she was disappointed.

I felt like a cat with nine lives; I had fully expected to die. At the time, my mind and body felt dissociated. My body was shaking, my legs were quivering, and my face was hot. But my mind was calm, as if I were watching the scene from a distance.

I had never read about orangutans using snags as weapons. I eventually concluded that this was a protocultural orangutan tradition in this part of Borneo. The behavior is not part of an orangutan's natural repertoire, but rather is passed from one generation to the next through learning. These traditions are an early (or "proto") form of culture. Much as some humans learn to speak French and others to speak Swahili, so some apes learn to fish for termites with sticks, others to crack nuts with stones, and still others (the Tanjung Puting orangutans) to use snags as weapons and signals.

I did not see Cara as a psychopathic murderer or a "killer ape." She was simply trying to rid her forest home of an unwanted intruder. Cara never came so close to injuring or killing me again, though she did occasionally push snags toward me. In a number of ways this scene typified Cara.

Cara was a handsome, broad-faced orangutan. There was nothing delicate about her. Vigorous, fast-moving, and decisive, she never cowered in the canopy at the approach of another orangutan, as Beth seemed to do. Cara took action, whether fleeing immediately or staying to confront the interloper. She moved through the trees energetically, causing the branches to shake and crack. After a time I could almost recognize her approach. As I learned on that near-fateful day, Cara could be quite testy, whether trying to eliminate me or chasing other female orangutans who got in her way. From the beginning, her strong character seemed to leap out from the canopy and down to me below on the forest floor.

After our first encounter I lost Cara's trail, but I had the feeling she was in the area. A few days later I stopped to remove a leech from my ankle. Out of the corner of my eye, I saw something shadowy in the undergrowth. As I moved in for a closer look, the "shadow" sped up a tree. A few seconds later I realized that the shadow was Cara. Her son, Carl, had been above her in the trees.

I followed them for the rest of the day as they moved rapidly from tree to tree. They began eating at the top of an emergent tree, one so tall it stands by itself above the top of the canopy. A storm was brewing. I couldn't see them clearly against the darkening sky, and my neck was aching from straining to keep them in view. I sat down to rest for a few minutes. The wind died down and I realized that the sound of fruit fragments falling to the forest floor had stopped. I jumped up and searched the emergent tree: no Cara or Carl. I ran in the direction they had been heading before they climbed the emergent. By luck I spied them two hundred feet away, walking stealthily on top of a very large branch. They had taken immediate advantage of my short lapse of attention to sneak away.

Cara seemed furious that she had been unable to escape my unwanted attentions. She broke and dropped half a dozen branches on me in her fury. But, true to character, she did not flee. Rather she made a nest in the very top of a tree and settled in. After hovering for a few moments, Carl moved in with her, and, judging by the silence, the two of them went right to sleep.

When I arrived at the nest the next morning, Cara displayed vigorously, dropping branches and again trying to topple a snag. Fortunately, it refused to budge. That day she was joined briefly by a large, unidentified subadult male. (I did not name an orangutan unless I observed him or her long enough, or saw some distinguishing feature that would enable me to make a positive identification on a subsequent encounter.) The new male feverishly checked Cara's swollen genitals, stayed with her for about an hour, and then moved away. Cara and Carl were by themselves for the rest of the day.

The following morning Cara and Carl were alone again, but not for long. Howard appeared and immediately checked Cara's swelling. It seemed as if the males needed to reassure themselves that she was "still" pregnant. Somehow, in the course of the inspection, Carl wedged himself between Howard and Cara. The three orangutans were sitting so close together on the branch, one could not have slipped the proverbial knife blade between them. Carl, who seemed very comfortable with Howard, had his own agenda: he wanted to play-fight. With one arm around each other the males pushed, shoved, and bit, then somersaulted over the branch in a ball of red-orange fur and, hanging by one arm, slapped each other on the shoulder and face with the other. I could see saliva shining on Howard's hair where Carl had tried to bite him. Though larger than Carl, Howard did not try to harm or overpower him. I wondered if Howard could possibly be Cara's older son and Carl's big brother. But, of course, there was no way to know.

By six o'clock that evening the sun had disappeared over the trees. The mosquitoes began to hum loudly. Cara made a nest and climbed in, followed by Carl. Howard made his own nest a few trees over and lay down. Soon all three were still. Minutes passed. The buzz of the mosquitoes became more intense. I watched a column of fire ants snake through the leaf litter and then fan out. The nests remained still. I began to think about a cup of steaming hot tea and a plate of rice. I sat beneath the nests, swatting mosquitoes, debating whether to leave or to stay.

On another occasion Howard had "tricked" me by making first one, then another, night nest, and then slipping away before dawn. I didn't want to lose Cara and Carl again, and decided to wait a little longer.

With no warning, a snag crashed to the ground, resounding through the forest like a crack of lightning. Seconds later a thundering long call reverberated through the trees, followed by loud crashing. Howard leaped out of his nest and slid down the tree in a single fluid motion. He stopped about twelve feet above the ground, his arms and legs wrapped around the tree, watching and listening intently. The uproar was moving closer. All I could see were branches heaving to and fro, as though some gigantic being from the forbidden planet were stalking through the canopy. After twenty seconds, Howard vanished.

The big male — the same one I had seen break up this trio before — came from the north. Apparently aware of my presence, he kiss-squeaked and broke branches, but proceeded steadily toward Cara's nest. He peeked over the edge. Then, as if satisfied by what he saw inside, he moved thunderously on his way. The roar from his inflated throatpouch — like the sound of water gushing through a steel pipe — never stopped.

Through this entire performance, Cara and Carl stayed in their nest. There wasn't the slightest ripple of foliage; not a leaf quivered. I couldn't believe that they slept soundly through the commotion, but clearly they did not feel threatened. I could only conclude that the big male's display was meant for Howard. Like a showdown in Dodge City or a barroom brawl, it was men's business, and none of their concern. Cara and Carl ignored them.

When I arrived the next morning, Cara and Carl were not in their nest, but I found them eating red berries nearby. I was slightly disappointed that they were alone. But Cara seemed to be a magnet for other orangutans. Within the hour, they were joined by an adult female and her large juvenile son, who was slightly bigger than Carl. Although I had not followed them for any length of time, I had seen this mother-son pair before and was able to identify them as "Priscilla" and "Pug."

Priscilla seemed prematurely aged, in both her manner and her appearance. Although the mother of a young male, she doddered about through the tree-tops like an orangutan octogenarian. Most orangutans move energetically and purposefully through the trees; Priscilla was slow and indecisive, first moving one way, then another, as if unable to make up her mind. She had a receding but definitely squarish hairline, with wisps of hair going in all directions as if she had not combed her hair that morning. Pug looked very much like his mother. Although I could never call an orangutan ugly, Pug came close.

In what was becoming a familiar routine, Priscilla dropped branches and vocalized when she saw me, but soon settled down to eat. Periodically, however, she stopped and stared into the treetops. Suddenly Beth and Bert materialized in the same tree, followed by a white-faced adolescent I couldn't positively identify.

The morning had begun with what I took to be the usual solitary pair of mother and offspring. Now, to my amazement, I counted seven orangutans in the same tree: Cara and Carl, Beth and Bert, Priscilla and Pug, and the unfamiliar adolescent. Seven wild orangutans together in one tree was unprecedented in my experience. The procession moved together from one food tree to the next, with Priscilla in the lead. In one, a medium-sized tree with many young leaves, all seven disappeared into the foliage. It was like a party in a closet. There was no sound of chomping or bits of food dropping. An unsuspecting person passing underneath would never have guessed that seven great apes were feasting overhead.

The troop of seven finally reemerged, reminding me of the circus act in which a seemingly endless stream of clowns pours out of a tiny Volkswagen. The parade continued on its way. Only Priscilla and the unidentified adolescent registered their annoyance at my human presence below; the others seemed unconcerned. As if moving on to the next ring of the circus, the seven proceeded to a large tropical oak and began devouring its flat acorns.

Without warning, pandemonium erupted. It was as if the peaceful, dignified orangutans had been replaced by a troop of banshees. Wild, guttural hoots and loud shrieks punctuated the air. In my many months in the forest I had never heard sounds like these. It took me several seconds to realize what was happening.

Priscilla and Cara were head to head. Their arms wrapped around each other's bodies, they were biting and pulling at one another's hair. After some minutes, they backed away from each other along the same branch, and Priscilla dropped down to a lower one. The spat ended as abruptly as it had begun. When Priscilla headed out to an adjacent tree, the entire troop followed her. It seemed as though peace had been restored.

Less than half an hour later, however, in a clump of red hair at the top of the canopy, Priscilla and Cara were fighting again. Once more wild whoops and sharp shrieks filled the air. This time, the squabble broke the party up. Priscilla and Pug left the tree in one direction. Led by Cara, the other five went in another direction, and I followed them. The unidentified adolescent later departed, but Cara, Beth, and their respective offspring stayed together for the rest of the day. That night they nested only about fifteen feet apart in adjacent trees.

The following day, in the dim light of early dawn, when the sunlight hit the tops of the trees but had not yet penetrated to the forest floor, Beth slipped away by herself, with Bert wrapped around her neck. Seeing Cara and Carl alone again, it was difficult to believe that only yesterday I had been observing a party of seven. Clearly, orangutan females were not always as solitary as previously believed. The world of the orangutan was slowly revealing itself to me.

Cara and Carl had left their night nest after Beth and Bert had hurried away. Later that morning, I heard an orangutan approaching, but could not see who it was. After listening attentively, Cara started moving off. Normally, Carl, who was almost half his mother's size, traveled independently, following his mother but not riding on her body. So I was startled to see Cara make a very solicitous gesture toward her maturing son. Cara reached out with one arm to grab the terminal branch of an adjacent tree, pulled it to her, and then froze, with her free leg dangling in the air. Without a moment's hesitation, Carl climbed across his mother's shoulders, as though she were a living suspension bridge. As soon as Carl was safely in the second tree, Cara let go of the first and pulled herself into the second with both arms. Cara seemed to know exactly what she was doing. Large as he was, Carl was still in his mother's protective care; but their relationship was changing before my eyes.

Shortly afterward, I heard intermittent but very loud squealing. The foliage obscured precisely what happened, but I soon realized that Cara was weaning her large son. Carl would approach Cara's breast and attempt to suckle. A moment later, his head would jerk back, as if she had pulled away or her milk had run out. Squealing, he would race down the branch, limbs flailing. The urgent squeals would gradually taper off. Soon Carl would head toward his mother's chest again, and the whole scene would be repeated, over and over.

Later that morning, Cara made a day nest in the leafy top of a pole tree. Carl, who was still nesting with Cara at night, followed her into the nest. About a half hour later, Cara left the nest, fed briefly on the end of a branch, then quickly made a second nest about ten feet below the first, and lay down.

Carl remained in the top nest, but kept peeking over the edge into his mother's nest below, as if checking up on her. Cara seemed to be sending Carl a message. I realized that weaning involved separation not only from the breast, but also from the mother herself. If Cara was pregnant, as she almost certainly was, this made sense, for she would soon have a new offspring to feed and carry.

For five months I had been looking *up* at orangutans usually high in the trees. If I needed a reminder, my cricked neck told me orangutans were indeed arboreal apes. Once I thought I had surprised Cara on the ground, but she had moved so quickly, I couldn't be sure. Perhaps I had only seen her shadow.

This day, shortly before noon, Cara was moving low in the trees, only ten or twelve feet off the ground. Each time I came close, she quickly moved away. When I stopped, to give her the space she seemed to want, she dropped to the ground and began walking on all fours toward a small clearing. The clearing, produced by a large dead tree falling over and pulling all of the smaller trees connected to it with vines down to the forest floor, was full of dead branches and rotting stumps. With one motion of her arm, Cara turned over the dead log and began eating.

I crept closer to get a better view. Preoccupied, she paid me no heed. Cara was sitting on the ground, holding on to the trunk of a small pole tree with one arm and clawing at the dirt with her free hand, pulling up what appeared to be clumps of roots. Carl was sitting in a tree thirty-five feet overhead, watching her every move.

Cara stayed on the ground eating for twenty-five minutes. Finally she stood, climbed up the trunk of the tree where Carl was waiting, and sat on a branch just below him, a clump of roots hanging from her mouth. Now I could see that the "roots" were actually a termite nest, which Cara dropped into one hand and picked at with the other. Every so often she held out pieces of the nest in her hand, and Carl helped himself.

After a few minutes, very little was left. Carl finished sucking termites out of the small clump in his hand and reached down for another piece. This time Cara abruptly moved her hand, holding the clump away from him. Carl erupted with a howling squeal of protest. He raced up the branch where he had been sitting, whirled around, and came back to his mother still screaming and thrashing. Cara acted oblivious. Then, casually, she allowed him a small bit before she put the last piece into her mouth. This was the longest bout of insect-eating I had yet seen.

Cara and Carl finished eating and moved on. An hour and a half later, the rain began. Cara moved quickly into a nearby tree, broke off two large, leafy branches, and held them over her head with one hand. The branches were almost three feet long, making an effective umbrella. Carl came over and nestled next to his mother. I later learned that orangutans frequently used "umbrellas" or overhead covers during the rain. This rarely has been observed among chimpanzees or gorillas. I vividly remembered seeing photographs of wet, miserable-looking chimpanzees huddling in the rain, unaware that they could reach into the surrounding vegetation, snap off one or two large leaves, and make themselves an umbrella. Cara had presented me with another orangutan first: tool use. Other animals may *seek* shelter in the rain; orangutans *make* themselves a cover. Like a chimpanzee, I huddled below, thoroughly drenched.

After a while, mother and son moved on. Cara stopped to claw at a termite nest on a trunk, then settled into a banitan tree. The pattern of Carl attempting to suckle or to extract a bit of nut from her mouth, and throwing a tantrum when Cara refused, continued. Sometimes she gave in. At one point she was sitting on a branch and Carl climbed up and hung above her by an arm and a leg. Cara turned and faced him. Carl bent his head to her chest and suckled for fifteen minutes, nursing almost upside down. But the second he let go of her nipple, Cara moved away. This battle of wills continued even after they settled into their night nest. Before I left that night twice I heard piercing squeals. Presumably Carl was trying to suckle and Cara was pushing him away.

Cara and Carl slept late the next morning, as orangutans sometimes do, emerging from their nest about an hour after dawn. Cara urinated, and then broke and dropped two small twigs, possibly in token acknowledgment of my presence. She did not, however, vocalize. Perhaps she was getting used to me.

Their first stop that morning was in a tropical oak, where Cara, standing on all fours as she chewed the large, flat, white acorns, allowed Carl to suckle briefly. Next they entered a banitan tree. Carl sat close to his mother, his hand on her mouth in a begging gesture. Carl's squealing was so regular that I didn't have to look up to know what was happening. When Cara succeeded in cracking a nut, Carl pried open her lips with his fingers and attempted to extract a piece for himself. If he did not succeed, he registered his protest with loud squeals and vigorous acrobatics.

A short time later Cara stopped, looked into the distance, and almost leaped out of the tree. Carl looked in the same direction, then scrambled after her, urinating and defecating. A large subadult male orangutan was approaching through the canopy. Cara kept very still, wrapped around the bottom of a pole tree as if trying to hide. But curious Carl, fifteen feet above, gave her away. The male stopped when he saw me and vocalized a long kissing sound, then continued his pursuit. Cara moved away, the squealing Carl behind her. I did not expect what happened next.

As the subadult male closed in, he approached Carl, not Cara, and the two began to play-fight, tugging and swatting each other. At the time, I thought Carl exceptionally outgoing. But I learned that all orangutans go through a gregarious stage as they become independent from their mothers. For several years after weaning they seek out playmates their own age, and sometimes follow other adult females, almost as if seeking a replacement for their mother. Carl was entering this stage.

The trio settled in a fruit tree, contentedly eating its tiny red berries. When Cara left that tree, Carl waited for the subadult male. When they all began eating young leaves in another tree, Carl sat next to the male, not his mother. The male looked down and watched me for a minute or two, giving me a chance to study him. He was a handsome, rugged fellow, with a large, heavy face, beetle brows, and lines running below his nose. He reminded me of Glen Yarborough of the "slightly fabulous Limelighters," and I decided to name him "Glen."

Antanas and Filomena
Galdikas, Biruté's par-
ents, 1945. (*Family
collection*)

*Far right:* Biruté Galdikas,
age two. (*Family collection*)

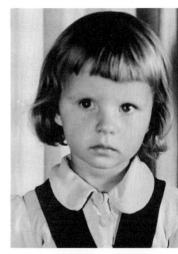

Biruté with her sister and
brothers, 1957. (*Family
collection*)

Biruté with her parents
and brother Al in Van-
couver, 1967. (*Family
collection*)

Excavating at Grass-
hopper site, University
of Arizona field school,
1967. (*Family collection*)

Biruté and Louis Leakey
just before their first
meeting at UCLA, c.
1969. Biruté is examin-
ing stone tools. (*Linda
Wolfe*)

*Below:* Louis Leakey, Jane
Goodall, and Biruté
Galdikas feeding Orcas at
Marineland. (*Joan Travis*)

*Below right:*
Biruté, Louis Leakey,
and Rod Brindamour
discussing the project at
Joan and Arnold Travis's
home. (*Joan Travis*)

Louis Leakey and Filomena Galdikas, Biruté's mother, 1971. (*Joan Travis*)

Biruté with Mary Leakey and Mary's dalmations at Olduvai Gorge, 1971. (*Rod Brindamour*)

Biruté with Sugito and Sobiarso, 1972. Sugito is nipping Sobiarso's hand. (*Rod Brindamour*)

Biruté and Sugito, age five. (*Rod Brindamour*)

Sobiarso in front, Sugito in back, 1972. (*Rod Brindamour*)

Biruté and Sugito in trees, 1972. (*Rod Brindamour*)

*Above:*
Biruté with Sugito, 1972. (*Rod Brindamour*)

Biruté stacking firewood at Camp Wilkie, 1973. (*Rod Brindamour*)

Sugito in front, Rio clutching Biruté's leg, Sobiarso on her arm, 1973. (*Rod Brindamour*)

Biruté, carrying Sobiarso, in front of the bark-walled hut that served as home for the first three years at Camp Leakey. (*Rod Brindamour*)

Rod and Biruté on a return visit to the United States. (*Vic Cox/OFI*)

Biruté and Sugito, age nine. (*Rod Brindamour*)

Biruté at first feeding station near Camp Leakey. (*Rod Brindamour*)

Mr. Binti holding Binti the Orangutan (nicknamed B.O.), while Cempaka clings to Biruté. Camp Leakey, 1975. (*Rod Brindamour*)

*Below:* Wild female Beth and infant Bert in a fig tree. (*Rod Brindamour*)

*Below right:* Biruté and Sugito in the forest. (*Rod Brindamour*)

Throatpouch, the first wild adult male Biruté habituated. (*Rod Brindamour*)

Cara, a wild female, and infant Cindy, stripping bark. (*Rod Brindamour*)

Georgina, a wild adolescent female. (*Rod Brindamour*)

*Below right:* Nick, a dominant wild adult male. (*Rod Brindamour*)

Ex-captives Gara and Kuspati at Camp Leakey. (*Biruté Galdikas*)

Princess, who learned to communicate with Gary Shapiro. (*Gary Shapiro*)

*Below:* Ex-captive Subarno, nesting. (*Rod Brindamour*)

*Below right:* Ex-captive female Akmad, 1974. (*Rod Brindamour*)

As Carl and Glen resumed play-fighting, Cara moved quickly out of the tree, as if seizing the opportunity to escape both her juvenile son and the subadult male. Unconcerned, Glen constructed a day nest and climbed in. Carl hung above, watching, then dropped down with him. Although I couldn't see them, it sounded as if they were play-fighting again.

Ten minutes later the male duo reemerged and caught up with Cara. They all spent the next hour moving and eating in typical wild orangutan fashion. Then Glen made another day nest. This time he and Carl stayed in the nest for only two minutes. Like human adolescents, no one activity engaged them for very long.

They were moving low in the trees when Cara suddenly disappeared. I wasn't concerned, because I knew Carl would find his mother for me. But he and Glen seemed to want to get away from me. I let them go ahead, and when they were about forty feet away, they descended to the ground. There was Cara. I followed the three orangutans as they moved along the forest floor, but I didn't want to intimidate them by getting too close. They started moving faster and faster, becoming more and more like shadows, blending into the darkness of the forest understory. Then they were gone.

I continued following in a straight line, along the path I projected the orangutans would take. When I couldn't find them, I stopped, listened, and watched intently, all my senses on alert. In the light drizzling rain, I saw slight movement in a tree about two hundred feet away. I ran to the tree and found the trio eating red berries again.

Sometime later Cara abruptly stopped eating, looked into the distance, and hooted. Then she leaned over and started pushing a snag. After several pushes the snag broke and fell to the ground with a resounding thud. The forest floor shook at the impact. Cara looked around, as though she were checking the snag's effect, then moved rapidly away. I could barely keep up with her. Even Glen was falling behind.

When Glen finally caught up with Cara, almost an hour later, she and Carl were in a banitan tree. While Carl whimpered, Glen inspected her white vaginal area. This was the first time I had seen Glen show sexual interest in Cara. Like the other males she had encountered, he seemed to know that she was pregnant and did not attempt to copulate. Not long afterward, Glen unexpectedly departed, racing southeast as though the devil himself were approaching. Apparently unconcerned, Cara and Carl moved on. Within minutes, Howard appeared. I puzzled as to why Glen would be afraid of Howard, and wondered whether something else had frightened him away.

Cara, Carl, and Howard were now in the banitan tree where I had first encountered them. This seemed to be a favorite rendezvous for Cara and Howard. Perhaps her earlier snag display had been a summons; or perhaps Cara wanted to keep other males at bay. Although I did not see him, the orange titan might have been in the vicinity, which would explain Glen's flight.

The threesome of Cara, Carl, and Howard had been traveling together for only a short time when still another, unfamiliar, subadult male appeared from the east. Cara took one look at him, made loud kiss-smacking sounds of annoyance, and began traveling again. As Cara crossed a gap in the canopy, she grabbed the top of a pole tree and bent it over, holding it low enough so that when Carl arrived a few seconds later, he could grasp the branches and cross the gap unaided. It was almost as if Cara were holding a door open for Carl, who was behind her. I had the feeling she would have liked to slam it in the new subadult male's face. As it was, Howard interceded, following closely behind Cara. Carl trailed behind Howard, leaving the new male to bring up the rear.

It was now late afternoon. The monsoon rain was so heavy I felt as though I were trapped under the sea, almost gasping for breath, hoping I wouldn't drown. At long last the orangutans started nesting. Cara and Carl were first, and Howard was second, nesting in an adjacent tree. The new male made his nest about a hundred feet away.

The next morning dawned cold and misty, but the rain had stopped during the night. When I arrived at the nesting area, all four orangutans were about a hundred feet away. Cara and Carl moved on by themselves, and I thought the group was breaking up. But shortly thereafter, the new male approached the tree where mother and son were eating young leaves. A minute later, Howard appeared, bypassing the other male and settling between them. He seemed to be keeping the interloper under surveillance. Carl engaged in two bouts of play-fighting with the strange male, once for two full minutes. But Cara kept her distance and I noticed that Howard's throatpouch, which normally hung loose below his jaw, was slightly inflated, perhaps a sign of tension.

By midmorning the new male had vanished. The rest of the day proceeded peacefully, with more stop-and-go feeding and traveling through the steamy, dark forest. With the other male gone, Howard seemed to relax and wandered farther afield. When the trio entered a banitan tree, Carl squealed like clockwork. Howard, sitting placidly on the other side of the tree, seemed not to notice. Cara allowed Carl to suckle, but only briefly.

The trio nested together, with Howard in an adjacent tree, that night. When I returned the following day, all three orangutans were gone. The heavy rain, which had kept up all night, had made their nests uncomfortable, so they had moved and made new nests during the night. This experience of losing an orangutan during a rainy night would often be repeated.

When I saw Cara and Carl again, a full month had passed. Rod and I were together in the forest, sitting by the trail, when we heard the sound of nuts being crushed by an orangutan's powerful jaws and teeth. Running in the direction of the sound, we quickly located the banitan fanatics. Cara and Carl were in their typical banitan pose, with Carl sitting right next to his mother, his hand on her mouth, trying to pry open her lips. I felt as though I had never left them. But I soon began to see subtle changes in their interactions.

Carl did not cling as closely to Cara as he had before. Sometimes he strayed as far as a hundred feet away, eating different foods in different trees. When they were approached by a large male, I was surprised to see Carl rush enthusiastically toward him. I was even more astonished when Carl hit him! Then I realized the male was Carl's "friend," beetle-browed Glen. At first Glen ignored Carl's invitation, but soon they were settled in the same tree, alternately eating and play-fighting. Within minutes, another subadult male joined them. Cara began hooting, then looked at me, as if she blamed me for all this unwanted male attention. The two subadult males looked straight at one another for a few long seconds. Then Glen turned away and resumed eating.

Cara made no attempt to hide her displeasure at the new male's presence, but moved vigorously away, vocalizing wildly and even knocking over a snag. The male responded by breaking branch after branch and voicing a string of unusually high-pitched kiss-smacks. Eventually, however, he left them. Cara calmed down. Carl and Glen wrestled and built play nests, as before.

Rod had been taking photographs, and we were watching the orangutans from different vantage points. It was late afternoon. The shadows were long, the forest swathed in darkness. Cara and Carl were moving very quickly, as was their habit. Glen was some distance behind, still eating bark in the tall thin tree.

Intent on observing Cara, I moved rapidly behind her. Rod stayed back to photograph Glen. As I ran through the jungle, my eyes upward, I almost collided with an enormous gray hulk on the forest floor. I stopped abruptly. A large adult male was sitting on the ground clawing up termite nests. I was only a few feet from him; I hadn't seen him and he hadn't seen me. In the dim light, the large cheekpadded male had turned into a shadow. For a split second I wondered if I was imagining things. Only when he climbed fifteen feet into a tree and let out a loud kiss-smack did I believe my senses. And then he disappeared — as the Melayu say, like a ghost.

That evening I saw another change in the mother-son relationship. Cara nested, but instead of joining his mother, Carl continued traveling through the forest. Less than two minutes later, Cara left her nest and followed Carl into a tree laden with succulent yellow fruit. A type of forest lichee, the oval, cherry-sized fruits have sweet, yellow, slippery flesh encasing a stone. The orangutans bite off the fruit shell, suck out the juice, then spit out the seeds with any remaining flesh. Occasionally they swallow the stone and pass it through their digestive system whole, so that it lands on the forest floor intact, with its own pad of fertilizer. Cara made a nest in an adjacent tree, but Carl continued to eat for some time afterward. It was a clear sign of Carl's incipient independence.

The next morning Carl and Cara were not in their nest. When I spotted them near a trail later that afternoon, Glen was traveling with them again. Before they nested that night, Carl attempted to suckle, but Cara apparently rejected him. Shrieking, Carl hurled himself headfirst down the branch. Suddenly he saw me. The sight of my upturned face sobered Carl instantly. He stopped shrieking and went back to his mother, shocked into forgetting the cause of his tantrum.

To this day, more than twenty years later, I feel I owe a debt to Cara and Carl. They revealed that orangutans are not as elusive or solitary as previously believed. Through them I was able to see interactions, the essential patterns of behavior that would tell me about relationships, family histories, and ultimately the social organization of the orangutan's world.

I was fortunate to have encountered Cara and Carl at a crucial point in their lives: Cara was pregnant, and Carl was being weaned. Mother and son were still a family unit, always traveling together and sharing their night nest. I wanted to know when Carl would leave his mother for the solitary life of an adult male cheekpadder.

Whatever Cara's charms, males seemed drawn to her. Yet they did not attempt to copulate. Perhaps the function of the white, swollen genitalia was to let males know that she was pregnant and that copulation was useless in terms of producing offspring. Of course, males wouldn't think that way. More likely, something about the genitalia — the swelling, the color, the smell — repulsed them, or at least cooled their ardor.

The males hovering around Cara highlighted another distinctive orangutan trait. Unlike their African cousins, the chimpanzees and, to a lesser degree, gorillas, orangutan females do not develop genital swellings when they are sexually receptive. They do not "advertise" their availability. Males have to infer sexual receptivity from females' behavior and other clues that might not be noticed by human observers.

Then there were the females Cara encountered. I had no way of knowing whether Cara was related to Beth or Priscilla. But they were "neighbors." I wondered whether the adult females whose ranges overlap interact in regular, predictable ways. So far I had followed only mothers and infant or juvenile sons; I longed to know more about mother-daughter relationships and how these changed as the daughter reached maturity.

Carl was coming of age, an orangutan preadolescent. Soon, I thought, he would be like Howard, Glen, and the other subadult males I had observed, independent, but drawn to females like so many moons or satellites, circling them in overlapping orbits. Then, years later, I speculated, Carl would be like the great orange titan, lord of all but friend of none. Females deferred to the huge adult males, and younger males fled from them. Did this mean they had "first rights" to the mature females in their ranges and fathered their offspring? What happened when two mature males entered the same area? crossed one another's paths?

I didn't have the answers yet, but I was beginning to formulate the questions. I had hypotheses to test with further observations. My data were assuming a useful shape. The stereotype of orangutans as passive, solitary beings was beginning to unravel. Since orangutans do not encounter each other very often, they interact and behave on a scale of time that almost seems to be in slow motion. But I was certain that eventually these infrequent encounters would reveal the inner workings of the orangutans' world. Flushed with the excitement of discovery, I was convinced that Cara and Carl would be the key that unlocked the orangutan universe. I never imagined that fate had another ending in store for them.

# 8
# SUGITO

It is dangerous to confuse children with angels.

— *David Fyfe*

What is lighter than a feather?
A child to his mother.

— *Grand Duke Gediminas of Lithuania*

---

**A**T THE END of our first week at Camp Leakey, after escorting Mr. Soegito to the airport, we stopped to see Mr. Aep, the English-speaking head of the Forestry Department in Kumai. As we sat sipping hot, sweet tea and chitchatting in the interminable fashion of the culture, Mr. Aep volunteered that his superiors had ordered him to be of every assistance to us. He said that our "every wish was to be his command." I instantly recalled Mr. Soegito's unsolicited statement about my releasing captive orangutans.

Rod and I looked at each other. We both knew what the first wish would be. We had heard that there were several captive orangutans in Kumai, including a tiny male.

"Why don't you confiscate the orangutan infant and give him to us to release in the reserve?" I asked.

The forestry official looked bewildered, almost as if we were asking him to take a sack of rice from someone's kitchen. But Rod and I persisted. We gave him a dozen reasons why it was *imperative* that he impound the infant immediately. Reluctantly, Mr. Aep agreed and took us to the house where the little orangutan was kept. In a dark corner we saw a small wooden crate. Inside, wrapped in rags smelling of defecation and urine, was a tiny orange infant. To my then untrained eye, the orangutan was less than a year old. Rod prompted Mr. Aep to tell the owner, in Indonesian, that it was illegal to keep an orangutan, and that he had come to confiscate it. A long, spirited conversation ensued.

The conclusion was that the man would give up the orangutan, but only if he were reimbursed for the milk and bananas he had fed the infant. The forestry officer refused to pay, but the owner was adamant. Rod was indignant: Mr. Aep must confiscate the orangutan, but we would not pay the man for breaking the law. We had reached an impasse.

I took Rod aside and quietly tried to persuade him that a token payment for the orangutan's food was not out of order. It would save face for the owner. What mattered was getting the little infant out of the dirty box and back to the forest. Finally, after more discussion, it was agreed that we would pay two thousand rupiah (then about five U.S. dollars) as compensation for the orangutan's food. Since the man probably had paid considerably more for the orangutan — the going price at that time was about a hundred dollars — this seemed a small amount to assuage the owner's pride. The small amount also ensured that he would not make a profit; a profit might encourage him and others to acquire more orangutans.

Although my Indonesian was rudimentary, I got the clear impression that the owner felt he was being unfairly singled out for harassment. The laws against keeping orangutans had been on the books for at least forty years, but they were rarely enforced. The forestry officer, for his part, seemed far less concerned with confiscating the orangutan than with maintaining a courteous atmosphere. On the one hand, Mr. Aep did not want to lose our goodwill, since we were guests of his superiors in Bogor. On the other, he did not want to make an enemy of the owner. Mr. Aep's dilemma reflected, in microcosm, the situation throughout Indonesia, where even government officials try to maintain harmony, delaying decisions or actions, often with discussion, for as long as it takes to achieve a consensus. I would encounter this predicament again and again, but the current problem was resolved.

I took two bills of one thousand rupiahs each and handed them to the owner. Then we all shook hands. Mr. Aep motioned to us to take the orangutan. I bent over and began pulling the squeaking infant from his crate. He was clinging to the wooden bars for dear life. He squealed piteously as, one by one, I unpried all four limbs. Once I held him, however, he clung to me with the same strength he had used to resist me seconds earlier. At that moment I felt no maternal affection for the smelly but firm-bodied bundle in my arms. Yet I felt exhilarated. We had saved the infant from almost certain premature death in captivity. Orangutans do not survive long as pets.

Triumphant, I walked out of the dimness of the house into the bright, streaming light of the equatorial afternoon, followed by Rod and Mr. Aep. The tiny orangutan, secure in my arms, watched everything intently from his new vantage point on my side. I looked down at the clinging infant, with his funny Popeye face and spiky hair. What does one do with a rescued orangutan infant? Neither Rod nor I had had much experience with infants, but the logical course was to give him some milk.

"Where do you find milk in Kumai?" I asked Mr. Aep, as we walked down the street on the edge of the river. Mr. Aep suggested we go to a *warong,* a stall-like restaurant. There I ordered a glass of milk. Fresh milk was not available then, as there was no refrigeration. Rather the stall owner served very sweet condensed canned milk mixed with boiled water. I offered some to the little infant, who drank with great relish. Then the rascal tried to escape! He went clambering off under the tables and chairs and was headed out the window when we finally retrieved him. Securely back in my lap, he drank a little more, squealed a little more, and, intermittently, urinated. By the time I carried him out of the small restaurant, I was soaked with urine.

While sitting in the *warong,* we decided to name the infant "Sugito." We wished to honor Mr. Soegito, who had helped us so much. Indonesian spelling had recently been simplified, to make it closer to the Malaysian national language. Names were not affected unless individuals wished. Although Mr. Soegito kept the original spelling of his name, we chose the simpler and equally correct spelling of "Sugito." Mr. Soegito had guided us to Borneo. Sugito would pioneer my rehabilitation program.

We left the *warong* and walked back to the forestry office. Hanging from the moving female body is what infant orangutans do naturally, so as I walked, Sugito molded his body to mine. I did not even have to touch him; he clung to me entirely of his own accord.

To me, it was an extraordinary moment. After only a week in Kalimantan, we had rescued a captive orangutan. Here I was with an infant orangutan on my hip, walking down a street in Kumai on the south coast of Borneo, as though it were the most natural thing in the world. As I looked down at Sugito's tiny bald head with tufts of orange hair sprouting on the sides, I hugged him more closely.

I wanted to get back to camp as soon as possible. Mr. Aep offered to send us back on the Forestry Department's *kelotok,* a diesel-fueled inboard motor-boat that resembled the *African Queen.* Loading our supplies, we chugged off in the late afternoon, accompanied by Mr. Hamzah, our cook, and Mr. Yu-suran, the forestry officer. Less than an hour after we embarked, the boat pulled over to a small hut in a clearing cut out of the nipa palms that lined the Sekon-yer River. The journey came to a standstill because the captain was hungry. In Kumai, we had urged him to leave immediately. Not wanting to refuse our request, he didn't tell us that he had not yet eaten his midday meal. However, he stopped at the first opportunity.

The local people offered us a meal of plain white rice and dried salted fish, washed down with sweetened tea. Food is precious in Borneo, and refusing a meal is considered impolite. Although we were eager to move on, we joined in the repast. Even Sugito had a bit of rice. By the time we began our journey again, it was getting dark.

We slept on the boat as it continued upstream. I discovered that as soon as I fell asleep, Sugito would wander off. Once I had to retrieve him from the pipes and pulleys and other "innards" of the small compartment that served as the *kelotok's* engine room. When I got up or moved around, however, he would squeal, rush back to me, and cling with all his might. Rod and I alter-nated sleeping and holding Sugito.

We were still on the river the next morning. As we traveled up the narrow Sekonyer Kanan toward camp, Sugito tried to catch the fronds of river vegeta-tion that brushed against the boat. He did not appear traumatized, but exhib-ited considerable curiosity, poking and pulling anything within reach as he clung to me or Rod.

We arrived at Camp Leakey with Sugito firmly installed on our bodies. Once in camp, Sugito clung tenaciously to whoever was holding him at the time. When he was passed to someone else, he squealed, urinated, and sometimes defecated, biting the person who was trying to take him off his "mother." When the original person tried to reclaim him, however, it was as if Sugito had amnesia. He would bite, squeal, urinate, and defecate all over again!

Mr. Yusuran, the forestry officer, made it clear that he had no interest in playing nanny to the little orangutan. During these noisy, messy transfers, he had a look of exaggerated horror on his face, worthy of an actor in a silent movie. In fractured English gleaned from his ever-present Indonesian-English dictionary, he suggested that we put Sugito in a cage. Later he commented that Sugito was spoiled, pronouncing the word "spoi-lèd," with the accent on the second syllable. I remember wondering what he was trying to say, and thinking "spoi-lèd" must be an Indonesian word. After two days, Mr. Hamzah became increasingly reluctant to share this experience. So the job of holding Sugito fell to Rod and me. We understood Mr. Hamzah's reluctance. Rod and I were covered in feces and urine. Having only five changes of clothing for the two of us, this was a persistent problem.

Each day, Rod took Sugito to a small, eight-foot-tall jackfruit tree planted by the people who had occupied the hut before us. Sugito refused to climb in a larger tree closer by, probably because the branches were so high that he would get too far away from his human surrogate mother. He eagerly climbed into the branches of the little tree, but came squealing down if Rod moved an inch. Rod had to stand motionless as a statue while Sugito played and swung in the low branches.

On the third day, Rod returned to the hut in less than ten minutes, a look of disgust on his face. At first he didn't want to talk about what happened. But after some urging on my part, he described how Sugito had dangled by his arms on a small branch above him and attempted to insert his penis in Rod's ear. Sugito also had tried to use Rod's hand to masturbate, moving it up and down over his genitalia.

After this incident, Rod's enthusiasm for Sugito dampened noticeably. The Garden of Eden had suddenly revealed a tiny viper; Rod never viewed Sugito in the same innocent light again. It was almost as if infant Sugito had made a sexual advance toward him, rather than trying to use Rod's fingers and ear as tools. I thought the whole incident — especially the appalled look on Rod's face — hilarious. Rod was not amused.

Several days later, Rod, Mr. Yusuran, Mr. Hamzah, and I decided to survey an area of dry-ground forest about two miles downstream of Camp Leakey. We took Sugito with us. After disembarking from our dugout canoe, we started walking along a narrow trail. At first, Sugito clung to Rod. Once the trail petered out, however, the men had to use their machetes to blaze a path. Since I had never used a machete before and Rod was proficient from his days in the British Columbia bush, I took Sugito. I walked with Sugito clinging to my body for several hours in the dense undergrowth of the great forest. Sugito did not stir. His eyes were bright, staring intently into the canopy and the foliage that surrounded us.

When we returned to the dugout, I still held Sugito. Back in camp, I wanted to take a quick bath with a dipper and a pail of water behind the hut. The walk in the forest had left me soaking with sweat. I asked Rod to take

Sugito. As he began pulling the infant off my body, Sugito squealed, urinated, and bit, as usual. But this time, try as he might, Rod could not pry him loose.

Something had changed. We realized from the ferocious way that Sugito was fending off Rod that the little orangutan's previous protests had been only token resistance. They had not had the full weight of infantile orangutan decision behind them. Sugito had decided that he wanted a mother of his own, and the mother he chose was me.

Members of each species have their own mandates and urges to express the behaviors that worked for their ancestors as the species evolved. Wild orangutans do not live in groups, and fathers do not stay with mothers, so orangutan infants spend all their time with their mother. The mother-infant relationship is extremely intense. Only the mother orangutan carries the infant. The mother is the infant's primary playmate. Orangutans simply are not used to multiple caregivers in the wild. Orangutan parent-infant relationships operate in the singular, not the plural. Furthermore, an infant orangutan who lost his or her mother would not survive very long alone in the forest. Infant orangutans are genetically programmed to cling to their mothers, and cling Sugito did.

The scene was getting ugly. Both Rod and I were covered with orangutan feces and urine, mixed with our own sweat. Rod was shouting. Sugito was squealing at the top of his lungs. I was exhausted.

"Stop," I implored Rod. "Leave him alone. Please. I'll take my bath with him on me."

By the time I had disrobed, put on a towel, and taken a quick bath, Sugito's agenda was clear, and the transformation was complete. Sugito had not only made the decision, he had implemented it as well. Walking in the great forest probably had stirred memories of what it had been like when he was with his birth mother, an orangutan female, as she moved through the green canopy. Without realizing the full significance of what was happening, and without going through labor and giving birth, I had become a mother.

In the odd quiet moment when Sugito was not squealing, squirming, biting, or urinating, I wondered how he had ended up in captivity like so many orangutans and other primates. I knew that our taking the infant from his "owner" had been right. More than anything, I wanted to return this little creature to the wild. Anything rather than let him languish and die in a cage.

At the time, there was no refuge in Kalimantan for confiscated, wildborn orangutans. As a result, laws against capturing and keeping orangutans could not be enforced. I wanted to create a refuge for these orphans. This had to be in a protected place, such as a reserve, or the orangutans would face the prospect of being captured again or even killed.

Little by little, I began to gain insights into the complex relationship between local traditions, modernization, and the killing and capture of orangutans. The Dayaks are the aboriginal or native people of Borneo, whose practices have been adopted to some extent by the Melayu. Dayaks were people of the forest. The forest was their life, and they had no wish to destroy it. The traditional Dayak way of life was based on slash-and-burn horticulture, sometimes called shifting cultivation. This method involved clearing a patch of forest by cutting and burning the natural vegetation, planting crops with a pointed stick, and then, after several years, abandoning those fields and clearing new ones. The Dayak also cut timber for family use.

Since aboriginal populations were low, and Dayak dry-rice fields small, the patches of forest quickly regenerated. In a decade or two, through the natural processes of secondary forest succession, the rice patch would once more become part of the mosaic of vegetation that characterizes the great forests of Borneo.

The Dayak kept a few domestic animals but much preferred wild game. The Dayaks' choice food animal was the bearded wild pig, which they hunted regularly. Pigs produce litters of up to twelve piglets each year, and so can tolerate heavy predation. Pigs are intelligent, omnivorous, and almost infinitely adaptable — very much like humans. Depending on conditions, pigs can be nocturnal or diurnal. They can be predators or scavengers. This opportunistic lifestyle — scavenging — is one our earliest hominid ancestors apparently adopted when they began venturing out of the forest. (Hunting came later.) In the depths of the great forest of Borneo, pigs are primarily fruit-eaters. But they can live on young shoots and roots if the forest is cut down, as well as hunt and scavenge. Perhaps our earliest hominid ancestors did the same when the tropical forests of Africa began to recede due to climate change. Because of pigs' and humans' comparable lifestyles, unwary paleontologists occasionally have mistaken pig molars for human teeth. Like humans, pigs are extremely difficult to eradicate. With their close kin, the peccaries of the New World, pigs are distributed throughout the world and occupy a variety of habitats, again like humans.

Pigs and humans stand in marked contrast to orangutans. The distribution of orangutans is highly restricted; today they are found only in the tropical rain forests of Borneo and northern Sumatra. Whereas pigs are opportunistic and flexible, orangutans are finely adapted to life in the forest canopy and limited in their choice of habitat. Whereas pigs survive and possibly even thrive under conditions of predation (which eliminates weaker individuals), orangutans are highly vulnerable. Orangutans have only one infant at a time and do not have another for years thereafter. Thus the slaughter of one individual, especially a female, has considerably more impact on the population as a whole.

Dayaks did not hunt orangutans unless little else was available. The main reason was practical: orangutans were too difficult to locate. If Dayak hunters did spot an orangutan, however, they saw the ape as just another meal. To the Dayaks, all animals are part of nature, and all nature is endowed with spiritual qualities. They would regard the idea of hunting for sport as sacrilegious. But the Dayaks did not grant orangutans special status just because they look so human; nor were they sentimental about the orangutans they occasionally killed or captured. The same is true today. In centuries past, the Dayaks were infamous as head-hunters; perhaps in those days the Dayak attitude toward the humans who met death at their hands was similar.

Hunting still provides the bulk of protein in the Dayak's diet. Dayaks probably eat as much meat as North Americans. Take away hunting, and the Dayaks either have to raise domestic animals or buy meat in the markets. Invariably, these two options result in poorer diets. The tropical rain forest environment will not support large herds of livestock, as Brazil discovered when it opened the Amazon to ranchers. Furthermore, the Dayaks have little access to the cash economy. This helps to explain local resistance to laws regulating hunting. As one Dayak said to me, "You call it poaching, but we call it survival."

With each passing year, Kalimantan is occupied by more people who are not native to the area and do not have the same reverence for the forests. The Indonesian government has a policy of moving people from crowded islands such as Java and Bali to Borneo, much like the Brazilian policy of moving peasants to the Amazon. Many people also come on their own, looking for land, jobs, and opportunity. In this process, local people are often pushed aside.

The entire tropical rain forest system is coming under tremendous pressure from commercial logging and permanent agriculture. The problem is insidious. People move into a previously uninhabited area. They build roads and cut down forests to create open spaces for living and for crops. Unlike the small, traditional Dayak gardens, more intensive agriculture exposes the thin tropical topsoil to erosion, so more land has to be cleared to maintain the food supply. Hand-logging with axes for personal use is replaced by mechanized logging with dynamite and bulldozers for plywood and paper mills as well as hardwood exports. More roads are cut to transport timber to coastal towns. The process feeds on itself: as the areas being cultivated and logged give out, more land has to be cleared, more roads have to be built, and so on and on. One consequence is to give poachers access to hitherto inaccessible forests.

Among the primary victims of "development" of the rain forest is the orangutan. For the first time, orangutan populations are being decimated. The main defense of these great apes is to hide silently in the forest canopy. If orangutans can't be seen, they can't be shot. However, with the destruction of tropical rain forests, the orangutans are inadvertently flushed out of the forest onto the ground and into open spaces where the large red apes are easy targets.

During millions of years of living high in the tropical rain forest canopy, orangutans have been shaped by evolutionary pressures. Orangutans are too large to walk along the tops of small branches. Rather, they hang and swing, in the hand-over-hand form of locomotion called brachiation. And hanging is easier if a large animal has four hands, not just two. On the ground, however, the orangutan's arboreal anatomy becomes a handicap. Running on four fists, orangutans are unable to move very fast. A person can easily run down an orangutan on open level ground. In the forest, the orangutan has the advantage. But when the forest is cut down the orangutan has no way to run, nowhere to hide.

Increasingly, orangutans must cross open fields and the wide, dirt logging roads that bisect their habitat. This brings them into contact with people, often with tragic results. I have heard several eyewitness accounts of brutal slaughter. In one instance, an American logger driving along a dirt road in Kalimantan Timur (East Indonesian Borneo) saw Philippino workers splitting open the head of an adolescent orangutan. A grizzled, laconic man from the Pacific Northwest, the logger described the incident as a "terrible sight."

Bloodthirsty though they may have been to our eyes, the Dayak did not kill animals gratuitously. Today's ape trade is far more dangerous to orangutans than traditional Dayak hunters ever were. Although no exact figures are available, the evidence suggests that thousands of orangutans have been killed over the past decade. This figure is supported by the numbers of captive infants and juveniles in Kalimantan, as well as the numbers smuggled out of Indonesia for sale on the black market (perhaps fifty or a hundred a year). For every orangutan put up for sale, at least eight or nine die. To capture an infant orangutan, one must first kill the mother. But captured infants rarely survive for long. A single survivor like Sugito represents three or four other infants who died in captivity, as well as four or five mother orangutans who were murdered during their capture. Wherever the forests have been cut down, virtually every town and village houses captive orangutans. Many other people tell of orangutan "pets" who died. All of this adds up to terrible slaughter. This slaughter, combined with habitat destruction, has pushed orangutans to the brink of extinction.

Three groups of people play a role in killing and capturing orangutans. The first are the poachers. Some are simply local farmers who kill orangutans who come near their fields, just as they would kill any animal threatening their crops. (This is one reason why opening up more land to permanent farmers is so dangerous to orangutans.) Other poachers deliberately murder female orangutans in order to capture their infants, tearing the orphans from their mothers' dead bodies. Sugito and Akmad were among the lucky ones who survived this ordeal.

Second are the traders who profit from the purchase and sale of young orphan orangutans, as Sugito's owner might have done had we not intervened. Some are "accidental" traders who happen on an orangutan infant and seize the opportunity to make a little cash. Others are established dealers who regularly purchase baby orangutans and sell the captives for a substantial profit. Many of the latter group are nonnative Indonesians who have connections abroad. A retired British soldier who had traveled along the southern coast of Borneo in the early 1960s told me of seeing eight infant orangutans kept in empty oil drums, several to a drum, so that they couldn't escape, waiting to be shipped out on logging boats.

The third group are the "owners," who purchase orangutans as pets. In Indonesia at the time I arrived, orangutan owners tended to exhibit a "colonial heritage mentality." The educated Dutch had liked orangutans because of their humanlike qualities; emulating their former colonial rulers, Indonesians saw orangutans as status symbols. Many owners treat their captive orangutans as favorite pets, or even surrogate children, try to keep their animals in good condition, and feed them properly. But few have any knowledge of normal orangutan behavior and development. Most do not think about the time when their cute, cuddly pets will grow into large, muscular, willful adults with powerful sexual urges — at which point they would have to be "disposed of," one way or another. (In reality, however, few privately owned captive orangutans survive even to adolescence.) Most orangutan owners would be horrified to think that half a dozen mothers and infants were slaughtered so that they could enjoy a pet, at least for a few years.

Indonesians are by no means the only people who seek orangutan pets; the market is worldwide. Neither are pet owners the only buyers of orangutans. Some are sold to laboratories, zoos, and entertainers. Orangutan skulls are marketed as souvenirs or as Dayak artifacts, engraved with traditional patterns in imitation of the old head-hunting culture. But private pet owners were the largest market for kidnapped orangutans when I arrived in Kalimantan, and still are today. Despite international treaties banning the traffic in endangered species (especially the Convention for the International Trade in Endangered Species, or CITES) and enforcement of local laws, a black market for orangutans still exists.

The irony is that our close kinship with the orangutan species is what makes them attractive as pets. We see them as "cute" because they are almost human. This, in turn, makes orangutans more valuable to poachers. The people who want a pet orangutan to "love" are directly responsible for their slaughter. If there were no market for orangutan infants, there would be no incentive to kill mothers and kidnap babies.

I learned how respectable, even fashionable, owning a captive orangutan was on a trip to the provincial capital of Palangka Raya a year after we confiscated Sugito. Rod and I needed to renew our government permits. We stayed in the home of Mr. Binti, whom we had met when we first arrived. While in the capital, we received an invitation to visit the regional army commander's wife. We accepted eagerly, not only because of her high position, but also because we had learned that she and her husband owned two captive orangutans. She apparently invited us because she knew we were studying wild orangutans and therefore considered us to be experts.

A forestry officer drove us to the house and waited outside. We were ushered into the spacious front room by an aide and asked to have a seat. Mrs. Alex entered a few minutes later, simply but elegantly dressed in a modest white blouse and a long, batik-patterned skirt. She was in her forties. Her black hair was carefully arranged in a chignon. She wore light-colored lipstick, but no other makeup. This was typical of local women: the natural skin tones of Indonesians do not need highlighting. The wife of an army commander in Central Indonesian Borneo, she could have stepped into a living room in any Western city on a summer's day and been well dressed.

The traditions of hospitality are strong in Indonesia. Usually, as soon as guests sit down they are offered something to drink. Mrs. Alex explained that this was Ramadan, the Muslim holy month, and she was fasting from dawn to dusk. We knew that during Ramadan, guests were not offered refreshment either, but we assumed this would be only a brief courtesy call.

Rod had become our spokesperson with Indonesians. Already he was fluent enough to carry on a relatively sophisticated conversation. Because I spent most of my time with orangutans, my Indonesian was more rudimentary. After chatting, mostly with Rod, for an hour, Mrs. Alex volunteered to show us her orangutans. She led us through the back part of the house into the yard.

To reach the orangutans, we passed a large enclosure where Mrs. Alex kept several sambar deer, native to Borneo and also found in other parts of south Asia. I was not offended by these captive deer. They were grazing on the grass, seemingly content. Indeed, Mrs. Alex told us that the deer would sometimes jump out of their enclosure at night, and then jump back in the morning. The orangutans had no such choice.

The orangutans were kept in a large cage constructed of wire hammered onto wooden poles, allowing them to stand and move around a bit, but little more. Adolescent males, both were much larger than the infant Sugito and would have dwarfed Akmad and even Cempaka, the captive female we saw on our first visit to Palangka Raya. Mrs. Alex seemed fond of her orangutans. Although she did not go into the cage with them, she put her hands through the wires to touch and pat them, and the orangutans immediately came over to her.

After a few minutes, to Mrs. Alex's visible embarrassment, the orangutans began masturbating with her hands. They inserted their little penises between her fingers, first looking at her intently, then gazing off somewhere in their own private reverie. They were using her hands as tools, manipulating her fingers into positions for maximum pleasure. Mrs. Alex's discomfort mirrored Rod's when Sugito had done the same thing to him. With some tugging, she managed to pull her hands away, then turned to us with a perplexed look.

"Is this normal?" she asked plaintively. "Are they perverted? Why do they do this?"

At this moment, a member of her staff arrived with rice, bananas, and milk. The orangutans abandoned Mrs. Alex, and began stuffing rice and bananas into their bulging cheeks, until they looked like overgrown chipmunks. We watched them eat.

Mrs. Alex guided us back into the house, where she continued to question us about her orangutans' emotional health. I tried to reassure her. After all, they were male adolescents. Mrs. Alex required a great deal of convincing. In retrospect, the scene was bizarre. There I was, trying to convince the owner of caged orangutans that her prisoners were perfectly normal and she was not doing anything wrong. In reality, this behavior was simply a sad reflection of their natural repertoire. In the wild, they would have been vigorously pursuing adult females, as Howard and Glen followed Cara, taking their chances with the big adult males. Confined to their small cages, and probably bored stiff, they fixated on their human owner.

Having convinced Mrs. Alex that she was not promoting orangutan perversity, Rod and I hinted at how nice it would be for these orangutans to go back to the wild. But when we broached this subject, Mrs. Alex suddenly found our Indonesian incomprehensible and continued the conversation as though she had not heard us. Diplomacy prevented us from confronting her directly.

Mrs. Alex asked if we would like to see a gibbon owned by the provincial chief judge. Though by now we were tired, hot, and thirsty, we obediently got up and followed. A snappily uniformed military man opened the front door as Mrs. Alex approached, then hastened to open the front door of the jeep for her. Rod and I clambered into the back of the jeep, opening our own doors. Neither the judge nor his wife were in. Nonetheless, Mrs. Alex was graciously received and ushered to the back of the house, where a medium-sized gibbon sat forlornly in a small cage. We "admired" the gibbon for a few minutes, then all got back into the jeep and returned to Mrs. Alex's house.

By now it was late afternoon and our hunger and thirst were becoming acute. But Mrs. Alex once more brought up the subject of the orangutans' "unseemly" behavior, and once more I repeated my reassurances. It was almost dark when Mrs. Alex indicated that our visit was over.

Rod and I returned to Mr. Binti's house, parched and ravenous. We broke our uninvited fast, then retreated to the privacy of our guest room. With the giddiness induced by eating after a long period of abstinence, we laughed uncontrollably. The contrast between Mrs. Alex's prim and proper demeanor and the young orangutans' blatant sexuality was hilarious. But there was a dark side to the day as well. If a military commander, a chief judge, and other high government officials openly kept captive apes, how could I convince local villagers and farmers that owning orangutans was both illegal and cruel?

Unknowingly, Mrs. Alex had shown me that the task I had set for myself — ending the trade in captive orangutans — would be far more difficult than I had anticipated. As a guest in Mrs. Alex's home, I could not even broach the subject directly. As a guest in Indonesia, how would I be able to take on the combined forces of lax enforcement of the laws protecting orangutans, economic pressures on local people, and traditional attitudes toward nature and hunting?

On the day we got Sugito in Kumai, I had decided that I would be the best possible orangutan mother I could be. Much of the time, Sugito gave me little choice. An orangutan infant constantly clings to the mother's body. No matter what I was doing or where I was going, Sugito was my inevitable companion, even when I was following wild orangutans in the forest. As I walked, Sugito clung to my side or wrapped himself around my neck like a prickly red scarf. When I stopped, he sat in my lap or moved into low foliage nearby. Sugito squealed piteously if I moved so much as a foot or two away from him.

Human babies do not demand this constant contact; nor do they cling in the same way. You can hand the baby to Grandma, put the baby in a crib, or even, like some Native American women did, hang the papoose from a tree. A human mother has some time off. Sugito was different; he needed constant physical contact. At times it became nerve-wracking to have this little ball of orange fluff permanently attached to my body. But most of the time I was enchanted by my adopted infant. I enjoyed the soft feel of his orangutan hair, which is like human hair in texture and fluffiness. I liked the firmness of his muscular body.

Because I was human and he was an orangutan, Sugito and I built a relationship that in some ways probably was more intense than what an orangutan infant would experience with his natural mother in the wild. Orangutan mothers rarely cradle their infants; the infants are expected to hang on to the mother's body on their own. The only time they are held is when they are newborn. After the first few days, it is the infant's responsibility to cling. Unlike a true orangutan mother, I continued to cradle and hold Sugito, particularly when I was walking, and he came to expect it. I probably spent more time looking into his eyes and playing with him than an orangutan mother would have.

He seemed to need me so much, it was almost unbearable. He clung to me night and day. While endearing, it was also claustrophobic, especially when I was trying to transcribe notes, clean the hut, or do other work. Changing clothes became an ordeal, with Sugito screaming at the top of his lungs, desperately trying to hold on to whatever piece of clothing was coming off. It took him weeks to get used to the idea that parts of me were disposable. Sugito looked hilarious tangled up in my maroon brassiere, holding on to it as if it were the very skin shed from his mother. He actually would try to put it back on me. Once or twice I spent the day in my pajamas because it wasn't worth the effort to peel him off my body. Bathing became a battle. Since Sugito was uncomfortable when wet, he clung even more ferociously to my bare skin, his strong little hands inflicting bruises where his tiny fingers and thick, sharp nails dug into my flesh.

Sugito refused to be toilet trained. In the wild, orangutans live in the tops of trees. They urinate and defecate where they are, but don't get soiled because the urine and feces fall to the ground. Orangutans typically do not urinate or defecate in their night nests. But when he first arrived, Sugito, who slept on my body in our loft, urinated indiscriminately during the night. A good night's sleep was impossible. I would be awoken repeatedly by a warm, stinging liquid drenching me. The warm liquid soon turned ice cold, leaving me clammy and shivering under my thin, wet blanket. Yet I knew if I got up to change clothes, Sugito would immediately wake up and start howling.

Even if Sugito had kept silent, I was wary of getting up in the middle of the night, when our hut became a prowling ground for snakes. Virtually every time I got up at night to go to the bathroom or to get a drink of water, I would find a snake somewhere in the hut, revealed in the pitch black by the beam of my flashlight. Most of the snakes were relatively harmless. Many were pythons, less than four or five feet long. Pythons are not poisonous but rather kill by constriction; a python under six feet is probably not a threat to a human being. I also saw cobras, kraits, and other poisonous species. The snakes were so numerous that I wondered if they sometimes slithered over us as we slept. But then I pushed the thought out of my mind. If snakes had been constantly underfoot, I might have felt differently. But snakes come and go. I had to live with them. I had no choice, and because I had no choice, I didn't think about it. Nevertheless, I did not want to tangle with snakes of unknown character, poisonous or not, at midnight; nor did I want to provoke Sugito's piteous screams.

Gradually Sugito stopped urinating in the middle of the night but waited until he woke up, sometime between five-thirty A.M., when it was still pitch black, and six, when the first light of morning broke. Every day, I would wake up at five-thirty and lie rigid, waiting for the torrent to start. If I stayed in bed I would be soaked, but if I got up I would have to deal with a screaming Sugito, who would urinate in any case. It was a dilemma only a tired mother would understand.

Sugito eventually reached the point where he would squeak first before urinating, so that I could hold him away from my body. If he was feeling very secure, he might leave me briefly and relieve himself through one of the cracks in the floorboards. I also took advantage of the fact that he and Rod had a somewhat contentious relationship. If I held Sugito's legs away from me, and Rod came close, Sugito invariably urinated and defecated. This meant I did not have to worry for the next half hour. With all these strategies, I still was soiled much of the time.

Once Sugito settled into a routine, I realized just how traumatized he had been during his first two weeks in Camp Leakey. Then, something as mild as an unexpected movement on my part would cause him to squeal and urinate. He urinated constantly in dribbles. Now, as he relaxed, he became more interested in food and his urination came in streams and more regularly. At meals Sugito began standing up on his spindly hind legs, one hand firmly clutching my shirt, his little face right next to mine, so that I occasionally felt his warm lips graze my cheek. He would stare insistently until I relented and gave him some food from my plate. He gargled with my tea and burbled my coffee.

Sugito's attachment to me, and his jealousy, remained a problem at night. He always slept between Rod and me. If Rod moved a hand toward me during the night, Sugito would instantly wake up, urinate, squeal, and angrily bite Rod. I couldn't touch Rod because Sugito monitored me as well. His squealing possessiveness became worse as he got older.

Through my observations of wild orangutans, I understood Sugito's jealousy. A wild orangutan female lives alone; her son would have no competitors for her affection and attention. A wild orangutan infant can relax. When I followed wild orangutans such as Beth and Bert, I was impressed with the serene, easy, mutual coordination between mother and offspring. Bert was approximately Sugito's age, but Bert already wandered to the other side of trees while his mother was eating, to forage, play, and explore by himself. But Bert had no rivals, no reasons for jealousy or fear. There was no male presence in Beth's life. Indeed, Beth avoided adult males.

Sugito, however, was thrown into a human situation where he was constantly surrounded by adult males. Especially during his first weeks in Camp Leakey, Sugito clung to me tenaciously, suspiciously eyeing Rod, Mr. Yusuran, and Mr. Hamzah whenever they approached, spoke to me, or even looked in my direction. His intense, high-pitched squeals ended with a loud piglike snort, a vocalization typical of immature orangutans when they are extremely upset.

Sugito's archenemy was Rod. Although Sugito was suspicious of Mr. Hamzah and Mr. Yusuran, they generally avoided him. Indonesians dislike conflict, and Sugito's squealing and biting kept them at bay. But Rod was frequently nearby, and once or twice a day I asked him to hold Sugito while I changed clothes or went to the bathroom. Rod, in the best Western manner, enjoyed a good confrontation. He began to see my requests to hold Sugito as a personal challenge. Rod took no "back talk" from Sugito. Once Rod determined that Sugito would be off my body, he would not stop until Sugito was actually off.

Not surprisingly, Sugito developed a strong personal dislike for Rod. The hostility gradually became reciprocal. Sugito made absolutely no attempt to ingratiate himself with Rod. As long as he was on my body, Sugito was not afraid of Rod. To the contrary, Sugito seized every opportunity to harass him. When Rod walked by me, Sugito's mouth would contort into a fierce grin and he would swat at Rod. Sometimes Sugito's sharp little teeth would sink into Rod's flesh.

A good-humored sort, Rod didn't understand. "I didn't do anything to him," Rod would say. "Why did he bite me?"

If Rod scowled, or threatened Sugito, Sugito would put on his innocent, poor-little-me performance.

"Rod," I would say indignantly, "why are you threatening Sugito? Can't you see how frightened he is? Don't be so mean."

Sugito's high-pitched, piteous little squeaks sounded like a fledgling bird. He even looked like an oversized, gawky, prehistoric fledgling bird with orange down. But like countless big-eyed offspring of numerous species, Sugito probably deserved an advanced degree in psychological manipulation of his parents, particularly his "mother," me. Within a few weeks, the belligerent tone of Sugito's relationship with Rod was set.

Under Rod's suspicious gaze, Sugito became my infant. Sugito's constant presence on my body strengthened my affection for him. There were moments when I glanced down at Sugito holding on to me, and for a split second I forgot that he wasn't human and wasn't my own biological child. Seeing a cute but malformed embryolike creature, an elf of a baby out of the corner of my eye, I would feel a surge of love for him. Instantly, I would remember that he was an orangutan and it was a mistake to judge him as a human. And then I would love him even more.

Sugito and I bonded, each day more deeply. My relationship with him became the most important relationship in my life, rivaled only by my relationship with my husband. Sugito was my child and my commitment: in addition to his own appealing individual self, he represented all orangutans. He symbolized my need, my responsibility, to help the orangutan species.

Although I had made the decision to adopt Sugito, it was Sugito who selected me as his one and only, his mother, showing the determination that only a small orphan fighting for survival can display. Yet who chose whom got all intertangled. Sugito chose me, and I also chose to raise Sugito, as nearly as possible, in the orangutan way. But there was another factor in the equation: a human male, Rod, who was not Sugito's father. This was the wild card. This is what decided Sugito's ultimate fate.

# 9

# THROATPOUCH

Some orang-utans have conspicuous cheek pads
and conspicuous laryngeal sacs.
Others have worse.

— *Will Cuppy*

Orang-utan sex is a prolonged and
erotic business.

—*John MacKinnon*

---

$S$EXUAL CHARM, whether in humans or orangutans, is an intangible and unpredictable quality. "Throatpouch" ("TP" for short), a wild male orangutan whom I judged to be middle-aged, was a case in point. He was a grouchy and irascible ape, who lip-smacked, kiss-squeaked, and bellowed, toppling snags and slapping vegetation at the slightest provocation. To my then unaccustomed eyes, he was bizarre-looking. Like the orange titan who had pursued Cara, he was humongous. It was difficult for me to imagine that cute little Sugito would ever become so monstrously large. TP's large, low-slung cheekpads made his eyes look close together and tiny. His back was mostly bare, with a fringe of hair on either side, as though he were wearing an evening gown with a very low cut back. But his most unusual feature was a permanently inflated throatpouch, which gave him his name. He looked as if he had a beach ball tucked under his chin.

By orangutan standards, however, TP probably was a decidedly handsome fellow. The object of TP's adoration was Priscilla. When I saw Priscilla with Throatpouch, she was even dowdier than I remembered. I thought that TP would have chosen a more comely female. But from the way Throatpouch pursued her, Priscilla had sexual charm to spare. TP was smitten with her.

⚛

One day I was alone at Camp Leakey, lying in bed with a fever. Rod and Mr. Hamzah were in the forest, cutting trails. Suddenly Mr. Hamzah burst into the hut, stammering that I had to get up and go to the forest. Rod had found three orangutans and, according to the cook, had ordered me to follow them. It was not like Rod to issue a peremptory summons, especially when I was sick. Something very significant must be going on.

I staggered down the ladder from our loft, threw on some clothes, and, grabbing a bottle of boiled water, raced to the forest with Mr. Hamzah behind me. Rod grinned when he saw me. He knew that, sick or not, I wanted to follow wild orangutans.

When Rod had spotted the adult female, Priscilla, her large juvenile son, Pug, and a subadult male about fifty feet away, he had sent Mr. Hamzah to get me. Soon after Mr. Hamzah had left, an enormous adult male had appeared. According to Rod, after being stared at by the adult male for some time, the subadult male had leaped to the ground and vanished. By the time I arrived, the adult male was sitting absolutely still in a low tree, watching Priscilla eat in an adjacent tree. I recognized Throatpouch. Throatpouch was watching the doddering Priscilla intently. He couldn't take his eyes off her. He didn't even bother to eat, so enthralled was he by her balding charms.

Adult males are twice the size of adult females, and TP completely dwarfed Pug's mother. Yet Pug looked unconcerned by the presence of this massive creature. TP, in turn, seemed oblivious to Pug. In TP's eagerness to get close to Priscilla, he did not seem to notice the large juvenile, and more than once almost stepped on him. Innocent Pug was forced to scramble out of TP's way each time.

I had been watching them for only a short while when another adult male appeared, unannounced, low in the trees. It was the orange giant we had seen with Cara. I had discovered that several fingers on one of his hands were thick and stiff, and named him "Handless Harry." These injured fingers were probably the result of battling other males; Harry was not one to be trifled with. TP didn't waste one second. He charged Harry in the trees. The two huge males grabbed each other like sumo wrestlers. Without letting go, they slid down to the forest floor, locked together in their battle embrace. When Harry tore himself away from TP and climbed another tree, TP followed.

TP and Harry fought nonstop for almost half an hour, grappling furiously, biting each other's shoulders, ears, and cheekpads. In the heat of combat, they fell out of the trees and onto the forest floor numerous times. Each time, Throatpouch chased Harry back into the trees, where they resumed wrestling.

Invariably, they came crashing to the ground again. Their backs glistened with beads of sweat, and the smell of their pungent perspiration lingered on the ground even after they were back in the canopy.

Several times they pulled apart and glared at one another, their faces only a few feet apart, as if trying to stare each other down. A deep rumbling issued from TP's throat. Arms around each other, face to face, chin to chin, the two giants fought. They were so engrossed in combat that I was able to get within four feet of them. Once Harry turned, looked at me, and lip-smacked before rejoining the battle; TP seemed not to notice me at all. From this close vantage point I saw that TP's throatpouch was almost completely deflated.

Finally the two combatants separated by about a foot. Lip-smacking, Harry stared at TP; TP emitted a low growl. Then TP moved away and started pushing a nearby snag. He shoved it several times, and as the snag started to fall, TP called. It was a vigorous, triumphant long call. His throatpouch vibrated with each bellow. Then there was silence. The battle was over. About a hundred feet apart in different trees, the two males seemed to be resting. In the distance I could hear Priscilla and Pug moving away through the trees.

I was watching TP. When I glanced at the spot where Harry had been sitting, he was gone. TP began moving in Priscilla's direction. He seemed winded, and periodically stopped to rest. TP had finally caught up with her and started eating when I heard the crashing sounds of an orangutan approaching from the northwest. To my surprise, TP sped south. After his victory over Handless Harry only an hour earlier, I couldn't imagine that he would now flee. I was correct. He wasn't running. He had raced to a nearby snag, and now pushed the snag over with a mighty shove and roared forth a long call. As if nothing whatever were happening, Priscilla and Pug continued to eat.

TP moved back toward his previous position. The sounds of approach had ceased, leaving only the whining of the cicadas, punctuated by the distant plaintive cry of an unseen trogan. TP sat very still, continuing to look toward the northwest. After about five minutes, he seemed satisfied. He returned to Priscilla, moving over my head as though I were either invisible or totally insignificant, which I probably was to him.

Priscilla, Pug, and TP were now all in the same tree, eating. It was almost dark. A movement high up in the canopy caught my attention. A subadult male was lurking behind the trunk of a large tree about seventy-five feet away. TP had moved out of the berry tree, and was sitting utterly still. Abruptly, he leaned over and shook the medium-sized tree next to him. Then he roared a long call, looking intently at Priscilla, his back to the subadult male. TP seemed unaware of, or unconcerned by, the younger male's presence. His long call seemed to be for Priscilla's benefit.

Priscilla started nesting under TP's watchful eye. When she finally lay down, Pug joined her, and TP started to make an enormous nest ten feet away in the same tree. I heard the sound of branches cracking far off. I assumed the younger male was nesting at a safe distance. About twenty minutes after darkness fell, the last sounds of branches and twigs being bent and twisted in TP's nest ceased. The buzz of mosquitoes filled my ears.

I had seen a combat between wild adult orangutan males, the first ever witnessed and documented by a Western scientist. Others suspected that the huge males were built for combat, but none had ever seen them fight. Evolutionary theory predicts that when lone males have to fight one another to gain access to females, the males tend to be much bigger than the females of their species. This rule applies to birds as well as mammals. The male's extra bulk is the bulk of aggression. And so it is with orangutans. The combat I had witnessed was preliminary confirmation of what the theory predicted.

The next morning, Throatpouch pushed over a snag and long-called immediately after leaving his nest. Priscilla and Pug emerged from their nest shortly thereafter. TP followed Priscilla very closely that morning. He was only thirty feet behind her, riding one pole tree to the next pole tree, as if he were walking on gigantic stilts. Had TP been any closer to Priscilla, he would have bumped into her.

After a while, Priscilla stopped foraging to rest. She and Pug sat side by side on the same branch. Although Priscilla and Pug often sat close to one another, they rarely interacted. Unlike chimpanzees and gorillas, wild orangutans do not engage in long bouts of grooming, probably because one of the functions of grooming is to bond individuals together into a group. Because orangutans do not live in groups, they have no need for bonding. When they do groom one another it is primarily for hygienic, rather than social, purposes. Moreover, Pug had been weaned. In contrast to Cara's juvenile son, Carl, Pug no longer attempted to suckle.

But now I watched a quiet moment of tenderness between mother and son. Pug reached over and took hold of the loose skin that bunched on Priscilla's throat. He held Priscilla's primate wattle in his hand for a few seconds; Priscilla vocalized a soft, owl-like *woo-woo*. Pug dropped his hand and started moving away. Priscilla *woo-woo*ed again, so softly it was scarcely audible. Pug turned around and went back to her. Priscilla then put her left hand on the top of Pug's head and, like a Catholic prelate with a papal ring, put her right hand in front of Pug's face as though she expected him to kiss her hand. Pug touched Priscilla's hand gently with his lips. It seemed as though Priscilla and Pug were reassuring each other that they were still a unit despite TP's ostentatious omnipresence.

Gestures that we see performed by captive apes, such as kissing, hugging, and hand-holding, are not learned imitations of humans, but common forms of expression that we humans share with the great apes. Apparently, kissing has a long evolutionary history.

The tender moment passed and Priscilla moved on, leaving Pug sitting on the branch. A few moments later she called woo-woo, and Pug immediately came to her tree. So did TP. I wondered if he thought she was calling him.

As yesterday, so today: TP spent most of his time watching Priscilla eat, consuming very little himself. Although he outweighed her by at least a hundred pounds, she was eating twice as much as he was. The morning passed quietly. TP continued to follow Priscilla as she traveled along in typical orangutan stop-and-go fashion. TP seemed the perfect gentleman. Only when she left a tree did he move in himself to eat. He was acting out the old adage Ladies first.

I had brought Sugito with me into the forest, as I often did. Most of the time he clung to my side or draped himself around my neck, though when I stopped, he might climb into the low foliage. At one point during the early afternoon, Sugito suddenly started squealing. Without glancing down, TP began a roaring long call. No other orangutan I followed reacted so strongly to Sugito. In fact, most ignored him. But Sugito's distress apparently touched a raw nerve in Throatpouch. While still bellowing, he moved into the tree where Priscilla and Pug were sitting close together, and plopped down a few feet from the mother-son duo.

Priscilla and Pug lost no time leaving, apparently sensing that TP was aroused. Priscilla moved as quickly as I had ever seen her travel. When Pug fell behind, she stopped and vocalized a soft woo-woo. Pug immediately caught up with her and the two moved on, with TP doggedly following.

Late in the afternoon, when the shadows were long and the red glint of the setting sun shone through the black lacework of tree silhouettes, I briefly glimpsed a second male in the distance. He was so far away I could not tell if he was an adult male or simply a large subadult. About twenty minutes later a snag crashed to the forest floor. TP paid no attention to the crash. After a while, TP entered the tree where Priscilla and Pug were eating tiny red berries. Priscilla continued to eat, seemingly oblivious to TP's approach. Pug, however, immediately moved to the opposite side of the tree, as far from TP as he could get.

Another snag crashed. There was no following long call. Then a third snag crashed, closer. Again, there was no call. It was a windless day; I was certain an orangutan had toppled the snags. TP, however, remained blasé. If he had heard the powerful sound of a ton of dead wood hitting the earth three times in a row, he gave no indication. Apparently unimpressed, he continued to eat.

About twenty-five minutes after the last snag crashed, Throatpouch suddenly bolted toward the southwest. Perhaps he had seen the snag-crashing intruder in the distance. Low in the trees, he raced nonstop for some five hundred feet. His hair stood on end, magnifying his size, and I glimpsed a smidgen of red through the hair in his groin, suggesting that he had an erection. Had TP been a dragon, he would have been breathing fire and chomping on horses. He stopped abruptly and sat down on a large branch staring toward the southwest, his back to me. Ten minutes passed before he heaved himself up off the branch. Moving slowly and laboriously, stopping briefly to eat in the berry tree, TP gradually caught up with Priscilla.

Priscilla promptly began making a night nest and, a few minutes later, TP began his. Barely had he settled down, when Priscilla left her nest and began to move rapidly away. TP left his nest, and followed Priscilla. A few trees later, Priscilla nested again. TP immediately nested again, this time constructing an enormous eagle's nest structure, with untidy edges and boughs sticking out at odd angles. Throatpouch flopped down on his back, obviously ready for a good night's sleep. The light was already gray, the colors fading from the forest. The whine of the evening cicadas had reached a deafening pitch.

Then I saw Priscilla quietly creeping down the trunk and along a large branch. Her movements were very deliberate: she was sneaking away. A minute later, as though hit by a bolt of lightning, TP sat straight up in his nest. He looked around as if he could not believe what was happening. He bolted out of his nest and followed Priscilla for another three hundred feet. Priscilla made another nest. This time TP was not going to be fooled. Rather than making his nest immediately, he sat in the top of a tree, loudly kiss-smacking. Finally, fifteen minutes later, he constructed his third nest for the evening. It was almost totally dark. TP uttered one loud kiss-smack and then began the low rumble, deep in his throat, that usually heralds a long call. The long call never came.

The rumble ended. The curtain of night fell. The whole episode, with actions both obvious and surreptitious, an orangutan here, an orangutan there, reminded me of the high farce of commedia dell'arte.

The next morning, TP and Priscilla left their respective nests at about the same time. They traveled together in typical wild orangutan style, stopping here to eat some leaves, there to eat some fruit. At one point they entered a fruit tree with four nests — two large and fresh, probably made the previous day, and two old and dry. TP and Priscilla sat in one of the newer nests together, eating small black fruits. Although I had not seen two adults sitting in the same nest eating before, this did not seem surprising for a male and female who were consorting. When the pair moved on, still together, Priscilla's mouth was bulging with fruit.

Later that morning, Priscilla was nibbling on leaves while TP sat at the same level in an adjacent tree, gazing at her. I heard the sharp sound of a branch cracking nearby but saw nothing. TP immediately moved into the tree where Priscilla was sitting. As he moved toward her, he long-called. Then he grabbed her by the hips and the next thing I knew, they were copulating, face to face. (Orangutans and bonobos are the only nonhuman primates who regularly copulate face to face.) Both were hanging from the branch above them by both arms. Priscilla was semireclined against another large branch. TP's rhythmic motion lasted ninety seconds, ceased, then continued for some minutes. Priscilla's expression was blank, as though nothing of significance was going on. But TP seemed totally absorbed. At one point during their copulation, Priscilla turned her face and stared at me uneasily. Had she been human, I would have said she was embarrassed at being observed in the act of copulation. TP appeared oblivious, his eyes turned up toward some faraway world.

After many minutes, Priscilla pulled away. She sat next to TP for thirty seconds, glanced at him as if to reassure herself that a decent interval had passed and he would not be insulted, and then moved to an adjacent tree and resumed eating. Much as TP seemed preoccupied with her, Priscilla seemed preoccupied with food. Pug had been eating in the same tree throughout the copulation. As far as I observed, he did not so much as glance up from the leaves he was busy stuffing into his mouth.

Throatpouch had not moved. Sitting exactly where he had been while copulating, he looked loose-jointed. He was holding on to the branch above him by both hands, dangling one foot below the branch on which he was sitting. He looked as though he had been hit by a truck. His throatpouch was even slightly deflated. Ten minutes later, TP moved a few feet along the branch and then flopped down again. He did not move or even twitch for the next hour.

While TP lay in a daze, Pug started lip-smacking and tried pushing over a small pole tree snag. After numerous shoves, he succeeded. He lip-smacked in triumph and moved over to where Priscilla was sitting, resting. He put his arms around her, his head face to face with hers. Priscilla lifted her hand and gently pushed his face away. But then she took his hand and started playing with his fingers. Pug lay down next to her on the branch. She took his head in both hands and groomed him for a while. Then her hands dropped and she sat motionless. Pug lay contentedly on the branch, both hands stretched out over his head.

This peaceful maternal scene ended abruptly when TP suddenly came out of his stupor. He moved toward Priscilla and grabbed her feet as she clung to the branches over her head with her arms. He pulled and twisted her, as though trying to break her grip, but she held on. TP was now directly below her, licking her genitalia and poking his fingers into her vagina. TP pulled and tugged her into a better position and, holding her by her feet, began to copulate again. Squirming, Priscilla tried to push him away. Several times she vocalized soft *woo-woo*s. TP withdrew, and then began copulating again, Priscilla still flailing at him. This time Pug rapidly departed.

Twelve minutes after TP's first movements, the copulation complete, Priscilla broke away. TP followed immediately, settling in the same tree. A while later I observed him sniffing the fingers of his right hand, as if he found them very intriguing. When, a few minutes later, Priscilla moved, TP followed.

At midafternoon, TP and Priscilla were eating on opposite sides of a berry tree. Pug moved into the tree, close to his mother. Priscilla put one arm around Pug's shoulder, and began exploring his back with her other hand. After several minutes they resumed eating, side by side. I was touched by these unusual displays of affection between Pug and Priscilla. Priscilla seemed to be reassuring Pug that all was well.

Late in the afternoon, Priscilla started nesting high in a tree. TP began to nest in an adjacent tree, and Pug made his own nest several trees away. Soon all were quiet. Then, some minutes later, I heard a soft *woo-woo*. I looked up and saw Pug on the edge of Priscilla's nest, peering in. He stayed there for a minute, then climbed onto the branch above her nest. Shortly after, the rain started. When I was able to look up again, I saw no sign of Pug. Apparently he had joined his mother in her nest. Far from driving them apart, Priscilla's consortship with TP seemed to be drawing mother and son closer together.

I had planned to continue observing TP, Priscilla, and Pug the next morning, but I couldn't. When I awoke before dawn I found that I couldn't move my hands. Covered with severe infections and tropical ulcers, they were immobilized, like claws. I couldn't even curl my fingers into a fist. Before the antibiotics took effect, I was forced to lie in my hammock for several days. The infections were probably scratched insect bites. In the tropical rain forest, the ceaseless humidity and perpetual damp cause every little scratch and minor wound to fester. I thought about some of my friends in North America, who made a fetish out of not taking antibiotics; the luxury of rejecting modern medicine was not an option for field scientists or local people in tropical countries. A full month would pass before my hands healed and I could write up my notes and return to the forest to look for Priscilla and TP.

I found Throatpouch again late one afternoon. TP had long-called, giving his presence away. When I located him, he shook a dead tree but did not vocalize. Priscilla and Pug were again with him. After eating in several different trees, the trio engaged in another round of musical nests, bedding here, bedding there, appearing and disappearing, before they all settled down for the night. TP flung himself into a large, old nest, without so much as bending a twig to improve it.

There was no way of knowing whether they had been together for the entire month; I suspected not. But the next day told me that time had not dampened TP's ardor. When I arrived that morning TP was in a new nest, built during the night directly under Priscilla's, and Pug had his own nest in another tree. The old routines resurfaced. The orangutans moved slowly through the forest, eating. As earlier, TP sometimes just sat admiring Priscilla while she ate. He seemed even more love-struck than before. In one instance, Priscilla was in the canopy, breaking bits of wood off the top of a snag and chewing them, probably for the termites encased within. Throatpouch sat in the sunlight watching her for a full twenty-five minutes. The sun seemed to set his coat ablaze. Throatpouch glowed. It was an unforgettable scene of natural glory.

Late in the afternoon, TP roared out a long call, then grabbed Priscilla and started copulating with her. After a few minutes, Priscilla tore herself away and moved on. An hour later Throatpouch was back. This time he pumped rhythmically for almost twenty minutes, a look of rapture on his face. Priscilla looked decidedly uncomfortable and lip-smacked repeatedly. As usual, Priscilla was the one who pulled away. Soon she and Pug were eating again. TP lay on a branch, belly up, his legs and one arm dangling below the branch, as if he had totally run out of steam.

Looking at TP, I thought to myself, "He must live on love." This saying is grounded in a biological truth. Ordinarily, orangutans spend perhaps 60 percent of their time eating. Given their primarily fruit and young-leaf diet, a huge orangutan male must consume large quantities of food to maintain his weight. Yet during the time I had observed TP consorting with Priscilla, he had barely done more than nibble. TP was not alone in this. Other large mammals, such as walruses and elephants, eat very little during their mating seasons.

We were already in the swamp. Gnarled knee roots, like so many short gray spears, rose out of the pools of black water. Tangled vegetation closed in around me, impeding movement. Small vines grabbed at my ankles and tripped me, hurling me against the hard points of the knee roots. Passage through the great forest is never easy, even on dry ground. But the difficulty of movement is magnified in the black waters of the tropical peat swamp forest. It made perfect sense to me that orangutans are arboreal. Watching the imperious passage of the orangutans up above, I felt like an odious, incompetent worm, crawling laboriously in the undergrowth. No wonder humans like to cut down the forest. In the great forest, orangutans are the masters of the universe. But once the forest is gone and the swamps are drained, then people assume their "rightful" place in the universe, as masters of all they survey.

TP had stopped to eat low in the trees. Priscilla and Pug were above and a little ahead of him. As I moved to get a better view of what Priscilla was eating, a thick, twisted vine barred my way. Without much thought, intent on observing Priscilla, I pulled my machete from its case and struck the vine as hard as I could. The vine fooled me; although it appeared thick, it was actually very light. The machete sliced through the vine like butter and struck my left knee, cutting to the bone.

I stared down in disbelief. The skin of my knee looked remarkably white against the bright red and pink of my exposed flesh. It was a clean cut; there wasn't much blood, and it was diluted by the dampness of my pants.

I looked at my torn jeans and gashed knee, debating whether I should continue the follow or go back to Camp Leakey. It was two-thirty in the afternoon. I wasn't in pain; my body was in a state of shock. But my knee looked raw. Regretfully, I decided to go back. In typical orangutan fashion, TP, Priscilla, and Pug neither noticed nor acknowledged my departure. Busy eating, they didn't even glance down.

I made my way back to the *ladang* and found the trail leading to camp. It was drizzling. As I slowly moved along the path in the open field, I looked at the forest in the distance. The field was very wide, perhaps a half mile or more across. Then my heart skipped a beat. From the thigh-deep grass along the edge of the path, a dark shape suddenly emerged. It was an orangutan, a large subadult male, lumbering along the ground on all fours. Without pausing, he crossed the path ahead of me. I stood absolutely still in the rain. He did not notice me. He disappeared into the grass on the other side of the path. I watched the movement of the grass until the ripples ceased.

I was awestruck. It was as though I had just seen an australopithecine making his way across some primeval African savanna at the dawn of time for the human race. This was the first time I had seen a wild orangutan on the ground in an open field. With their long, hooked hands and feet, orangutans simply are not built for life on the ground. Who would have imagined a wild orangutan a quarter of a mile from the closest tree, moving across an open field!

I limped back to Camp Leakey and excitedly told Rod what I had seen. Rod was duly impressed. I also told Mr. Hamzah and several Melayu who were gathered in his hut. They did not seem in the least surprised. Mr. Hamzah told me that once he had been crossing a *ladang* so broad that the trees were no longer visible on the hazy horizon. In the middle of this *ladang,* he came across several orangutans sitting on the ground, feasting on the purple *kremunting* berries found on low shrubs in open fields.

I was disappointed by Mr. Hamzah's blasé reaction, but then I thought about it. Much of what we scientists "discover" is known by local people. If I had told them that I had seen an orangutan swimming or flying, the Melayu would have reacted differently. That would have been extraordinary. But an orangutan on open ground was old news. Having lived there all their lives, they had seen it before. As anthropologists, we are trained to view apes coming down from the trees as a major event in hominid evolution. Having decided in advance what is important, we are ecstatic when we find it. But the Melayu did not know that traveling on open ground was thought to be a major event in human evolution. Neither did the orangutan; he was simply traveling from here to there. For me, it was a sobering lesson in guarding against preconceptions.

The Melayu were not particularly impressed by my wound, either. Most local people carry scars from accidents with machetes. Nevertheless, I decided to seek medical treatment. I bound up my leg, and Rod and I set off for Kumai. We left in our small outboard motorboat about two hours before dark, thinking we would get to Kumai just as the sun set. Halfway down the river, the motor broke. It took Rod most of the night to fix it, with only a flashlight for illumination. We arrived at Kumai twelve hours later, as dawn was breaking.

We went straight to the home of Mr. Yusuran, the forestry officer who had been posted at Camp Leakey during our first months. Mr. Yusuran was no longer working for us, as we had no funds to pay him. But he and Rod had remained good friends. Mr. Yusuran assured us that he would get a vehicle to take us to the local hospital in Pangkalan Bun within the hour. We waited twelve hours. A vehicle finally came that evening. We arrived in Pangkalan Bun some thirty hours after my machete accident. As the local doctor stitched up the gaping edges of the wound, he cheerfully told me that I would bear the scar for life, and asked why I hadn't come sooner.

A month and a half had passed since I last saw Throatpouch. My wound had healed, leaving a white oval surrounded by tendrils where the stitches had dissolved. One evening at Camp Wilkie, after nightfall, I was drinking a cup of tea when I heard TP's long call. TP's call was unmistakable. The urgency of his bellow fit his jumpy, ornery temperament. Probably he had just bedded down in his nest but called before he went to sleep. An hour after midnight, his foreboding, gloomy bellows punctuated the darkness once again. Half awake, I listened to his distant call, haunting against the faint clicking sounds of insects that filled the night. Among day-living primates, only the adult male orangutans regularly issued their loud, wailing call in the middle of the night.

Lying in my hammock at Camp Wilkie in the total darkness of the forest, looking at the glowing embers of the evening's dying fire, I sometimes heard as many as three different males calling in the distance, seemingly answering one another. Some calls were barely audible in the distance, others were clear and booming, as if magnified by the still night air, while yet others were tossed and almost obliterated by a sudden chill wind. I wondered what these males were saying, what messages they were sending back and forth. Was it reassuring to a male to hear his brethren, to know that he was not alone in the universe? Or was it troubling to him to realize that his competitors were within earshot? I got goosebumps when I thought about how other, similar, orangutan calls had reverberated at night in these forests many thousands of years ago.

Orangutans are an ancient species. Studies indicate that genetically modern orangutans have been on the earth for more than two million years. Modern humans, more or less indistinguishable from ourselves in anatomy, have walked this planet for less than a hundred thousand years. Ancestral humans probably listened to orangutan calls in the night. Who knows how these ancient hominids interpreted the calls. In Sumatra today, the long calls of adult male orangutans are sometimes attributed to tigers, embellishing the great striped cats' mythical stature.

The long call of the adult male orangutan never ceases to impress me, no matter how often I hear it. It is the loudest and most intimidating sound in the Bornean rain forest. The long call lasts at least one minute and sometimes as long as four minutes. This is what prompted John MacKinnon, who studied orangutans in northern Borneo in the late 1960s, to call it a "long call." The name stuck. The call begins with a series of low grumbles that build until they break into loud bellows. I used to compare the sound to an ungulate having a nervous breakdown, or an inebriated elephant charging the world in a drunken stupor. I had yet to hear a lion roar, except for the MGM lion at Saturday movie matinees when I was a child. But from Hemingway's description in "The Short Happy Life of Francis Macomber," and from what people have told me, an orangutan long call equals or even surpasses a lion's roar in volume and intensity.

The local Melayu, living in small villages scattered on the edge of the forest, usually hear only the peaks of the bellowing in the distance at night. They say, "The orangutan is sighing because his bride left him on his wedding night."

Certainly, the orangutan's long call has its mournful side, but to me, the power and grandeur of the call predominate.

TP called shortly after dawn, as I was waking. From his verbosity during the night, I knew that he would call again at some point during the day. Rod and I decided that we would both search for him, I close to Camp Wilkie, Rod farther afield. I tramped the forest trails near camp all morning, knowing that TP was close at hand but hidden like a shadow in the foliage.

In the early afternoon, I went back to camp and made some hot tea. I sat on Camp Wilkie's raised platform for almost half an hour before lowering myself back to the ground to begin searching again. Barely had I left camp when Throatpouch called close at hand. TP frequently gave himself away in this manner. I learned that the long call was, among other things, a form of self-advertisement. In the dark, dense forest, how else could an adult male let receptive female orangutans know where he was, and warn male competitors to stay away? As I walked through the forest, I imagined that TP was calling, in his forlorn yet assertive mode, for Priscilla.

Fifteen minutes after I left Camp Wilkie, I found TP. Or perhaps he found me. There he was, spread-eagled between two trees just a few feet off the ground, looking at me. He seemed irritated that I had passed close by without noticing his massive presence. TP defecated several times. At this precise moment, Rod called in the distance. His voice was so faint, I estimated that he was half a mile away. I answered four times. Four hoots was our prearranged signal that the caller had found an orangutan. My hooting seemed to annoy TP. He kiss-squeaked loudly looking directly at me.

Throatpouch swung around the tree and stared at me again. Rod had not answered my call, so I hooted again. This time TP seemed even more annoyed. He kiss-squeaked menacingly. When I repeated the four-hoot call a third time, TP became infuriated. He climbed around me and, passing several trees, came to a large rotten stump that towered twenty feet in the air. He shook the stump, then pushed it in my direction. The snag landed a few inches from my feet. If it had hit me on the head, I could have been killed instantly. There was always a danger of severe injury or even death from orangutans who heaved or dropped dead wood because they didn't like being followed.

TP's action with the snag was so sudden I froze. It was difficult to believe that I had just missed death by inches. As the snag crashed to the ground, TP called. After his call, he seemed less tense, and began eating young leaves. By this time Rod had arrived, flushed and short of breath.

Rod had called me from the top of a tree, sixty feet off the ground. We often attempted to re-create for ourselves the experience of orangutan daily life by tasting the fruits they ate and spending time in trees. When I announced my discovery of TP with four hoots, Rod tried to respond instantly, but found that climbing down took much longer than climbing up.

Shortly after Rod arrived, TP called again. Then, as if nothing had happened, he began eating a small, burrlike fruit. Twenty minutes later, after leaving the burr tree, he called again. Even for the highly vocal TP, this many calls was unusual. I wondered if Priscilla's absence had anything to do with it.

A heavy wind began to blow, and it became very dark. Within minutes, the thunder that had been in the distance was overhead. But the rain did not come, and although it remained dark, the thunder eventually stopped. TP was busily eating the large, round, soft green fruits of a vine. I heard a very faint long call, but TP neither looked up nor stopped eating. Soon he moved to another burr tree and began eating high in the canopy.

All this time, I had been carrying Sugito. Earlier, he had climbed off me but stayed low in the trees. Now he began climbing higher and higher. Soon Sugito was up in the canopy, level with TP, who was a few trees over. Sugito had reached a stage of development analogous to a two-year-old human child. Often he would climb away from me, high into the canopy, and become so interested in what he was observing that he seemed to forget that I was not climbing with him. I marveled at his audacity as he swung around and played in the branches, practically under the nose of the feeding TP. I suspect naive little Sugito thought that this big orange fellow would make a fine playmate. TP seemed oblivious to his antics.

Unsuccessful in attracting TP's attention, Sugito suddenly seemed to notice that I was far away. He started climbing down toward me. But as Rod had just discovered, climbing down was more difficult than climbing up. Halfway down, Sugito emitted one tiny whimper, so soft I barely heard it. But the sound enraged TP. Like a crotchety old man, TP did not like unexpected sounds in his vicinity. Now he flew down the tree after Sugito. Sugito was terrified. He slid down the last few feet of the tree as though it were a greased pole and leaped into my arms. TP was right behind him.

I stood up, panic-stricken. Still unnerved by TP's pushing a snag at me earlier, I had a vision of me rolling on the forest floor with TP, fighting over who was to get Sugito. Sugito was holding on so tight that he seemed to have become a part of me. As far as he was concerned, no power on earth was going to separate him from me.

I started slowly backing away. TP kept coming. Had Rod not been there, I think I would have run for my life. Doubtless, TP would have chased me.

But Rod, who had been sitting beside me on the ground, calmly stood up, machete in hand. He looked directly at TP. With one decisive stroke, Rod sliced through a small sapling directly in front of him, continuing to stare at TP. Rod's action had the desired effect: TP stopped abruptly. He was only six feet away, hanging directly over us from some slender branches that looked incapable of supporting his weight. Apparently ready to drop on us at any moment, TP glared down menacingly. His hair erect, he was an awesome sight. Rod continued to stare. Finally, TP broke eye contact, climbed to a high perch, and bellowed forth a long call. So far, this was the closest we had come to being attacked by a wild orangutan.

After the long call, TP charged back to the burr tree as if still irritated. He nested almost immediately afterward, taking great pains in the nest's construction.

I was mortified by the whole incident with Throatpouch. Without think-ing, I had let my feelings for Sugito overwhelm me to the point where I might have fled from a wild orangutan. If I had run, almost certainly I would have been attacked. Most local people knew of someone who had been badly mauled by an orangutan. They claimed a male orangutan was forty times as strong as a man. A zoo director later told me that a male like Throatpouch was probably eight times as strong as a person. He added that of all the animals in the zoo, only male orangutans could open coconuts with their teeth. But it was not the fact that I might have been injured that upset me; rather, it was the fact that I might have fled.

I was mortified because I had violated my own principle: You never run, you always stand up to a challenge. But if Rod had not been there, I might have turned tail and fled. It was a reaction I did not expect from myself. I was depressed about the whole episode.

Rod was puzzled by my reaction. In his typical, no nonsense way, he helped me to understand my own behavior.

"Why are you so bothered by this?" he asked. I couldn't say.

"How many times did you fight with other girls in high school?" he con-tinued.

"Actual fights?"

"Yes."

"None," I answered.

"Well, there you go," Rod replied. "Girls don't fight; boys do. I was always shorter than many of the other kids in my class. I learned to fight and I learned to bluff. Don't worry about it. Bluffing takes practice."

I vowed that next time, like Rod I would stare down any charging orang-utan. My feminist principles had been challenged.

That night TP long-called after midnight. His call was answered twice by another male from the southeast. Lying in my hammock, I thought about how dealing with physical threats and challenges is part of being male. Several months before, I had watched TP fight off a competitor; today I had watched Rod stand up to TP's charge. While I admired Rod for his courage, I felt deprived. Why hadn't I learned to deal with aggression as he had? Why hadn't I learned when to fight and when to bluff? Boys have an advantage in that their natural aggression is sanctioned.

But I also wondered how much difference Sugito's vulnerable presence on my body had made. Under the circumstances, my retreat behind Rod's masculinity might have been adaptive. Primate females almost invariably carry their infants on their bodies when they move. For a female with an infant to fight a much larger male would mean putting that infant at risk. When a huge, angry male came at me from the treetops, I didn't think about my principles, all I thought about was saving my infant. Pride and principle have their place, but care and responsibility for one's infant come first. I had behaved like a normal primate mother.

The next morning, as TP left his nest, he long-called for more than two minutes. His voice cracked from the exertion of what was for him an unusually long call. Priscilla was nowhere to be seen. Perhaps his longing for her was taking its toll. He called several times again that morning, looking off into the distance. If, as the Melayu say, he was calling for his bride, he got no answer. TP spent the rest of the day alone.

By now Rod was spending much of his time documenting wild orangutans on film. Whenever he came into the forest, he carried ten pounds of photographic equipment in a weather-tight aluminum box with a leather shoulder strap. The box clanged as he walked, and permanently pulled down one shoulder. The next morning he decided to come with me to follow TP.

When we arrived at his nest, TP showed his displeasure by snapping and dropping a dead branch as he kiss-squeaked. He moved off quickly, making it difficult to follow him. But then TP found a branch in the sunlight and settled down for a nap. Like a cat napping on a sunny windowsill, TP sat curled on his haunches, intermittently opening and closing his eyes as though it were an effort to stay awake. Down below, in the damp and dark, Rod and I, more pedestrian creatures, were still shivering from the cold morning dew that had soaked us as we pushed through the thick vegetation on the forest floor. It was still difficult for me to accept that here, in the middle of the Bornean jungle, only two degrees south of the equator, we were constantly battling the cold in our fingers, toes, and joints. Ensconced on his branch in the sunlight, TP's arboreality put him in a different universe.

TP could not have picked a spot more conducive to photography. The sky was almost shocking blue behind him, and the sun picked up the bright orange of his coat and intensified it. The colors were worthy of van Gogh. Although TP was high in the trees, Rod was able to take several pictures of the big orange male while he dozed. I still have the pictures, and the vividness of his coat never fails to impress me.

This day I had brought Sugito with me to the forest. TP had roused himself and was eating *merang* — a sweet red fruit the size and texture of a large cherry tomato — when Sugito whimpered. Instantly, TP leaped out of the tree and charged down a nearby trunk. But this time he stopped about twenty feet above us and monitored the situation. Much calmer than he had been on the previous day, he sat on a small branch, produced two *merang* fruits from his cheeks, and began to chew as casually as if he were lighting up a cigarette. He sat there chewing and watching Sugito for several minutes. Sugito seemed to know he was being watched. Almost swaggering, the little show-off climbed into the small saplings a foot or so away from me. TP continued to chew.

I wondered if I had misread TP. Perhaps it was not just irritation at Sugito's whimpering that brought him flying down out of the trees but a need to protect this infant of his own species. Whatever the answer, he seemed to be getting used to us.

That afternoon around two, TP descended to the ground and ran away without once looking back at us. When he was thirty or forty feet away, he simply vanished into the dark maze of tree trunks and ground vegetation. The brilliant orange coat that had shown so vividly against the bright blue equatorial sky disappeared. Because the light no longer caught the shafts of his hair, it was as if the orangutan had shed his orange coat, retaining only his dark skin. TP's dark form melted into the shadows of the rain forest and was gone.

When TP's long call led us to him, three hours later, he was still alone.

The next morning, TP seemed unusually agitated, even for TP. He charged through the treetops, broke branches, rocked snags, and long-called several times. Later he began to move through the forest purposefully. He seemed to be listening for something. He would move, stop, listen until he heard something in the distance, then move in that direction. Shortly after he crossed into the swamp, I spotted Pug. At TP's approach, Pug climbed higher up in his tree. TP just sat, watching intently. Two minutes later, Priscilla emerged out of the foliage. I soon realized that their relationship had changed. Whereas TP was uncharacteristically silent, Priscilla and Pug produced an incredible cacophony, kiss-squeaking, hooting, breaking branches, and toppling snags. Only when it began to rain heavily did they stop. When orangutans displayed, I usually assumed the hostility was directed at me, the human observer. But from TP's meek demeanor, perhaps he felt that it was directed at him.

TP followed Priscilla and Pug for the rest of the day, but the next morning he was alone again. He long-called repeatedly that afternoon. But the only creatures he encountered were a troop of four or five red leaf-eating monkeys. Normally, their coats blazed crimson or glowed a golden yellow, depending on the light. But on this rainy afternoon, their coats were drab and dark, giving the uninitiated observer no hint of their sartorial splendor in the sunlight. The monkeys showed no special reaction to TP, but when one of them spotted me, they immediately leaped away.

TP had better luck locating Priscilla and Pug the next day, but received no warm welcome. Pug greeted him with a snarling growl; Priscilla simply ignored him. I realized that there were other orangutans in the trees: Howard, the quiet subadult male I frequently had seen with Cara, and a boisterous adolescent female I named "Noisy." Noisy put on a wild display, whether to impress me and Rod, TP, or all of us, I didn't know. Throughout this uproar, TP sat watching Priscilla as though he were totally enraptured. When she moved, he followed.

I got the distinct impression that Priscilla had decided their consortship was over. A little later I discovered why. Priscilla's genitalia were now white and swollen: she was pregnant. TP and Priscilla had been traveling together, consorting and mating, for at least three months. During that time, I had not seen TP with another female, nor had I observed Priscilla with another male. Almost certainly, he was the father. What effect would her pregnancy have on TP? Would he abandon her once she convinced him that she was no longer sexually receptive? Would he continue to monitor her protectively? Would he become a devoted father? I knew the latter was unlikely, but I still longed to observe their changing relationship for myself.

By now Rod and I, with Sugito, were in the deep swamp, up to our thighs in black water. TP and Priscilla were resting separately in the canopy. It was midday, and the usual sounds of the forest had thinned from the morning. The whine of cicadas was punctuated every so often by the shriek of an unseen bird.

At precisely one-thirty, an unbelievably loud sound exploded out of the sky. The forest was thrown into total silence. Sugito leaped soundlessly into my lap and clung desperately. Rod and I sat stunned, as did Throatpouch, Priscilla, and Pug above us. Even the insects were still.

It was as if God had shouted "Shut up!"

Whispering, Rod and I talked about what the sound might be and where it came from. We concluded it must have been a sonic boom. Our hypothesis was correct. Listening to the radio that evening, Rod learned that, indeed, the Concorde had flown overhead on a demonstration flight from Europe to Australia.

In the days, weeks, and months ahead, I frequently thought of TP and Priscilla, and the coming infant. Only in later years would I realize the full significance of that sonic boom. The Concorde itself would not change the world, but it heralded, in dramatic fashion, the global and technological forces that were bringing the world together, for better or worse; forces that increasingly impinged on the silence of nature in the least trampled places on earth. The sonic boom represented one of the culminating achievements of human technology, an aircraft that traveled faster than the speed of sound, reducing the Atlantic and Pacific Oceans to the size of mere puddles. Humankind was trying to supplant God in the ordering of time, nature, and the earth. Priscilla's yet-to-be-born infant would grow to maturity amid ever-increasing reverberations of the sonic boom. The sounds of human domination and destruction — buzz saws, chain saws, bulldozers — were coming ever closer to the orangutan's unsullied tropical paradise. For orangutans and their fellow creatures of the forest, the sonic boom, representing the triumph of human technology and the economic shrinking of the globe, was an atomic bomb.

# 10

# GEORGINA

This magic moment . . .

— *sung by the Drifters*

. . . perplexed by no conflicts,
troubled by no philosophical questions,
beset by no remote ambitions.

— *Margaret Mead*

---

THOUGH JETS were flying overhead, Borneo had yet to enter the postal age. Mail delivery was sporadic at best. The post office in Pangkalan Bun would give our mail to whoever passed by and agreed to accept it. Sometimes our letters would end up in the hands of friends or relatives of people who knew us; other times we would have to track down total strangers. Occasionally, a few pieces would be given to our assistant, Mr. Hamzah. But often we received no mail for months.

Mail became an obsession. Aside from Rod's radio, it was our only link to the outside world. We had none of the usual sources of information — books, magazines, newspapers. At times we felt as though the rest of the world had abandoned us. We regularly wrote to family and friends, but got no answers. The few letters we did receive confused us. Leakey admonished me to write to my mother; good friends begged for a few words. Only much later did we learn that almost none of the letters we wrote during our first six months in the field reached their destinations. Rumors that we were "lost in the jungle" had begun to circulate. I had always thought of myself as an independent, self-reliant sort of person, who could get along without much contact with other people. Now I yearned for an old magazine, for a postcard, for any word at all from the outside.

Informal, haphazard methods of delivering the mail were typical of Kalimantan at the time. Even so, I was surprised when, one day in mid-May, hand-loggers working illegally about two hours upstream were the mail carriers. Rod handed me the letters when I returned from the forest that evening.

All three pieces of mail were memorable, but for different reasons. The first was an alumni newspaper from UCLA. It reminded me of something I had read in one of Cindy Adams's books. When she was in Indonesia, working on a biography of the country's first president, Dr. Soekarno, letters from her parents, friends, and family never seemed to get through. But one time a department store flyer, mailed third class, reached her in record time. Hungry for news from home, she read it over and over. Likewise, I read and reread every word of the UCLA alumni newspaper, until I knew it by heart.

The second piece of mail was a welcome pat on the back from the original chairperson of my doctoral committee, Dr. Joe Birdsell. Dr. Birdsell was pleased that I was sighting wild orangutans.

Then I got an unpleasant jolt. The third piece was a short note from Louis Leakey, attached to a long article on orangutans that had just appeared in a scientific journal. The author was John MacKinnon, a young Englishman who had first studied insects at Gombe and then, in the late 1960s, gone on to study orangutans in Sabah, in northern Malaysian Borneo, for his doctoral studies at Cambridge. Leakey had told me about him before I left for Indonesia, but MacKinnon had not yet published the results of his orangutan study. I started reading the article immediately, while there was still light.

MacKinnon's monograph was brimming with information. It was the first article ever published that described how orangutans lived in the wild. Before that all we really had were informal observations and sketchy surveys. Clearly, MacKinnon was not only an intrepid investigator but also a careful and astute observer. I found the article fascinating.

But when I finished, by candlelight, I became profoundly depressed. My worst fears were realized. In the mountainous region of northern Borneo where MacKinnon had conducted his study, the wild orangutans were migratory. He had difficulty recognizing individuals, because they moved constantly.

My plan was to study orangutans the same way that Jane Goodall was studying chimpanzees and Dian Fossey, mountain gorillas. I wanted to compile life histories of individual orangutans. This meant that I had to be able to recognize individuals, habituate or get them accustomed to my presence, and then observe them over the years, to see what patterns their lives would take. But I could do this only if the orangutans stayed in one place. Given the deep swamps and trackless forest, it would be impossible to follow wild orangutans over long distances for several months, much less for years. Even if I had wanted to equip individual orangutans with radio transmitters, and had unlimited funds, I wouldn't have been able to follow them in a jeep or even a small plane. If orangutans were migratory, as MacKinnon believed, my study would be over before it really began. I was devastated.

When I received the article, I had gone ten straight days without spotting a single wild orangutan. The ones I had begun to know — Beth, Cara, Priscilla, and Throatpouch — seemed to have disappeared. I wondered if I would ever see them again. Perhaps the faint long calls I had heard in the distance were TP's final goodbyes. I prayed that MacKinnon was wrong. But I suspected that he was right. After all, he had studied orangutans for one and a half years. I had been in Tanjung Puting less than six months.

⁂

The next day, as most days, I walked the forest alone, pores open, dripping with sweat, hair caked against my neck and scalp, breathing heavily, suffocating in the dense humidity. I grew so weary that even lifting one foot and placing it in front of the other became an effort. I was truly discouraged. I had almost convinced myself that the wild orangutans had left the area, and I would never see one again. But I could not even cry: all the excess fluid in my body disappeared in sweat. Rod and I hardly saw each other these days, except in the evening when we both were exhausted. That night we decided to take a day off. Instead of my searching and Rod's cutting trails, we would walk together along a trail cut a few years earlier by the provincial forestry department to mark the boundaries of the reserve.

We left Camp Wilkie shortly after dawn, and walked for hours. It was a brilliant day. Sometime in the early afternoon we surprised a trio of gibbons. We saw the gibbons for only a few seconds, but we could still hear their alarm calls for minutes afterward. They seemed to be warning and reassuring each other simultaneously. As they took flight, evaporating into the canopy, I thanked the fates that I hadn't chosen to study gibbons.

It was well past midday when we turned back. The late afternoon shadows were already enshrouding the forest when we walked under a tree that stood directly in the middle of the trail. Then I noticed the remains of freshly eaten fruit. Drops of bright red juice still glistened on the green fruit skins. "Do you remember seeing these fruits on the ground this morning?" we asked each other simultaneously. The answer was "No."

"I bet the orangutan is still close by," said Rod. We looked up and there she was, a furry adolescent female, an orangutan Goldilocks.

The orangutan sped out of the fruit tree overhead, stopped a few trees over, and looked at us in frank disbelief. Grasping branches with her hands, she pulled herself into an *aru* tree. Unlike most trees in the Bornean tropical rain forest, *aru* is not a flowering plant, but rather a gymnosperm. Gymnosperms, which predate flowering plants, covered the earth in the days of dinosaurs. Typical gymnosperms are pine and fir trees, which the *aru* resembles. On an *aru* tree, a branch is the functional equivalent of a leaf, attached to the trunk with a ball and socket joint. The floor under an *aru* is littered not just with needles but with whole branches.

It probably was no accident that this large adolescent female chose to move into an *aru* tree. Because of its design, the branches are relatively easy to remove. Kiss-squeaking indignantly, she began to systematically denude the tree. She would tear a branch from its socket and throw it at us in an underhanded fast-pitch, sometimes swinging the branch back and forth a few times to build momentum before she let it go. Even after she had stripped the *aru* of branches, she stayed in the tree and continued vocalizing, making long, passionate kiss sounds followed by loud grunts.

It was growing dark and we only had one flashlight between us. I volunteered to go back to Camp Wilkie, start a fire, and get water boiling for rice and tea. Rod would stay with the orangutan until she nested. Afraid of getting stranded in the dark without a flashlight, I raced to Camp Wilkie. As I ran, I decided to name the adolescent female "Georgina," after my landlady in the dusty Macedonian village of Anzabegavo in the former Yugoslavia, where I had done archaeological research.

I was overjoyed to have found a wild orangutan, especially an adolescent. The other females I had followed were all adults. I would never know how old they were, how many offspring they had had prior to the ones accompanying them now, or other vital details. It was as if I had opened the books of their lives in the middle. But Georgina was still in her youth. She offered me the opportunity to study a wild female orangutan's reproductive career from the beginning.

Georgina was an exquisite creature. Her long hair parted in the middle, almost as if it had been styled, and fell down the sides of her face, framing it. Her narrow, delicate face was dominated by large, liquid brown eyes with thick lashes. Although her snout was dark, her eyelids and a small circle around her eyes were still light-hued, a sign of youth. An orangutan female's face becomes totally dark, losing the last vestiges of white on her eyelids, sometime in her mid-twenties. (The same process occurs in males.) Actually, I didn't know this at the time. But although Georgina was almost adult in size, her fresh, unlined face, her ruff of bright hair, and her bouncy, spirited behavior told me that she was still an adolescent. I just knew it, the way one knows that a Great Dane or St. Bernard puppy is a puppy, even though the puppy is enormous.

Georgina was the first adolescent female I habituated. She was also the first wild orangutan who actually was curious about me. Even during our first encounter, when she stripped the *aru* tree of branches, she had come closer and closer as she displayed. The adult females seemed genuinely outraged when they displayed at me. Georgina seemed to be enjoying herself, as if she were showing off her prowess at the adult business of chasing away intruders. Periodically, she checked Rod's and my faces, as if to see how her performance was being received. For the first few days I followed her, Georgina displayed now and then, tossing branches and producing loud kiss-squeaks. But I got the feeling that she was playacting, at least in part. Georgina did not seem wary, like Beth, or bold and aggressive, like Cara. Nor was she irritable, like Priscilla, who continued to display at me furiously, off and on, for twelve years. Georgina went about her business apparently undeterred, foraging and resting as she liked.

Very early in my association with Georgina, a singular incident took place. In all my years of studying wild orangutans, this incident has no parallel. I knew at the time that this was an extraordinary moment, but I didn't realize that it would never be repeated.

Several days after we found her, Georgina was sitting quietly in the trees. Rod had come with me to take photographs. We were standing on the edge of a small clearing, waiting to see whether Georgina had stopped to rest or would travel on. Rod happened to have his camera out.

To my astonishment, Georgina descended from the canopy, climbing straight down a pole tree until she was about four or five feet off the ground. When she stopped, she was almost level with us. I stood frozen in amazement. Holding on to the pole tree with both hands, Georgina looked directly at us across the open space. She was only seven or eight feet away, but she seemed much closer because no vegetation stood between us. I scarcely dared breathe; I wanted the moment to last. After so many months of trying to get a clear look at wild orangutans, I got my first unobstructed view of a wild orangutan because she wanted to see her human observers.

Georgina was motionless. Unblinking, she looked at us intently, as though trying to understand who we were, or what we were. I can't recall whether the moment lasted for one minute or five. Georgina just looked. Her eyes betrayed nothing. There was no hostility, no emotion, just curiosity. She seemed to be drinking us in. Then, abruptly, Georgina left, climbing back to the top of the canopy. She did not look down. In the thirty seconds or so before she began climbing, Rod took one picture. The click of the shutter was so loud, it seemed almost sacrilegious.

No other wild orangutan has ever behaved the same way. Often they stared for a minute or two or even more, but once they convinced themselves that I was neither dangerous nor interfering, they lost interest. No other wild orangutan has ever climbed down level with me just to look at me. I now see Georgina's intense scrutiny as an expression of the friendly, curious nature that typifies adolescent orangutans.

I met her when she was on the verge of adulthood but still exhibited some of the recklessness of youth. Like the human teenager who jumps into a car and speeds down the freeway at ninety miles an hour, secure in the myth that he or she is invulnerable and immortal, Georgina threw caution to the wind when she descended from the canopy to look at us. It was reckless behavior on her part. If we had been Dayak hunters, she would have been dead.

Older females had discovered the boundaries of their lives. Beth, Cara, Priscilla, and the others I had briefly observed all had one or more offspring. They seemed to know that they would spend the rest of their days caring for offspring and seeking food. Now and then, their lives would be punctuated by consortships with adult males. But, if they were lucky, life held few surprises. My presence in the undergrowth might be irritating, but it was basically irrelevant to their adult roles: rearing offspring and finding food.

For Georgina, the possibilities were still infinite. She had seen adult females and their offspring, of course. But she did not know this was the shape her life almost certainly would take. Because she was an orangutan, her mother never sat her down and told her the facts of life. Suspended between childhood and motherhood, her days were full of new experiences. Rod and I were one of those new experiences. Unlike the adult females, she hadn't yet formed an opinion about human observers.

But her youthful, reckless curiosity was tempered by her emerging maturity. She did not attempt to interact with us on that or any other day. Having looked us over, she returned to the safety of the canopy.

My first impressions of Georgina as young, sweet, and gay were confirmed in the days ahead. Without offspring, she led the seemingly carefree life that one imagines young adolescent girls must have led in paradise. It was reminiscent of the lives Margaret Mead described in *Coming of Age in Samoa*. Georgina liked company, particularly the company of adolescents like herself. She encountered other orangutans more often, spent more time with them, and interacted with them more directly than any of the adult females I had followed. When adult females traveled together, they moved in a stately procession, maintaining a rigid distance between one another. There was a formality in their interactions, and sometimes more than a little tension. Almost the only time they physically touched was when they fought. By comparison, Georgina and her pals seemed easy and casual. They moved along willy-nilly, sometimes brushing against each other, sometimes swinging apart, with no apparent agenda or rules. They might quarrel, but they did not seem afraid of one another. Georgina traveled with other adolescent females, particularly the three I named "Fern," "Maud," and "Evonne," and with both subadult and adult males. But she was leery of adult female orangutans, and seemed to avoid them when she could. As a result, it was impossible to determine which, if any, of the adult females in the area was her mother.

On the second day I followed her, Georgina met up with a large, fully adult male with cheekpads, whom I provisionally called "Bearded" in honor of his prominent beard. (Beards and partial baldness are two distinctive, sex-linked traits males of the human and orangutan species share.) When Bearded appeared, Georgina was eating *kubing* fruit. The *kubing* tree is a member of the Ficus family, a family characterized by its sticky white sap. The branches of trees in this group frequently ooze latex when cut. The fruit skins also seemed to contain the white, syrupy goo. Georgina picked a fruit. Rather than eating it immediately, she pulled off the stem with her hand and held the fruit upside down, as if to drain it first. I later saw another female take four fruits, pull the stems off each one, and lay them on a branch. She waited several minutes before eating the drained fruits leisurely, one by one.

When Bearded entered the *kubing* tree he stared at me but did not vocalize. Then he settled down to eat. At first Georgina seemed to ignore him. But by the time she had eaten several fruits, she subtly had maneuvered herself, through a series of imperceptible steps, to within two feet of the large male. Without further ado, Georgina moved over to Bearded and, standing on all fours, put her snout right next to his. She stared intently first at his mouth, then at the contents of his hand, which he was holding next to his mouth.

Bearded continued chomping away as though she wasn't there. About a half minute later, Georgina casually moved away, sat down, and resumed eating.

The vision of the adolescent female with her snout pressed against the mouth of the cheekpadded male stayed with me. Although I did not realize it at the time, she was probably indicating interest in him, not the food he was eating. In human terms, we would say she was flirting. But like the teenybopper who pursues a rock star, she got nowhere.

The next morning Bearded had departed, but Georgina soon met another fully adult male. He was massive, with exceptionally large cheekpads that seemed to meet above his forehead and form a dome. Unlike Bearded, he kiss-squeaked furiously when he saw me, using a foot as well as his hands to break off branches and drop them. The large male started a long call. Then, apparently thinking better of it, he yawned, pulling his lips way back. Next, he began bouncing on a branch less than ten feet away from Georgina. Finally, after more than half an hour, the cheekpadder moved off. Had Georgina been an adult, she would have fled. But she seemed to pay no attention to his antagonistic display, and she stayed close by, a subtle clue that she found him interesting. When he left, however, she went in the other direction and spent the rest of that day, and the next, alone.

Early the following morning, Georgina encountered the adult female I had named "Fran," Fran's infant, "Freddy," and her adolescent daughter, Fern. The tiny infant clung to her mother's side, and Fern rode on Fran's back. This was the first and only time that I ever saw a wild orangutan carrying two offspring simultaneously. Much later, I watched poor, harried Akmad struggle to carry both her biological infant, Arnold, and the large four-year-old female she had adopted, Carey. When I saw Fran carrying Fern and her infant, I did not know how unusual this behavior was.

The infant Freddy was so tiny and such a light color compared to her mother and older sibling that she must have been only a month or two old. The way she clung tightly to her mother's side as though glued there was another indication of her very young age. When infants become slightly older, they frequently shift positions on the mother's body and loosen their tenacious grip. Infant Freddy's eyes were wide open, unblinking, staring straight ahead, as if a flash bulb had just gone off in her face.

Fran, Freddy, and Fern slowly moved past Georgina, vocalizing loudly and dropping branches as they went. Clearly they did not appreciate our presence. Rod followed the noisy trio while I stayed with Georgina. Hurrying out of adult Fran's way, Georgina moved into a fruit tree.

Five minutes later, a subadult male appeared in the tree where Georgina was eating peacefully. Although not fully grown, he was much bigger and huskier than she was. I named him "Bearded Without Cheekpads," or "BWC" for short. BWC glanced in the direction of Fran and her brood, whose vocalizations and crashings could still be heard in the distance. Then he approached Georgina and sat right next to her. She ignored him. But then BWC grabbed her roughly by both legs and lifted up her bottom, which he began nuzzling with great interest. Clinging to a higher branch by her arms, Georgina squealed sharply, then produced a hybrid whimper-squeal that resembled the sound that Sugito made when I stared him straight in the eye after he had wrecked something. When she squealed, BWC released Georgina in an offhand manner, left the tree, and vanished into the foliage. I was surprised that he released her without a struggle.

I thought that was the end of the encounter, but in fact it had just begun. Georgina ate a few more fruits, then left in the same direction BWC had taken. A few minutes later, as if by magic, BWC reappeared. He was unusually calm. He looked at me, but did not display. The loud commotion from Fran and her brood, still audible even though they were more than three hundred feet away, seemed to puzzle him more than my presence did. He kept glancing in their direction, as if wondering what was going on.

BWC and Georgina began traveling together, eating in the same trees. Georgina seemed relaxed in the subadult male's presence. Although she had rejected him sexually, she did not reject him as a friend. She seemed to like his companionship. At one point she sat with her leg dangling, holding on to a branch above with her left arm. BWC sat above her, on a branch about ten feet higher. They seemed comfortable in one another's company.

It was high noon. Although the sun did not penetrate the maze of foliage on the forest floor, it was blazing directly overhead; it must have been hot in the canopy. Down below, where I sat on a log, sweat flies congregated on the back of my drenched shirt. Typical of a lazy, hot afternoon, the silence of the forest was overwhelming, broken only by the ebb and flow of cicadas whining, moving through the forest in waves of sound.

Georgina snapped and bent six or seven branches to make a day nest. She climbed into her nest and sat upright for a minute or two, then lay down gingerly, as though not quite trusting the nest. With one arm holding a branch above her, she lay in the nest without moving for almost an hour, which almost certainly meant she was asleep. BWC sat quietly on a branch above her, occasionally making a movement that suggested he was flicking away a fly.

Suddenly, as if he had sniffed something, BWC moved down to Georgina and put first his hands and then his head into her nest. Georgina squealed and started to leave. But BWC backed off and moved to a branch five feet away, where he sat with his back to Georgina and casually ate something. Georgina settled back into the nest. Fifteen minutes later, BWC moved higher into the same tree, and then sat very still as though he, too, were resting. The sun was very hot; the air was very still.

Georgina rested for a total of an hour and a half. This turned out to be typical of Georgina. She was one of the few females who almost invariably left her nest at dawn, rested in the late morning, and then foraged until dusk, often nesting after dark.

After Georgina left her day nest, she sat in the sun high in a tree. BWC approached her, reached out and, with his hand, gently touched her face, near her mouth. She squeaked, but did not move away. BWC dropped his hand and moved to a lower branch in the tree and began to eat tiny burrs. It started to rain, but Georgina and BWC continued to eat on opposite sides of the tree. The rain became heavy, then finally stopped. But the drizzle-and-leaf scatter continued. After a rain, minuscule puddles of water remain on the leaves. The slightest movement or even a hint of wind scatters the drops, creating a type of localized after-rain, which may continue for hours. I heard thunder in the distance, but could not see lightning.

Georgina and BWC ignored the weather. By this time I knew that eating was an orangutan's first preoccupation. Wild orangutans spend up to eight hours a day munching, chomping, processing, bending, picking, sorting, and devouring foodstuffs. Watching Georgina and BWC eat the small, burrlike fruit was an education in the sophistication of orangutan food-processing techniques. These berry-sized fruits contain two crunchy seeds attached to a bit of orange pulp. I found the pulp a little too sour, but that may have been because I was picking up pieces from the forest floor, tasting what the orangutans had discarded.

To eat these particular fruits, the orangutans had to get past the burrs — insidious, microscopic glasslike slivers. Orangutans had several techniques. First they would pick a number of the burr-berries. Once they had a collection of the tiny fruits in the palm of one hand, they would slap the palm against the top of the other hand and rub vigorously in all directions. A second technique involved vigorously pressing and rolling a palmful of burrs on a small branch. At one spot where Georgina was eating, the branch seemed shiny from wear. She seemed to have chosen this branch as her burr-processor.

The one time I tried to process burrs myself, I screamed in pain. Lacking the thick skin of orangutans, I only managed to pound the burrs into my hand. I learned not to sit directly under burr trees when orangutans were eating there, because an invisible rain of microscopic slivers would penetrate my shirt, making my skin itch and burn for days.

After several hours eating burrs, BWC hastily constructed a nest and lay down. Only a few minutes later, he sat up and strode along a branch toward Georgina, low rumbles emanating from his throat. Georgina started whimpering. This time ignoring her protests, BWC wrapped his legs around Georgina's torso. She tried to push him away, but he brushed her hands aside and kept trying to position her with his legs. She continued to whimper and push him away. They grappled this way for about five minutes.

BWC's movements were slow and deliberate. There was nothing rough. He acted as if he had all the time in the world. Finally, she was facing away, squeaking and breaking twigs. He was holding her by the legs, and adjusting himself under her. He pulled and pushed at her body until she was half facing him, but she kept twisting away. He finally achieved penetration, and pumped rhythmically for about a minute. But again, Georgina twisted away.

Apparently giving up, BWC moved several trees away, made a night nest, and went to sleep. I was somewhat surprised to see that rather than attempt to flee Georgina approached BWC's tree. She settled in an adjacent tree, incorporating two bent-over pole trees into her nest.

Georgina's relationship with BWC opened my eyes. I had seen orangutan copulation before, with Priscilla and Throatpouch. Using that pair as my model, I had assumed that mating took place within the context of ongoing consortships between "consenting adults." Priscilla and TP would spend several days together, separate when she lost interest in mating, then get back together a month later. Georgina and BWC clearly had a different kind of sexual relationship. BWC forcibly copulated with Georgina. Yet, unlike TP, he made no attempt to guard or monopolize her. In fact, the day after this incident he was gone.

There was an ambiguous, teenage quality to their relationship, as if they were just fooling around. Like many adolescent girls and boys, Georgina and BWC seemed to have different agendas. Georgina liked his attention and wanted his friendship, but did not want to copulate. BWC didn't mind the friendship, but basically what he wanted was sex. Their last encounter resembled the stereotypical scene in which the teenage girl protests "Don't, don't," while the teenage boy insists "Why not, why not?" In effect, BWC had committed date rape. I do not want in any way to trivialize date rape among human beings. I know from friends and acquaintances how traumatic, and how alarmingly common, this is. But sex does not have the same meaning for orangutans that it does for humans. We view sex through cultural and moral lenses. For an orangutan, sex has no more meaning than eating. It is an expression of biological urges. An adolescent orangutan female may not enjoy forcible copulation, but neither does she suffer guilt and self-recrimination afterward. Clearly, Georgina did not hold BWC's actions against him. But unlike the mature Priscilla and TP, neither of the adolescents seemed to be sure of what they were doing. Adolescent ambivalence is something our two species share.

Georgina not only was "dating" and traveling with males her age, but she also was traveling with other young females. These associations clearly were friendship, but friendship by orangutan standards. To the untutored human eye, Georgina's relationship with other young females might not have seemed special, but from an orangutan perspective she had pals.

Early the next morning, Georgina met Fern, the adolescent she had encountered with her mother, Fran, a few days before. This time Fran was nowhere to be seen. Fern was much smaller than Georgina and may have been three, perhaps four, years younger. Her face — her snout as well as the skin around her eyes — was still pinkish-white.

Georgina and Fern traveled together, primarily eating burrs. The next day, the two adolescent females stayed together for the entire day, moving through the forest in their rambunctious, distinctively adolescent way. Swinging from here to there, running instead of walking, climbing and then dropping, their behavior was more playful and less purposeful than that of the older females.

In the afternoon Georgina and Fern were joined by a boisterous male adolescent, younger than BWC. The trio bounced along together, in constantly changing combinations, for the rest of the day. Unlike the more sedate adults, they never stayed in one tree, or one combination, for very long. The three orangutans ate until it was pitch dark. I couldn't see them nest, though I could hear the sounds of branches breaking and cracking.

By the next morning, the adolescent male had disappeared. Georgina seemed to be alone, but met Fern again in midmorning. They traveled together for the next two days. The second day Georgina groomed Fern briefly, running her hand through the hair on Fern's back as the other adolescent hung from a branch. I have never seen two wild adult females groom one another, no matter how friendly they seemed to be. Several times, Georgina approached Fern and put her snout next to Fern's mouth as Fern chomped on vine stalks, as if she were begging for food. She had done the same with the large adult male Bearded. It seemed to be a gesture of friendship. Georgina was trying to intensify the interaction.

Georgina and Fern were eating peacefully in the top of an extremely tall tree when a large subadult male with a fat face and a beard appeared lower down. He probably was coming from the ground. His intentions perfectly clear, he climbed directly to Georgina, pulled her legs, and positioned her so that she was facing him directly. Squealing, Georgina batted his hands away. For some seconds it looked as though they were playing handsies. Fern came closer, as if to verify what was happening, defecated, and then quickly left the tree, watching from a distance.

The big male pumped rhythmically for more than four minutes, occasionally pausing to reposition himself. After the copulation, when Georgina pulled out of his grasp, Fern fled even farther away. Because Georgina was older, she probably was more desirable, but Fern was taking no chances.

Big and burly, the new male was almost the size of a cheekpadder. He had enormous brow ridges and a long flowing beard, but no cheekpads yet. He looked so formidable, I named him "Beast." (After all, Georgina was the beauty.) I saw Fern make a nest that night, but Beast and Georgina were still eating burrs when it turned dark, Beast comfortably ensconced on an eating platform made by bending together three branches. When I arrived the next morning Georgina and Beast were gone, whether together or alone, I didn't know. I followed Fern, who traveled alone for the next two days, then lost her, too.

A pattern was beginning to emerge. Georgina had approached adult male Bearded, and quietly observed a second, highly aggressive, adult male display. Clearly, she was attracted to the mature cheekpadders. But these fully adult males ignored young Georgina. Subadult males, however, were drawn to her and two—BWC and Beast—had forcibly copulated with her. I saw a similar pattern several months later, when I followed another adolescent female in a different part of the study area.

"Lolita," as I named her, was an unusually small adolescent female, with very prominent brow ridges, a brush cut, white lips, and a distinct wattle. To my human eye, she was not very appealing. Georgina seemed infinitely more attractive. But I was a mere human and not a true connoisseur of orangutan pulchritude. Judging by the number of males that clustered around her, Lolita oozed sex appeal. Perhaps it was her vigor and chutzpa, not just her looks.

Nearly every time I saw her, Lolita was accompanied by at least one, and sometimes two or even three subadult males. Energetic and feisty, Lolita seemed to relish her popularity with the young males. But in human terms, she was a tease. She encouraged the subadult males to follow her, then rejected their sexual advances, playing hard to get. Instead she threw herself at an adult cheekpadder who seemed, at best, ambivalent about her. "Fingers" was so-named because part of one of his fingers was missing, probably the legacy of a fight with another male over a female. Majestic and dignified, with full cheekpads and a long, flowing, pointed beard, he gazed down at me almost benevolently, rarely displaying. Fingers's attitude toward Lolita was equally nonchalant. I realized that Lolita was chasing him, not the reverse. Although Fingers did not appear totally enthusiastic, he was allowing himself to be pursued.

Over the three days I observed them together, Lolita's attempts to seduce Fingers were blatant. She scrambled to him whenever he long-called. (Long calls sometimes precede copulation.) She groomed his back and arm intently with her fingers and lips; she put her arm around his neck and clung to him. She dangled suggestively in front of him, her bottom inches from his face. Once she climbed above him, grabbed his cheekpad with her foot, and firmly pulled his face between her legs. Then, to make certain he understood, she took his hand in hers and placed it directly over her genitalia. Even then, Fingers remained uninspired.

Several hours later, however, the magnificent male finally responded. When Fingers began rumbling, Lolita immediately climbed under him, and they copulated for four full minutes. As I circled under the tree, trying to find the best vantage point, I saw Fingers and Lolita clearly. Fingers seemed totally consumed in the mating, thrusting like an enormous piston, machinelike in his efficiency. His eyes were rolled heavenward. Lolita lay on her back, playing with a twig. Had she been human, I would have described the look on her face as one of self-congratulation. But her triumph was short-lived. The next day Fingers chose to sit and eat on a branch with the now very pregnant Cara, ignoring Lolita totally.

At first I was puzzled. I had watched TP, an adult male in his prime, moon over the middle-aged, balding, feeble-looking Priscilla. Now Lolita, young and nubile, was actively, almost desperately, courting an older male who acted as if sex were the last thing on his mind. Yet Lolita spurned the eager, younger males who attempted to mate with her. I realized that I was thinking in

Western cultural terms, where youth and beauty are highly prized. Gradually, as I observed different orangutans, the pieces fell into place.

Female orangutans of all ages are attracted to mature cheekpadders. These males prove their virility (or fitness) by chasing off younger males and, when necessary, fighting other mature males, as TP had done during his consortship with Priscilla. Cheekpadders, in turn, are attracted to mature females, especially those who have demonstrated their capabilities as a mother by rearing at least one healthy juvenile. Female orangutans begin searching for their Mr. Rights in adolescence. Over the years, I would discover that there is a cheekpadder in every orangutan female's life. Rejected by females young and old, subadult males resort to forced copulation. The ultimate goal of all these activities, of course, is reproduction. But perhaps orangutan mating patterns served other purposes as well. My observations of the two adolescent females and their admirers, of Priscilla and Throatpouch, as well as pregnant Cara and the multitude of males who hovered around her, demonstrated that sex was a powerful force drawing orangutans together.

Georgina had one of the most distant ranges of any wild orangutan I followed for a week or more, far from Camp Wilkie and Camp Dart. This, plus the fact that she usually rose at dawn and stayed up past dark, made her difficult to find and follow. After my initial ten-day follow, I did not see her often again while she remained an adolescent. But when I did, she was usually traveling with other adolescent females. One day I was watching Georgina, Fern, and another of her young companions, Maud, when the adult male "Ralph" appeared. A recent arrival in the area, Ralph was built like a tank. He was the kind of orangutan male who caused one to tremble involuntarily, he was so powerful and immense. As the three adolescent females foraged in the same tree as Ralph, Georgina ate on the same branch, very close to him. Then I noticed that Georgina's genitalia bulged in the telltale sign of pregnancy. There was something in the comfortable, easy way she moved next to Ralph that suggested she knew the gigantic male well. Perhaps he was the father of Georgina's unborn offspring.

Although soon to become a mother, Georgina would remain for me the quintessential adolescent female, in her sweetness, her curiosity, and her friendliness. First impressions tend to linger. When I think of an adolescent female orangutan, I think of Georgina as she was then.

Adolescent Georgina was highly gregarious, even to the point of showing interest in her human observers. Her activities and behavior were clearly

different from those of Beth, Cara, and Priscilla. Free from both the surveillance of her mother and the responsibility of offspring, Georgina rose early,
napped at midday, and stayed up nights. Her behavior had playful, experimental
qualities that I had not seen in the adult females. Some of this behavior might
have been due to her temperament, but much was related to her stage in life.
As an adolescent, she was finding her way, establishing her home range, and
generally setting up her life.

One of the important and distinctive features of orangutan adolescence is
"friendship." Orangutans may not form cliques and gangs like human teen-
agers, but they do go through a period of hanging out with their peers. The
four days Georgina spent with Fern showed that orangutans, especially females,
do not live in a social vacuum. Orangutans have not repudiated their pongid
heritage; they have refined it. Georgina's social knowledge of who was who
and how they were likely to behave probably was as complex as that of a
group-living chimpanzee or gorilla. Or possibly even a human.

Georgina was, up to that point, my longest follow. I had found her when I
was at an emotional low point, convinced that the critics were right, that
orangutans were elusive and unsociable, impossible to study. She gave me hope.
Her very presence showed me that even if orangutans were migratory, as John
MacKinnon had concluded, some remained in my study area. With her net-
works of contacts and encounters, she convinced me that a long-term study
of wild orangutans was possible — and necessary. Clearly, orangutans behaved
differently in different stages of their life cycle. There were again weeks when
I could not locate wild orangutans. There were days when orangutans whom
I had known for years died or disappeared. Orangutans grew up and moved
away. But the study continued. As she grew out of her adolescence, Georgina
still had surprises for me.

# 11

# COMINGS AND GOINGS

Across the river and into
the trees.

— *Ernest Hemingway*

Absence and death are the same. . . .

— *Walter S. Landor*

---

TWO DEGREES BELOW the equator, the length of day varies by less than twenty minutes over the course of the year. Dawn breaks promptly at six, the black sky whitening to blue, the gray morning mists lifting. But the forest awakens from slumber much earlier. The trees come alive with the voices of creatures large and small rehearsing and preparing for the day. This predawn chorus frequently begins with the red leaf-eating monkey male's staccato call summoning his troop to the travels of a new day. Gibbon males sing solo, endlessly repeating glorious soprano songs that reverberate for miles. The forest crackles and hums with energy as hungry birds, mammals, and insects awaken, eagerly anticipating their first meal of the day and announcing their presence to conspecifics. At dawn, the airways so buzz with songs and voices that even an orangutan's distant long call becomes faint in the tumult. The cicadas are particularly loud, as though seeking to outdo the voices of other creatures who are normally silent.

Dawn is the busiest and loudest part of the day, unless it rains. On gray, wet mornings, the usual sounds are stilled. The silence, even of the gibbons, makes the forest reek of expectancy.

By midmorning, the show is over and the forest lies still, baking in the heat of the tropical sun. Among primates, only the orangutan male and the gibbon female regularly break the silence. The gibbon female often issues a spectacular crescendo of sound, warning her mate of intruders and summoning him to vigorous territorial defense.

The gibbon female's soaring vocal performances contrast with the orang-utan female's silence. But then, their worlds are very different. Gibbons have only one mate, from whom they never stray. Not only do male and female gibbons both call, but both are approximately the same size. In some species of gibbon, males and females also look very much alike. This is typical of monogamous species. In contrast, the orangutan female is relatively silent, and relatively small.

In the nineteenth and early twentieth centuries, naturalists regularly shot orangutans, and then sometimes weighed them. According to their figures, a typical orangutan female weighs seventy-five pounds, while an adult male might be a hundred and fifty pounds or more. I suspect that TP weighed closer to two hundred. Moreover, this was solid muscle leveraged in a way that makes the average human being seem weak and puny by comparison.

The adult male orangutan is singular. He is as different from an adult female orangutan as a male peacock with his brilliant, fanned tail is from the drab peahen. Some aboriginal people in Borneo claim that the adult male orangutan is a different species of animal from the females and subadult males, who lack cheekpads. Indeed, some Dayaks have different names for the various age and sex classes of orangutans.

It isn't just his enormous size, his cheekpads, and his long call that make the adult male unique. According to local people, adult male orangutans frequently become so large in old age that they can no longer climb trees and live on the ground. During the first six months I was in Borneo, I never saw a wild orang-utan on the ground for more than a few minutes. But I had spent very little time observing lone adult males. I longed to follow one for as long as I had followed Georgina in May, but this goal proved elusive.

In June, however, I followed TP for several days. He was totally alone now. No more Priscilla or long-suffering Pug. TP was on his own. His behavior had changed, too. Earlier, when consorting with Priscilla, he had stayed in the canopy; now, increasingly, TP came close to the ground. Before he had not shown much interest in his human observers. Now, whenever he came close to me, or to Rod, he stared — not in the calm way that Georgina stared, but in an impatient way. TP appeared fidgety and irritated every time I came near him. He would look at me intently, almost as if sizing me up for combat. Rod reported the same experience when he followed TP by himself. Obviously, TP was anxious about us.

In laboratory experiments, orangutans demonstrate insight learning, or the "ah–ha" experience often represented in cartoons by a lightbulb over the character's head. The orangutans do not use trial and error; rather they seem to contemplate the problem posed by the experimenter and suddenly (insightfully) hit upon a solution. TP's acceptance of his human observers, in its abruptness, seemed to be an example of insight learning.

I remember clearly the moment TP made his decision. Rod and I had been following him together. We were sitting on a log near the trunk of a tree where TP was feeding. TP had been in the crown of the tree for some time. It was midday. Unlike the busy morning, sunny afternoons are usually lazy. This was the hottest time of day. There were no breezes, not a leaf stirred. Most creatures of the forest were resting. Only TP, trapped by the need to sustain his large adult male orangutan body, could not rest. He continued eating.

We could not see TP clearly in the dense foliage. But we were reassured that he was still above us by the constant rain of fruit remains and twigs, as well as glimpses of an orange arm occasionally bending a branch. I was obsessed with the thought that during those unavoidable moments when I couldn't actually see an orangutan, he or she was doing something that would totally revolutionize our understanding of great apes. I was afraid to miss anything. To relieve the pain in my neck, I frequently lay on the forest floor, looking upward with my binoculars balanced on my face.

TP gave no warning. Suddenly he came crashing down the trunk of the fruit tree. He stopped on the ground at the base of the tree and looked at us. He was just six or seven feet away.

His demeanor said, "You're not going to stop me."

He stared directly into my eyes. I thought to myself, "It's all over, TP is going to rip me to shreds. He's had enough — he doesn't want to be followed ever again."

I waited for TP to charge. Rod seemed frozen beside me. A microsecond passed. Maybe two. I had often joked that while male orangutans had enormous fangs, we humans carried iron fangs, our machetes. But neither Rod nor I had brought a machete that day. Not that it would have done us that much good. The local Melayu told us stories of people fighting with orangutans, particularly adult males. The orangutan invariably was the victor. In one case the orangutan caught the man and bit off half his hand, then turned him upside down and tore off part of his foot. It turned out that the man had been chasing the orangutan with dogs. A full accounting of incidents like these always led to the same conclusion: invariably, humans who were bitten or wounded had provoked the orangutan.

Perhaps inadvertently we had provoked TP by our constant following. Breathlessly I waited for TP's charge. TP looked angry. His hair stood on end. His eyes blazed.

TP did not charge. Rather, he turned his back to us in one resolute motion and sat down on a log just below the tree. I gasped; Rod was wide-eyed. Apparently, TP had decided that our presence was not going to disrupt his normal routine. He was asserting his right to be there on the forest floor, eating termites from the rotten wood of the fallen stump of some long-dead tree. What I interpreted as aggressive intent was simply bravado. Somewhere in the canopy, before TP had come down, the lightbulb had turned on. "I don't care, I'm going to do it," I could imagine TP thinking. "They've been hanging around for months. They're harmless." He had made his decision, come what may.

From that point on, TP came down to the ground regularly. I followed him for twenty-three days straight during August and September, by far my longest continuous follow yet. TP became my guide to the peculiarly solitary life of the adult male orangutan. During those twenty-three days, TP encountered other orangutans only three times. He met up with Carl and a very pregnant-looking Cara, who seemed remarkably serene, especially for Cara, gliding quietly past TP and going on her way. That same day, TP also crossed paths with "Dale," an adult female I had followed briefly from time to time. Another day TP ran into Beth and her infant, Bert; true to her timid nature, Beth hastened away.

TP seemed to take these adult female orangutans for granted. Unlike the subadult males, who sometimes pursued females with or without invitation, TP showed little overt response to their presence. His main concern seemed to be other adult males. Once, TP was traveling on the ground and stopped cold. Another large orangutan was approaching low in the trees. He wasn't clearly visible, but I could see branches shaking and hear him coming. The orangutan paused for about ten seconds, then continued his advance. Still on the ground, TP charged toward the approaching orangutan. The other orangutan slid to the ground and ran away. TP long-called, but his call was peculiar. He sounded as though he were gulping for breath. He bellowed at a very fast pace, but the bellows were high-pitched, and not particularly loud. I later termed this version of the long call the "fast call." The call was given only if another adult male was in the vicinity, or if the crash of dead wood or an abrupt sound startled the orangutan. The fast call seemed to be directed at other male orangutans, while the long call was more a public statement, directly to whoever was in the vicinity.

After the fast call, TP walked slowly along the ground, stopping and listening. A quarter of an hour later, he was still walking in this stop-and-start fashion, evidently searching for the other male. He put his hand on his lips and grumbled. Then he started walking again on all fours, a deep rumble percolating from the depths of his throat. Finally, some minutes later, he sat down on the forest floor and began pulling up the inner shoots of a wild ginger plant.

As TP became used to me, his forays on the ground stretched longer and longer. The distances he traveled on the ground increased as well. Soon he was spending more than six hours a day eating ground plants and termites on the forest floor. His ease on the ground was remarkable. When he moved over dry ground from one swamp to the next, TP could cover half a mile in a matter of minutes. He ran so fast and seemed to find clearings so easily that I wondered if he were following pig trails. To follow him, I sometimes had to bend over and run for all I was worth. If I tried to run upright, I got ensnared in tangles of vines. TP had no such problem. He moved on all fours, like a squat bulldozer, snapping vines right and left.

TP easily could have escaped me; what stopped him was curiosity. Whenever I got too far behind, he couldn't resist stopping, standing upright on two legs, and looking back to see whether I was still following. This gave me a chance to catch up.

Clearly, TP had become habituated, but so, I realized, had I. The process was reciprocal. Gradually, TP and I worked out an unspoken agreement. If he didn't want me to advance, he would angrily slap or shake the vegetation near him until I stopped moving. I learned that if I didn't make eye contact with TP, I could come within ten feet. So I would walk head down, my eyes to the forest floor. Otherwise TP would go wild, kiss-squeaking and bouncing, slapping and snapping branches. I grew proficient at pretending that I hadn't noticed that he had come to a stop and was standing ahead of me, staring at me. As soon as our eyes locked, I would act surprised at his presence and look elsewhere, as if I were distracted by an unusually fascinating piece of foliage or a crawling insect nearby. Satisfied, TP would then resume foraging or continue moving.

TP seemed thoroughly familiar with the study area and appeared to know exactly when a particular tree was fruiting, which berries were bursting, and where termites were hatching. Sometimes he walked purposefully up to a fruit tree and climbed straight up the trunk to the crown, where the fruit burdened the branches. During my long follow of TP, he spent a good deal of time eating a thick-skinned white fruit called *penjalin*. *Penjalin* is perfectly round and sometimes as large as a grapefruit. TP ripped open the thick skin of the fruit with his teeth and jaws in one or two easy chomps. The heart of the fruit consists of smooth, creamy, sweet white flesh adhering tenaciously to long oval seeds. Orangutans sometimes swallow the seeds.

I soon learned how tasty this fruit was. Rod and I started craving it, perhaps because of our monotonous diet of rice and sardines. But we also learned that the fruit had to be ripe; otherwise, it pursed one's mouth like an unripe lemon. TP had several *penjalin* trees that he visited every few days, in turn, to harvest the newly ripe fruits. Other orangutans, and possibly Malayan sun bears or pig-tailed macaques, also visited those trees. Frequently, unripe, baseball-sized, rock-hard gray fruits were scattered below, left behind as inedible by previous animal visitors. The fruits below the tree ripened in a few days, providing food for deer, pigs, and other creatures unable to climb into the treetops.

One day, Rod and I gathered all the unripe fruit under a particular *penjalin* tree while TP foraged in the canopy above. TP even dropped a few fruits our way after testing and rejecting them. We constructed a pyramid of fruits over a foot high on the forest floor. When TP left the tree that afternoon, he didn't even glance at the ordered pile. Rod and I looked forward to an hour of gorging on the luscious fruits the next time TP visited the tree, probably in a few days' time.

Right on schedule, three days later, TP walked along the forest floor in a direction we recognized, heading toward the *penjalin* tree with our mound of fruit beneath. Rod and I almost salivated in anticipation. Apparently, we were not the only ones planning a succulent feast. Without pausing for a second, and without veering from his initial course, TP walked directly to the pile of now ripe fruit, plopped down, and noisily devoured every single one. Not a morsel was left. I could only assume that TP had spied us busily piling up the unripe fruit and had another "ah-ha" experience. I could imagine him laughing to himself over human gullibility as he consumed the fruits of our labor.

One reason why I was able to follow TP for so long was that it was the dry season. This may also have been one of the reasons why TP was spending so much time on the ground.

When I arrived in Kalimantan, I had no experience in the tropics. "Dry season" and "rainy season" were mere abstractions. I didn't know what to anticipate in terms of weather. I was suspicious about the dry-ground forest in the study area. I had read that orangutans prefer swamps. Perhaps the dry ground would turn to swamp as the rainy season progressed. At every opportunity, I grilled local people about the climate, but they seemed baffled by my questions. They simply could not grasp the extent of my ignorance.

There was one trail in Tanjung Puting when we arrived, used primarily by the wild-rubber tappers who worked in the area. The trail led from the temporary Melayu settlement on the lake about a mile from Camp Leakey into the forest and continued for some distance. We named the trail *Jalan Toges* in honor of one of the tappers, Mr. Toges, whom we frequently encountered there. (*Jalan* means "trail," "road," or "street.") *Jalan Toges* became our primary trail as well, since it followed a ridge of dry ground and avoided the swamps. I called *Jalan Toges* the "spine" of my study area.

One afternoon, I met a tapper on his way home from the swamps with a heavy load of white latex that made him bend forward as he walked. He put down his load and we talked. Inevitably, the conversation turned to the weather. I knew this was the wet season; it rained every day and sometimes through the night. I wanted to know if the dry-ground forest was ever inundated. Despite my faltering Indonesian, the rubber tapper seemed to understand the questions. I asked him how high the water got in this forest during the height of the wet season.

The tapper answered solemnly, "Deep. The water here gets very deep." He motioned with his hand to his waist. Then he said, "Sometimes it gets even deeper."

I was horrified.

"Here in this forest?" I asked. "Deeper?"

"Yes," he answered, "right here in this forest."

I had a vision of standing on *Jalan Toges* up to my armpits in water. I didn't want to believe him, but the tapper must have known what he was talking about; he had lived here all his life. I remembered reading about the Amazon basin, where hundreds of square miles of forest turn into shallow lakes and swamps, providing breeding habitat for dozens of species of fish during the rainy season.

Rod and I watched and waited for months. We fully expected the dry-ground forest to be flooded. It didn't happen. But we noticed that the swamps became deeper and deeper as the wet season progressed. The dry-ground forest remained dry, but I was convinced that with a turn of the cosmic wheel the whole forest would be flooded and my orangutan study submerged.

Rod was not one to wait passively for something to happen. He and Mr. Hamzah engineered a raised bridge over a tiny creek in a low-lying, swampy area. Constructed of pole trees lashed together with vines, the bridge took a full week to build. But Rod, like me, was convinced the low-lying area soon would be covered with water.

The rubber tapper used this bridge to come in and out of the swamp. He had no choice, for it covered the trail. But the bridge was rickety. One day the tapper lost his footing, fell, and spilled a day's worth of rubber onto the forest floor. He complained to us, in a good-natured way, about the bridge. Little did he realize that his bruises and spilled rubber were the direct result of his answers weeks earlier to my questions about the wet season.

It was a classic example of cultural misunderstanding. The Melayu tapper had answered the questions that he thought I was asking to the best of his ability. It probably never occurred to him that I could be so ignorant as to ask whether the permanently dry forest could ever be flooded. Belatedly, I realized that he had been referring to the water levels in the swamp, which did reach shoulder height close to the rivers. Mr. Hamzah never said a word about our "bridge to nowhere." However, he laughed heartily when he heard that the *jelutung* tapper had fallen. I later wondered if Mr. Hamzah thought that our building the bridge was some elaborate practical joke on the wild-rubber tappers.

By July, the dry season was upon us. The pools of standing water in the swamp had disappeared, but the mud still sucked my legs into it, embracing me up to the knee. With every step I had to pull hard to retrieve my leg from the swamp. At times I almost missed the wet season, when I waded through pools of black water. By August, the dry season was in full force. Even the leeches disappeared. The swamps dried up, the mud dried up, the earth was hard. It was eerie, walking in the hollows of the dried-up swamp, looking up at the exposed stilt roots of the trees.

The sun shone every day. The morning light had a hard, harsh quality. In the forest, the leaf litter began to crackle under our feet. The normally soggy earth now betrayed even the passage of the minuscule mouse deer as the deer's tiny hooves tapped the dry leaves. The forest seemed full of ghosts, as unseen squirrels, birds, and other animals, which ordinarily moved invisibly, without a sound, were now announced by their crunching footsteps.

One night during our long follow of TP, it finally rained, long and hard, breaking the weeks of dryness. The next morning when we left for TP's nest, the forest did not seem wet from the night's rain, but the air was cold. I was beginning to understand the cycle of seasons in the forest. During the wet season, the cloud cover trapped the heat of the day. During the dry season, the skies were clear, and at night the heat evaporated. Lying in my hammock under a single blanket, I shivered.

I was chilled when I walked to TP's nest that morning. We sat under the nest, waiting for TP to emerge. We had not brought rain capes. No sooner had the sun come up than the rain began once again. Buckets of water poured out of the sky. It was the cold hard rain of the dry season. Rod and I huddled together, sitting awkwardly on a tiny stump. We simply could not keep each other warm. I was soaked to the bone. My shirt and jeans were as wet as though I had been immersed, fully clothed, in a bathtub for three hours. By the time the rain stopped at ten o'clock in the morning, I was so chilled that I could barely move. I hadn't dared to abandon my precarious perch on the stump, because it offered the best view of TP's nest. I already understood orangutans well enough to know that they were somewhat unpredictable in the rain. Had TP left his nest during the downpour, there would have been no auditory cues, which usually alerted us to an orangutan's movement and guided our eyes.

After this one harsh, cold downpour, it did not rain for the entire month of September. I followed TP for the rest of the twenty-three days in brilliant heat. I had intended to follow him for a full month, but it was not to be. On the twenty-fourth day, Rod relieved me by following TP alone while I took a rest. Rod inadvertently lost him. TP was on the ground, sucking termites from a nest he had dug up. The previous evening, I had asked Mr. Hamzah to clear a trail nearby. Mr. Hamzah was at least a quarter-mile away in the forest. It was ten-thirty. He must have just arrived. Rod heard Mr. Hamzah's machete strike wood. There was one sharp blow. Before the next blow came, TP was gone. He dropped his termite nest and fled. By the time Rod got up to follow him, he had disappeared. It seemed as if TP knew what caused the sound. I wondered how much experience TP had had with the local Melayu who frequented these forests, cutting and burning them for their dry-rice fields. It was the first time we had seen an orangutan spooked this way, by the sound of human activity.

During September, the dry season stretched so long and seemed so severe that I began to wonder if this were normal. I asked Mr. Hamzah. He and the occasional local Melayu who came to Camp Leakey confirmed that it was a dry season like no other. In fact, older people said they had not seen such a dry season since Dutch colonial times, well over thirty years ago.

Following TP one day, I came across the dying embers of a large fire. The fire had raged almost a mile inland from the river, following the dry-ground forest in and sweeping through a small *ladang* that had been made just a few years earlier. I was shocked by the fire. I had assumed that the tropical rain forest was impervious to fire. Although lightning sometimes set trees ablaze, the dampness of the foliage and soggy, rotting wood on the forest floor usually prevented fires from spreading. But this fire was only the beginning.

By late September the sky was gray, filled with the smoke of countless fires gone astray. I knew that the Melayu and Dayak farmers used the dry season to burn the trees that they had cut down to make their dry-rice fields. The ash provided fertilizer. The surrounding forest, wet with rain, contained these fires. But the expected rains were late. Later I learned it was not Melayu or Dayak fires sweeping the forests, but rather fires made by newcomers to Kalimantan from other islands in Indonesia. The newcomers did not know how to read the weather or how to control fires. Nor did they have the traditions of respect for the great forest that the aboriginal Dayak people did.

That year the red sun hung low in the gray, smoke-filled sky. Clouds of locusts scattered upward as I walked along the *ladang*. The whole scene, with the sun a large red orb, reminded me of a Japanese print that only used a palette of black, gray, white, and red. The river level fell so low that it took us twenty hours to get back to our camp from Kumai in our outboard-motor-powered longboat. The local Melayu all agreed: it was the longest dry season in living memory.

In October, I learned that Louis Leakey had left this earth. Rod was a devotee of "Voice of America," the BBC, and the U.S. Armed Forces Radio, which broadcast out of South Vietnam. When we weren't in the forest, he listened to the radio all day. I found the crackling of the radio difficult to understand, and usually didn't pay full attention as Rod fiddled with the dials.

This morning Rod was outside and I was half listening to a rundown of the day's headlines. Above the static, I heard the voice announce "prominent anthropologist dies in London." I knew instantly it was Louis. Louis Leakey and Margaret Mead were the most famous anthropologists in the world at that time. But the Kenyan Louis, who was of British descent, spent much time in London. The American Mead probably spent little time there. Still, I prayed it wasn't him. I flew outside to get Rod.

We rushed back inside. Holding our breath, we listened silently as the full stories unfolded. The last item was about Louis Leakey. He had just died. We heard the news as soon as anybody else did, even though we were in the forests of Borneo. Louis's death was a true loss, although not unexpected. He was not only a scientist, but a visionary. As we mourned him, I was grateful that he had believed in me, and that his belief in me had been vindicated. I had contacted the orangutans.

In November, the rains finally started. I found TP again, and followed him on his usually solitary rounds. There was no hint that changes were in store.

One afternoon in December TP long-called, staring at a point in the distance. I followed his eyes and saw a large adult male sitting absolutely still, low in the trees. TP moved toward him, calling again and hurling dead wood onto the forest floor.

When I got a good look at the other male through my binoculars, I was astonished. One of his canines cut through his lip to the outside of his face. The large, glistening two-inch fang curved over his lower lip. I called him "Tusk." His tusk might have been the result of a fight, but most likely he had been born that way.

TP moved boldly and confidently toward the intruder. Tusk began a long call, but didn't finish it. Now TP was low in the trees, while Tusk had climbed higher, stopping about eighty feet up in the canopy. Moving toward Tusk, TP puffed his cheeks in and out, expelling an angry chomping sound. Tusk sat motionless.

I was prepared to see another combat. TP was about fifty feet from the other male and charging toward him, when suddenly TP slid to the ground, turned, and ran away as fast as I had ever seen him move. I was stupefied. To this day, I do not know what made TP turn tail. Buddha-like, Tusk remained sitting very still in the trees.

I followed Tusk for several days, but he never got used to me. I nicknamed him "Houdini" for his ability to be sitting at the top of a tall tree, and then abruptly vanish. I suspect Tusk slipped noiselessly down to the ground behind large tree trunks. After one of Tusk's disappearing acts, days would pass before I found him again.

For the next month or two, Tusk and TP alternated calling at each other.

Then, in January, I began encountering adult males more and more frequently. Up to that point, I had seen only one or two in the study area at one time. Now there were as many as half a dozen. I noticed that most of the adult males had physical anomalies. In addition to the size and shape of their cheekpads, the deformities made each male distinctive. The middle and index fingers of TP's left hand were stiff. Fingers, the adult male Lolita had courted, was missing half his right index finger, and one of his toes was turned backward. A newcomer, "Knobs," was missing an eye. Although I could not know for certain, a reasonable hypothesis was that all had been injured in fights with other males.

In mid-January I had to make a decision. Mr. Hamzah, our first assistant, had returned to Kumai with his new wife. Our new assistant, Mr. Ahmad, had spotted Tusk while cutting a trail. The same day, Rod had located TP, while I had been following Fern. Since Mr. Ahmad had not yet been trained to take notes, I had to decide which two of the three orangutans we would follow. I wanted to continue following Fern, to fill out my picture of adolescent females. I had to choose between TP and Tusk for Rod's follow.

Rod and I discussed the problem over cups of tea, sitting next to the fire in our kitchen hut at Camp Wilkie. We had known TP for nearly a year. During that year, he had stayed in one area of the forest. We had become familiar with his haunts. We knew the trees he periodically visited. We recognized his breathy, throaty call. His low-slung cheekpads and two stiff fingers were engraved on our brains. After a year, we felt we could safely say that TP was a permanent resident of the study area.

Tusk, on the other hand, was a newcomer. His strident long call seemed newly minted. He was young and vigorous. Recently arrived, he might not stay. We decided that we could learn more about orangutan behavior if Rod followed Tusk.

The next morning Rod and I awoke in heavy blackness, an hour or so before dawn. After we dressed, I started the fire while Rod checked his photographic equipment. It seemed like a routine morning until, in the darkness, a strange howling began. I cannot describe it. The howls stopped and started, sometimes turning into sequences of snarls and high-pitched shrieks. The unearthly cries swirled through the darkness into our open-walled hut and enveloped us.

The sounds were so loud and overwhelming that at first Rod and I were immobilized. When we recovered our wits, we rationally discussed what it might be. There are no tigers in Borneo. Could it be a clouded leopard, or a bear? an orangutan? The howls continued for almost half an hour, as Rod and

I resolutely and calmly prepared for the day ahead. I had less to fear: Fern's nest lay south, away from the sound. Both Tusk's and TP's nests, however, were relatively close by, within a quarter mile of camp. Rod would be going directly into the swirling wall of sound.

We did not hurry. By the time we were ready to leave, the howling had died away. When we later described the sound to the local Melayu, their eyes widened. They knew exactly what we had heard. Each and every local person we ever asked said exactly the same thing. It was the sound of Satan.

Tusk was not in his nest that morning. Rod could not find him or TP. We wondered if the "sound of Satan" might have been the sounds of two adult male orangutans fighting, amplified by the predawn darkness. That was the best explanation. At one point that day I heard an adult male orangutan calling from the north. It was too far away to be sure, but to me it sounded like Tusk.

As the months passed, we occasionally ran into Tusk and followed him. We saw the large, magnificent male Ralph, who had associated with Georgina. We also met Handless Harry, Cara's orange titan, again. But traveling on the ground, Harry left the study area, crossing the narrow Raden River by means of natural log bridges. Soon Ralph moved toward the edge of the study area and disappeared into the swamps. Not long afterward, Tusk followed him. Another adult male, whom I had not seen before, appeared and then disappeared along the same route. The invasion of males that had begun in January ended as suddenly and mysteriously as it had begun. The male orangutans in the Tanjung Puting area seemed to confirm John MacKinnon's migration theory, but the females did not. I saw no pattern of coming and going among the females; rather, they stayed put.

By the beginning of the new dry season, in mid-June, the forest seemed strangely quiet. As I lay in my hammock at Camp Wilkie, I heard only the mechanical sounds of insects. One, in particular, sounded like a small bell jingling. There were other sounds borne on the night air that I would learn to recognize only later, such as the high-pitched screech of the flying fox. But I heard no long calls.

We had last seen TP in mid-January. Since then, Rod and I had been busy following wild orangutans, both adult males and females. But as the weeks and months passed, we began to wonder why we weren't encountering TP, and stranger still, why we no longer heard his distinctive long call. We began looking for him. We searched all his old haunts. We went everywhere he had ever taken us. He was nowhere to be found. There was no familiar long call. There was no trace of his once ubiquitous presence.

Perhaps he had migrated out of the study area, as other males had done. But they were merely passing through; he had been in residence for at least a year. Why would he suddenly leave? Where would he go? Perhaps Tusk had frightened him off. I wondered if the satanic howls we had heard that morning were related to his disappearance. I feared the worst.

One night I had an exceptionally vivid dream. In the dream I was in the forest, and I came across an old nest in a tall tree. I climbed an adjacent tree up into the canopy and peered into the nest. The nest held a skeleton, lying on its back. The bones were bleached white. It was an orangutan. My heart stopped. The index and middle fingers of the ghostly hand were stiff. It was TP's skeleton.

The dream ended when I woke up in a cold sweat. The dream certified my fears: TP was dead. But I still couldn't believe it; he had looked so healthy the last time we saw him. TP became an obsession. Rod and I talked endlessly about what might have happened to him.

In June, when all the other males were leaving for parts unknown, a new male appeared. This magnificent young adult was different from the others, especially from TP. While TP had the nervous jumpiness of a street fighter, the new male always seemed relaxed and in repose. Like a born aristocrat, he had the aura of one who never doubted his rightful place at the top of the heap.

The new male made his entrance almost casually. I was following Maud, the adolescent female who was an occasional companion of the sociable Georgina. Maud was traveling with her mother, "Martha," and a younger sibling. I heard an orangutan approach behind us. It was an adult male. He pushed over a tall snag and watched it crash to the ground. Then he dropped a branch. The females vanished when he was about a hundred feet from them. The male proceeded calmly on his way.

From our first encounter, I was impressed by the new male's serene self-confidence. When he first saw me, he did not kiss-squeak or vocalize. Rather, he looked down at me for a few minutes and then tried pushing down a large dead branch that was caught in some vines. He tugged on the dead branch several times but was unable to free it. TP would have been hopping mad. The new male merely moved away from the branch as if he didn't give a hoot. He began to eat, but every once in a while he turned and looked down at me, as though surprised that this pale apparition was still there.

My second encounter with the newcomer, two days later, was much the same as the first. He casually broke and dropped several branches. Not seeing any reaction, he resumed eating. Then he looked at me, opened his mouth, and held it open for one minute, exposing his fangs. He displayed this way two more times, but again getting no reaction from me, he simply resumed eating. I decided to name him "Nick," after an equally unflappable fellow graduate student at UCLA.

Nick seemed considerably younger than TP and the other males who had passed through the study area. Nick's face was unlined and unscarred. His cheekpads were round, relatively flat, and regularly shaped. In contrast, TP's cheekpads were low, almost drooping. Nick's back was partially bare, but the bald spot did not cover most of his back. TP's back was almost totally nude, except for the narrow band of thick fringe that lined either side. It was as if someone had run a lawnmower down his back. Had they been men, TP would have been bald, but Nick still could have camouflaged his bald spot by combing his hair across it. In sharp contrast to the older male, his throatpouch was not prominent. I first saw Nick six months to the day after we had last seen Throatpouch.

Nick moved into the study area as though he already owned it. He virtually never vocalized except for the long call. He long-called regularly, sometimes several times a day. His long call was impressive. Reflecting Nick's character, it was calm, assertive, leisurely, powerful, and well-paced, very different from the breathless call of the irascible TP.

When Nick first arrived, very little fruit was available in the forest. Nick spent much of his time eating bark and young leaves. He seemed inordinately fond of *sindur* bark. He would bite the tree trunk sideways with his front teeth. Then he would clamp down like a vise with his teeth and rip yard-long strips of bark off the tree. I enjoyed following Nick because he was calm, nested early, and didn't wander far during the course of a day.

Over the next several months, Nick met most of the females whom I already knew. Nick's interactions with the females were nonchalant. He usually long-called before he approached. Although I had seen females race away from subadult males in great alarm, most seemed unruffled by Nick's appearance. Although the females did not enter a tree where he was feeding, neither did they scramble away when he entered theirs. Rather, they exited gracefully, avoiding a close encounter. They respected him, but they were not terrified by him. Nick did not impose himself. When the females moved away, he did not follow.

By the end of the year, Nick appeared to have replaced TP in the study area. Nick seemed to be everywhere. We almost couldn't avoid him. We encountered him in the forest, even when we weren't looking for wild orangutans. We heard his long call. When we were following other orangutans, he frequently appeared. Once I found Nick sitting on the ground eating termites. He saw me approach, looked up briefly, and went back to the termites. He did not move off the ground for another half hour. He was calmer and more self-assured than his predecessor.

If the study area forest near Camp Leakey and Camp Wilkie was the kingdom, then clearly Nick was now king of the castle. No other adult male was so omnipresent. But I still was consumed with curiosity. Was TP actually dead? Or would he come back to claim his throne?

# 12
# ALL IN THE FAMILY

One does not meet oneself until one catches
the reflection from an eye other than human.

— *Loren Eiseley*

Men are what their mothers made them.

— *Ralph Waldo Emerson*

---

WHEN WE LEFT FOR INDONESIA, Rod and I had no immediate plans to start a family. Yet within months of our arrival in Borneo, our hut was filled to the brim with "children," furry orange children to be sure, orangutans, but "children" nonetheless in that all considered me their mother. I was a cross-species mother.

Sugito was my first child, my initiation into orangutan motherhood. My goal was to give him as normal an orangutan upbringing as possible to prepare him for the brutally competitive life of an adult male orangutan in the wild. I didn't want to housebreak, train, and coddle him, as people do with pets. Sugito wasn't destined to be my lifelong companion, a tropical version of woman's best friend. He was born free. I wanted him to return to the forest and to the life of a wild orangutan. But like humans, orangutans require a long period of nurturing. And like an infant, Sugito took over my daily life.

Wherever I went, Sugito went. When he first arrived, I judged him to be six months old. But I was comparing him to captive orangutans, who are much larger than wild orangutans the same age. Sugito probably was one or two years old. Even so he was tiny, weighing at most four or five pounds. His minuscule size enabled him to transform himself into a mobile orange-haired lump on my body.

At times, I would almost forget he was there as I went about my daily routines. Other times, however, an uncontrollable rage would well up within me. I would pull Sugito off my body and run away. He would screech piercingly and run after me. The word "run" does not accurately describe Sugito's locomotion. He moved somewhat like a crab, in halting, awkward sideways steps, and sometimes tumbled head over heels, arms thrashing, in his fury to get to me. Invariably, I would relent after only ten or twenty seconds, stop, let him catch up with me, and gather him in my arms.

If I held him away from me he howled piteously. When I persisted and did not let him back on my body, he threw a temper tantrum. Climbing away from me, he would fall, seemingly purposefully, and repeatedly bang his head against our bark floor, screaming all the while. Since I did not yet have children of my own, I had never observed a full-blown human toddler's tantrums. At the time, I thought Sugito's behavior verged on autistic. Later I realized that this display of hysterics was a highly evolved and effective way for an orangutan infant to manipulate his mother. Carl behaved much the same when Cara began to wean him. But Carl was well beyond infancy, and Cara was a more experienced orangutan mother than I was. Great gushes of guilt would flood over me at the sight and sound of Sugito's heart-wrenching displays.

Day by day, Sugito insinuated himself into my life. Gradually I became accustomed to the clinging; I grew used to the warm, sometimes moist, bundle on my body. Sugito became my child and I no longer resented my loss of freedom. The sudden impulses to dash away from him subsided, and I grew to treasure the little orange creature whose eyes fastened on mine first thing in the morning and who attended my every move. Sugito gave me the highest compliment any man or woman can receive. To him I was, by far, the most important individual in the universe.

I often took Sugito to a grove of small trees with short trunks and sprawling horizontal limbs, close to our hut. I would climb into the lower branches and pretend to go to sleep. In the hazy, lazy warm afternoons, lulled by the buzz of flies and mosquitoes, I sometimes did fall asleep. When I awoke with a start, Sugito would still be clinging to me. He might clutch at a twig or swat at a butterfly, but he always kept one hand or foot firmly clutching my body. After a week or two, he began letting go. If I remained frozen, he would move a few hesitant steps away. But if I shifted position even slightly, he raced back to me. Gradually I was able to leave the tree and sit at the base of the trunk. By the end of his first month at Camp Leakey, I could sit on a bench beneath the cluster of jackfruit trees in front of our hut, while Sugito played overhead. But if I stood up or even slid along the bench, Sugito would hurtle down from the trees. Nonetheless, he seemed to be gaining confidence. The arrival of other wildborn ex-captive orangutans added new dimensions to his rehabilitation.

The second wildborn ex-captive orangutan given to us for release was a large male juvenile who had long been kept in an outdoor cage. The owner felt the orangutan was too dangerous to be handled, so he was never allowed out of his cage. We named this somewhat melancholy male "Sinaga."

The names "Sugito" and "Sinaga" caused no end of merriment among the local Forestry Department officials. In Indonesia, animals simply were not named. The concept of dogs and cats with names was hilarious to locals. When we told them that in North America people named their goldfish and canaries, they howled with laughter. They didn't know how to react when I told them that some North Americans cried over the deaths of their pet goldfish. (Indeed, the death of her goldfish was a major trauma in Dian Fossey's childhood.)

Orangutans, however, were human enough that Indonesian owners some-times gave them names, but the names were not those commonly given to humans. When I named Sugito and Sinaga after respected government offi-cials, some people didn't know what to think. I explained that I was honoring Mr. Soegito and Mr. Sinaga. But local people were not convinced. I realized that some of them assumed I had a hidden motive, though I never completely understood what they thought my motive was.

When Sinaga (the orangutan) first arrived, he was probably eight or nine years old, roughly the same age as the wild orangutan Carl. In the wild, Sinaga would now be beginning to travel on his own. Sinaga seemed to verify what I suspected: that wildborn ex-captives, if old enough, would eagerly return to life in the forest with little or no prompting. The moment we freed him, Sinaga climbed into the jackfruit trees in front of our hut.

Sugito was fascinated by the new arrival. Clinging to my neck, he stared intently at the older male. As soon as I clasped the trunk of one of the trees, my signal for Sugito to climb, he scampered along my arm after Sinaga. Sinaga climbed higher. When Sugito caught up with Sinaga, he reached up and gin-gerly touched one finger to Sinaga's stomach. Sinaga looked at the infant, then reached down and gently hooked his fingers around Sugito's chin. He scruti-nized Sugito's face for several seconds, then, apparently losing interest, he dropped his hand and looked away. Although Sugito continued to show great interest in Sinaga, and continued to follow him through the trees, Sinaga ignored him. Within a half hour of his release, Sinaga disappeared into the great forest near Camp Leakey.

"We'll never see him again," I predicted, naively. Sinaga was back the next day, raiding our hut for food. His raids continued for about a month. He would lurk in the trees until Rod and I went to the river to bathe, then he would strike. We would return to find our hut in shambles. But Sinaga spent most of his time in the forest. The only time he actually came into camp to visit, as opposed to raid and run, was when I was alone. Sinaga, like Sugito, reacted totally differently to me than to Rod. Sinaga cowered and squeaked when Rod strode into view. Sinaga also seemed to be intimidated by Mr. Hamzah and Mr. Yusuran, but not as much as by Rod. The two Indonesian men had a gentle, self-effacing manner. By comparison, Rod swaggered. After he left high school, Rod had made friends with several members of "outlaw" motorcycle clubs. Something in Rod's walk and the way he held himself brought these old chums to mind; something indicated that Rod was not to be taken lightly. Orangutans take their own adult males very seriously. Rod fit right in. He only lacked cheekpads.

Thus far, following Sinaga was the most independence Sugito had shown. I was relieved. At least there was a possibility that I might not be burdened with my little orange appendage forever. Akmad's arrival, the day after Sinaga's, had an equally electric effect on Sugito. I might have been his "mother," but Sugito clearly was drawn to his own species.

Akmad was five or six years old when she came to Camp Leakey. After she was brought to our hut, she stood still for a moment, her liquid brown eyes serene beneath her exceptionally thick lashes. Then she climbed into the rafters, her face attentive and alert as she surveyed the hut from her vantage point just below the roof. Sugito was fascinated. He immediately left me and climbed into the rafters after her. Akmad did not even briefly acknowledge Sugito's presence. But Sugito kept touching her and pulling at her hair, apparently trying to get Akmad's attention. Akmad, in her benign way, ignored him.

Akmad spent her first afternoon in Camp Leakey exploring the rafters of our hut. Sugito clumsily followed her, incessantly touching and pulling at her hair. The contrast couldn't have been greater between the delicate, composed Akmad and the roughshod, rowdy Sugito. Self-assured and aloof, Akmad seemed utterly disdainful of Sugito. Scrambling after her, Sugito looked ludicrous. She moved nimbly through the hut, a delicate, adroit, silent shadow. A well-mannered guest, Akmad did not touch anything except food. She was a lady. Sugito, however, grabbed, clutched, pulled, and tore apart everything within reach. Although some of the difference probably was due to their ages and sex, and some to their individual personalities, I suspect their behavior also reflected their different histories. Akmad, recently captured, had lived most of her life in the wild; the younger Sugito had spent proportionately more of his life with humans and therefore was more oriented toward objects.

At dusk I lured Akmad outside with a bowl of rice. I wanted her to nest in a nearby jackfruit tree. She climbed into the lower branches and sat silently looking at me for a minute or two, then she climbed to the top of the tree and began to build a nest. Sugito could hardly restrain himself. He left me, followed her to the top of the tree, and sat on a high branch, watching Akmad crack branches and make her nest.

It was now quite dark. All movement in the nest had ceased. To my surprise, Sugito did not come down. I went inside, leaving Sugito with Akmad. But about fifteen minutes later, when I stepped outside, I heard terrible screeching. It was Sugito, dangling from the lowest branch of the jackfruit tree. I plucked him from the branch and carried him inside. This was by far the most independence he had shown. The new, larger orangutans totally intrigued him. Sugito recognized his own kind; he knew that he was an orangutan, even though his adopted mother was a human.

The next morning Akmad descended silently from the jackfruit tree to eat from a bowl of rice I had placed at the base of the trunk. After she finished, I held out my hand. Without hesitation, she took it. She held my hand gently as the two of us sat next to each other at the base of the tree. As usual, Sugito was glued to my side. I soon became uncomfortable sitting on the uneven, rough ground, and slowly pulled back my hand so that I could get up. Akmad came with the hand and moved onto my body. Even at age six, Akmad still needed a mother. Now I was carrying two orangutans.

Sugito looked very unhappy with this new development. He put his hand on Akmad's foot, the appendage closest to him, and vigorously pushed it away. His kiss-squeaks and chomping vocalizations made him sound as if he had acute indigestion. Despite my efforts to put Akmad back up in the trees, she continued to cling, wrapping herself around my neck like a furry collar. It was virtually impossible to pull her off my body when she was in this position. But Akmad was always gentle; she never clutched or clawed or screamed like Sugito.

Akmad didn't always cling to me, but she asserted her rights as my "daughter." Sometimes as I sat on my bench at the rough wooden table under the jackfruit trees, Akmad would descend from the branches. Her lower jaw jutting out, she would take my arm and carefully put it around her shoulders and chest, and lean back on my arm. Sugito, in the crook of my other arm, would peer anxiously out at her from his side of my body. Akmad would casually reach over, put her hand on Sugito's face, and push it back. It reminded me of James Cagney pushing a grapefruit half into the face of his movie girlfriend.

Once, as I was sitting at the table, Sugito briefly left me to get some rice. After he stuffed his mouth as full as he could, he rushed back to me. Akmad casually leaned over and bit his hand. Then she pushed his hand away, preventing him from returning to my body for a few seconds. Sugito went berserk.

This sibling rivalry began on the first day of Akmad's arrival. In human families, children have stressful reactions when a new baby enters the household. But at least the new baby isn't bigger and stronger and doesn't beat them up or bite them. Poor Sugito. Not only did he have to share me with another orangutan, but one who, in all fairness, was cuter, sweeter, and fluffier than he was. On top of that, she could push him around. Sugito had to fight back. He couldn't intimidate Akmad, but he could manipulate me, psychologically. When a new sibling appears, human babies frequently regress, exhibiting behaviors typical of a younger age. The day after Akmad arrived, Sugito began acting in a way I had never seen before. He would go limp like a rag doll, compelling me to scoop him up in my arms and clutch him to my bosom so that he would not slide out of my arms onto the ground. If I released my grip, even slightly, he would fall out of my arms. Of course, I responded by hugging him even more tightly, not thinking about the fact that I was reinforcing his behavior.

Yet Sugito appeared to be torn between jealousy of Akmad and fascination. The second day after her arrival, he seemed unusually stressed. He frequently made chomping vocalizations, he fell limp, and he rubbed my fingers on his genitalia repeatedly (one of his responses to stress). But Sugito couldn't decide whether to leave me and follow Akmad into the trees or to stay with me and ignore Akmad. This indecision resulted in frantic dashes up the tree after Akmad and equally frantic returns to me ten seconds later.

Several times Sugito nosed up to Akmad, as if begging for food. Then Sugito positioned himself below her as she sat eating in the jackfruit tree and started poking her genitalia with his finger. Akmad darted a withering look in his direction that, had she been human, would have told him that she thought him totally worthless. But Sugito persisted. Although still in his infancy, Sugito seemed to want it all: food, sex, and attention.

Sugito's fascination with his "big sister" soon won out over his jealousy. Now that he had an orangutan playmate and role model, he no longer glued himself to my body night and day. He and Akmad would spend hours play-fighting. Akmad was ideal, because although she was twice as large as Sugito, she was much gentler. The rougher Sugito could hold his own with her and not get hurt. I had never seen Sugito so active. He followed Akmad everywhere in our hut and investigated everything she touched. Akmad was remarkably tolerant of Sugito — most of the time.

One morning Akmad snuck into our hut. I lured her out with a few uncooked eggs. She ate the eggs and dropped the shells. Akmad always dropped food remains and fruit skins very gently and slowly. She would put her hand behind her back as if to hide what she was doing, as though she didn't want to be caught littering. When Akmad dropped the eggshells, Sugito scurried to the spot, picked up a large one, and began sniffing it and putting it to his lips. Akmad immediately moved to Sugito and with her thumb and forefinger demonstrating an exquisite precision grip, pinched Sugito's hand, hard. She showed no mercy. Sugito squealed and dropped the eggshell. Akmad did not retrieve it but simply moved away. When it came to what interested her — food — Akmad was subordinate to no one.

Several days after Akmad's arrival, I was alone in my hut when Sinaga appeared. I tossed Sinaga a banana from the doorsill. Akmad, who was in the hut behind me, raced out, ran toward Sinaga, and snatched the banana from under his nose. The second time, I put the banana in Sinaga's hand. I gave him a second and then a third banana. Sinaga turned away slightly to eat his bananas. This is typical of orangutans. Eating seems to be a private matter for them. Turning away also hid the food; he had no intention of sharing. Akmad was watching closely. Finally, she couldn't stand it anymore. She leaped onto Sinaga's back and started wrestling him for the banana. Since Sinaga was at least twice Akmad's size, she was unable to pry the banana from his tightly closed hand. What surprised me was that Sinaga did not bite Akmad, or even appear to be angry. He simply pushed her away and scampered a few feet off to finish his banana.

I got my notebook, came outside, and sat down at the table under the jackfruit trees. Sinaga soon ambled over and climbed onto the table. For the first time since I had known him, Sinaga no longer seemed sad. I sat there with Sugito on my side, Akmad sitting on the bench next to me, and Sinaga dozily sprawled in front of me. Sinaga soon fell asleep. I didn't dare move; it all seemed so perfect. I realized that Sinaga felt calm because all the men were gone. They had left Camp Leakey in the early morning to go upriver. Sinaga might have watched them leave from his night nest, or perhaps the sound of the boat motor had told him. For the first time, Sinaga was totally relaxed.

As I sat under the jackfruit trees, I felt to the marrow of my bones and to the depths of my soul that the apes surrounding me were refugees from paradise, a paradise that we humans left behind to seek our destinies on the savannas and open lands of the earth. These apes were survivors of Eden. What else could explain their benevolence, their ease with each other, and even their lack of overt need for each other? The sky was sparkling. A warm breeze was blowing from the Java Sea only twenty miles away. I slowly reached for my pen and notebook. Akmad quietly left and made a nest in the jackfruit boughs above me. Sugito followed and tried persistently to get into her nest, but she gently pushed him away. Gently but emphatically. A tiny tailor bird, so minuscule that one could hide in a closed fist, warbled a two-note song close by. I started writing and lost track of time.

Suddenly I noticed that Sinaga was standing on all fours watching me intently as I moved my pen across the page. Instinctively, I reached out to touch him, but he moved back, avoiding my touch. He only came forward again to watch me when I dropped my hand.

I sat there looking at him. I hadn't eaten yet, so I reached over and pulled out an inner frond from a ground plant called *rasau* and started eating. The fronds reminded me of celery; I liked their crisp texture and mild taste. The *rasau* looked like a pineapple plant without the pineapple fruit. Sinaga watched me, and then he leaned over to another *rasau* plant near him and pulled out a stiff leaf and ate the white inner part of the frond, which was hidden in the bosom of the palm. I don't know whether Sinaga regularly ate *rasau,* but it seemed to be a case of social facilitation, the process where if one individual does something, like drink water, it encourages others to do the same. Then Sinaga continued to stand absolutely still next to me.

Akmad soon came down from her nest. She reached over to some bananas that were near me. The sudden sound of branches cracking caused Akmad to start. She reached for Sinaga's arm and held on to it, as if to reassure herself that everything was all right. Only when Sugito came into full view did she let go of Sinaga. Her gesture of seeking reassurance seemed so humanlike. Then Sinaga shifted his weight and put his mouth next to hers as though he were begging for food. This didn't make sense to me, because the bananas were right next to Akmad and Sinaga easily could have gotten one for himself. But he seemed much more interested in the mush in Akmad's mouth. Then, very gently, Sinaga carefully put one finger in Akmad's vagina. He pulled out his finger and put it to his nose and sniffed. Akmad ignored him. Then he put his mouth next to her face again. Only when he reached over and tried to take the rest of the banana dangling from her hand did she move her hand away. A struggle erupted, with the two of them biting each other's hands. Akmad kept the banana.

Sinaga then moved into our hut. I was alone. I had visions of the large Sinaga running amok inside the hut, tearing everything apart in his search for easy pickings. I took an ax handle with no head and banged it loudly on the floor to make as intimidating a sound as I could. I fully expected Sinaga to yawn, baring his huge canines as a threat. Instead, he climbed up and hung from the rafters of the hut. I banged, yelled, and even prodded him. But he wouldn't leave the hut. As I stood my ground below Sinaga, glaring, Akmad took advantage of this wonderful opportunity to explore the hut. And perhaps to show off for Sinaga! She roamed the rafters and rattled the pots and pans, after carefully opening the lids and checking for contents. Then she discovered Mr. Hamzah's bedroll, a reed mat rolled around a pillow. (He and Mr. Yusuran still slept in the hut with us.) Akmad tossed the bedroll over her head, then opened it, rolled it out, and fell asleep, stretched out on her back for comfort.

Sinaga just sat there in the rafters, as if he had all the time in the world. He flicked his leg back and forth. He seemed perfectly comfortable with me. I suspected that he wanted to investigate the contents of the hut, just as Akmad had done, but he didn't want to annoy me any more than he had to. He easily could have ransacked the hut; I couldn't have stopped him. But he didn't. The two of us just sat there — me, tense and wound up, and Sinaga, loose, relaxed, yawning occasionally in an easy manner. Clearly he enjoyed sitting there. This stalemate continued for three hours.

Finally, in the late afternoon, Rod and the assistants appeared. They must have paddled in, because there was no sound of a motorboat. To my surprise, Sinaga did not flee. Rather he emitted a few feeble squeals, moved up and out of the hut, and sat on the main roof pole, which jutted out horizontally. He just sat there, looking like the carved wooden figurehead of a ship. Only when Rod and Mr. Hamzah crawled up onto the thatch roof to rout him did Sinaga flee into the jackfruit tree whose boughs brushed the roof.

Clearly, orangutans responded differently to men and women. If two women, rather than two men, had climbed onto the roof, I'm sure Sinaga would not have moved. Intellectually, I wasn't surprised that orangutans saw males and females differently, for in their own species, the difference is enormous. But the reality of it shocked me. In human terms, orangutans were decidedly sexist. It went against everything I wanted to believe about male-female relationships. I had come of age during the 1960s, the decade when women in North America began saying for the first time that they were no different from men. One of the last books I read before I went into the field was Germaine Greer's *The Female Eunuch*. The fact that orangutans so clearly differentiated between men and women was almost alarming. Louis Leakey had said that male great apes would react differently to males and females, and that a woman observer would not excite the aggressive tendencies of a male ape. Indeed, Louis thought that male great apes might react protectively toward human females. I wasn't so certain about protection, but if Sinaga were any indication, male orangutans certainly were more comfortable with me than with Rod or the Indonesian men.

In January, we brought to Camp Leakey a tiny, one-and-a-half-year-old infant even smaller than Sugito. She had been owned by an air force officer in Pangkalan Bun who was extremely protective of her. It took hours of nonstop talking to convince him to release her into our care. The officer and his family were worried that we would take the infant and deposit her in the forest, where she might starve or be eaten, or that we would put her in a cage and deprive her of the cuddling she clearly needed. I countered each of his arguments patiently and at length. Finally, after nearly five hours, he handed her over, saying, "I am convinced that this is the right thing to do." On the way back to Camp Leakey, I decided to name the new infant female "Sobiarso" after a police official in Palangka Raya.

Sobiarso became my second infant. Akmad and Sinaga were no longer infants; both were well on the road to independence. Sinaga rarely visited Camp Leakey, and Akmad often disappeared for days at a time. But the new orangutan was a baby. As I did Sugito, I carried Sobiarso everywhere. Instead of one furry orange infant, two now shared the bed with Rod and me. Like siblings everywhere, Sugito and Sobiarso squabbled.

Tiny Sobiarso was adorable. With her smooth pinkish face and luminous brown eyes surrounded by soft, fluffy, bright orange, almost yellow, hair, she was like an orangutan doll created by toy manufacturers to elicit the "cute response." Psychologists have discovered that humans frequently have an involuntary protective response toward small, rounded, big-eyed creatures. We want to cuddle and love them. The bigger the eyes and head, the more closely the animal resembles the proportions of a human infant and the stronger our response. Mickey Mouse, for instance, when first drawn looked more like a rodent than he does now. Over the years his eyes have become larger, his forehead proportionately bigger, and his snout smaller, as cartoonists took advantage of the cute response. Sobiarso elicited the cute response par excellence. Perhaps this was the real reason the air force officer and his family worried so much about her welfare.

Sobiarso had a sweet-natured temperament to go with her sweet face. Yet from the first, she was much more independent than Sugito. Sobiarso liked to cling, but after a while, if I was just sitting still, she would start exploring, climbing, and wandering. Her wide, lustrous eyes shone with curiosity and a sense of wonder at all she was discovering. Unlike Sugito when he first arrived, Sobiarso would climb into the trees and play contentedly, secure in her knowledge that when it was time to leave, I would call. Sobiarso was guileless, feisty, and self-confident.

Sobiarso also transferred readily from one person to another. Indeed, she frequently initiated the transfer, especially if the other person had food in his or her hand. She moved away from me instantly whenever she spotted food. She was so light that I scarcely noticed when she slipped off my neck or my side, particularly if I was busy or engaged in thought. Often I would look up, glance over to another part of the hut, and there she would be, playing with some cloth or vegetation on the floor, totally engrossed.

Gentle Akmad's reaction to tiny Sobiarso was quite different from her easy tolerance of Sugito and Sinaga. Akmad got her first look at Sobiarso the morning after the new infant arrived. Akmad had left her nest and entered the jackfruit trees. She gazed down at us. Sobiarso looked up and then climbed toward the top of the tree, apparently curious about the older female. Akmad watched her ascend.

For at least five minutes, Akmad sat motionless, never once taking her gaze from the younger female, as if she were evaluating Sobiarso. Then, very deliberately, Akmad moved over to Sobiarso and started biting her hands. Next, she flipped tiny Sobiarso over and methodically bit one foot, then the other. For the coup de grace, Akmad fiercely bit Sobiarso's rear end in the vicinity of her genitals. At this, Sobiarso's hesitant squeaks turned into loud squeals.

Poor Sobiarso was upside down, hanging on to the branch with only her feet while Akmad inflicted this punishment on her. The way Sobiarso was shrieking, I expected blood to start dripping down from the tree.

I stood helpless below. The tree had no low branches, so I couldn't climb up to rescue Sobiarso. I called Akmad's name as loudly as I could, over and over until I became hoarse. After about two minutes Akmad abruptly released Sobiarso, who flew down the trunk of the tree into my arms, still whimpering. I was shocked: I never expected gentle Akmad to behave this way toward an infant.

I inspected Sobiarso for damage. Much to my surprise, there was none. The only evidence of Akmad's seemingly furious bites were clumps of Sobiarso's hair plastered together by Akmad's abundant saliva. I concluded that Akmad's uncharacteristic aggression was due to the fact that Sobiarso, unlike Sugito and Sinaga, was a female. That same day Akmad repeatedly inspected Sobiarso's genitalia, pulling the reluctant Sobiarso toward her, positioning her precisely, and then picking at Sobiarso's clitoris the same way Akmad picked at everything, especially particles of food. Akmad gently put her thumb and forefinger around Sobiarso's clitoris, then put her two fingers first to her mouth and then to her nose for inspection. She seemed to have a powerful need to verify and reverify that Sobiarso was, indeed, female.

Surprisingly, Sobiarso never became afraid of Akmad. After that first day, Akmad returned to her usual gentle, tolerant self. Up until now, Akmad had dominated the food, sometimes even excluding the much larger Sinaga. But Sobiarso fiercely bit Akmad whenever Akmad drank milk or ate food that Sobiarso wanted. It was as if Sobiarso had experienced the worst that Akmad could deliver and was not intimidated. Nor did Akmad ever retaliate. I later learned that an initial attack to establish dominance was Akmad's pattern. Once she established her dominance, the matter was finished. Sobiarso was probably the spunkiest and most fearless orangutan I have ever known. She refused to be subordinate to anyone or anything. But at the same time, she shared Akmad's sweetness and gentility. Akmad was gentle, serene, and beautiful. Sobiarso was sweet, spunky, and cute. Akmad glided. Sobiarso bounced. And bubbled. It wasn't just their age difference. It was also their personalities.

Akmad and Sobiarso, in turn, were different from Sugito and Sinaga. Akmad never raided our hut as Sinaga did, for example, and Sobiarso did not throw tantrums like Sugito. My sample was tiny: four ex-captive wildborn orangutans. But, nonetheless, the two males were clearly different from the two females in temperament. I wondered whether this was the common pattern among orangutans or just "sampling error."

The three orangutans, Akmad, Sobiarso, and Sugito, became my family. I spent not only my days with them but my nights as well. Sugito always slept with me, but gradually over the weeks Sobiarso settled into a large green washbasin lined with a thick, pink mosquito net. I did not let Akmad stay inside the hut for the night, so she nested in the trees nearby. But during the day she often entered the hut, with or without an invitation. Shunning the front door, Akmad preferred to enter through the roof. Her constant comings and goings, through the roof and through the matting on the front of the house under the roof peak, left gaping holes. She particularly liked to sit on the rafters and sometimes, at the sound of approaching rain, would stand up and push her hand or head out to check if it was raining, leaving more holes. This was not the only damage she did. Once while sitting under the roof waiting for the rain to end, Akmad scored a direct hit on a pile of freshly laundered, neatly folded dry clothes, soaking them with urine.

When I went into the forest searching, I frequently carried both Sugito and Sobiarso. When I was actually following a wild orangutan, however, I usually left Sobiarso behind. Unlike Sugito, Sobiarso was happy to play by herself in the hut or the trees nearby, and there was always someone in camp to look after her. Akmad at this stage oscillated between dependence and independence. Sometimes she disappeared for days. When she was in camp, however, she monitored me closely, and anxiously followed if I strayed from the vicinity of the hut. On days when I searched for wild orangutans, I started leaving camp earlier and earlier so that Akmad would not discover that I was leaving.

Without any planning on my part, not only had I become a mother, but Sugito, Sobiarso, and Akmad had become a family. They squabbled like birth siblings while clinging to my body, pushed and poked at each other while eating, and shoved and tugged while going to bed. They laid claim to the loft, perhaps because it was above ground, which is where orangutans spend most of their life, or perhaps because there were pillows, blankets, and sheets to roll around in. Shortly before sunset, all three would stealthily climb up and congregate under the mosquito net that hung from the roof.

I gloried in being a mother to Akmad, Sobiarso, and Sugito. It felt like the role I was born for. In the middle of the forest, in a tiny hut with no electricity or comforts of civilization, I spent all my waking hours mothering (when I was not searching for or observing wild orangutans). Eventually, after my first year, I even started carrying the trio to Camp Wilkie and back whenever I overnighted for more than a few days at the inland camp.

The mothering became even more intense when, about six weeks after his arrival, Sugito discovered my thumb. A nursing female orangutan does not have visible breasts unless she is plump. But she does develop large nipples, which can be about the size and shape of a woman's thumb. The discovery enthralled Sugito. Once he started sucking my thumb, his whole world seemed to revolve around it. He sucked constantly, sometimes for a half hour at a time. No other finger would do. It had to be my thumb. He sucked at night before he went to bed, in the morning after he woke up, and at various intervals during the day. He sucked after he was apart from me and he sucked when we were together all day. My thumb became his major source of comfort. He became more relaxed and calmer. But when I denied him the thumb, he had a fit. I soon learned that it was easier to give him the thumb on demand than to try to ration it. When I withheld his "pacifier," Sugito would scream hysterically nonstop as he destroyed every object within reach. Soon, Akmad and Sobiarso discovered the joys of the thumb, too, but they never depended on it like Sugito did. Like a chain-smoker, Sugito couldn't get enough. Akmad sucked occasionally, but never for very long. Sobiarso treated the thumb more like a luscious, rich dessert which she relished, but only in moderation. For all three of them, nobody else's thumb would do. It had to be mine.

Intellectually, I knew there was nothing abnormal or perverse about Sugito's craving. Orangutan mothers allow their infants to suckle on demand. Even so, my puritanical upbringing made me uneasy about the thumb-sucking. When I was growing up, thumb-sucking and, for older children, nail-biting were considered wicked. Somehow I felt ashamed that my adopted orangutan offspring were getting such deep satisfaction from sucking my milkless thumb. It provided too much intense pleasure, especially to Sugito. Strange to say, I felt like I should be reading them bedtime stories, doing something more civilized, rather than allowing them this pagan pleasure. My guilt combined with pain. Although I alternated thumbs and tried to ration them, the intense sucking made my thumbs hurt so much that I frequently wanted to scream in agony when Sugito sucked.

❦

The wildborn ex-captives gave me insight into the most important mammalian relationship — that between a mother and her offspring. We humans, mammals to our core, intuitively recognize the crucial nature of the mother-child bond. But in the animal kingdom as a whole, this pattern is an anomaly. For most nonmammals (and hence most living creatures), there is nothing particularly special about the mother-offspring bond after birth. Most fish, amphibian, and reptile mothers do not take care of their young at all, but rather lay eggs by the hundreds or even thousands and promptly abandon them. Among fish, in the exceptional case where the young receive parental care, it usually is the father who is the devoted single parent. Among birds, where parental care is the norm, both parents usually participate in caretaking after the young have hatched from their shells. Only among mammals does the female, with her milk-producing mammary glands — which give the name to the entire class of animals — have an exclusive relationship with her young, from which the father may be excluded. Biparental care, where both mother and father participate in rearing their offspring, is the exception. (Even in our own order, Primates, fewer than 30 percent of species practice biparental care.) Orangutans are a clear example. In the wild, orangutan males play virtually no direct role in the care of their offspring.

True to this primate pattern, Rod did not play a constant role in the daily care and nurturing of the orphaned orangutans. To be fair, the orangutans, who have an exclusive relationship with their mother in the wild, did not invite Rod's attention. But neither did Rod make an active effort to overcome their natural jealousy. Though he often helped, he saw meeting Sugito's, Sobiarso's, and Akmad's continual demands as my business. The young ex-captives were my family, not our family.

For many years, scientists believed that an infant mammal's attachment to his or her mother was based on the association of the mother with the satisfaction of bodily needs, especially hunger and thirst. The British psychiatrist John Bowlby called this the "cupboard theory" of mother love, for it essentially reduces the mother to a feeding station. Then, in the 1960s, the American psychologist Harry Harlow performed a series of experiments that upset the cupboard. Harlow took infant rhesus macaques from their mothers at birth and reared the young monkeys in isolation. The poor infant monkeys spent most of their time huddled in a corner of their cages, clutching their own bodies and rocking. Then Harlow gave the young monkeys a choice of two wire "mother" substitutes, one equipped with a bottle and one covered with foam rubber and terry cloth. Without exception, the baby monkeys chose the "contact comfort" of the cloth mother over the cold, wire mother with food. But these mother substitutes did not compensate for the loss of "mother love," in Harlow's phrase. As adults, they responded to other monkeys with exaggerated fear or aggression. They did not exhibit normal responses to sexual approaches.

The few females who did mate and conceive tended to abuse or neglect their own infants.

From the monkey's point of view, Harlow's laboratory was a chamber of horrors, with isolation cells, a variety of cruel "iron mothers," and even a "rape rack," used to artificially inseminate females and so produce more ill-fated subjects for research. At the time, the torture and sacrifice of hundreds of monkeys for the sake of science was almost routine. The infant monkeys were seen as objects for research, not as living creatures with feelings and emotions. Only a few people protested the psychological and physical pain inflicted on the innocent orphans. Today many groups and individuals are fighting the sometimes unnecessarily cruel experiments performed on laboratory animals for minimal scientific gain. How ironic that it took infant abuse to convince science of the importance of mother love!

Harlow's experiments caused scientists to reevaluate the nature of the mammalian mother–infant bond. As other experiments were carried out and more detailed observations made, researchers discovered, for example, that the licking of infant rats, or pups, by the mother rats is a prerequisite of normal development. Animal research does not necessarily illuminate human behavior, but in this case it did. Some years later, researchers discovered that premature infants, isolated from their mothers in sterile incubators in neonatal hospital wards, benefited tremendously from massages several times a day. The infants grew faster and developed better muscle coordination than did premature babies who had no physical contact with a human being.

Gradually, scientists began to understand that a mammalian mother provides not just milk and warmth but the very environment in which the infant's normal development takes place. As much as physical care, infants need a responsive mother, one who lets them know that they have an effect on the world, that their expressions of need are understood, that their emotions are reciprocated, whether by smiling back when they smile or comforting them when they cry. Without this interaction — without the responsive presence of the mother herself — normal development is difficult if not impossible.

When separated from his or her mother, the infant does not just miss the mother, but rather experiences severe psychological and physical withdrawal symptoms. The attachment between infant and mother is so strong and so pleasurable and so loaded with multisensory (visual, auditory, thermal, tactile) input, that the infant is addicted to the mother. Like an addict needs heroin, so the infant needs mother. Suddenly and irrevocably separated from his or her mother, an infant goes through the equivalent of "cold turkey."

Instinctively, as a female primate, I provided the maternal environment for the three orangutans who became members of my forest family. I didn't lick them, I combed them. I didn't suckle them, but I allowed them to suck my thumb and I provided them with milk. I hugged, carried, caressed, and loved them. They became addicted to me and I to them. Their physical warmth, their soft squeals, their expressions, their feel became part of my daily life in the forest. My life was grounded in my family. They made me laugh and they made me cry. They weren't human but they were close enough. Akmad, Sugito, and Sobiarso were not like pet cats or dogs whom I had loved. In my childhood I was attached to my cats as companions. But the cats never let me forget that they were cats and members of a different species. Orangutans are great apes, and share almost 98 percent of their genetic material with humans. The two percent difference began to matter less and less until it gradually disappeared. I was their mother, a mammalian mother, a primate and hominid mother, and it didn't make much difference that I couldn't climb and swing in trees or open heavy, thick-skinned fruit with my canines. It didn't make much difference to them that I was human. It didn't make any difference to me that they were orangutans. It was enough that Akmad, Sugito, and Sobiarso became my forest family, and the forests of Kalimantan, my home.

# 13

# A DIFFERENT
# REALITY

---

T O THE AVERAGE NORTH AMERICAN, death is a distant reality.
Modern medical science treats death almost like a curable condition, to be
avoided or postponed at all costs. Our comfortable life with advanced sanita-
tion systems, abundant (government-inspected) food, and highly specialized
medical care cushions us from the stark, ultimate reality of death. When I
arrived in Kalimantan, I had attended only one funeral, that of Rod's father. In
my sheltered life, Rod's dad was the only member of my immediate circle of
friends and family who had died. Death happened to other people, people I
didn't know.

Like most North Americans, I believed in science and technology. I grew
up with the conviction that diseases have natural causes and that modern medicine cures all (or would in time). Today AIDS has altered the equation somewhat, as have the burgeoning rates of cancer, tuberculosis, and new superinfec-
tions, which resist most antibiotics. But, at least for middle-class people,
ordinary, garden variety infectious diseases have been defeated. Western people
rarely die from diphtheria, pneumonia, influenza, or measles any more. The
plagues that devastated whole continents are no more. (The debate over destroying the last sealed batches of smallpox virus is largely an ethical one. Do

we have the right to deliberately render a species extinct, even if that species is harmful to humans?)

In Kalimantan, I entered a different universe. The difference wasn't just the absence of comforts, modern hospitals, supermarkets, cars, buses, telephones, electricity, sidewalks, running water, and daily mail. It was deeper. Just as there is no separation of the natural from the supernatural in Kalimantan, so death is not separate from life. The native people, both Melayu and Dayak, lived in the constant shadow of death's black wing. I learned the omnipresence of death from talking with the women, who invariably asked me how many children I had. When I asked them in return, inevitably the answer would be something like "Eight: five alive and three dead."

It wasn't just children. It was also adults. One day I shook the hand of a senior air force official in Pangkalan Bun. He was perhaps in his late thirties and looked fit. A week later he was dead. The story was that he had eaten mangosteen with red sugar. Mangosteen is a round, thick-skinned, dark purple fruit with luminescent, almost transparent pulp. The fresh fruit is a true nectar of fairies, materialized into a light, unearthly sweetness. For some reason, local people seemed obsessed with the idea that if you ate a mangosteen with sugar, you died. The local army doctor told me the air force official had died of hepatitis.

During my second year, I hired a young local man as an assistant, a slim, soft-spoken Melayu whose name was the exact word for "thank you" — *Ačiv* — in the Lithuanian language I had spoken at home as a child. He worked for me for several months and then left. About six months later, I heard he had been on a small boat off the coast near Kumai when he started vomiting. Before the boat reached Kumai, he was dead. He was only twenty-one. I suspect that he died of cholera. The brackish waters of Kumai Bay are a natural breeding ground for the disease, which is more common during the dry season, when wells dry up and people use other sources of drinking water.

Naively, I imagined that the story of my forest family of orangutans would have a fairy tale ending. But I soon joined the chorus of Melayu mothers: "Six orangutan 'children': four alive and two dead." When we first arrived, Rod and I had visited a local Chinese merchant who owned a juvenile female orangutan. The orangutan was kept in a cage, but when taken out, she was frisky and energetic. We asked if we could take her back to the forest, but the Chinese owner was reluctant. "Later," he said. "I'll give her to you when she is older." Later, however, became sooner. Within months, we heard a rumor that the merchant's orangutan was very ill. The next time I went to town, the owner could not give me the orangutan quickly enough. In only six months, the lively juvenile had become a walking skeleton.

I named her "Barbara" in honor of Barbara Harrisson, who had rescued orphaned orangutans in northern Borneo. I was determined to nurse Barbara the orangutan back to health. When I wasn't in the forest, I spent every minute with her. I gave her antibiotics, I gave her vitamins. I took her to the local doctor, who kept asking, "Will she bite me? Will she bite?" Barbara was so weak she could barely move.

I spent hours trying to coax Barbara to eat and drink. I considered getting her to swallow a spoonful of sugared water or a few grains of rice a major triumph. Intellectually, I knew that Barbara was dying; I knew that I wouldn't be able to save her. But I refused to acknowledge this emotionally. I kept denying the reality to myself. It was a "reality" with which I had virtually no experience.

After Barbara died, I cried all night. I tenderly wrapped her in my best sarong before we buried her. I cried because her death was so unnecessary. Had Barbara's mother not been killed, then Barbara herself would have lived. Ordinarily Rod had little use for tears or emotional weakness, but even he was shaken.

A juvenile male orangutan was next. Someone's chance remark pointed us to his owners, in a village near Pangkalan Bun. A Forestry Department official agreed to take Rod to the village on a motorbike. The owner was not in the house, but his family was there. At first the family was unwilling to hand over the young orangutan, but when Rod threatened to bring the police they backed down. Rod left a letter explaining to the absent owner the laws concerning orangutans. He admonished the family, "Don't tell the owner that you gave away the orangutan. Tell him that we *took* the orangutan." As the forestry officer translated for Rod, he grinned at Rod's audacity.

I named the new arrival after my father, Antanas; the anglicized version of his name is "Tony." Tony was three or four years of age. Although not as emaciated as Barbara, he was thin and ate very little. Exceptionally lethargic, he spent most of the day sleeping. He preferred to sleep on me, but if I was too active, he would crawl off my lap and find some quiet place to snooze. He would creep along the floor of the hut on his elbows for a bit and then just stop, resting on the spot on his stomach, all huddled up as though the exertion were too much for him. Unlike the other orphan orangutans, whose faces were pinkish white, Tony's face had a yellow tinge.

Even so, I was optimistic. During the first few weeks, he showed marked improvement. His appetite improved and he stopped losing weight, his coat looked healthy, and his eyes were bright. But Tony never played. One day he spent the entire day sleeping in our hut, encased in my blue jeans, the waistband framing his body. Another day, while Tony was sleeping, Sobiarso accosted him as though she wanted him to play. Tony got up and left the hut. A minute later, I went after him, but it was too late. I looked for him in the thick elephant grass next to the hut but couldn't find him. I became frantic. I was terrified that a bearded pig or a large python would find him asleep on the ground and eat him.

It was still early afternoon when I began searching. Akmad, Sugito, and Sobiarso all trailed behind me. I called Tony's name as I walked. After several hours, I stopped calling. A few minutes later I heard a faint squealing sound. I found Tony some twenty-five feet away from a trail in a patch of forest more than two hundred yards from Camp Leakey. He was on the ground. Less than a week later, Tony was dead.

Tony's death, only two months after Barbara's, devastated me. Given his condition, I should have been prepared, but I wasn't. Irrationally, I had kept hoping that he would recover; irrationally, I felt I had failed him. Not knowing what else to do, I created a bit of superstition. Since the two orangutans who had died had Western names, I decided that henceforth I would give Indonesian names to all wildborn ex-captive orangutans I received (though not to wild orangutans). I wondered if the numerous local superstitions had arisen in similar ways, as attempts to prevent or forestall the inevitable. Human beings have a powerful need to *do* something, to make sense out of tragedy and thus regain their feelings of control over events.

These deaths, I convinced myself, were an aberration. I still had not grasped the cruel justice that rules this world. Here life feeds on death, and death is the normal order of things. Being Western, and thus relatively immune with my still well-nourished body, my inoculations and booster shots, and a store of antibiotics in my medical kit, I had not grasped the essential reality of Kalimantan. For me, as for most middle-class North Americans, death was just a tremor far down, far away at the end of a very long road, not something lived with every hour of every single day.

Between Barbara and Tony, mercifully, we had received "Wildie." Wildie had been captured only days earlier at a logging camp a few miles from Camp Leaky, outside the reserve. She was Akmad's age, but the difference in personality could not have been greater. While Akmad's liquid brown eyes were calm and gentle, Wildie's eyes blazed. She clearly knew who the enemy was: humans. Although she weighed less than twenty pounds, it took four men to force her into a burlap sack. This did not improve her disposition. Mr. Hamzah, who carried Wildie on his back, was bitten through the sack for his trouble.

Wildie needed no instructions for returning home. Upon release, she climbed into the jackfruit trees, snarled, hooted, and ran away. Her case is the way release should work.

Around this time Rod and I had to go to Jakarta for three weeks to renew our permits. I hated to leave but I had no choice. In those days the trip was an ordeal. To get to Jakarta we had to travel by boat to Kumai, ride a truck to Pangkalan Bun, fly to Banjarmasin, the capital of South Borneo, stay there a night or two, then catch a flight to Java. There were times along the way when, like Wildie, I wished I could flee into the forest.

I remember sitting at a crossroad in the back of a truck piled high with bales of rattan and containers of congealed wild rubber and crowded with laborers, in the screaming sun of high noon. At that time, open trucks were the only form of public transportation between Kumai and Pangkalan Bun. There were only a few trucks and only one road. As I waited for Rod, a crowd gathered.

After a year, I was still a local curiosity. An ordinary, young, somewhat emaciated pale North-American woman with long, light brown hair, wearing old, faded, torn and patched blue jeans, I still attracted crowds wherever I went. As long as I kept walking, people only stared. But if I stopped to buy fruit or vegetables at the market, a crowd of men, adolescent boys, and children would stop in their tracks. The men and children rarely jostled me. Still, their staring, frozen faces disturbed me. I felt my humanity dissolve in their piercing stares. No travel guide, no explorer's account, had prepared me for this. I was a spectacle.

Rod didn't attract a quarter of the interest that I did. Perhaps it was because he was a man. Or perhaps it was because, in my faded jeans and khaki shirts, I was a Western woman dressed like a man. The German nun was the only other Western woman in the area. Dressed demurely in cotton print frocks past her knees, her long brown hair tied sedately in a bun at the back of her head, carrying a parasol, she seemed to fade into the background. She was the archetypal brown wren of a woman who flitted by without attracting notice. But the nun had been there for a number of years; she was also securely middle-aged.

In Pangkalan Bun, I never felt animosity. In Banjarmasin, where we spent the night on the way to Jakarta, curiosity was tinged with hostility. Groups of children gathered outside the door of my tiny room in the *loesman* (small hotel) and stared nonstop, forcing me to retreat. Little boys threw stones at me in the marketplace and yelled seemingly rude things that I couldn't understand.

Jakarta was still bewilderingly large, and the traffic seemed to have become worse during the year that we were gone. But at least the Javanese had a few hundred years' experience with foreigners, and people did not find the sight of Westerners so amazing. But Rod and I did! Except for the German missionary and his sister, the only people we saw during our first year were the slim, golden-skinned Melayu. In Jakarta the sight of another white face came as a shock.

I relished the relative comforts of Jakarta. We ate ice cream, drank Coca-Cola with ice, and enjoyed the electric fan in our little room in the local *loesman*. But Jakarta still was not home. Indonesian homes and hotels did not have Western-style bathrooms. The toilets were squat toilets, rather than flush toilets with a raised seat. Instead of tubs and showers, bathrooms were equipped with large cisterns of water, and you bathed with a dipper. (Uninitiated Westerners have been known to climb into the cistern, thereby spoiling the water for everyone else.) But after washing from a bucket or in the river for so long, this was a luxury. I couldn't buy any clothes or shoes in Jakarta because I was too tall and too big-boned. In those days, there weren't enough tourists and other visitors for Indonesians to make clothes in Western sizes. So I went to government meetings in a clean pair of jeans. Indonesians are very careful of their appearance. Even the poorest person has one good set of clothes for special occasions. But because I was a young field researcher, government officials considered my neat, casual dress appropriate, even in their offices.

The trip back to Camp Leakey was as unpleasant as the trip out. I began to dislike Kumai with a special passion. The young men invariably wore black velvet mosque hats and colorful sarongs, which they moved around their firm brown bodies as though they were unfolding the wings of enormous butterflies. The look in their eyes was hostile, even contemptuous. I wanted to disappear.

After this trip I retreated into the forest, and Rod handled the managerial aspects of the project and made the shopping trips. I sometimes went for six months without setting foot in Kumai or Pangkalan Bun.

The whole time we were in Jakarta, I wondered how Sugito, Sobiarso, and Akmad would react to my return. When we finally arrived at Camp Leakey, we found Sugito and Sobiarso confined to a cage. Our new assistant, Mr. Ahmad, told us that the terrible duo had been raiding the storeroom. Our hut was a shambles. Everything we had left behind was torn, smashed, or missing. There wasn't a map or a picture left hanging on the wall. Fortunately, at that point in our lives, we had very little, and had taken most of our possessions with us in our backpacks.

When Sugito saw me, he uttered a little squeal and, as soon as the cage door swung open, ran to me. A second later, Sobiarso fiercely grabbed my leg and sat on my foot, refusing to let go. Akmad came from the forest the next day.

In November, we were given another wildborn ex-captive orangutan, whom we named "Rio." Rio was at least a year younger than Sobiarso and half her size. After Barbara's and Tony's deaths, I was very apprehensive about Rio. He had a ravenous appetite, but he was very thin and had only a cape of hair fringing his back. His skin was wrinkled and slack. Although he was active in the morning, Rio spent most afternoons just lying in the hut while Akmad, Sugito, and Sobiarso played nonstop. I watched Rio constantly. Barbara's and Tony's lovely, innocent faces still haunted me: Barbara, sweet even as a living skeleton, still seeking affection, and Tony, mild and listless, seeking only sleep.

A week after Rio arrived, he started projectile vomiting. He became feverish and diarrheic. His appearance changed dramatically in a matter of days. With his round, distended stomach and stick limbs, he resembled the starving children of Biafra, whose pictures filled the newspapers at that time. Then the seizures started. Rio was sitting with me under the jackfruit trees near our hut when suddenly he fell over backward from the bench onto the ground. For a second, I thought it was all over. His face assumed a grotesque expression, his lips pulled completely back in a horrific grimace, as if in absolute terror. Huge tremors convulsed his body. I eventually forced some chloroquine pills down his throat, thinking he might be suffering from malaria. (Orangutans do get malaria, but it's a different species of parasite from the several species that affect humans.)

For the next few days, Rio stopped drinking milk or water. He would eat only dry milk powder. He continued to vomit but stopped defecating. We took him to the doctor in Pangkalan Bun. The doctor suggested hepatitis but admitted he really didn't know what was causing Rio's symptoms. We treated Rio with antibiotics and vitamins but saw no immediate improvement. Although the tremors stopped, Rio continued to be feverish and listless, sleeping much of the time. During an entire month, he made a play face only once.

His somnolence contrasted with the bouncing, boisterous antics of Sugito and Sobiarso and with Akmad's more graceful acrobatics. Rio was virtually nude, the long red fringe having fallen off his feverish body.

But slowly Rio's condition improved. After about two months, he started making play faces, swinging in the trees, and joining in Sugito and Sobiarso's games. Rio's recovery created a new set of challenges. At times I felt like a crazed housewife trapped with a bunch of mindless, mischievous kids. I understood why housewives rarely win Nobel prizes or run governments or armies. With four lumbering, orange toddlers stumbling and rolling around, tearing into everything, climbing the walls (literally), I could never finish even a brief letter to my parents or a report to the government (due every three months) without major interruption.

Combining research and rehabilitation was a constant problem. Like every working mother I faced the problem What do you do with the kids? Akmad, after a year, came and went as she pleased. But Sugito, Sobiarso, and now Rio, still infants, were clinging and quite dependent. Sometimes I would take them with us to Camp Wilkie, and Rod and I would alternate going into the forest and staying with the young ex-captives. Other times I would leave them with the assistants at Camp Leakey. Occasionally I took Sugito with me into the forest, and less often, Sobiarso as well.

Gradually the orangutans and I worked out a routine for the days when I remained in Camp Leakey. In the morning, immediately after breakfast, I would take Rio, Sobiarso, and Sugito to the trees and vines about twenty-five yards from our hut. There the orangutan trio would climb and play. Sometimes Akmad would join them. These particular trees and vines had a view of the hut's front door. As long as I didn't leave the vicinity of the hut, the orangutans would stay in the trees until the early afternoon, giving me a few precious hours of daylight to work and reflect. Then they would mass together, clutching each other's backs for moral support, drop to the ground, and shamble back to the hut.

Once back in the hut, they refused to leave unless I went with them. Since the alternative was staying in the hut and keeping them under constant surveillance, I would take them walking in the forest. This became one of our favorite pastimes. It was idyllic. Often we walked for hours. Sometimes I climbed into small trees with them. More often, I sat at the bottom of trees while they climbed into the canopy and foraged for fruit and leaves.

During these walks, the young orangutans began to familiarize themselves with the forest, their original home. They learned the way branches and trunks of different trees bend, snap, and sway. They practiced making nests, sometimes with comical effect. They bounced in the vines. They probably memorized arboreal pathways and the locations of certain fruit trees. They tasted fruits, flowers, and young leaves, sometimes gingerly, sometimes with great gusto. Even though we rarely met with wild orangutans on these walks, we were in their shadow. They were teaching the little wildborn ex-captives indirectly, via their food droppings. Just as it was clear to me, it probably was clear to Sugito, Rio, and Sobiarso when a tree's fruits had been eaten by wild orangutans. Monkeys and other tree-dwelling animals left different signatures on their fruit remains. Only orangutans left a carpet of branches, twigs, leaves, skins, fruit stones, and uneaten fruit under a tree when they finished foraging. The litter of skins and stones provided a lesson in how the fruit should be eaten.

Akmad now periodically disappeared into the forest for weeks at a time. Sugito, who was approaching five years of age, had just undergone a growth spurt that transformed him from a large infant, easily carried, into a small juvenile. Although I had to carry him to and from Camp Wilkie, when I was following wild orangutans Sugito traveled on his own. He would follow his earth-bound "mother" on the ground, just as wild orangutan juveniles follow their mother in the trees. The slow, stop-and-start pace of wild orangutans as they moved leisurely through the canopy facilitated Sugito's independence in the forest. Everything seemed perfect. I was finding wild orangutans, the older ex-captives were progressing, and I even had time to work uninterrupted.

By the end of the year Rio had grown much larger than Sobiarso, even though he was younger. However, the relationship between Rio and Sobiarso remained the same. She was senior despite their difference in size. Rio clung to Sobiarso for comfort and security. They frequently slept together, played together, and traveled together. Sobiarso took the lead while Rio, hanging on to her by one hand, followed. In some ways, they became inseparable.

Sobiarso was quick, volatile, intelligent, nimble, sweet-tempered, and active. Rio was much more docile, sluggish, food-oriented, and somewhat slow-witted. Rio wasn't retarded, but neither did he seem particularly smart. Had he been human, he probably would not have won spelling bees or science contests. But down at the country fair, Rio would have won all the pie-eating contests. He was big and gentle, an orange, tropical version of the Jolly Green Giant. For me, he captured the essence of what it is to be an orangutan. I could never get angry at Rio; there wasn't a mean or malicious thought in his head. How very different he was from the quick-witted, destructive, tool-using, sexually precocious Sugito.

Although the orangutan trio — Rio, Sobiarso, and Sugito — had survived, the deaths of Barbara and Tony, and Rio's slow recovery, had battered my Western feelings of safety and certainty.

On a rare trip to Pangkalan Bun, I was finishing an evening meal of rice and chicken broth with sundry chicken parts (including the head) floating on top, at a small *warong* or food stall. A young local woman approached me. She wanted to talk about her pet gibbon. I knew that many people in Kalimantan kept gibbons as pets. With their delicate, flat faces, thick hair, bipedal walk and (usually) mild-mannered dispositions, at least before maturity, gibbons are popular pets. Natural acrobats with dainty habits, they are interesting to watch.

The young woman told me that her pet gibbon was an adolescent female from the interior of Borneo. She had bought her six months ago from a wood carver. She wanted to know if it was legal to keep the gibbon and whether her pet might be confiscated. I told her that gibbons were protected and, technically, could not be kept as pets. I also explained that while gibbons were sweet-tempered in their youth, as adults they became increasingly territorial and started attacking people other than their owners or keepers. With their razor-sharp canines and lightning speed, gibbons could be very dangerous. We had an earnest, woman to woman conversation for more than half an hour.

I asked the woman whether the gibbon showed any signs of sexual maturity. A hard, cold smile came over the woman's face. "There is no gibbon," she said. "I don't have a gibbon. But I am thinking of buying one and I wanted to know whether there was a risk that the gibbon would be confiscated. I know you take orangutans."

"What?" I asked, incredulous. "You don't have a gibbon? But what about the story you told me?"

"Oh," she replied, "I made it all up. I just wanted to see your reaction." Then she continued, "Why are you so surprised? You know you should never believe anything anyone tells you."

I wasn't merely surprised. I was shocked. I was shocked because I was a credulous Westerner, who *did* believe what people told her. I was shocked by the woman's directness and by her total lack of remorse for having fooled me. It was beyond my comprehension.

This was another aspect of Kalimantan reality. Over time I discovered that what the young woman did was not unusual, except perhaps in her immediate admission that she had fabricated her story. I learned that people would look you in the face and lie. They lied unblinkingly. They lied convincingly. They probably could pass lie detector tests, because reality for them became whatever was most useful at the moment.

Like Homer's ancient Greek heroes, traditional peoples in Kalimantan were not concerned with good and evil. Good and evil were irrelevant. What mattered were strength and weakness. Whereas strength earned respect, vulnerability invited scorn or even abuse. They liked to test the state of the universe. They liked to probe the strength and weakness of others periodically, just to have that information handy.

Paradoxically, Rod and I, two young Westerners in tattered blue jeans, striding tall in the manner of our culture, were empowered by the conviction that we were doing good. Saving orangutans from certain death in captivity and keeping loggers out of the orangutans' habitat became our dogma. Our conviction grew out of our perception of the orangutans' vulnerability. We knew that if we didn't save them, nobody would.

To the local people, we became powerful figures. We were inexplicable, because it didn't make sense that someone would squander their power on orangutans and trees. Local people sought all kinds of explanations for our behavior. In Indonesia, especially in Kalimantan, it is considered a form of weakness to let other people know what really is important to you. Nothing is as it seems. Appearances are meant to deceive.

At first most people didn't believe that we cared about orangutans. They thought we were showing our power for other, hidden, reasons. Gradually a few government officials figured us out. One of the first was the chief of the Sekonyer Village. People from his village saw us day in, day out, in the forest. They saw us ministering to sick orangutans. They saw us chasing loggers out of the reserve. The chief came to the startling conclusion that we were transparent. That we did what we said and we said what we did. Their respect for us grew. Our directness, in itself, implied power. Only people who were very certain of their strength would be so disconcertingly honest. At the time, however, we didn't grasp this. We knew people viewed us with a certain amount of respect, but we thought it was because they recognized the unassailable truth of our position, that the orangutans and the tropical rain forest had to be protected. Truth and goodness by themselves had little to do with it.

Life at Camp Leakey now was falling into a familiar, comfortable routine. Sobiarso and Rio remained constantly together. When they came back from the forest, they looked like a six-legged creature, with Sobiarso walking on all fours and Rio with both hands on her back, holding on to her for dear life.

She became his mother substitute, even though she was only a year older than he was. When they slept, Rio would use Sobiarso's round tummy as his pillow. Sobiarso never objected.

Akmad, Sugito, Sobiarso, and Rio played incessantly, often in our hut. Sobiarso still liked to sit in her green washbasin, comfortably ensconced behind the front door of the hut. Sugito had learned on his own to bring me a container if he wanted some milk. Whenever I made milk, Sugito would inundate me with an assortment of cans, cups, and bottles, trying everything in his impatience to get his share. He also learned to pull up the sweet potato plants in our new garden to search for the edible tubers, which he liked to eat raw.

Akmad seemed totally at home in the forest, but Sugito, Sobiarso, and Rio still came back to Camp Leakey each afternoon. Watching them travel along a thick, horizontal vine in the canopy revealed their different levels of development, as well as their individual personalities. First came Sobiarso, totally fearless, dangling by one arm and flinging herself through the air like a somewhat awkward gibbon. Rio followed, brachiating cautiously hand over hand, his legs and body dangling below the vine. Finally Sugito appeared, very ill at ease, hanging by all fours, slothlike, upside down and moving one foot or one hand at a time so that at least three limbs clutched the vine at all times.

We received another juvenile orangutan, a male we named "Subarno," who had been captured near Pangkalan Bun. We kept him in a quarantine cage for two weeks and then opened the door. He refused to leave the cage until everyone had left the vicinity. Like Wildie, Subarno disappeared into the forest, though later he occasionally appeared for feedings and nested close by.

When Rod and I returned from our second annual trip to renew our permits in Jakarta, we brought back the orangutan "Cempaka" from Palangka Raya, the provincial capital. Two years earlier we had left Cempaka at the top of a coconut tree, refusing to come down. A year earlier I had asked the elderly couple who kept her to release her to us. They declined. On this trip, I asked again. Without comment, as though they had decided long before, the old man laboriously unlocked Cempaka's cage and his wife took Cempaka out and held her. With a sharp gleam in her eye, Cempaka hugged the old lady's body closely. Then she came to me immediately, showing no remorse in leaving her "mother." Cempaka seemed to understand what was happening.

Cempaka was my introduction to that peculiar "hominoid," an almost mature orangutan who had been reared by humans. A few rambunctious orangutan infants and a gentle forest-living juvenile sharing our hut was one thing. A sixty- to seventy-pound adolescent orangutan who thought she was human and insisted on her rights, was another. More than any other orangutan I had known up to that point, Cempaka taught me how alike orangutans are to humans, but also how different. She showed me how readily ex-captive orangutans may imitate human skills, then use them for orangutan purposes; how humans and orangutans can live together yet inhabit different realities.

Arriving at Camp Leaky in the evening, we let Cempaka out of her box. She was like quicksilver. All the energy that had been compressed by her ten or more years of captivity burst forth upon her release. She rampaged through our hut. Discovering the loft, she pulled off the sheets and blankets, overturning the mattress in the process, then rolled them all together in a bundle, which she put on top of her head. Then she followed Mr. Ahmad through the dark to his hut, where she ran amok again, even biting Rod on the heel. After a half-hour struggle, the three of us forced her back into her travel box for the night.

The next morning I released Cempaka again. Taking her by the hand, I walked her to the closest trees. She was probably about eleven or twelve years old and had spent virtually her whole life in captivity, but she needed no instruction with regard to trees. As soon as we came within fifteen feet of the trees, she dropped my hand and leaped into the branches. She refused to leave the trees. Only several hours later when I brought her some rice and milk did she very cautiously venture down and quickly take some food. Then she scrambled back up into the canopy, as though she thought this wonderful opportunity could vanish at any moment.

I left her in the trees for the day. When I came back in the afternoon, she leaped down on me. I carried her back to the table just outside our hut. Until now, Cempaka had seemed astonished and frightened by the smaller orangutans. She ran up tree trunks whenever she saw one of them approaching. She shook branches and vocalized ferociously if they came too close. She reminded me of "Washoe," the first chimpanzee to be taught sign language. When, after years of living with human beings, Washoe first saw chimpanzees, she invented a sign for them: "black bug." But now, sitting comfortably in my lap at the table, Cempaka calmly appraised her conspecifics. It was as if sitting around a table with a human and other orangutans behaving in a civilized way, she felt at home. Sugito immediately scrambled over and tried to determine Cempaka's gender. She responded by cupping her hand under his chin and bringing his face closer to hers as if to examine him further. It was an uncannily human-like gesture. But thirty seconds later she made an unmistakably orangutan motion. She reached out with her long arm and pinched his anus.

Cempaka spent her first night of freedom in the canopy overlooking Camp Leakey, hooting from time to time. Dawn came, but she refused to leave her perch. Not until midmorning did she finally lower herself from the vines. Looking around for a minute, as if to check for strange orange creatures, she leaped out of the trees and dashed into my arms. I carried her back to our hut. Inside the hut, she became frantic. She was a quivering mass of doubts and contradictory impulses — should she explore her new surroundings or seek security in my arms? The moment she made up her mind to do one thing, she wanted to do the other. She reminded me of Sugito during the first few weeks after he decided that I was his mother. But Cempaka weighed at least ten times what Sugito had weighed when he first arrived.

That evening Cempaka showed me her mettle. I was so relieved to get her off my back — literally — that I let her go up into the loft unsupervised. She quickly made herself a fine nest by piling the sheets, blankets, and pillows into a mound and then very carefully tucking in the ends of the mosquito net. But this was only the beginning. Next she searched the hut, grabbing anything she could get and putting it up on her mound: batteries, bottles, candles, pans, anything. I quickly retrieved what I could and put the objects into our storeroom under the loft. Before I finished, Cempaka had opened a pillow and begun eating the kapok seeds encased within. ("Silk-cotton trees" are found throughout the tropics. Their kapok "down" is harvested for stuffing and insulation, while the seeds are pressed for oil used in cooking and in soap.) I immediately grabbed the second pillow from Sugito, who was trying to open it, apparently imitating Cempaka. I had never seen Sugito attempt to unstuff pillows before. He then joined Cempaka in picking out the seeds from the first pillow, every now and then stopping to nuzzle her genitalia.

Cempaka reached out and tried to grab the storm lantern, which was lit. I had visions of the hut going up in flames as the lantern fuel spilled across the floor. In my panic, I was quicker than she was. While I was righting the storm lantern, Cempaka discovered our bottle of sweet Chinese wine, or *putau*. By the time I wrestled the bottle away from her, the wine had spilled all over the mattress. Cempaka grabbed the wine-soaked sheet and started sucking, pulling the sheet off the mattress in the process. Then she started sucking the wet part of the mattress. Soon she had torn an enormous hole in the mattress and begun pulling out the stuffing to search for more kapok seeds.

I had had enough. I raced up the ladder. Cempaka leaped off the loft and swung rapidly along the roof beams. The hut vibrated and shook as if it were going to collapse. A cup of tea and a container of malaria pills fell from the table, producing a soggy mess of medicine tea. I finally chased Cempaka out of the hut by waving a stick at her. After climbing around on the roof, Cempaka moved into the adjacent jackfruit trees, accompanied by Sugito. I followed, calling Sugito's name to lure him down. Sugito refused, but Cempaka leaped into my arms. Unable to pry her off, I brought her back into the hut. She sat there clinging to me quietly as the two of us looked at the havoc she had wrought.

While I attempted to clean up, Cempaka climbed back into the loft and wrapped herself up in the sheet. Soon Sugito followed her and began pulling Cempaka's legs in the "rapist" fashion typical of subadult males. She pushed him away, but he was insistent. After a while, I intervened, pulling Sugito away. Cempaka lay down. Finally, the hut was quiet.

By the time Rod returned from the forest, not only was he exhausted, but so was I. We ate quickly and prepared to go to bed. Cempaka refused to relinquish her place on the loft. She became infuriated when we pulled on the sheet in which she had wrapped herself (our sheet). Rod, in his no-nonsense way, decided that the only way to get her off the loft would be to toss her down to the floor in one, quick jerk. This he did. At this point I was down on the floor, and Cempaka tumbled six feet into my arms (not a long distance for an orangutan). When Rod looked down at her, she drew in her head like a turtle and squeaked piteously. But then she climbed right back up to the loft. Rod allowed it because he was going to teach her the same lesson again. But she had already learned it. This time when Rod tried to toss her down to the floor, one of her feet was securely wrapped around a pole. It's difficult to say who won. Cempaka did sleep on the floor of the hut, but wrapped in our sheet like a mummy. No wonder the old couple in Palangka Raya were not reluctant to see her return to the forest!

I had thought that the infants and juveniles were destructive, but Cempaka showed me that they had been amateurs. She took whatever she could lay her hands on. She turned on radios and tried to carry off lit storm lanterns, items in which the other orangutans had never shown the slightest interest. When I chased her, she didn't immediately drop the stolen item as the others did, but rather ran with it clutched in her foot, mouth, or hand. She had no fear of humans, but rather acted as though people had been created for her to taunt.

Cempaka even attempted to "cook." She would fill a glass with handfuls of flour and sugar. Then she would steal one of the eggs we tried (unsuccessfully) to keep hidden, break the egg into the glass of flour and sugar, and stir vigorously. She was following, almost exactly, our cook's recipe for pancakes. I am certain that if we had allowed Cempaka into the kitchen area, she would have poured the batter into a pan and put the pan on the fire, very likely setting the hut ablaze in the process.

Cempaka's vigorous, mischievous behavior deceived me. In Kalimantan the appearance of health can be an illusion. Cempaka's eating habits were peculiar. Only two types of food interested her — onions and sweets. She might swallow a spoonful of cooked rice or a quarter cup of milk, but then pushed the rest aside. She savored sugar, however. She ran off with one-pound cans and sat in the trees with her prize, taking her time, dipping her fingers in the sugar and then licking them.

Our scale confirmed that Cempaka had lost weight since she arrived. Not knowing what else to do, I put antibiotics in her food. But she didn't eat or drink enough to mask the taste and refused to eat anything that had been doctored. So I started giving her penicillin shots, two injections a day. At first she protested, but by the end of the second day she barely blinked when the needle went into her arm. She was the only orangutan I have known (not close to death) who did not need to be held when we injected her. Almost like a person, she thrust out her arm and ostentatiously looked away at the approach of the needle. Within a week, Cempaka's health began to improve. Within six months, she had gained twenty pounds. I was enormously relieved that she was well.

Having grown up in a human environment, Cempaka's forest skills were poor. Her attempts to find a sleeping place at night were sometimes hilarious, sometimes almost painful to watch. Some nights she just sat on a branch, leaning against the tree trunk all night long, her discomfort publicized by occasional snorts. Other times she invaded a young ex-captive orangutan's nest, expelled the nestmaker, and then tried to squeeze her large adolescent body into a nest two sizes too small. Once she occupied an old nest of Akmad's for two days, apparently delighted with her hand-me-down.

But orangutan nests were not all she coveted. Shortly before Cempaka arrived, Mr. Ahmad's wife, Mrs. Bahriah, had given birth to her eighth infant (and sixth surviving child). Cempaka was fascinated by the baby and often sat absolutely still, watching as Mrs. Bahriah pulled out her breast and let her baby suckle. One night there was a terrible commotion from the assistants' hut:

babies and children screaming, adults shouting, things dropping and thumping, people dashing about. I ran over to investigate.

Mr. Ahmad, Mrs. Bahriah, some visiting relatives, and their children all had been asleep in the hut. The new baby was sleeping, papoose style, in a cloth sling like a cozy hammock suspended by strings from the ceiling. This is the traditional way Indonesian babies are lulled to sleep, and the babies love it. So, apparently, did Cempaka. Around midnight, she stealthily entered the hut, crept to the cloth swing, pushed the baby out onto the floor, and climbed into the swing herself. The baby, rudely awakened, howled when he hit the floor. Everyone in the hut awoke. The children started screaming. The adults rushed about. Since the only light was a small kerosene-soaked rag in an old sardine can, they couldn't see what was causing the uproar. Meanwhile, Cempaka left the swing and scampered up the wall, upsetting and overturning objects as she went, and exited through the thatch roof.

It took the children almost an hour to calm down. The baby was unharmed. In fact, when he grew up he became known for his bravado. I think he was influenced by Cempaka, who frequently invaded Mr. Ahmad's hut, sending adults and children fleeing. Mrs. Bahriah told me that as this baby grew older, he often charged at people, orangutan-style, just like Cempaka.

Nothing was safe around Cempaka, the overgrown toddler. But she had survived. Why Barbara and Tony had succumbed were questions no one could answer. Infants of every species are vulnerable. Indeed, Barbara and Tony shared the fate of many human infants in Kalimantan. As a Westerner, I found the precarious balance of life and death difficult to accept.

Kalimantan reality is all-pervasive: psychological, cultural, and physical. The tropics nurture countless microscopic organisms, many unknown to medical science, all seeking a hospitable environment, such as the human body. The person who did not have some infection, virus, or parasite lurking in his or her system was rare.

Watching the doctors work in Pangkalan Bun left one with the unmistakable impression of men and women grappling with unseen figures in the dark. They used a hit-or-miss strategy. I once went to the doctor and received eight different kinds of pills. When I asked what they were, the doctor explained that three were simply vitamins and minerals, one was an analgesic, one was for inflammation, and two were antibiotics. The other was never identified. The doctors were neither careless nor amateurs. But without proper laboratories and diagnostic equipment, they never were able to tell for certain what was wrong with the patient. They knew that many if not most people in the area suffered chronic subliminal vitamin deficiencies. So the doctors medicated with a shotgun approach. Sometimes it worked; often it did not.

In a world where death hovered in the air like an invisible, ravenous bird of prey, even the doctors measured their victories in terms of today, because tomorrow was unpredictable. The patient you saved from malaria today might drink a glass of unboiled water tomorrow and die of typhoid. No wonder that local people had very strange expectations. Every person I met in Kalimantan had a story of someone who was perfectly fine but took a bath in the river when he was feeling hot and died within the hour. This belief arose not from ignorance but from the experience of apparently healthy people suddenly dying.

The Dayak and Melayu of Kalimantan were not alone. Years before, when I was in the former Yugoslavia, traditional Serbs and Croats issued dire warnings about going outdoors after you washed your hair. It seemed as if everyone there had a grandmother who had died from washing her hair! As in Borneo, this improbable sequence of cause and effect simply acknowledged that death may strike anyone, anywhere, anytime. In Kalimantan, local people didn't distinguish between what, to us, was a "harmless" flu and a dangerous condition such as hepatitis or cholera. In the tropics, an apparently minor disease can wear down a person's resistence, making him or her more vulnerable to a more serious condition. A minor cold may be the beginning of the end.

I finally understood why, during my first week at Camp Leakey, our Indonesian escorts had seemed terrified of the rain. If you have the malaria parasite in your body, getting wet, cold, overheated, overtired, or even stressed will bring the malaria parasite out of the organs where it hides and into the bloodstream, causing chills and fevers. Rod and I were protected by antimalarial pills. But most local people carried the malaria parasite and experienced flare-ups from time to time. If they were weakened by other conditions, an attack of malaria could be fatal. Death was always a possibility. Hardly a week went by without someone I knew, or a relative of someone I knew, dying.

The Kalimantan reality is crystalized in the *Hindu Kaharingan* religion of the native Dayak people. Just as there are many North American "Indian" or native tribes, so there are numerous distinct Dayak cultures in Borneo. But perhaps because Borneo is smaller than North America, the Kenyah, Ngaju, Iban, and other Dayak cultures share a basic worldview. Only after I had been in Kalimantan for a number of years did I begin to appreciate Dayak art, attend Dayak rituals, and talk to shamans and others about their religion.

*Kaharingan* is an ancient, animistic religion, which has a deep philosophical cosmology but acknowledges the supremacy of nature. I am often struck by the similarities between Dayak beliefs and rituals and those of other technologically primitive cultures. Animistic religions around the world — in Siberia, the Americas, New Guinea — have so many elements in common, it seems very likely that they have a common origin, perhaps dating back to the Paleolithic.

The word *"Kaharingan"* originates from the word for a species of fig tree, whose deep roots and enormous branches represent the tree of life, similar to the tree where Buddha found enlightenment. Like other animist religions, *Kaharingan* teaches that ordinary animals and objects have souls or consciousness, that spirits play an active role in daily events, and that nothing happens by accident. Unlike the historic religions — Judaism, Christianity, Buddhism, Hinduism, and Islam — *Kaharingan* does not draw a sharp distinction between this life and the life hereafter, the natural and the supernatural, religious and secular activities, priesthood and laity. Religion is part of the fabric of everyday life.

At the heart of *Kaharingan* is the concept of a parallel universe, the other, darker side of reality. The universe we see is a mirror image of the other. One might compare the two universes to a film negative and a photographic print; what is black here is white there, and vice versa. Unlike heaven and hell in Judeo-Christian and Islamic teachings, the parallel universe is not a distant place, accessible only in the next life. The parallel universe is real; it exists in the here and now. Humans can go there while still in this life, through dreams and visions. This is how shamans acquire special powers. But ordinary people may travel back and forth as well. The female god who rules the parallel universe is represented in this universe as a serpent-dragon. Some Dayaks believe that crocodiles are the dragon god's helpers, sent from the parallel universe. Only when they cross over into this universe do they assume the form of crocodiles. The parallel universe is as real to followers of *Hindu Kaharingan* as antimatter is to physicists, or negative numbers to mathematicians.

In Dayak culture, death is an integral part of life. Indeed, death is considered more real than life, as if everyday experience were the dream, and death the awakening. Whereas Westerners view life as having a beginning and an end, Dayaks see life and death as part of a cycle. In their worldview, life is regenerated through the destruction of life. Like the Aztecs and even the ancient Hebrews, the Dayaks appease the gods with blood sacrifice. In the Sun Dance, the Sioux reach the gods by torturing themselves. But the meaning and purpose of these different rituals from different times and cultures is much the same.

In Kalimantan Tengah, the most important rituals are the funerary ones, usually called *tiwah*. The core of the *tiwah* is the bone-cleansing ceremony, held sometime after a person dies. Whether it is held a month after a person dies, or forty years later, depends on the particular Dayak group and on the circumstances. Immediately following death, the body may be buried or cremated. In the *tiwah,* the bones are exhumed for ritual cleansing. In the past, human beings were sacrificed during the *tiwah;* today, animals are substituted. After the proper ceremonies are performed, the bones are placed in an ornately carved ossuary and reinterred in elevated, elaborately carved hardwood family mausoleums, shaped like a house or a boat. At the *tiwah,* masks frequently are worn to guard against evil spirits (and, admittedly, to entertain). The grotesque, garish, red and black wooden masks, with yellow or red and white curlicues, remind me of the nightmarish Satanic gargoyles on Gothic cathedrals.

Many Dayaks believe that when a person dies, part of the soul stays with the body or bones, and the other part enters the parallel universe ruled by the serpent-dragon god. The *tiwah* reunites the two parts of the soul, and sends the dead on their way. If this ceremony does not take place, the body's soul may remain in limbo and become a ghost. The *tiwah* thus serves both the dead, by making the soul whole again, and the living, by sending away a potentially malevolent spirit.

The *tiwah* embodies Kalimantan reality. You can't fight death; you can only acknowledge and embrace it. Dayaks view life as borrowed time. Ironically, because they accept death, they live joyously.

I was too Western to accept such a verdict. I had long ago decided that since I was not born Indonesian, I could not knowledgeably judge what happened in Indonesia. I made no judgments. I talked, as did Rod, to every government official I met about orangutans and tropical rain forest conservation. But politely. And calmly. When I wasn't searching or following wild orangutans in the great forest, I nursed sick orangutans. I didn't ask anyone else to do it; I just did it. Rod, whose primary objective was to create a visual record of wild orangutans, was occupied with his photography.

To many Indonesians, our attitudes and behavior made little sense. Our mission to protect orangutans and their forest habitat was incomprehensible. Because we were incomprehensible, we were considered unpredictable. Because we were considered unpredictable, we were assumed to be powerful.

Local officials, including the *bupati* and the Sekonyer Village chief, as well as high-ranking Forestry Department visitors from Jakarta and the provincial capital of Palangka Raya, visited Camp Leakey. Officials always wanted to see for themselves. They constantly went on "fact finding" tours. Given the local assumption that you could only believe what you saw with your own eyes and had to be careful about believing what people told you, this was not surprising. Officials usually came in borrowed logging company speedboats. They would spend a few hours, play with the ex-captive wildborn orangutans, who were becoming a sensation locally, and talk to us.

These visitors were a captive audience for our proselytizing concerning orangutan and tropical rain forest conservation. Rod seemed to bond well with Indonesian men; he fit right in. Officials tended to be more formal and distant with me, as befit relationships with a married woman in a predominantly Muslim society. They also respected the fact that I didn't complain and didn't give in or give up, but kept to the path I had set for myself. This is what they told me. My idealism and single-mindedness about a "mere" animal species was foreign to the fatalistic and multifaceted Indonesians. They were fascinated and puzzled at the same time.

After many years in Kalimantan, I am still Western in my belief in science and natural causes, and in my sense of justice and outrage at injustice. But Kalimantan exposed me to a different reality, to a nature that knows no pity, to death without reason, and to a view of life where truth is not absolute. I once talked to a Dayak woman who commented that *Hindu Kaharingan* makes sense in Kalimantan, but seems to lose power in the modern city of Jakarta. I knew what she meant.

Despite one's Western cultural armor, when you live in Kalimantan for any length of time, Kalimantan reality becomes your reality. You may not believe in spirits and spells, but you are forced to acknowledge how much you cannot see and how much you cannot control. The omnipresence of death and deception undermines your faith in a benevolent deity and your trust that tomorrow will be a better day. Your optimism becomes grim determination. You learn to expect that the next knock on the door will bring news that someone you love is dead, or that a long-fought battle you thought you had won is lost. You learn that behind the smiles and gentility of the beautiful, lithe, golden-skinned people of Kalimantan, and the majesty and grace of the forested, riverine panoramas, Nature rages, and when she turns, sometimes — just for a second — as one catches a fleeting glimpse of her face, her visage wears the black and red mask of Satan.

# 14
# CARA'S FATE

Food is life.

— *Harry Wu*

This is the way the world ends
Not with a bang but a whimper.

— *T. S. Eliot*

---

"CINDY," wild orangutan Cara's newborn infant, was the fluffiest, cutest bright orange creature imaginable. Through my binoculars, I delighted in her wizened little pinkish white face with chocolate brown eyes resting against the dark red hair of her mother's side. Cindy could have been a child's plush toy, created to elicit a cute response.

I said to Rod, "She's so adorable; I'd love to hold her in my arms."

Rod smiled. "Me, too," he replied. Usually so detached and objective, he almost looked as if he meant it.

In medieval Europe, wise people cautioned that sometimes the worst thing that could happen was that God answered your prayers: Be careful what you wish for; it could come true.

Almost a year had passed since I first encountered Cara, during 1972. Because *Jalan Toges,* the main trail in my study area, cut through the middle of her home range, I saw Cara more often than any other wild female orangutan. Despite her initially aggressive reaction to my presence, she was one of the most completely habituated orangutans I had studied. I was familiar with her comings and goings, her likes and dislikes. I had become very fond of Cara. I spent more time alone with her than with any other individual. Even when I was alone with Rod I wasn't really alone, because the ex-captive orangutans were there and something was always going on. When I was alone with the ex-captives, I was always with a group, rarely with a lone infant or juvenile. Only with Cara did I enjoy a one-to-one relationship. Because of this, Cara assumed a special importance for me. I looked forward to finding her and observing new developments in her life the way one looks forward to reading the next chapter in a compelling book. Cindy would be my first opportunity to follow the life history of a wild orangutan from birth.

When I first saw Cara with her newborn, Cara herself seemed thin. Her hair looked scraggly and her face, pinched and gray. I knew that human mothers need at least a few hundred extra calories a day for their infants' milk supply. Getting the extra calories at the supermarket is one thing. It's another to find them in the tropical rain forest, calorie by calorie, fruit by fruit, leaf by leaf. Several months passed before Cara looked herself again.

Carl continued to follow Cara, staying within a hundred feet of his mother. When Cara stopped, Carl often came and sat beside her. Age eight or nine, Carl was about half her size. For orangutans, Cara and Carl seemed particularly affectionate now. One afternoon, while Cara was resting, Carl stretched out in front of her. Cara immediately started grooming him — unusual behavior. While being groomed, Carl looked at Cindy and Cindy looked at him. Then Cindy started tugging at Carl's right foot. Carl opened his mouth and pushed some fruit he was still chewing to the front of his lips, as if to show his little sister. When she did not react, probably because she was too young to notice, he pushed the mush further out on his flexible, rubbery lower lip, looked at it himself, then pulled it back into his mouth. After a few minutes, Cara gathered up Cindy and moved away.

Another day, Carl came over and put his head to Cara's chest right next to Cindy. Then he lay down, using Cara's foot as a pillow. Carl frequently turned Cindy upside down, as if to check her gender, and sometimes groomed her. Neither Cara nor Cindy paid him much heed. For a time, Cara, Cindy, and Carl seemed to be a close, happy family.

Carl still seemed attached to his mother. But Cara was gently pushing him toward independence. She seemed to be leaving him behind more often; only if Carl protested vigorously did she wait for him to catch up. Cara still shared food with Carl, but when she wanted to, not when Carl begged. At dusk Cara would make a large night nest and allow Carl to climb in. Then, after a few minutes, she would move out, leaving Carl in sole possession, and make a new nest for herself and Cindy.

Most surprising, Cara and Carl began playing together, something I'd never seen them do before. Usually Carl was the instigator. He might pull on Cara's arm. Cara would make a play face, her upper lip covering her teeth in a broad, open-mouthed grin. Hanging from an overhead branch, mother and son would twist and turn as they tussled. (Cindy would be tucked securely out of the way on Cara's far side.) The sight of the dignified, almost austere Cara playing with her immature son seemed incongruous. Perhaps Cara was reassuring Carl that her pushing him away wasn't personal. Cara and Carl's play-fighting continued for more than a month. Sometimes their play was so intense that I thought I could hear throaty huffs that mimicked human laughter.

The new infant had not improved Cara's general disposition, however; she was as irritable as ever. One day Carl surprised a colugo, a "flying lemur." These animals are among the most alien-looking mammals on this planet and belong to an ancient order with only two surviving species, both in Southeast Asia. Flying lemurs are not lemurs, nor do they fly. But they are the most perfectly adapted of all gliding mammals, with membranes stretching from the tips of their fingers and toes to the ends of their tails and the points of their chins. The colugos cling vertically to tree trunks, then suddenly leap into the air, open their gliding membranes, which may be one and a half feet wide, and alight on another tree trunk as far as two hundred feet away. The colugo in a glide looks like an oversized starched white handkerchief floating in the air. The size of a small house cat when folded up, colugos melt imperceptibly into tree trunks. The mottled gray, brown, and white and scalloped edge of the colugo's gliding mantle blends perfectly with the bark — only in glide is their white underside exposed. The head resembles a knob of wood. Their camouflage is so extraordinary, it is difficult to see a colugo even when you know one is there. Grotesque and homely, yet also somehow cute, they remind me of E.T.

At Carl's approach, the colugo glided into another tree. When Carl followed, the colugo glided into a third tree, and froze on the bark. Cara suddenly moved in, grabbed a small tree, and furiously swung it against the tree trunk where the colugo was sitting. At the last possible moment, the colugo glided off and seemingly vanished. Cara stopped, empty-handed. The scene reminded me of a distraught housewife trying to squash a large spider in her cupboard.

Even though Cara was often grouchy, I never expected her to turn on her son. But one morning they were eating close together in the same tree when, without warning, Cara leaped toward Carl. Shrieking in terror, Carl tried to run away, but wasn't quick enough. Cara caught his hand. She did not bite it, but shook it hard. Then she let him go. A few minutes later, Carl started knocking down dead wood from the canopy in what seemed to be frustration or redirected aggression.

Later, Cara and Carl were traveling with Beth, her son, Bert, and the semi-independent adolescent Maud. Cara was quietly eating in a small fruit tree about forty feet off the ground. Suddenly, the entire top of the fruit tree broke off, sending Cara and Cindy hurtling to the forest floor. Cara succeeded in grabbing hold of a branch from an adjacent tree as she fell. But the branch snapped and came down with her. Cara landed on her back less than ten feet from where I sat with my open notebook on my knees. Close up, Cara seemed much darker and much larger than I expected. She picked herself up, trotted to the nearest tree, and climbed straight up about thirty feet. Then very carefully, she lifted Cindy off her side and inspected her, limb by limb. Her examination was as meticulous and unhurried as a medical specialist performing a test of neurological function. Apparently reassured that Cindy was fine, Cara resumed eating.

Less than an hour after her fall, Cara attacked Maud. Faster or perhaps more alert than Carl, Maud escaped, although Cara chased her for more than 150 feet. Maud uttered a piercing, undulating, high-pitched squeal as she ran. After the attack, Maud did exactly what Carl had done. Looking toward Cara, she climbed into the canopy and pushed down pieces of wood.

The six orangutans — Cara and Cindy, Beth and Bert, Carl and Maud — moved on together. But Maud never entered a tree with Cara, and Carl followed close behind Beth and Bert. Both adolescents seemed to be avoiding the testy Cara. A while later another orangutan appeared in the distance. Beth and Cara were in the same tree about five feet apart. As both gazed intently in the direction of the newcomer, their postures and expressions were identical. Beth and Cara could have been twins. The new orangutans were adult Fran and her infant, Freddy.

Cara leaped to the ground and raced in Fran's direction. Soon she and Fran vanished in the undergrowth. Although I couldn't be sure, I suspected that Cara attacked Fran. I was surprised, because Cara always had seemed wary of Fran. But then Cara was never totally predictable.

Left behind, Carl began squealing at the top of his lungs, his squeals followed by piglike snorts. Leaving Beth, Carl moved east, almost running through the trees, squealing as he went. Soon he was moving north by northeast. After stopping to eat in a few trees, he turned and began retracing his arboreal path. Nearly three hours later, Cara, Cindy, Beth, Bert, and Maud appeared moving due east. Carl squealed and then whimpered. But he did not immediately move to his mother; perhaps he knew better. Rather, he went over to Beth, who was drinking water from a small natural cistern in the forked trunk of a tree. Water dribbled from Beth's mouth. Carl put his mouth under her chin and drank.

Carl must have known where Cara was going; that was the only possible explanation. After she vanished, he had a locale in mind and headed in that direction. When he didn't find his mother there, he retraced his steps. Cara was going where Carl had predicted, but not as fast. Eventually, she reached the trees where he had turned around. Although Cara's plans were not discernable to me, they were clear to Carl. After years of traveling with Cara, he knew her habits and seemed able to read her mind. Later that evening Cara and Beth nested side by side on the same branch less than three feet apart. Carl noiselessly entered his mother's nest. As if to make up for her earlier disappearance, Cara did not protest.

From Carl's extreme reaction, I judged this to be the first time that mother and son had ever been separated. I was so immersed in Cara's family saga that my relief when Carl encountered Cara again was almost as great as his. But Carl's troubles were only beginning.

The next day Carl was innocently eating fruits about three feet from Beth and Bert. Out of the blue, Beth grabbed Carl and bit his foot. I had no clue as to why the normally benign Beth turned on him. Cara moved rapidly through the trees and sat about two feet away from Carl, as if assessing the damage. Her protective motherly feelings toward Carl were still operating. Carl sat in the tree licking his right foot with an exceptionally glum expression on his face. When he finally moved, he was very careful not to put the flat of his foot down on any surface. I could imagine him wondering why all the normally gentle adult females in his life had suddenly turned grouchy.

Beth's son, Bert, was almost five years old and had gone through the growth spurt that transformed him from a small infant to a young juvenile. Beth still suckled him on demand and nested with him at night, but she wanted him to travel behind her on his own from tree to tree. Bert still wanted to be carried. I sympathized with Beth more than she will ever know. Sugito was about the same age as Bert, and much heavier than before. Although I didn't object to Sugito sucking my thumb, I felt weighed down when I had to carry him long distances. "He can walk," I kept telling myself, as Sugito used every wile to entice me to carry him through the forest.

Bert was experiencing the first separation crisis in a young orangutan's life. Beth was insisting that he walk (and swing), not ride. What is remarkable is that this first push toward independence occurs so late in the orangutan's development. Young chimpanzees go through their first crisis at around age one, when their mother forces them to ride on her back rather than cling to her belly. By age four, young gorillas are weaned. In contrast, orangutans this age are still nursing, still nesting with their mother, and still occasionally being carried. I often wonder if this long period of maternal indulgence helps to account for the serenity of adult orangutans.

The second separation crisis in a male orangutan's life begins around age seven, when the mother starts to wean the juvenile, pushes him out of her nest, sometimes refuses to share food, sometimes refuses even to share trees, and, if he doesn't leave of his own accord, eventually chases the young orangutan away. Carl was nearing the end of this second, and final, separation. The male orangutan's long, exclusive relationship with his mother contrasts sharply with the adult male's isolated existence, making the final break especially traumatic. (I later learned that mothers do not push daughters away as emphatically or with the same finality.)

As Cindy approached her first birthday, Cara was becoming increasingly unfriendly toward Carl. The mother-son play sessions had ended. Carl was no longer sharing Cara's nest at night. Rather than passively allowing Carl to become more independent, Cara was now actively, aggressively, pushing him away. In her orangutan way, Cara was doing her duty as a mother, preparing Carl for his solitary destiny as an adult male.

During Cindy's infancy, Cara frequently traveled with other females. Indeed, when I first saw Cindy, I had been following "Ellen" and her offspring. Like Cara, Ellen was a vigorous, middle-aged female, probably in her thirties or even forties. Her high-spirited daughter, "Evonne," named for the brilliant Australian tennis player Evonne Goolagong, was about Carl's age. Ellen also had a newborn infant, whom I named "Eve."

The orangutan mothers traveled leisurely together for four hours. The two adolescents, Carl and Evonne, seemed to particularly enjoy the company. At times they switched mothers. Thus, Carl and Ellen ate *ubar* fruits in one tree while Evonne foraged in another tree with Cara. Other times, Carl and Evonne occupied the same tree, eating and playing together. At one point they were in a *pintau* tree, a wild relative of the commonly cultivated jackfruit. *Pintau* fruit is about the size of cantaloupe and covered by a thicket of bright yellow prickles when ripe. Evonne was just about to open one when Carl approached her. She held up the *pintau* fruit as if exhibiting a prize. Carl took the offering from her hand with his mouth. He took a bite of the fruit and then dropped it. Their easy camaraderie reminded me of the good-natured interactions between Akmad, Sugito, and the other wildborn ex-captives in camp. Only a young orangutan would play with food.

In contrast, during their whole time together, adults Cara and Ellen did not visibly interact or touch one another. David Agee Horr, a pioneering field researcher, once commented that wild orangutans in the crowns of trees were like "ships passing in the night." To a human observer down below, orangutans often appear oblivious to one another. But perhaps they communicate by means of subtle changes of expression and posture that we can't see. The more I watched these females and their young, the more convinced I became that something was going on. I was impressed by how similar their emotions seemed to human emotions and by how much I understood intuitively. Orangutans differ from humans in countless ways. But in their lack of ritualized or stereotypic responses to each other, orangutans and humans are very similar.

A distinct individual, Cara had friends and enemies, good moods and bad moods, and her own personal style. I liked her decisive, no-nonsense manner. I had seen the softer, maternal side to her brusque exterior. Although I could never predict how Cara would act toward a particular orangutan on a given day, her behavior made sense to me.

Of all her female acquaintances, Cara seemed to have the easiest relationship with Beth. Cara and her retinue and Beth and her large infant, Bert, sometimes traveled together for days at a time. Typically, Beth followed Cara one or two trees behind. But they frequently ate in the same tree, often on the same branch, and nested in adjacent trees at night. When Cara and Beth were together, I got the impression of two old friends. Totally relaxed in one another's presence, their behavior appeared synchronized. When Cara traveled with other females, it usually was for only a few hours and their interactions seemed more guarded.

Cara's relationship with "Martha," in particular, seemed complicated and uncertain. Martha was a very black faced, middle-aged orangutan, slower and probably older than Cara. Although Martha seemed to harbor no animosity toward Cara, Cara seemed ambivalent toward her.

On one occasion, Cara was traveling with Martha, her infant son, "Merv," and her daughter, the adolescent Maud. Martha and Cara were next to each other eating bark along the same branch. Cara looked up at Martha's face and flinched. I saw nothing untoward in Martha's posture or behavior. Indeed, Martha reached out and reassuringly put her hand on Cara's back. For a few seconds Cara sat immobile, with Martha's hand touching her. Then Cara sped out of the tree as if she were in mortal danger. Martha casually resumed eating bark. As soon as Cara left, Carl came and sat next to Martha, watching her intently. Martha ignored Carl, but little Merv moved off his mother's body and put both hands on Carl, apparently inviting him to play.

Cara had moved to an adjacent tree. She was sitting below Maud, who was peacefully eating young leaves. With no apparent provocation, Cara attacked Maud. So swiftly did Maud flee that she didn't actually start squealing until she was out of Cara's way. Martha came closer and watched, but she did not intervene. The next day, as Martha and Cara continued traveling together, Maud fled whenever Cara so much as moved in her direction. But this precaution wasn't enough. Maud and Cara were ten or twelve feet apart in different small trees when Cara suddenly flew at Maud, who squealed and ran away. Again, Martha just looked on passively.

A few hours later, Martha and Cara were eating bark on opposite sides of the same trunk. There were only a few inches between them, they were so close. Both seemed preoccupied with eating. Then Martha paused and stared at Cara, something she normally did not do. Indeed, wild orangutans rarely look directly at one another. A second or two later, Martha moved ever so slightly in Cara's direction. Cara backed down the trunk and hastened out of the tree, as if Martha had attacked her. I saw no malevolent intent on Martha's part, but then Martha's face was not inches from mine. Martha continued looking as Cara backed away, but did not move. Then Cara did her usual maneuver. She attacked Maud. This time Cara showed no mercy. She chased Maud for more than three minutes. Martha moved one tree over and watched, passively. When Cara moved away, Martha did not follow.

Cara's dislike of Maud was almost palpable. She had attacked the hapless adolescent three times in less than twenty-four hours. I couldn't tell whether Cara was sending a message to Martha, whom she didn't dare attack directly, whether Cara found Maud annoying because Cara was burdened with a son of approximately the same age, or whether Cara simply did not like Maud as an individual.

A researcher who had studied orangutans briefly in East Borneo wrote, "Orangutans are hardly more social than any mammal must be." He had observed wild orangutans in groups for only 1.65 percent of his total observation time. John MacKinnon noted that he had never observed two adult females with offspring traveling together. David Agee Horr also reported that contact between adult female orangutans was infrequent.

Cara was breaking the rules; she was not behaving in the way orangutan females were described as behaving in other areas. Although her social life lacked the elaborate ritualized behavior of wild chimpanzees, and the groups in which she traveled never reached double-digit numbers, Cara impressed me as gregarious. I decided to observe her for a month. That would give me a good sample of her social behavior and let me document Carl's growing independence and Cindy's development.

During the thirty-one days I followed Cara, I expected a rerun of her energetic encounters with other females. But Cara, Cindy, and Carl were nearly always alone. There were a few fleeting encounters — a glimpse of an orangutan in the distance, an agitated female I did not recognize briefly chasing Cara out of her night nest, an encounter with the adult male Knobs, who displayed furiously at me while Cara swung lightly away. Once Cara and her offspring traveled with Ellen, Eve, and Evonne for several hours. But adolescents Carl and Evonne did not play once, and mothers Cara and Ellen barely looked at each other.

Then for nine days straight, Cara, Carl, and Cindy were totally alone in the forest, meeting no other orangutans. There wasn't even the sound of long calls in the distance. It was as if a chunk of the planet with Cara, Carl, and Cindy had broken off and was floating in space. On the tenth day, Cara entered a tropical oak where ancient Alice and her large adolescent son, "Andy," were eating. Alice and Andy seemed to be in their own isolation capsule. As far as I could tell, neither Alice nor Cara even noticed that the other female was there. Nor did Carl and Andy play.

In all, these encounters scarcely added up to a full day. Only her few hours' association with Ellen could be termed remotely "social." The other contacts took the form of avoidance or total disinterest. Cara was confirming what other researchers believed. Orangutans are basically loners, the Greta Garbos of the higher primates.

I had vacillated between the prevailing view that orangutans are solitary and the possibility that they were more gregarious than anyone suspected. Now I realized that it wasn't an either/or question and that both were true. Sometimes orangutans are solitary, sometimes not. Rather than calling them "solitary," as other researchers have done, I prefer to think of orangutans as being "semisolitary," or sociable but solitary.

Orangutans remind me of New Yorkers moving past one another on a crowded sidewalk without exchanging greetings or even making eye contact. Observing such a crowd, an anthropologist from another planet might conclude that human beings are asocial. But if New Yorkers stopped to socialize with everyone they encountered on a single midtown block, they would never get anywhere. And so, as a matter of survival, they develop psychological blinders.

Similarly, orangutans moving through the treetops are busy making a living, which for an orangutan means finding food. Because food sources are relatively sparse and widely scattered in the tropical rain forest, and because orangutans are large animals who require large amounts of food, they cannot afford to congregate in one place or to travel and feed in groups of any size. A single orangutan may consume all the ripe fruit or edible flowers in one spot. If orangutans fed in groups they would have to travel longer distances, find more food sources, and perhaps waste energy competing for what they found. Foraging alone is more efficient. Their mostly solitary lifestyle is not so much an expression of the orangutan's nature as an adaptation to circumstances. As the ex-captive orangutans at Camp Leakey demonstrate, orangutans can be quite social when conditions allow or require it. It just so happens that conditions in the tropical rain forest favor solitary foraging.

The orangutans' self-sufficiency makes them unique among higher primates. For orangutans, eating comes first; socializing comes second, if at all. For chimpanzees, the reverse sometimes seems true: socializing seems to come first, and eating, second. Chimpanzees are political animals. They devote much time, energy, and intelligence to learning the social hierarchy and social etiquette of their community, monitoring and manipulating the emotions and loyalties of other chimps, forging alliances, staging coups, and resolving disputes. Living in a group plays a key role in the chimpanzees' adaptation to their environment, just as maintaining distance is a central part of the orangutans' adaptation.

Because adult orangutans do not need one another, they do not use or manipulate one another. This is why they seem so benign to us, and so innocent. When chimpanzees befriend other chimpanzees, they invariably have ulterior motives: the more friends a chimpanzee has, and the more powerful those friends, the better. But adult orangutans have nothing to gain from associating with one another. Their motives are pure. When Beth and Cara travel together it is simply because they like one another's company. Chimpanzee friendships require constant affirmation. A primary reason why chimps spend hours carefully, almost compulsively, grooming is to reassure one another that they are still friends. Unburdened by expectations, orangutan relationships are less volatile, and therefore less demonstrative. Orangutan companions are like old, old friends who don't need to talk to enjoy being together.

To human eyes, orangutans may seem distant and aloof. After all, they rarely groom one another, rarely share food with one another, and virtually never come to one another's aid in a spat. But we humans, who share almost 99 percent of our genes with chimpanzees, are more like chimps in our emotions and social behavior. Our motives are never entirely pure, and we can never completely trust one another. Orangutans display an honesty and candor that humans and chimpanzees cannot afford. In their social machinations, chimpanzees remind us of ourselves. In their innocence, orangutans remind us of the Garden of Eden we left behind.

Cindy was now one year of age. Her bright orange hair glowed as if she were carrying her own sunshine. She was a little bundle of energy and activity, reaching out and exploring. She frequently strayed several feet from Cara. Already she was sharing food, drinking water from her mother's mouth, and reaching for pieces of bark in Carl's hand as well as Cara's. Cara's relationship with Carl had taken another turn. Apprehensive, he stayed away from her during the day when she was eating and sometimes squealed when she so much as looked at him. Only when Cara was sitting, relaxed, would Carl approach her. Then it was Cindy who would tug at him and do somersaults just above his head as though enticing him to play. I remember Carl holding Cindy's foot with his own foot as he inspected her back with his right hand. He groomed Cindy's back for one and a half minutes. When he let go of her foot, she examined the foot herself, as though looking for Carl's imprint.

Shortly after Cindy turned one, Carl left Cara for the first time to travel on his own. He teamed up with Evonne on what probably was her first excursion away from her mother, too. The two adolescents spent most of their time eating, occasionally stopping to play. The dry season had ended. But this year the dry season was barely discernible from the wet. There had been little fruit and the orangutans had been eating primarily bark and young leaves. Now once again there was some fruit in the forest, and Evonne and Carl hastened to sample everything. But they still spent most of the day eating bark and leaves. Perhaps there wasn't enough fruit to sustain them.

I didn't see Cara, Carl, and Cindy again for another month. Soon after I began following the trio, they met up with Beth and Bert. Comfortable traveling on his own now, Bert was becoming somewhat impetuous. When Beth and Bert arrived, Cara was sitting with a broken branch in one hand, picking burr fruits with her other hand, cleaning them, and popping them into her mouth. Bert ambled over and started picking burr fruits off Cara's branch. Had he been Carl, he would have been attacked immediately. But Cara good-naturedly paid Bert no heed. Later Bert even slyly put his hands to Cara's genitals. Cara twitched. Bert withdrew his hand but then tried again. Cindy moved down to where Bert was sitting and watched intently. Bert lost his nerve and moved away a few feet. A few minutes later, however, he was back.

The drizzling rain became heavier. Cara collected Cindy and moved into another tree. Bert raced after Cara. But when Cara nested to get out of the rain, Bert returned to the burr fruit tree where his mother, Beth, was still eating.

I had been observing Cara and Bert and had not paid attention to Carl, who was also in the burr tree. When I saw him, I did a double take. Carl looked hideous. He had lost all the hair on his head and shoulders. His bare skin reminded me of elephant hide, thick, leathery, and deeply folded. I was shocked. Carl seemed to have some kind of mange, but I did not know enough to be sure. Aside from his skin and coat, Carl seemed normal. Perhaps that is a bit like saying, aside from a patient's breast cancer, she's healthy.

The only change in behavior I noticed was that Carl was scratching much more than usual. In fact, whenever he stopped moving, he scratched. I hadn't noticed this earlier because most orangutans scratch a great deal. Some of their desultory scratching doesn't seem to be related to itching at all. It is almost as if they have an inordinate need to keep their hands busy and, since unlike humans orangutans do not smoke or carry worry beads to fiddle with, they scratch. Sometimes they scratch their heads; sometimes their knees. Any spot seems to do. But Carl's scratching was different. He scratched repeatedly with long, intense strokes. He sometimes stopped eating to scratch. I wondered if Carl's condition was contagious.

I started monitoring Cara closely. She also scratched a great deal. But so did Beth and Maud. The rainy season had arrived, and the wet clothes on my damp skin made me itchy, too. Perhaps Carl was suffering from a nonlethal, noncontagious disease like eczema.

Rod and I discussed the fact that we were objective observers. It was not our place to interfere with the phenomena we were studying. In the classes I had taken at UCLA in the mid- and late sixties, budding anthropologists and primatologists learned to put their emotions aside, observe, and not interfere. Even if we had decided to treat Carl, we had no way to capture him or to identify his condition. There were no veterinarians in Kumai or Pangkalan Bun, and the two doctors in the area were poorly equipped for diagnosis; they had been of little help with infant orangutans Barbara and Tony. A trip to Jakarta could take a week or more, and once we were there, who would we talk to who would recognize Carl's symptoms? We told ourselves that Carl's condition was probably transitory. Perhaps the mange was a psychosomatic reaction to the stress in his life. Or an allergic reaction. He might recover spontaneously.

Although I was very anxious about Carl, I was relieved that Cara and Cindy did not seem to be affected. I was wrong. Three weeks later I met the trio again. My heart sank when I saw Cindy. She was now just a skeleton, and half her hair was gone. I could see the vertebrae of her spinal column through her skin. Whereas previously Cindy was full of energy, always jumping off Cara the moment Cara stopped, now she clung to her mother constantly, her eyes closed. I wanted to weep. I had never seen Cindy lose her grip, but now holding on seemed all she could do. Every so often, she would slip down Cara's body. Cara would gently lift her up, nuzzle her face, and put her back in a more normal position such as on her shoulder.

The next day Carl left Cara. A few hours later he encountered Martha, Maud, and Merv. Much to my surprise, when Carl began eating on the same branch, Martha charged him. He fled silently. First his mother, then Beth, and now even Martha! But Carl didn't even squeal in protest. The next time Carl saw Martha and Merv in the distance, he quickly moved away. For several days, Carl was alone. Then he encountered Cara briefly, but it could have been any adult female orangutan for the interest they showed in each other. When they moved on their separate ways, I decided to follow Cara.

I never saw Carl again. Had I known that would be the case, I would have followed him ceaselessly. But as worried as I was about his condition, I never imagined that he would die. At age nine or ten, Carl was well past the stage of infant vulnerability. Although he looked terrible, as far as I could tell, he had not lost his appetite or his energy. The last time I saw him he was moving in the trees about 150 feet away.

For the first time, Cara was scratching vigorously. Although she still had all her hair, I knew that whatever Carl had, Cara had too. Less than three weeks later, I found Cara again in the late afternoon. I saw Cindy on Cara's neck and wondered why she was so still. In the fading light, it was difficult to see clearly. The next morning Cara left her night nest alone. My heart stopped. Cara defecated and then scratched her back by rubbing it along a branch. She moved back to the nest, picked up Cindy, and put her on her neck. My heart broke. Cindy was dead. Cara went about her business of foraging and moving between trees as vigorously as before. There was no change in her foraging routine. But Cara seemed distraught; she kept looking at Cindy. Clouds of flies buzzed around Cindy's body. She must have been dead for some days.

While Cindy was alive, Cara had groomed her only occasionally. Now she groomed the little body a dozen times a day for several minutes at a time. Cara inspected Cindy's body with her lips, then put her lips to Cindy's mouth. I was deeply moved by how devoted she was to Cindy, even in death. Her tenderness was tragic and horrific. Cara would gently pick up Cindy's hand in her hand, and lift Cindy's head and look at her face. From the forest floor sixty feet below, I caught whiffs of rotting flesh. I wanted to vomit.

The fourth morning that I followed Cara, she left Cindy in her night nest. After Cara nested that evening, I ran to Camp Leakey and brought back Rod and Mr. Ahmad. They retrieved Cindy from the nest. Cindy's body was petrified; she was just shriveled skin and bone. She looked like an Egyptian mummy, cut loose of its wrappings. Amazingly, Cindy's body was free of maggots. By constantly grooming her and then leaving her in a very high nest, Cara had protected her from the flies.

Be careful what you wish for. It just possibly could come true. My wish came true. I held Cindy in my arms as I carried her body back to Camp Leakey. I was numb. So was Rod. It was as if we had stumbled into a nightmare and couldn't wake up. The next morning we took samples to find out what had killed her. Deprived of Cara's careful grooming and the high nest, Cindy's body was now covered with maggots.

In my archaeology days I had learned about taphonomy, the study of what happens to animal bones after death. The reason for studying bones is to better understand the distribution of fossils. Paleoanthopologists have long puzzled over why so few hominid bones are found in forest environments. I decided to measure the rate of deterioration of Cindy's bones. I needed to do something, to make her death meaningful. Since Cindy had been left in the trees by her mother, we decided to put her back. We made a little nest about eleven or twelve feet high in some small trees near camp. The nest was low enough that we could periodically climb up and monitor Cindy's bones. In the Kalimantan way, our plan came to naught. A few hours after we put Cindy's bones in our carefully constructed nest, a wild pig came by, pushed over the small trees that supported the nest, knocked Cindy to the ground, and ate her whole. Not a scrap of Cindy was left.

❧

Cindy's death, Carl's disappearance, and Cara's illness left me desolate. In a way only people who have spent much time alone can understand, the wild orangutans had become almost family. Rod and I each did much of our work alone during these years. Often we alternated observing the same orangutan. Sometimes we simultaneously followed different orangutans in different parts of the study area. For days at a time, except for the hour or two in the dark of early morning before we each trudged out to a nest and the hour or two in the dark after we returned to camp for supper, most of our waking hours were spent in the company of the wild orangutans.

Humans are gregarious primates. We even have a word for those rare individuals who choose to live in solitude, "hermit." Those who dedicate themselves to the church, whether nuns or monks, frequently sever their normal relations with other people. It is considered one of the greatest sacrifices a human can make. We humans have an exceptional capacity to bond. Not only do we bond with each other, but we bond with other species. Witness a man and his cat; a woman and her dog. I remember once seeing an episode of a TV science fiction series where a spaceship goes to a distant planet to pick up a stranded scientist who had crashed years earlier. All his crewmates had been killed in the crash. Alone for twenty years, he had bonded with a robot, an "android" who crashed with him, and refuses to leave the robot behind. Alone in the forest day after day, I bonded with the orangutans.

Cara was the female I had followed most intensively. I looked forward to seeing her in the morning. I became deeply involved in her relationship with Carl. It was like the daily unfolding of a soap opera, and like many soap opera fans, I became addicted. It wasn't just me. One day Rod returned from an all-day follow of Cara. He was wet and cold, his clothes plastered to his body like a second skin. Nonetheless, he was grinning broadly. "You know," he said, as he peeled off his wet clothes, "that Cara's kind of cute. If I were an orangutan, I could really go for her."

"Cute" is one of the last words I would have used to describe the hot-tempered, strong-willed, almost imperious Cara with her black face and steely gaze. But I understood what Rod was saying. In the absence of other companions, I, too, had begun to depend on Cara, Beth, and Georgina for "human" contact. Fourteen hours by myself in the depths of the forest made me lonely in a way that few human beings experience.

The relationship between a free-ranging orangutan and a human will always be asymmetrical. Our species needs contact; we crave other human beings. The orangutan is a universe unto herself, with only her dependent offspring of any account to her. Cara's relationship with me could never be reciprocal. I needed Cara much more than she would ever need me. The emotional aloofness of the orangutan females was alien to me. I couldn't have penetrated their universe even if I could have climbed up into the canopy with them. We were divided by at least ten million years of separate evolution.

Yet I had come to depend on Cara, Beth, Georgina, and other orangutan females I followed alone in the forest. I was very attached to the ex-captive orangutans, too, but our relationship was one of parent and offspring. The adult female orangutans were more my peers. Rod was a devoted spouse, and I was grateful to have him. But no matter how close you are, one person cannot fill all your emotional needs. I developed relationships, single-sided ones but relationships nonetheless, with the wild adult female orangutans.

After Cindy's death, I saw Cara one more time. Her mangy appearance reminded me of Carl when I first noticed that something was wrong with him. We had sent skin samples and organ tissue from Cindy's body to a group of U.S. Navy medical researchers who were working in Jakarta, hoping they could tell us the cause of her death. The medical researchers found nothing. I began to suspect that Cindy had died of starvation. If her mother was sick, as Cara now appeared to be, perhaps her milk supply had dried up. That would account for Cindy's skeletal condition. But we still had no clue as to what was wrong with Carl and Cara.

Rod and I talked for hours about what we should do. We wrote long letters to people in North America who we thought might be able to help. I watched other orangutans for symptoms. We searched for Cara and Carl, hoping to encounter them one more time. But over the weeks and months, no matter how often we searched or where we searched, we couldn't find either one. At every new encounter with a wild orangutan, my heart would race. "Is it Cara?" "Is it Carl?" But it never was.

After many months, Rod and I reluctantly concluded that Cara and Carl must be dead. But I felt the uncertainty of a wife whose husband is missing in action. There was no conclusion. There was no goodbye. But there was no body, so there was always hope.

As years wore on, I wondered if what had happened to Cara, Cindy, and Carl had been anomalous. I vowed that the next time, no matter what, I would not sit and just observe. If a wild orangutan needed help, I would spring to action no matter what the cost.

Four years after Cara's disappearance, some of my assistants observed a wild female with little hair, apparently starving, on the edge of the study area. The new assistants were Dayaks, who have a strong tradition of hunting. The skills and techniques they had developed for hunting proved invaluable in studying and saving orangutans. The Dayak assistants made a lasso of vines, climbed up into the trees, and lassoed the sick orangutan female. We now had an extensive inventory of medicines in camp. Rod treated her with an antimite solution, vitamins, and antibiotics, and released her. We didn't know her, and orangutans look very different once their hair grows back, so I can't say positively that she lived. But we think she did. This time, we were ready. When Carl and Cara were stricken, we weren't prepared.

Nothing in my life to that point devastated me more than Cara's, Carl's, and Cindy's deaths. TP's abrupt disappearance had been a shock, like hearing that a friend who had boarded a small plane for Borneo's uncharted interior was missing and feared lost. Though unlikely, it was not impossible that he might reappear. Cara's loss was traumatic. It was like watching helplessly as a relative slowly dies of cancer.

Rod, too, was flung into depression. In retrospect, I can see that this was a turning point for him. Gradually, his attitude toward the wild orangutan research began to change. He lost interest in the ongoing stories of the individual orangutans we had been following. Before, Rod always had been eager to discuss and analyze our research findings; now his attitude seemed to be, "So what? You already know that; you already understand orangutans." Up 'til then, Rod had been my staunchest supporter, the one who urged me on when I was discouraged. Now he began questioning the importance of long-term studies in scientific disciplines as diverse as biology and astronomy. Once very motivated and idealistic, he started evaluating scientific research entirely in terms of cost-benefit.

Looking back, I think that on some level Rod felt that he had failed Cara, that he had failed in the role of male protector of females and their young. Rather than mourning Cara, he threw himself almost with a vengeance into the fight to save the forest from loggers. Daredevil action and risky confrontations were his painkiller. At the time, however, I was too numb myself to understand what Rod was going through.

We would never be quite the same again. Our idyllic Garden of Eden existence had been shattered. We had been living in a delusion brought about by our youth, our isolation, and our North American upbringing. Like so many Westerners, especially the flower children of the 1960s, I had been partially seduced by the "naturalistic fallacy." Nature was pure and noble, beautiful and bright. Nature produced happy endings. In traveling to the tropical rain forest, Rod and I were fulfilling our generation's dream of "going back to nature," returning to the Garden of Eden. But gardens are made by humans, to please human sensibilities. To maintain a garden, one must keep nature at bay — weeding, pruning, spraying, watering, fencing. A garden is Nature tamed, domesticated, civilized. In the beginning, there was no garden, there was only Eden. Our original home was not a garden but a wild place, where Nature reigned. I was learning that Nature clean and pure was also Nature brutal, ruthless, and savage.

As I looked at the artwork that filled every corner of traditional Dayak life, I saw everywhere the motif of the serpent-dragon, Nature herself. She appears on everything from kitchen utensils to burial monuments. I couldn't get away from her. In Dayak cosmology she represents the earth and is the ultimate protector of humans. But it was the serpent in Judeo-Christian tradition who offered Eve the apple from the tree of knowledge. That apple symbolized the beginnings of culture, hunting and gathering, the domestication of plants and animals, and ultimately modern science and technology. For the first time, I was glad that Eve had tasted the forbidden fruit. Nature had offered humans a way out, through the development of culture. We have clothes, shelter, cultivated food, medicine. As I visualized one lone nest swaying somewhere in the green canopy with Carl's bones and another with Cara's maggot-ridden remains, I wept. Nature had not offered them a way out.

The impact of Cara's death on my research also was devastating. I had committed myself to studying individual life histories. A year earlier Throatpouch, my most habituated adult male, had vanished. Now the adult female I had observed most often had died. Had I been studying a troop of baboons, I would have habituated the whole group. If one or two individuals had died or disappeared, I still would have had the troop. The study could have continued uninterrupted. But orangutans must be habituated one at a time. The fact that TP or Cara had accepted my presence did not mean that another orangutan would allow me to observe him or her. With each new orangutan I had to start from the beginning. I had invested the better part of three years in TP and Cara, and now they were gone.

I decided that as much as I wanted to collect detailed life histories of specific individuals, I could not afford to put all my scientific eggs in one basket. I decided that unless there was a strong reason to observe a particular individual continuously, such as consortship or pregnancy, I would limit my follows to five days (which I later extended to ten days), then look for another orangutan. I knew that this decision was scientifically correct, but it did not ease the pain of TP's disappearance and Cara's death. I kept wondering what I was doing wrong. Was something happening that I hadn't seen?

Sometime later, when I was analyzing data for my Ph.D. thesis, I began to see a pattern. During the few months before Carl had fallen ill, fruit in the forest had been exceptionally scarce. An unusually dry year, which local people characterized as the worst in living memory, had been followed by a very wet year in which the fruit failed. The flowers didn't develop properly, rotted, and fell. I didn't see another good wild durian crop for several years. I never saw such a paucity of fruit, before or after. Fruit is the orangutan's mainstay. When there is much fruit in the forest, over 90 percent of the orangutan's diet may consist of fruit, and there are many days when the orangutans eat nothing but fruit.

For months, Cara and Carl had been subsisting primarily on bark. The other orangutans in the area whom I frequently observed, such as Beth, Ellen, and Georgina, survived the fruit famine. But Carl, who was traveling and feeding on his own for the first time, Cara, who had just weaned Carl and was now nursing Cindy, and Cindy, who was a tiny infant, were all in vulnerable states. I will never know exactly what killed them, but starvation played a role in their premature deaths. I had not understood how close orangutans live to the edge. As a sheltered Westerner, I had not understood the saying, "Food is life."

But I saw it when ex-captive orangutans, after a year or two in the wild, suddenly returned bone thin, seeking food in camp. I saw it when one of my Dayak assistants stumbled upon the freshly dead body of an emaciated stranger, a wild adult male orangutan who had arrived in the study area only days earlier. I began to understand that the tropical rain forest, packed to the brim with life, was a deadly place where the competition for food was paramount.

One or two of the people to whom I had written in anguish about TP's disappearance and Cara's death wrote back, admonishing me to "let nature take its course." They implied that I was being sentimental; that I was getting too involved with my subjects; that, in trying to save orangutans, not just study them, I was behaving too much like a woman. Lacking the skills and experience to do anything, Rod and I partially succumbed to the belief that scientists can study nature objectively, from a distance. But this, too, is a fallacy. Humans have already interfered with the natural world to such a degree that almost everything that happens on the earth now bears our fingerprints. We hold the smoking gun. The question is not whether to interfere, but how to interfere, for what purposes. Of all the people who wrote back, Jane Goodall was the most forceful on that point: "By all means, you must save them." But by that time it was too late.

Although I couldn't pinpoint the cause of Cara's death, I was convinced that, ultimately, somehow, humans were responsible. Cara wasn't killed by poachers, her head and hands hacked off for sale as trophies, the fate of Dian Fossey's beloved mountain gorilla "Digit." Cara did not die of an infectious disease imported by humans, as may have been the case with a number of chimpanzees at Gombe Stream during the 1966 polio epidemic. Cara had not been kidnapped as an infant and deprived of maternal care, like Tony and Barbara. Cara was a seemingly healthy, vigorous orangutan in her prime. She had raised her son, Carl, to the point of independence and given birth to an alert, lively infant, Cindy. Of all the orangutans I had observed, Cara seemed to be one of the most competent and determined, one of the ones I would have picked as a survivor. And then she died.

Most likely Cara's death was the result of a chain of small events that deprived her and her offspring of some essential vitamin, mineral, or other nutrient, weakening her immune system. People who are malnourished or suffering from vitamin deficiencies are disadvantaged in fighting off infections, whether bacterial, fungal, or viral. Sometimes the body turns on itself. The first link in this deadly chain may be something small and apparently insignificant. I was reminded of an old parable:

> For want of a nail, the shoe was lost; for want of a shoe, the horse was
> lost; for want of a horse, the rider was lost; for want of a rider, the battle
> was lost; for want of a battle, the kingdom was lost.

In natural systems, small changes can have enormous impact. A tidal wave begins with a ripple, a hurricane with a breeze.

Digit's murder at the hands of poachers was horrifying and tragic. The chimpanzees at Gombe suffered cruelly from polio. But in these cases at least we know the cause of death and can attempt to prevent future deaths from the same causes. Cara's death from unidentified causes is more common, more insidious, and more dangerous. Countless individual animals and plants slip into oblivion every day, their deaths unnoticed and unexplained. With relentless regularity, whole populations and entire species vanish. We know something is happening, but we don't know what it is, how it started, or where it will lead.

I am convinced that Cara was the victim of human encroachment, however indirectly. Experiments with rats and dogs support the conclusion that Cara's death was related to malnutrition. In laboratories, it is difficult to infect healthy, well-nourished animals with mange. However, if certain vitamins are missing from their diets, rats and dogs get mange easily. We all intuitively recognize that mange is the sign of an unhealthy animal. In our everyday experience, the condition is linked to the image of a half-starved stray dog. Mange itself is not life threatening. But mange usually is a symptom of a deeper, underlying problem having to do with nourishment and the immune system.

Cara's death was caused not only by the unseen hand of natural selection, but also by the visible, iron-fisted hand of human progress. The rain forests of Kalimantan had remained almost untouched through the 1950s. This changed in the 1960s, shortly before I arrived. Now massive, large-scale logging began in earnest. Perhaps the destruction of the forest fifty or a hundred miles away from Tanjung Puting played a role in Cara's death, for example, by increasing the orangutan population around the reserve and hence competition for food. Cara's death came after an extremely dry season, followed by a year of constant torrential rain. Perhaps this unusual weather pattern was related to global warming, and Cara was a victim of human interference in the biosphere.

Doomsday predictions have become all too common. Dire warnings about global warming and acid rain, and urgent appeals on behalf of endangered habitats and endangered species, have become almost routine. We ban aerosol hairsprays. We recycle. We spend a hundred dollars to attend a star-studded fund-raiser or a rock concert to Save the Earth. We make a donation to help save the whales or the elephants. And then we go about our daily business more or less as before.

Cara's death brought me face to face with the bleak reality. Unless she had older offspring whom I did not know, Cara left no survivors. She and her family had vanished from the universe. Cara's family line was extinct.

For me, Cara's fate symbolized the fate of all orangutans, and perhaps all species, including our own. After Cara's death, I was even more convinced that saving individual orangutans was not enough. Each orangutan, particularly a female who generally stays in the same area of forest for her whole life, needs reliable sources of food. Food, for orangutans, means mature fruit trees, trees that in some cases may be hundreds of years old. Saving orangutans means saving old growth primary rain forest. I became convinced that if the tropical rain forest that constitutes the orangutan's only habitat were not saved, there would be numerous other Caras who quietly slipped into oblivion. I realized that if I wanted to return ex-captive orangutans to the wild, that there had to be enough wild for them to return to. That "going back to nature" means having enough real nature to go back to. Rod and I redoubled our efforts on behalf of the forest. We owed a debt to Cara, Carl, and Cindy, whom we had observed but could not save.

Rod and I didn't help Cara and her offspring, because we didn't know what was wrong with them and didn't know what to do. We rationalized our inaction on the grounds of "scientific objectivity." But when we turn our backs on compassion, because compassion is too difficult and its execution too complex, we risk our own humanity. We turn our backs, once again, on Eden and the state of grace given us there by the unseen hand of God. We owed a debt to Cara and her offspring simply because we are human.

# 15
# TANJUNG PUTING

Defeat is not the worst of failures.
Not to have tried is the worst of failures.

— *George Edward Woodberry*

Orangutans, Biafrans, giant sequoias, and
impoverished Brazilians are interchangeably sacrificed
so that the rich may dine on caviar or so that the
middle class may watch Monday Night Football
in an air-conditioned rec room.

— *John Nichols*

---

W HEN EUROPEAN EXPLORERS first ventured onto the shores of Borneo at the close of the Middle Ages, they found the third-largest island in the world. The island was almost entirely covered by lush primeval tropical rain forest. On Borneo's coasts, the Europeans discovered opulent, sophisticated Malay sultanates, the legacy of Hindu kingdoms whose rulers later converted to Islam. Aboriginal Dayaks, living much as their ancestors had for hundreds, perhaps thousands of years, occupied the heart of the island. A Portuguese explorer circumnavigated Borneo and mapped the outline of the island in 1627, but the interior remained unknown to the West until the late nineteenth century.

Even today, centuries after the first European explorers sighted the lush green shores of Borneo, 90 percent of the island is covered by forest. Timber fuels the economic engines of Sabah, Sarawak, and the provinces of Kalimantan. Only minuscule Brunei Darussalam, with its gargantuan oil reserves, has been able to spare its forests from the ax and the buzz saw. The human appetite for wood seems boundless. Today we consume approximately four billion cubic yards of wood each year. This is enough to girdle the globe several times if placed end to end. Enough, perhaps, to begin a plank trail through space toward Mars.

This wood comes from both temperate and tropical forests. About half, or two billion cubic yards, is burned as fuel each year. In much of the undeveloped world, wood is the only source of energy other than muscle and sweat. In the tropics, most wood is burned simply to cook food.

The other half of the wood consumed annually is cut commercially and turned into paper pulp, boards, and plywood. Paper pulp consumes only 20 percent of the commercial total. Until recently, virtually all paper pulp was produced from temperate softwoods. Softwood comes from the coniferous trees which ring the northern temperate zones, trees such as pines and firs, which have needles and are evergreen. Hardwood comes from deciduous trees, or trees with leaves. Hardwoods are found both in the tropics and in the temperate zones. Until the invention of enormous chipping machinery in the mid–1970s it was almost impossible to grind hardwoods into the chips that are pulverized into pulp. Now tropical trees increasingly provide raw material for paper pulp. The pulp ends up as paper, packaging, and convenience products such as paper towels and toilet paper.

Much of this wood still originates in the world's temperate zone forests. But as deciduous hardwood forests in the temperate zone are being depleted, the world is turning to the tropics. For the tropical rain forest nations, whose hardwood exports have skyrocketed in the last forty years, forests mean wood and wood means easy money. Who says money doesn't grow on trees?

When I went to Tanjung Puting, the huge mechanical chippers were not yet grinding their way through the world's rain forests. But Borneo's forests already were being cut down for logs, boards, and plywood. In the mid-1970s, a team of Canadian forest experts examined the logging situation in Borneo. The word in the corridors of local government was that the Canadian foresters had proclaimed that Borneo's rain forests were being cut down "too soon, too fast."

The conservation situation in the Kumai area when I arrived appalled me. A village of several hundred people, the Sekonyer Village stood inside the boundaries of the Tanjung Puting Reserve, right on the Sekonyer River. Other villages were located on the other side of the reserve in the east. Smaller settlements of extended families dotted the reserve. Hand-loggers worked openly in the reserve, and small local logging companies with legal concessions employed hundreds of men. Some of these companies, too, operated within the reserve. Local people from Kumai and the Sekonyer Village were practicing slash-and-burn horticulture within the reserve boundaries. All of this was legal, because Tanjung Puting was a game reserve, where only the animals were protected by law. This meant that trees could be tapped or cut and vegetation could be burned. Only the animals themselves could not be touched.

I didn't accept the concept of a game reserve. "How can a reserve protect the animals without protecting the habitat?" I asked every government official I met. It didn't matter that Tanjung Puting was officially a *suaka margasatwa,* a game reserve. I insisted that game reserves had to be de facto nature reserves in order to protect the game. In those days, my young idealistic mind wasn't choked by legalities. Tanjung Puting was a *cagar alarm,* a nature preserve, or it was nothing.

In reality, it wasn't a nature reserve, and it wasn't even Tanjung Puting. The official name was the Kotawaringan-Sampit Reserve, but this seemed un- wieldy. Tanjung Puting, the name of the peninsula that juts out into the Java Sea, was the alternate title, put in brackets after Kotawaringan-Sampit Reserve. I decided that Tanjung Puting was more appropriate and less confusing. On the dozens of reports I wrote the government, I exclusively used "Tanjung Puting" as the name of the reserve. I noticed that in their own reports and discussions, officials also started using Tanjung Puting. I hoped that someday the entire peninsula would be encompassed by the reserve, including the coastal areas currently outside it.

The western border of the reserve was the Sekonyer Kanan River, which ran past Camp Leakey. Several hundred people, mostly loggers and some farm- ers, lived upriver. The river was their only "road" to town. Along with other craft, log booms occasionally wound their way downriver past our camp. Be- cause I spent most of my time in the forest, away from the river, only getting back in the late afternoon, I had little contact with the traffic up and down the river.

One day, in my second month at Camp Leakey, I was sick. This was the first day I had not gone to the forest. As usual, Rod and Mr. Hamzah left shortly after dawn to cut trails. Mr. Yusuran no longer worked with us, having re- turned to Kumai. I spent the day alone in camp, lying on a reed mat on the flat top of our enclosed storage room. We didn't yet have a mattress on our loft. I had one of those "mysterious fevers" that Barbara Harrisson had warned me about when I had visited her years earlier in Ithaca, New York, in prepara- tion for Borneo. I was half dozing when I began to hear strange sounds. I couldn't imagine what they were; they sounded like thunder or cannons being fired. I heard the sounds at least a dozen times; they seemed to originate relatively close by, just north of Camp Leakey.

When Rod and Mr. Hamzah came back to camp that evening, I described the sounds. A knowing look flashed across Rod's face. "Trees!" he said. "Someone is cutting down trees! In our study area!"

"Are you sure?" I asked, not wanting to believe him. "How can you tell?"

A look of chagrin came over Rod's good-humored, open face. "I have cut enough trees in my life," said Rod, "to know the sound of falling timber. No doubt about it." As a teenager he had worked for logging companies in British Columbia during school holidays.

In my naivete, I was shocked that people were cutting down trees within earshot of Camp Leakey, inside the reserve. The Forestry Department in Pangkalan Bun had assured us that Tanjung Puting was a reserve and that no cutting was going on. I felt as though an ominous black cloud hung over Camp Leakey. I had just begun my orangutan study, and my study area was already being logged.

Rod decided that the next morning he would take our dugout canoe upriver and stop whoever was logging. That evening, by candlelight, we sat on the bark floor of our hut and, using our English-Indonesian dictionary, constructed a few sentences for Rod to memorize. The next morning I was still too ill to go with Rod, but I staggered down the slight incline to the shallow lake where we tied our dugout. It was only an hour or so after daybreak and the morning was still cool. A few lingering wisps of mist floated on the surface of the lake and shrouded the vegetation in mystery. In the distance, the soaring call of a gibbon reverberated through the treetops. Rod, weighed down by a large aluminum camera box, a machete, and a water container, teetered awkwardly on the slippery, shimmering logs, coated green with fungal slime, that we used as "trails" in the swamp. The logs rose a mere quarter of an inch out of the black water. I held our dictionary in my hands and coached Rod on the sentences he was still memorizing. "*Pemerintah,*" I repeated. He was having trouble with some of the longer words. "*Pemerintah.*" "Government." Rod planned on telling the loggers that he would report them to the government if they didn't cease. At the last moment, I handed him the dictionary as he got into the dugout. After adjusting his gear, he put the dictionary in his camera box and paddled off alone in the direction of the Sekonyer Kanan River, two hundred yards away.

I went back to the hut and lay down. The raging fever continued. Shortly after Rod left, I heard the first trees crash to the ground. The trees continued to fall intermittently all morning. Then, in the afternoon, the crashing stopped.

The afternoon gradually became evening. I waited and waited for Rod. My apprehension grew. It became dark. I became anxious. Worst case scenarios formed in my mind: Rod's body, chopped to mincemeat by loggers, floating on the river, Rod lost alone in the tangled vegetation, Rod held captive by vicious outlaw loggers who gloated over their felled Western prize.

Isolation frequently brings heightened affection and emotional intensity. By the time Rod and I finally went to Borneo, we had been together for more than five and a half years. While we loved each other greatly, the honeymoon was over. The waiting period in North America had been emotionally bruising. We couldn't make any plans because we thought we might depart for Asia at any moment. The constant uncertainty had battered our life together. But now, in the forest, Rod and I were each other's sole companions. We grew increasingly united and totally dependent on one another. We became each other's television, telephone, and newspaper. Sometimes weeks would go by without Rod or me seeing another human face.

In the darkness of our hut, relieved only by the flame of a single homemade lamp, an old cloth sticking out of a sardine can filled with kerosene, I contemplated losing Rod. I should have stopped him. I should have insisted that Mr. Hamzah go with him. Perhaps, despite my fever, I should have gone with him myself. My regrets grew. I felt tearful. What would I do without Rod, my husband and best friend? The prospect was too dreadful to contemplate. In my fever, I dozed off into a fitful and uneasy sleep.

Suddenly, the door burst open. Rod stomped in. With his camera-box strap and his machete belt crisscrossing his bare chest, he looked like a Mexican bandito. He was wet and barefoot. Behind him in the darkness were a dozen or so Melayu men. Two or three of them wore shirts and long trousers, while the rest looked bedraggled and in tatters. None were smiling. All had machetes. A few had axes.

"Who are they?" I asked.

"Loggers!" said Rod triumphantly. "I'm taking them to town tomorrow to see the Forestry Department chief."

Mr. Hamzah came to our hut. He looked hesitant and worried. He said to me, "Big trouble. These are important people. Their leader is the brother of the Sekonyer Village chief." I didn't say anything, but I thought to myself, "It doesn't matter who their leader is; they still got caught logging in the reserve." Mr. Hamzah quickly boiled some rice and fried some sardines for the group and made cups of hot sweetened tea. We didn't have enough tin cups and plates to go around, so the loggers ate in shifts. Rod and the village chief's brother ate together last. Too sick to act as host, I went back to bed. Rod spent half the night talking in the flickering light with the better-dressed men in the group. The loggers were crammed into our tiny hut, sleeping on the reed mats that covered the bark floor. Relieved that Rod was back, I fell asleep almost immediately.

After breakfast, Rod left with the loggers in the motorized longboat we had acquired recently. He came back two days later. Finally, we had a chance to talk. Most of the loggers had insisted on being let off at the Sekonyer Village, Rod told me, and he let them go. But he took two of the leaders to Mr. Aep, the forestry chief in Kumai. Mr. Aep acted embarrassed and wouldn't look Rod in the eye. Finally Rod took the village chief's brother alone to Mr. Aep's boss, the Forestry Department chief in Pangkalan Bun.

The official didn't say much. He listened uncomfortably, shifting in his seat and avoiding Rod's gaze, while Rod told his story. Finally, when Rod was finished, the official leaned over to the village chief's brother and said firmly but quietly, almost as if he hoped Rod wouldn't hear, "Don't embarrass me again, especially in front of Mr. Rod and Mrs. Biruté. Don't log near Camp Leakey again." That was it. The official rose to let Rod and the logger know the meeting was over. No fines! No indictments! Rod was disappointed, but there was nothing more he could do.

It did not surprise me that Rod could round up a group of loggers and bring them in, single-handed. In our short time in Kalimantan, I had discovered that we seemed to have an electric effect on local people. It was just the way things were. People acted as though we were apparitions.

I remember once sitting in the swamps at dawn, alone beneath a wild orangutan's nest. The orangutan hadn't stirred. Suddenly I heard the faint crunch of feet on dead leaves. I glanced up to see a Melayu wild-rubber tapper picking his way along the tree roots, carefully avoiding the black pools of the swamp. He was oblivious of my presence. Over his shoulder he held the long, razor-sharp metal stick he used to slice open the bark of wild rubber trees. On his back was a homemade *kiba,* a wood and rattan backpacklike container to hold his wild rubber sap. He was barefoot. His white shorts were made of cloth retrieved from a flour sack, and his shirt was so threadbare and worn that the colors could not be discerned. In contrast, tightly wrapped around his waist was a new-looking, brightly colored sarong, sewn together to form a loose tube. Now he wore the sarong as a belt, but at home in the evening it would serve as a wraparound skirt (which both men and women wore); at night it would become a blanket. On his head was a black velvet mosque hat. His machete was strapped to his side with a coarse rope.

The tapper continued carefully high-stepping toward me in the shadows. He was very close, but he still hadn't noticed me. Conscious of the need to be polite, I said cheerfully, "*Selemat pagi, Pak*" ("Good morning, Sir"). The Melayu rubber tapper jumped three feet into the air. He jumped so quickly and so high, the expression "jump out of your skin" came to mind. Then he turned and shot across the swamp, giving new meaning to another expression, "walk on water." I continued sitting under the orangutan's nest in the shadows amid the vegetation. My visage must have seemed eerie, like a washed-out hallucination. I was sitting silently under a tree, in a place where people rarely go. When the local Melayu went into the forest, they often sang and chanted loudly, as though to keep the wildlife — and the spirits — at bay. I sometimes did the same to keep my courage up when I walked in the forest in the total darkness of early morning. I am convinced the rubber tapper thought I was a ghost. I doubt that he returned to the area. This was not an isolated incident; several times we heard rumors that a new, pale ghost (namely me) had appeared in the forest.

Before Tanjung Puting could be protected, everyone had to agree on the reserve's location. When we arrived in Indonesia, Mr. Sinaga, the head of P.P.A., Indonesia's Nature Conservation and Wildlife Management Agency, had loaded us down with maps. Some of these were copies of old Dutch maps made early in the twentieth century. When the Dutch colonial government and the Sultan of Kotawaringan, in his capital, Pangkalan Bun, created the Kotawaringan-Sampit Reserve in the 1930s, no ground surveys were made. The sultan and the Dutch merely drew lines on a map.

On one of my first days exploring the forests around Camp Leakey, I unexpectedly found a trail. It was absolutely straight and a yard wide, with every single tree obstructing it cut down. When I inquired, I was told that this was the northern boundary of the reserve, cut by the Forestry Department a year earlier. About every two hundred yards was staked with a painted black and white ironwood marker. The trail was everything a reserve boundary should be.

There was only one problem. The boundary was in the wrong place. According to the old Dutch maps, Camp Leakey was well within the reserve. But according to the Forestry Department's own beautifully demarcated boundary,

Camp Leakey was several miles north of the boundary. This meant that legally my camp and even much of my study area were outside the reserve. Clutching the ancient Dutch maps like sacred scrolls, Rod and I leaped into battle for the forests of Tanjung Puting.

The first struggle was with groups of local loggers and farmers like the ones Rod had brought back to camp while I was sick. These men were hand-loggers, equipped only with machetes and axes. They laboriously chopped down trees with traditional iron tools that probably had been used for thousands of years. A dozen men could cut down perhaps a dozen trees in a day. But it took weeks to drag the cut logs out. The hard labor sculpted the small, slim bodies of the Melayu into gleaming bronze works of art, with every sinew taunt. When Rod and I heard trees crashing, we investigated and evicted the loggers. Even so, by the end of the year, many of the magnificent trees that had risen out of the lake downstream from Camp Leakey were gone. They had been cut down to use as floaters for the heavier ironwood and *ramin* logs being brought downriver. The giant silhouettes of these tall trees, which I had glimpsed through the gray rain on my first day on the Sekonyer River, had been eradicated.

Without discussion or a conscious decision, Rod and I had divided up the work. I concentrated on the wild orangutan research and the rehabilitation of wildborn ex-captives, and Rod took charge of protecting the reserve, chasing the loggers whenever we encountered them. The loggers soon learned to keep out of earshot of Camp Leakey. Gradually, Rod went farther and farther afield on his patrols.

Rod assumed with passion his heroic role of evicting illegal loggers. He was born to it. Rod was short by North American standards, barely edging five eight in stocking feet, but in coastal Kalimantan his powerful, stocky body made him a giant among the diminutive, slender Melayu men who wore their colorful sarongs with almost feminine grace. I, too, confronted loggers when I came across them in the reserve. What made us effective was that we didn't have the slightest doubt about our mission or the righteousness of our cause, protecting orangutans and their tropical rain forest habitat. We were so sure of ourselves that local people assumed we had the right to evict them from the reserve.

I remember an encounter with five or six men I discovered along a swamp-edge trail, splitting a newly cut *ulin* ironwood log into roof slats. The log was about six feet in girth and probably represented a three-hundred- or four-hundred-year-old tree. *Ulin,* or ironwood, is a very heavy wood that does not float. As calmly and politely as I could, I explained that logging was not permitted inside the reserve. The men stood absolutely still, their bodies gleaming with sweat, their faces sullen. I did the talking; they listened. A slight noise caught my attention. I glanced over and saw another man crouched in the bushes, hiding. I continued my speech, asking them politely if they understood. The men did not respond. A cold fury swept over me. For some reason, the sneakiness of the crouching man bothered me. Did he intend to ambush me? I strode to the bushes, grabbed the man who was hiding by the collar, and pulled him to his feet.

"What are you doing there?" I demanded. "Why are you hiding?"

"Oh, I'm just watching the leaves," he said, smiling brightly.

My adrenalin still pumping, I let him go. I don't know what possessed me. There I was, in the middle of nowhere, a lone, unarmed woman surrounded by half a dozen men with machetes and axes. I looked around the circle of men again, then turned on my heel and walked away. I could already feel the machete I expected to hit my back at any moment. My back quivered. The machete never came. I walked away untouched. When I returned to the spot the next day, the men had gone, taking their roof slats with them.

Later, as I replayed the scene in my mind, I realized that, striding unexpectedly into their midst, I must have struck the loggers as some unholy being. The man in hiding probably had been trembling like a leaf, terrified. I called him *Tuan Daun,* or "Mr. Leaf." After this incident, I saw *Tuan Daun* near the Sekonyer River several times. The moment he saw me he would leap to his feet, smile broadly, and wave. Other loggers would also return my greeting, as if we were the best of friends. Local people may not have understood who we were or what we were doing, but they seemed to accept our right to protect the reserve. Our confidence that we were doing the "right thing" was our power.

The confrontations with local loggers continued. Our primary weapon was talk. Our Indonesian rapidly improved, because we talked to every local person who would listen. Indonesian democracy is based on the concept of *musyawarah,* discussion and deliberation. Many Indonesians believe that majority-style democracy as practiced in the West is simply tyranny of the 51 percent over the 49 percent. Indonesians believe that decisions have to be unanimous.

Consensus, or the appearance of consensus, is crucial. It's also very important that everyone be given a chance to speak. Everyone's opinion matters, although, of course, the opinions of older people, or of people with more status, matter more.

As befits a traditional society, when local people speak in groups, they speak formally. The ability to speak eloquently and extemporaneously is highly valued. I was astonished how Indonesians, who never pushed themselves forward, would nonetheless stand up and pontificate in a polished manner for an hour as though they had spent days preparing their speeches. The ability to persuade with reasonable and rational arguments was very important.

In Indonesia I learned to talk. I learned that no matter what happened, if you talked you postponed the inevitable, and possibly you postponed disaster. As long as you talked, you had a chance to persuade. In Indonesian society, talk became a weapon in the defense of forests and the orangutans.

Rod had always liked to talk. Indonesia is a tolerant but predominantly Muslim society, where men sometimes speak for the women in their family, so Rod often took the lead. But since women may speak for themselves, I also talked to anyone who would listen. I talked to local loggers; I talked to local officials. I talked to local men; I talked to local women. We talked so much that the Maduran *Bupati,* Major Rafii, who was the highest local official in the region, started bringing official visitors to Camp Leakey, turning them over to us and whispering, "Take them to the forest and give them your speech." Meanwhile he could sit back, relax, and take a breather from the numbing round of ceremonial duties required of government officials. Of course, the ex-captive orangutans at Camp Leakey always stole the show. They never failed to captivate local visitors and officials as well. Sugito's antics, stealing food, holding hands with visitors, and showing off with acrobatics in the trees and vines, punctuated our talks on the importance of orangutan conservation.

The local people listened. They understood. One man who farmed in the upper reaches of the Sekonyer above Camp Leakey coined the phrase *gudang biji* to explain why the reserve was important. He explained that Tanjung Puting was a "storehouse of seeds" for the future.

Two years after our arrival, we felt satisfied that real progress had been made in preventing local logging. We knew we were having an effect when local loggers began arriving in Camp Leakey to ask our permission to cut stands of trees in the Sekonyer Kanan River catchment area. On one occasion a man who had a crew of twenty or more loggers came to see us. The man was relatively well educated, dressed entirely in Western clothes (no sarong wrapped around his neck or waist), and wore shoes rather than sandals. He made us a formal offer. On the edge of my study area, deep in the forest by the Raden River, a small tributary of the Sekonyer Kanan River, was a place where *kruing* proliferated on a bit of dry ground. A member of the dipterocarp family of trees, *kruing* provided valuable timber. The proximity of these *kruing* trees to the river meant he could transport the logs to Kumai economically. He formally offered us 10 percent of his gross sales if we allowed him to cut the *kruing*.

By now, Rod and I were dressed in rags. We were covered with weeping sores. We were feverish with malaria and weakened by parasites. Almost certainly, we were malnourished. Rod and I looked at each other in amazement. We shook our heads. We said as politely as we could that while we appreciated his thinking of us, we did not have the right to give away the trees in the forest. Our simple answer was "No." Nobody could log this forest; this was a reserve. It was a place reserved for orangutans and all other plants and animals. This was a *gudang biji,* a storehouse of seeds for the future. I explained to the logger that when all the forest in Kalimantan was gone, his grandchildren would still be able to find ironwood and *kruing* trees in Tanjung Puting. If all the mature *kruing* trees were chopped down, where would people get the seeds? At least one place had to be protected for the future. That place was Tanjung Puting. I also explained that while he couldn't log here with his twenty men, neither could anyone else. The forest was protected for everyone's grandchildren.

It was almost dark when the logger finally got into his small motorboat, started the engine after a few false tugs on the rope, and began chugging down the river. Although we saw him in Kumai occasionally, we never again saw him or his crew on the Sekonyer Kanan River. Those *kruing* trees still stand tall in the depths of the forest next to the now overgrown Raden River, where virtually no humans have trod for twenty years. The trees have had twenty years to become taller, more magnificent, and even more valuable in a world starved for timber.

Ironically, just as we were convincing local people that Tanjung Puting was for orangutans and trees, not for logging and farming, a new and more powerful threat materialized.

We had been at Camp Leakey for more than two years. The Sekonyer Kanan River area was almost free of loggers. But rafts of logs still floated downstream toward the sea on the other branches of the Sekonyer River. One day we noticed that the log booms suddenly had stopped. It was spooky. Abruptly, the Sekonyer River, which had been clogged with booms, boats, and people, was empty. Because I spent most days in the forest, Rod noticed the change first. We couldn't imagine what was going on.

It was the rainy season, which made searching for wild orangutans especially difficult. The whoosh of rain and wind created a thousand phantom orangutans moving through the treetops. Orangutans seemed to be everywhere, yet they were nowhere to be found. The torrential rains typical of wet season afternoons penetrated to the forest floor. I knew that during the rain orangutans typically huddled under a fan of leaves or in a hastily built nest in the treetops. Sometimes they looked so cold and miserable I wanted to rush out and embrace them. Of course, I knew I could not. They were too high up and too shy and wary. But I also knew their discomfort would end quickly. As soon as the rain ended, the relatively coarse hair of the orangutans would dry out within minutes, as if they had blow-dryers. I, on the other hand, would remain soggy, my clothes clinging to my skin like enormous Band-Aids, until I reached camp in the evening, peeled off my wet clothes, and dried myself with a towel.

Even so, I welcomed the downpours. After sitting out the rain, orangutans become hungry. At the first opportunity they race to the nearest food source. Sometimes they do not even wait for the rain to end. The best time to see and hear orangutans on a rainy day is when the rain peters out, the clouds lift, and the birds and insects begin to sing.

Just after a heavy rain, I spied adolescent female Noisy with subadult male Howard traveling rapidly through the trees. I walked through the forest, observing the two wild orangutans. Slumped and tired from a full day's search, I crossed a slash line. The slash line was like a slap in the face. It was brand new. The whiteness of the newly exposed wood where the trees had been slashed and the bright red of the newly painted numbers seemed almost alive, like flashing lights in the deep dimness of the forest. The slash line had been made only hours earlier. Whoever made it was confident and bold. Out in the open. I had been in Borneo long enough to know that it was a logging company's "cruise line." Someone was "cruising" for timber right in the middle of my study area, marking off sectors for cutting.

I stopped following the wild orangutans, hoping that I could find them again before they nested for the night. I followed the cruise line for over an hour, but I didn't see anyone along the line, nor did I hear voices in the forest. I noticed that the damp earth of the cruise line only had footprints going in one direction. Obviously the cruisers had not left the forest. But it was getting late. Confused, I started walking along *Jalan Toges,* listening for the sound of people. Then I turned a corner of the trail and saw a line of men coming toward me. Upon seeing me, the first man in the line leaped behind the second man in the line, cowering.

The second man obviously was the team's leader. He was instantly identifiable by his bright yum-yum yellow hard hat and high-top logging boots with thick soles. He did not seem particularly surprised to see me in the forest. We spoke. My initial suspicion was correct. The line had been made by a major logging company named Kayu Mas. He was a Kayu Mas employee from the East Borneo boomtown of Samarinda. The other men with him were locals, which explained why one of them had jumped behind the leader in fright upon seeing me. I explained that no logging was permitted in this area.

"Oh, is this your concession?" asked the hard hat from Samarinda, a mild tone of curiosity in his voice.

"No," I replied. "It is a nature reserve." I then launched into a long-winded explanation of what a reserve was and why logging was not permitted. He looked uncomprehending, as though I were relating a private fantasy.

The next day he and his crew marched into the forest again. We couldn't stop them. Several days later the Kayu Mas representative was on a plane out of Pangkalan Bun to Banjarmasin and on his way back to Samarinda, his task of surveying trees accomplished. Talking to local people we learned that the Forestry Department had stopped all local logging, whether authorized or illegal, because the rights to the whole northern part of the reserve and beyond, including my study area, now belonged to Kayu Mas. This was why the traffic on the river had stopped. From what I could understand, a consortium of military officers in Java had been given a concession to log the area by the forestry directorate in Jakarta. Since the military officers did not have logging expertise or machinery, the officers contracted out the timber rights to Kayu Mas. In return, Kayu Mas would pay the consortium a fee for every tree felled. For members of the consortium, the forests of Kalimantan, which probably few of them had seen, represented a fortune.

Our local victories had lulled me into believing that we had won the battle for the forests of Tanjung Puting; in fact, the war had not even begun. As if by unspoken agreement, Rod and I never discussed the possibility that we would lose and that my orangutan study and rehabilitation program would be ruined. Mentally, we dug our trenches and, using the only weapon we had — talk — went on the offensive.

The logging company, Kayu Mas, established offices in Kumai. They brought their heavy machinery in and built dirt roads through the forests north of Tanjung Puting Reserve. I was painfully aware that the study area was now theirs. I protested to whoever would listen. The *Bupati,* shrugging his shoulders, said he would do his best, but remarked that he was only a major and the people holding the concession were generals.

One day a colonel suddenly appeared at Camp Leakey in a speedboat. He was from Jakarta but had been in Kumai for some weeks, preparing for a helicopter inspection that the generals were going to make of their concession within the next few days. The colonel was as close to hysteria as I have ever seen a member of the armed forces. He had talked to the *Bupati,* who asked him not to allow logging in my study area. To ignore the *Bupati* would be politically impolite, but the generals from Jakarta were extremely powerful. Somehow the colonel had to justify to the generals why the Sekonyer River area should not be logged. He pleaded for maps, regulations, anything that would be useful when the generals came. He said that he knew we were an international project and that he himself realized the project's importance but that he needed ammunition to sway the generals. We gave him what we could.

The nightmares began soon after his visit. They were so vivid that sometimes, for a split second or two during my waking hours, I would remember part of the nightmare as if it had actually happened. In my nightmares, townhouses were put up in neat rows with manicured green lawns and sidewalks along *Jalan Toges.* Trucks roared down the paved road in front of the townhouses. Sometimes I would wake up in the middle of the night gasping for breath, drenched in sweat and terrified.

Eventually two personal appeals bore fruit. Typing by candlelight on the floor of our hut, I wrote to Mr. Sinaga, the head of P.P.A., explaining the situation and asking for help. I trusted Mr. Sinaga. There was a gruff openness and hearty smile on his face. After our first year in the field, we had visited him at his home in Bogor. As soon as he saw me, Mr. Sinaga said only three words: "*Hasil atau tidak?*" "Success or not?" I knew he only wanted a brief immediate answer, so I simply said "*Hasil*" (success). A smile covered his face just as a volcano's lava obliterates the landscape. His whole face became the smile. "Oh, I am so glad," he said, "I so much wanted you to succeed."

We had been in Bogor to renew our annual permits. Mr. Sinaga took me completely by surprise. "I like you," he said. "I know how troublesome bureaucracy can be. Rather than give you permission to stay in Tanjung Puting a year at a time, I will give you permission to stay in Tanjung Puting forever. I will not always be in charge. This way, if you later run into a P.P.A. official who doesn't like you or doesn't like what you are doing, he can't get rid of you simply by not renewing your reserve permit." Mr. Sinaga had just learned of Louis Leakey's death. He knew Louis Leakey was my mentor. He had corresponded with Louis. Now that Louis was gone, Mr. Sinaga was more protective than ever. Even though the P.P.A. permit was only one of many that I needed to continue my work, Mr. Sinaga's generous gesture removed one bureaucratic hurdle.

But Mr. Sinaga never answered the first letter I sent him outlining the gravity of the situation in Tanjung Puting. Nor did he answer my second letter. Many of the letters I mailed from Pangkalan Bun in those early days never reached their destinations. I assumed my appeals to Mr. Sinaga had gone astray. I was wrong.

When we finally arrived in Jakarta many months later, Mr. Sinaga told me that he had solved the problem. He had summoned the Chinese-born president-director of Kayu Mas to his home in Bogor. There, in his front room, on a Sunday afternoon, Mr. Sinaga extracted a personal promise from the elderly owner. Kayu Mas was logging a sizeable portion of another Kalimantan game reserve in East Borneo. They had been allowed to build a large road through the middle of that reserve. In return for concessions on the East Borneo reserve, Mr. Sinaga demanded that Kayu Mas leave Tanjung Puting alone. The Kayu Mas owner agreed. "That is the bargain," Mr. Sinaga explained to me. "As long as you continue your orangutan work in Tanjung Puting, Kayu Mas and the concession holders agree not to log." This gave me an impression of how things worked in Southeast Asia. It was important to maintain balance. If a reserve lost in one case, a reserve should win in another case. It was also important to keep score. The modus operandi was a favor for a favor.

I resolved then and there that I couldn't leave Tanjung Puting. I had always intended to stay, but this put an end to any thoughts whatsoever about leaving. It sealed my destiny. To ever leave Tanjung Puting would be to betray it. I now realized that every forest needed a guardian.

The next morning we drove to P.P.A. headquarters, an old, cream-colored colonial building in Bogor, to see Mr. Soegito, the official who had escorted us to Camp Leakey on our arrival. We literally ran into him when we pushed open the swinging doors to his office. Mr. Soegito was uncharacteristically excited.

"I have something to show you," he said jubilantly. "I don't know how this happened, but it did. Let me get the file."

He darted into his office, reached into his file cabinet, and produced a slim manilla folder. He opened the folder and pointed. I read eagerly. The letters inside were a consequence of our special relationship with a couple in Kalimantan Tengah.

Rod and I had been "adopted" by an assistant to the Dayak governor of Kalimantan Tengah. Years earlier, we had met Mr. Binti in the governor's office in Palangka Raya, the provincial capital, when we made a courtesy call with Mr. Soegito. The governor, Mr. Sylvanus, had not been very talkative, so we ended up conversing with Mr. Binti. He was a short, stout, middle-aged, outgoing Dayak, originally from Mandomai. He beamed constantly; it was the normal expression on his face.

The second time we met the governor and Mr. Binti was one year later in Banjarmasin, the capital of Kalimantan Selatan (South Borneo). We were returning from Jakarta. Since there were no direct flights to Pangkalan Bun, we stopped in Banjarmasin. We needed to visit Palangka Raya in order to get permits. After that we would return to Camp Leakey. Our first day in Banjarmasin, while checking into our cubbyhole hotel room, we heard that the governor of Kalimantan Tengah was in town. Everyone knew where he was staying. We called and got a seven A.M. appointment the next morning. From eight o'clock on, the governor had a full-day conference with the other three governors of Kalimantan. Early morning was the only time he could see us.

The next morning, Governor Sylvanus came into the room wiping his mouth. He had just finished eating breakfast when we arrived. Mr. Binti was with him. After some pleasantries, we said we had heard that the governor was returning to Palangka Raya the next day and asked if we could join his party. The governor asked us how much luggage we had. I replied, "Two large backpacks and several boxes of supplies."

There was an immediate rapid-fire exchange between the governor and Mr. Binti in a language other than Indonesian. I surmised that they were speaking their own native Dayak dialect, *Kapuas*.

Governor Sylvanus then turned to us and said that he would not be returning to Palangka Raya tomorrow. Besides, the governor would be using a speedboat, and our baggage would not fit. But Mr. Binti was leaving the next day and would be happy if we joined him, backpacks, boxes, and all.

We left at five the next morning in mists so thick on the still water that the cigar-shaped longboat plowed through the darkness as though through waves.

Mr. Binti stood on the bow holding a large flashlight whose rays barely penetrated a few feet into the blackness. The mists and fog swirled around us like whirlpools. Rod and I were so worn out from our trip that we promptly went to sleep, putting our fate in the hands of Mr. Binti and his flashlight.

By the time we awoke, we were well on our way to Palangka Raya, which was twelve hours from Banjarmasin. The route had taken us from the Barito River, so wide that from the middle you almost cannot see either bank, to the narrower Kapuas and Kehayan Rivers, two mighty waterways that emerge from Borneo's heartland. The river route from Banjarmasin to Palangka Raya was obviously an old, well-traveled pathway with cluster after cluster of houses and huts hugging its shores. The forests on either side had long been settled. Only in one or two places did I catch momentary glimpses of desultory troops of gray, long-tailed macaques, the smallest of the macaque genus of monkeys, sitting in the branches of low trees. During the whole trip I saw only one bird, a brown and white brahmany kite soaring eaglelike above the river. At Mandomai, Swiss-style A-frames galvanized me. I peered eagerly from the longboat, but saw no other sign of European missionaries. Mandomai was the site of a massacre of missionaries by the Dayaks in the latter part of the nineteenth century. At the time I didn't know that it also was Mr. Binti's home village.

When we arrived in Palangka Raya, Mr. Binti invited us to stay at his home. However, he had to check with his wife first. We waited at the dock for some minutes while he went home in a waiting car. The car returned soon afterward for us and our belongings.

As befitted Mr. Binti's high position in the provincial government, he had a spacious home with Western-style furniture and large paintings of Jesus on the walls. Mr. Binti had converted from *Hindu Kaharingan* to Christianity as a child, when he first attended school. We had our own bedroom, with a double bed and chest of drawers, as well as our own Indonesian-style bathroom, with a cistern of water and a dipper for bathing.

Mr. and Mrs. Binti's hospitality was so genuine that sometime during our stay I told Mr. Binti that we felt awkward that someone older and as respected as himself would call us "Mr." and "Mrs.," even though this was routine for the culture.

"Just call us Rod and Biruté," I told Mr. Binti.

Mr. Binti seemed startled by the suggestion. For a second or two, he looked at me intently, as though gauging the seriousness of my proposal.

Finally, he said, "All right, I will do so, but only if my wife and I can adopt you."

Rod and I agreed, and from then on, Mr. and Mrs. Binti proudly introduced us to everyone as their adopted children. We stayed in their comfortable home whenever we visited Palangka Raya. As our adoptive father, Mr. Binti personally escorted us to various government offices.

During that first visit, Mr. Binti explained the special place of Kalimantan Tengah in Indonesia's history. After independence, central Kalimantan had initially been part of the province of Kalimantan Selatan (South Borneo), whose capital is Banjarmasin. The predominantly Muslim Banjarese had long held sway over the Dayaks of central Borneo. In the 1950s, however, the Dayaks persuaded President Soekarno to grant them their own province, Kalimantan Tengah. A new city, Palangka Raya, was erected as the provincial capital, in the manner of the planned city Brasilia. My adoptive father had been part of that historic process.

Mr. Binti visited Camp Leakey numerous times. Since he was a provincial government official, his duties sometimes took him to Pangkalan Bun, which was a *kabupaten,* or regency capital. On one of these trips, we had explained to him the problem regarding Kayu Mas and logging in my study area. We had urged him to speak to the Forestry Department. His answer had startled us. He had said, "I can't speak to the Forestry Department directly. It is not my place. As a member of the governor's staff, I can only report to the governor. But I will tell him about the urgency of the situation. The governor can order the provincial head of the Forestry Department to take action." It seemed that channels had to be followed, no matter how high ranking the officials. Almost as an aside, Mr. Binti had added, "I don't want to be beaten up." The comment was so strange, I didn't even ask him about it. But I never forgot it.

Mr. Binti had not seemed hopeful. His usual sunny smile had faded.

"I will try," he had said. "I will do all I can, but I promise nothing."

The three letters spread before us in Mr. Soegito's file in Bogor did not mention Mr. Binti. But I knew they were the results of his efforts. The first letter was from the governor of Kalimantan Tengah to the provincial head of forestry, Mr. Widajat. The governor requested the restoration of the Kotawaringan-Sampit (or Tanjung Puting) Reserve boundary to accommodate the presence of the orangutan researchers. The second letter was from Mr. Widajat to the director general of the Forestry Department, Dr. Soedjarwo, proposing a temporary reserve boundary adjustment northward. The last letter was a decision by Dr. Soedjarwo himself, temporarily moving the reserve boundary northward well past our study area!

My nightmares of bulldozers along *Jalan Toges* ceased. Tanjung Puting was safe, at least for the moment. It had taken a double-lock process, both formal and informal, to protect the reserve: the formal process was the Forestry Department's officially moving the boundary northward, and the informal process was the agreement made in Mr. Sinaga's living room with the head of the logging company. Neither alone would have been sufficient. The Forestry Department, the logging company, and the local officials had all agreed in harmony. Because agreement was virtually unanimous, the pact would be upheld. In Indonesia, I would learn, getting as many parties as possible to agree was crucial to any undertaking.

Rod and I were jubilant. Indonesia had saved the reserve, at that time we thought, forever.

There was one major sore point left concerning the western part of the reserve: the Sekonyer Village at Tanjung Harapan was approximately one mile inside the reserve boundary. We repeatedly mentioned this to the local Forestry Department, asking them to move the village outside the reserve across the Sekonyer River. Moving the village seemed like a simple proposition. After all, the huts were constructed of wood, covered by bark walls and roofed with nipa thatch. Construction of new huts across the river would not constitute major hardship. There was only swamp on the other side of the Sekonyer River, which meant that the villagers would have to change from dry-rice to wet-rice agriculture when they made the move. However, it could be argued that changing agricultural practices would benefit the villagers. The villagers opposed the move, not because of their huts or fields, but because of their cemetery. Yet somehow I knew that if the villagers stayed inside the reserve, local logging, poaching of deer, and other illegal economic activities would continue unabated. Moving the village was imperative.

Mr. Binti's longest visit to Tanjung Puting was in 1974. He stayed for almost a week. On that visit he recommended to the *Bupati* that the wild-rubber tappers not be allowed within Tanjung Puting. "This kind of activity is not fitting inside the reserve," he said. The *Bupati* ordered them out.

Mr. Binti also had been appointed the head of the tourism committee for the province. I welcomed tourism, I told him. "Better tourists than loggers." Mr. Binti's committee came several times, inspected Camp Leakey, and wrote reports.

"What do you need for tourism?" Mr. Binti asked.

"A bridge," I replied, "so visitors can have easy access to Camp Leakey from the river."

Not long afterward, the provincial government of Kalimantan Tengah built a six-hundred-foot (two-hundred-meter) causeway from Camp Leakey to the Sekonyer Kanan River. A beaming Mr. Binti personally supervised the construction. The causeway still stands today and still ushers visitors and camp staff into Camp Leakey. We no longer had to wade in mud up to our thighs in the dry season, and in water up to our armpits during the wet season, to get to the river. And throughout it all, Mr. Binti kept saying, "You are my adopted daughter. Never forget that means that you are a child of Kalimantan Tengah and thus a child of Indonesia."

# 16

# WATERSHED

The woods are lovely, dark and deep. But I have promises to keep . . .

— *Robert Frost*

Destiny . . . is a matter of choice.

— *William Jennings Bryan*

B Y 1975 I had been in the field four years. The bridge linking Camp Leakey to the Sekonyer Kanan River had just been built, eliminating some of the camp's isolation. The bridge symbolized the various ways in which my work at Tanjung Puting was linking up to the outside world, through papers, trips to North America and Europe, and an expansion of the orangutan rehabilitation program. Camp Leakey would soon be transformed from a makeshift outpost into an established field station, recognized both in Indonesia and in the Western world.

The few previous studies of orangutans had lasted only a year or two. My uninterrupted four years were now the longest study of wild orangutans ever achieved. With 6,800 hours of observations, I felt I had more than enough material to begin writing my doctoral thesis.

I had left Indonesia briefly in 1974 to attend the Wenner-Gren Conference on Great Apes in Austria, where I presented a paper on orangutans. The conference was my first opportunity to meet other orangutan researchers. Richard Davenport, who conducted a pioneering field study of orangutans in the 1960s, was there, as were three younger men who had completed their studies just before I left for Kalimantan. David Agee Horr was outgoing and charming.

John MacKinnon was wickedly funny, with dark, dancing eyes and a cutting, brilliant British wit. John had just published a popular book on his orangutan studies, *In Search of the Red Ape,* and brought a copy for us to peruse.

Peter Rodman was quiet and serious. One evening after dinner, Peter and I sat in the lounge area, talking. I told Peter I was studying orangutans simply because I wanted to understand them; I didn't have an academic career plan. This seemed a revelation to him. His eyes focused on the distance as he mused about his own feelings while in the field. "All I wanted to do," I recollect him saying, "was collect my data, finish my thesis, and get a tenure-track position." At the time I thought to myself that this is the difference between men and women: Caesar said, "*Veni, vidi, vici,*" "I came, I saw, I conquered," and then he left. But a woman would have said, "I came, I saw, I stayed."

I was delighted to see Jane Goodall and Dian Fossey again. Although I had met Jane several times, I had spent very little time with Dian. Now Dian was almost maternal toward me. I had a large, festering tropical ulcer on my hand. During the eight days and nights that about twenty scientists were sequestered in an Austrian castle, in constant contact, only Dian noticed my oozing sore. When she saw my hand, she immediately marched me to her bathroom, washed the ulcer, and medicated it, all the while muttering, "How could you do this to yourself? Don't you know that this could be dangerous?"

Dian was fretting over a wicked-looking but ultimately minor tropical ulcer on my hand, when she had just had a bone in her leg reset. She had broken the leg some months earlier, but had let it heal by itself and it had not set properly. Coming out from Africa, Dian had been persuaded, at great effort by friends, to get her leg examined. The physician had to break the bone again in order to reset it correctly.

Dian's room was next to mine in the castle. One evening I knocked on her door rather timidly. Dian welcomed me so matter-of-factly, as if she had been expecting me, that I began visiting her frequently. I liked Dian. She was warm and energetic. She was also hilarious. When people describe Dian they tend to focus on her pain and her anger. What I remember is how much fun she was. She had a flair for slapstick, and used her tall, angular body to great comic effect. I can visualize her mimicking a hapless tightrope walker, teetering along an imaginary rope, arms outstretched. She loved double entendre, and often made sly, offhand comments that were easy to miss. Once, when Dian and I were traveling together, a porter handed her the baggage tags. Dian asked if the tags were for both of us. The porter said, "You're friends, aren't you?" Dian replied, "Well, yes, for now we are." That was typical Dian. I think one of the reasons some people found Dian "arrogant" was that they didn't pick up her dry sense of humor.

When we talked about our field experiences, Dian didn't mince words. She described how, during her first months in Africa, civil war had broken out in the Congo (now Zaire) and she was captured and held in a cage for public display. The other people in the cage were killed, but she was spared. Then she said, "Biruté, I was raped; I was raped," repeating the phrase as though she were reliving the experience. I got the strong impression that this was not the first trauma in her life, but had reopened an older wound. Dian had resumed her study in Rwanda. When she repeated the seemingly abusive phrases she exchanged with government officials there, I was incredulous. She would say, "Your mother's milk is white, but you're still black and you'll always be black."

"Dian!" I gasped. "How do they react when you say something like that to them?"

"Oh," Dian said, "they love it!"

"They like it?" I repeated in disbelief.

"They love it and ask for more!"

I was shocked. I kept thinking there must be something I was missing, something I didn't understand. Now I realize that what I was missing was an African sense of humor. This kind of banter, based in creative insults and one-upmanship, was African to the core. Dian fit right in. Obviously self-confident, Rwandan officials were not defensive about mere skin color.

A tall, coltish woman, Dian hovered at about six feet. Whereas I attended the conference in blue jeans and a simple cotton shirt, Dian wore pleated wool skirts, cashmere sweaters, and pearls. She was always well groomed and fastidiously dressed. In her own room after dinner, Dian put on a white lace, full-length dressing gown with a tightly tied waist, sprayed herself with expensive French perfume, and redid her coiffure and makeup.

I was astonished that this scientist, whom I almost revered, was so preoccupied with femininity. She had faced four-hundred-pound adult male gorillas in the wild, yet she seemed to define herself in terms of female attractiveness. I attributed this to her growing up exceptionally tall in the 1940s and 1950s, when such height was not yet in vogue for women. No doubt, some tall women from those times compensated for their "unfeminine" height by exaggerating the traditional pretty-woman-frilly-lace-and-ruffles effect. But it was more than a game of "dressing up." At times Dian's sexuality filled the room like a pungent aroma. In her own lair, her sexuality was so strong that even I felt it.

Late one evening I was in her room when one of the older, distinguished

American scientists knocked at her window, a wine goblet in his hand. He peered through the pane and, spotting me, quickly turned and stumbled away. "Biruté," Dian said firmly, "you must stop interfering in my sex life!" This was typical of her wit. It showed the double edge of African humor, where you make fun of an incident and at the same time trick the listener into thinking you might be serious.

Dian the sensitive, patient woman who had earned the trust of the wild mountain gorillas, Dian the swaggering mountain woman who bullied local officials, Dian the genteel Southern lady, and Dian the courtesan seemed totally at odds. But as I got to know her better, the different pieces of the puzzle began to fit. Although she was in her early forties, there was something child-like about Dian. She hid her vulnerability behind a tough, raucous exterior. It was a cover-up. Dian always seemed skittish, as if ready to flee at a moment's notice. Her perpetual watchfulness gave her the air of a fawn. But her wariness also made her furious in attack, as though she were fighting for her life.

At the conference Dian rarely spoke, but when she did, it was with bravado. Conservation was not on the agenda. However, during a brief discussion one afternoon, I mentioned a meeting with Indonesia's then vice president, the sainted Sultan Hamengkabuwono IX. Dian looked up from the round, green felt-covered table and said emphatically, "Biruté, I don't speak to vice presidents; I only deal with presidents!"

There was a long silence. Everybody in the room stiffened. I struggled to keep from laughing. The "putdown" was a soft version of the cutting humor she practiced with Rwandan officials. I recognized it as the act of a gentle woman who had learned the hard way that in Africa, niceness was equated with weakness, and the facade of toughness had to be maintained at all costs.

Jane Goodall and I spoke privately only a few times at the castle, as Jane was preoccupied with the conference and spent most of her time with Dave Hamburg, who was co-coordinator with her. It was he who told me that Jane was getting a divorce from Hugo van Lawick and marrying Derek Bryson, an older man of English origin, prominent in independent Tanzania's government. I was only mildly surprised. I remembered the moody van Lawick sitting alone in the kitchen at the Earl's Court Mansions flat in London five years earlier.

After the conference in Austria I flew to the United States. I spent two days in Washington, D.C., talking to Mary Griswold Smith and others at the National Geographic Society. Mary once told me that the reason she was assigned to

Cempaka, digging a hole with a stick. (*Rod Brindamour*)

Subadult male Rombe in one chair; Princess with her son, Prince, in the other, 1985. (*Noel Rowe*)

*Below left:*
Biruté and Rod with Sultan Hamengkubuwono IX, then vice president of the Republic of Indonesia. (*OFI*)

*Below:* Biruté with ex-captive male Gundul. (*Rod Brindamour*)

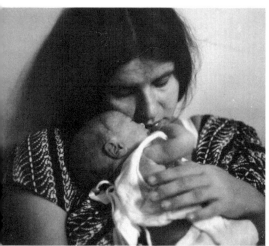

Biruté with her first son,
Binti Paul, eleven days
old. (*Rod Brindamour*)

Binti, age one, with Princess. (*Rod Brindamour*)

Binti, age two, standing
with Akmad. Siswoyo
is sitting in front. (*Rod
Brindamour*)

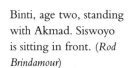

Binti watching Rio with
dipper at Camp Leakey.
(*Rod Brindamour*)

Biruté with doctoral committee members Bernard Campbell and Rainer Berger, after turning in her Ph.D. thesis, 1978. (*Joan Travis*)

Gordon Getty with Dian Fossey, Jane Goodall, Biruté, and Don Johanson, the discoverer of "Lucy," at Cal Tech in 1981. (*Joan Travis*)

*Below:* Gary Shapiro and Biruté with adolescent Rio on Biruté's knee. Gary is teaching sign language. (*Rod Brindamour*)

*Below right:* Biruté with Indonesian government official from Palangka Raya and orangutan. (*Rod Brindamour*)

*Above left:* Rio as a juvenile. (*Biruté Galdikas*)

*Above:* Biruté with Binti in the forest, watching wild orangutans. (*Rod Brindamour*)

*Left:* Biruté and *Pak* Bohap with their son, Fred, one week old. (*Biruté Galdikas*)

*Pak* Bohap and Fred, age one. (*Biruté Galdikas*)

Jane, three days old, with Biruté, Fred, and Binti in Vancouver, 1985. (*Family collection*)

*Above left:* Fred and ex-captive adult orangutan, Siswoyo. (*Biruté Galdikas*)

*Above:* Sam, a wild adult male. (*Michael Charters*)

*Left:* Biruté, Dian Fossey, and Jane Goodall. (*Joan Travis, OFI*)

*Above:* Camp Leakey from the air. (*Biruté Galdikas*)

Biruté (in hat) with Earthwatch volunteers. Gary and Inggriani Shapiro are in matching T-shirts in front. (*Biruté Galdikas*)

Jane, age two, at Camp Leakey. (*Biruté Galdikas*)

Jane, age four, with ex-captive orangutan Asep. (*Biruté Galdikas*)

Joan Travis, Biruté, Jane Goodall, and Dian Fossey. (*Linda A. Flynn*)

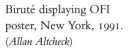

Biruté displaying OFI poster, New York, 1991. (*Allan Altcheck*)

Ralph, a wild adult male. (*Les Greenbaum*)

*Above:* Siswi, daughter of ex-captive Siswoyo, and Brooke, a young ex-captive male. (*Noel Rowe*)

*Left:* Biruté and Binti, age fifteen, in New York to receive Biruté's Eddie Bauer "Hero for the Earth" award. (*Ann Tompkins*)

Biruté, Jane Goodall, and Kelly Stewart, who studied mountain gorillas at Karisoke, at the Second International Great Apes Conference, Pangkalan Bun, Kalimantan Tengah, Indonesia, 1991. (*Biruté Galdikas*)

Jane Goodall's first story was that she was a female and about Jane's age. Louis Leakey met Mary when he was visiting Dr. Melville Grosvenor, the president of the society. Louis had liked Mary, and a few months later she was on her way to Gombe to help plan photographic coverage of Jane's study of chimpanzees, then in its second year. During my visit, Mary looked at Rod's photos and convinced other editors that it was time for a *National Geographic* magazine story.

Then I returned for a few days to Los Angeles. The smog was as thick and pervasive as I remembered, but on days when a breeze from the ocean cleared the air, the skies turned a brilliant Mediterranean blue. I was surprised by how much I had missed my family. I was delighted to see friends from UCLA. I couldn't tear myself away from the newspapers and news magazines in my parents' house.

Although I had been away only a few years, I felt a little like Rip van Winkle, awakening to find that decades had passed and the world had changed. At the Los Angeles airport I innocently picked up a "woman's magazine," flipped open the pages, and discovered a foldout of a naked man at the center. I was flabbergasted. Obviously, I had missed an important change in North American women's attitudes toward men. I also remember an interview with a reporter who was interested in my work. Suddenly a disembodied noise emerged from his clothes. I leaped out of my seat. For some reason, my first reaction was that the beep had something to do with a bomb. The reporter patiently explained that it was his pager, and then what a pager was. I didn't know such devices existed.

While I was in L.A., I discovered that my feet had widened considerably, probably because I went barefoot or at most wore sandals in Kalimantan. I simply could not squeeze my feet into the dress shoes I had left in California, and I had packed only running shoes and plastic sandals. I was scheduled to give a talk to supporters of the Leakey Foundation. Unable to fit into my shoes, I presented the lecture barefoot. I think Dian had similar problems. I have a clear memory of Dian, dressed in a well-cut Chanel-type suit and stockings, kicking off her shoes in mid-lecture.

Wearing a long, loose batik gown, I thought my feet would be hidden. Later I was surprised to learn that my bare feet caused almost as much comment as my orangutan research. I wasn't going native or making a statement. I just wanted to be comfortable. It was bad enough that a steel band was tightening around my head. By the end of the dinner before the lecture, I was sweating profusely even though I felt chilled. I knew it was malaria, so before I spoke I rushed to the washroom to take some malaria pills, as the doctor in Pangkalan Bun had instructed.

With my four-week exit visa about to run out, I had to return to Indonesia. I stayed in Jakarta for a short time, then flew back to Pangkalan Bun on August 17, Indonesia's Independence Day. I returned to Camp Leakey the next day.

⁂

During 1975, we embarked on a building program at Camp Leakey. Barbara Harrisson provided much of the inspiration for this expansion, as well as help in raising funds.

Barbara had visited Camp Leakey in 1973, when I had been in the field for two years. It was fitting that she was our first Western visitor. At that time, many considered her the world's expert on orangutans. In the late 1950s and early 1960s, while living in Sarawak, Barbara had studied wild orangutans and raised orphaned orangutans. Her book *Orang Utan* was the first book dedicated entirely to the red ape, and I had studied it closely before coming to Kaliman-tan. Barbara spent a week in camp. As usual, we received the telegram saying that she was coming long after she had left.

Barbara Harrisson was in her early fifties when she came to Camp Leakey. She was tall and lean and had close-cropped hair. She chain-smoked, drank her coffee black and hot, and brought along a bottle of whiskey. She wore a plain white T-shirt, tight blue jeans, and an armload of pure gold bangles. Barbara slept on a mattress directly on the floor of our hut. Almost every night she got into blanket-tugging contests with the ex-captive orangutans who shared our quarters.

Having raised orphan orangutans herself, Barbara was accustomed to their antics. What inspired her was my wild orangutan study. One morning I took Barbara to see Cara, Carl, and Cindy. As Barbara and I sat on the ground, Cara, who usually was belligerent and standoffish, suddenly descended to a branch right over our heads. Cara was as close as she had ever been to me. She ate bark off a small *habu-habu* tree with great abandon, seemingly oblivious to our presence. Barbara watched in awe. She continued staring as minutes passed, stretching into a half hour.

As we sat speechless, watching Cara strip the *habu-habu* tree with her pow-erful jaws and teeth, something happened. Barbara stopped looking at Cara and began to look at me with the same expression of wonder. It made me uneasy at first, but then I realized what had happened. The "crown" had passed. Barbara passed it to me. Barbara Harrisson was looking at me with a strong, steady gaze that signified new respect. Some of the awe she felt at seeing Cara so close was transferred to me. Looking straight at me, she said, "I promise you, I will help you." We talked very little in the forest, as was my custom around the wild orangutans. But at dinner that evening, Barbara said that in all her years in Borneo, she had never been so close to a wild orangutan. She promised to alert the world to our difficult situation. She was appalled by our living conditions. "Nobody should live like this," she exclaimed repeatedly. In truth, our hut was deteriorating. Barbara pulled out her checkbook, saying, "You must build a proper house. How much would it cost to build something that would keep your books and papers dry during the rain?" I ventured a guess: "Three hundred dollars." Barbara promptly wrote a check for that amount. She repeated that she would help find us funding once she returned to North America.

When Barbara left Camp Leakey, Rod and I accompanied her. Halfway to Kumai, we stopped at the Sekonyer Village to pay a courtesy call on the village chief, who was vigorous and middle-aged, with a pockmarked face and bright, dark eyes with a sly look.

The most famous American in Indonesia at that time was not the U.S. president or a movie star. Rather she was a self-proclaimed "anthropologist" from California. Wyn Sargent became notorious by marrying a warlike local chief in Irian Jaya, the Indonesian sector of New Guinea. "American marries tribal chief" read the local headlines, titillating the Indonesian public for years. When I first arrived in Indonesia, people on the street would ask me if I knew the famous Wyn Sargent. Indonesians never tired of talking about her and speculating about her motives. Wyn Sargent assumed almost mythical proportions.

She and her tribal warrior played the part. I saw fuzzy photographs of them in Indonesian newspapers and magazines. She was tall, lanky, and good-looking in her jeans, cowboy boots, and hat. She was as American as they get. He was naked and stocky, with a bone in his nose and a two-foot-long penis sheath. His naked body was covered in war paint. He would have been an award-winning cover for *National Geographic.* She could have been a cover girl for *Glamour* or *Mademoiselle.* She was white. He was black. She smiled. He scowled. She came from the most technologically advanced society in the world. He came from the Stone Age.

Wyn caused a sensation. There were very few North Americans in Indonesia at that time. "Mixed marriages" of this kind simply didn't happen. Indonesians invariably married within their social class and their religion. Wyn and her tribal chief repeatedly explained that the marriage had never been consummated. The chief had too much respect for Wyn to go to bed with her. After a short "honeymoon," Wyn went back to California, where she disappeared from public view.

Barbara had asked me about Wyn Sargent. With a twinkle in her eye, the recently divorced Barbara said that if she were twenty years younger, she'd marry a Bugis sea captain and travel leisurely in his schooner through the myriad islands of Indonesia. The Bugis were known as "sea gypsies."

When we arrived at the house of the Sekonyer Village chief, we introduced Barbara as our eminent guest from America. Barbara jangled her armload of gold bracelets to accentuate the point. As we sat drinking the inevitable cups of sweetened tea, a crowd of villagers gathered. Those who could not squeeze into the chief's hut hung from the windows and crowded the doorway. The village chief, probably to keep the conversation going, apologized that his wife wasn't there to greet Barbara. His wife had been in Kumai for some time. Barbara decided to have some fun.

"You need a second wife," Barbara said. "One who will keep you company in the village." She knew a Muslim man was entitled to have four wives if he could treat them all equally.

"Oh no," said the village chief. "Who would want me?"

"I do," said Barbara. "I'll be your second wife."

"Oh," he said cautiously. "Why should you want me? I am a poor man. You are a wealthy woman." He looked pointedly at her gold bracelets. The crowd of villagers was absolutely still, staring in wide-eyed astonishment. They understood the repartee because Barbara spoke Malay, which is so closely related to Indonesian that the two languages are mutually intelligible.

"What is wealth if a man and woman are interested?" Barbara rejoined. "Besides, you are young and vigorous."

"No," said the village chief, "I am old and poor. You don't want me, because I am poor. You are rich. Why should you want me?" Barbara had him on the run. She flashed her most dazzling smile while he squirmed in his seat, repeating, "I am a poor man. Nobody wants a poor man." The scene clearly enhanced his standing among his villagers. He was shrewd enough, however, to ensure that the exchange ended in a stalemate.

Rod and I saw Barbara off in Pangkalan Bun. I rarely went to Pangkalan Bun, but Rod had asked me to come for a specific reason. During his last trip to town, he had been approached by an air force officer. The officer invited Rod to his house to see a *kris* that his wife wanted to sell. If the wife couldn't sell the *kris* soon, she planned to send it to a dealer in Jakarta for sale there.

A *kris* is the traditional dagger that used to be carried by all men of high birth in Java and still is used on ceremonial occasions. The ivory, metal, or wood handle is ornately carved with figures to ward off evil spirits, and the blade is pounded and twisted into a spiral, said to produce a deep, jagged wound. Before a battle or an assassination, the owner would treat the blade with arsenic, and sometimes snake venom, to make the weapon more deadly. *Kris* lore runs deep in Indonesia. There are many stories about a *kris* talking, flying, turning into a snake, even fathering a human child. But most important, a *kris* often belongs to a class of objects called *pusakas*.

A *pusaka* has magical power. *Pusakas* stay with their legitimate owner; they cannot be stolen, because they eventually return to the man (or woman) who has the power. At the same time, the person who attains the power cannot forget the *pusaka*. Possessing the *pusaka* is crucial. It's almost like the Calvinist version of God's grace, which holds that you can tell who is meant for God's kingdom after life only by who is successful in this life. Similarly, you can tell who has magical power only by seeing who acquires and is able to hold on to a *pusaka*. Indonesia is full of stories about people who misjudged *pusakas*. For instance, a lowborn warrior won a battle and usurped a throne, but, being a commoner, he didn't realize the cosmic significance of the royal *pusaka* and allowed the family of the previous ruler to flee with it. The usurper wasn't king for long. "The *pusaka* always comes back to its legitimate owner," was a constant refrain. To many Indonesians, it is a law of nature.

Rod and I knew that some old, traditional artifacts could be bought in Pangkalan Bun. But we were hardly in a position to become collectors. The fact that Rod was excited by the *kris* intrigued me. Rod was not dazzled by aesthetics or the beauty of objects. He was more interested in function. He liked machines — he liked their precision and was quick to understand how they worked, how best to use them, and how to repair them. Motorcycles, planes, cameras, and computers all fascinated him.

When I saw the *kris,* I understood why Rod had been impressed. With a teak handle ornately carved in precise geometric patterns, a silver sheath embroidered with the graceful, flowing lines of Arabic script, and an extraordinary blade with two sinuous dragons curling along each side, the *kris* was magnificent. I bargained with the air force officer's wife and finally brought the price down to one hundred dollars. This was an enormous sum for us, but Rod and I both felt the same urgency. If we didn't buy the *kris,* it would probably be sold far away.

Mr. Binti, my adopted father, had told us of plans to restore the old sultan's palace in Pangkalan Bun as a museum. When it was done, Rod and I planned to present the museum with the magnificent *kris* so that it would remain in Kalimantan forever. Later an older friend in Pangkalan Bun translated the Arabic inscription on the sheath. Sometime in the nineteenth century, the *kris* had been sent from the sultan of Banjarmasin to a prince of Kotawaringan, the prewar sultanate whose capital was Pangkalan Bun.

After Indonesia became independent, the last sultan of Kotawaringan had taken much of his wealth and moved to Solo. But he left several sisters behind in Pangkalan Bun. One destitute sister lived in the decaying hulk of the enormous black ironwood palace, selling the remaining royal porcelain to eke out a living. Without asking, I assumed that the *kris* had been sold to the air force officer's wife by a member of the sultan's family. I dismissed as superstition the notion that the *pusaka* always returns to the rightful owner. Yet I never felt that the *kris* was mine. I believed strongly that I was merely a temporary guardian. For reasons I could not fully explain, I felt that the *kris* had to be kept in Kalimantan. Much later I learned that this particular *kris* was meant to pass through my hands.

True to her word, Barbara Harrisson went back to North America and campaigned on my behalf. Jane Goodall had already spoken to the New York Zoological Society about my study. When Barbara reinforced the appeal with a firsthand account of my work, they immediately offered a grant. Barbara also made an impassioned plea to the Leakey Foundation in Los Angeles, whose board promptly awarded me an eighteen-thousand-dollar renewable annual grant, with an implicit understanding that the grant would be continued until I obtained my Ph.D. When I received the letter announcing this decision, I literally jumped for joy. Eighteen thousand dollars to support a year's research seemed like a fortune. Adding to our bonanza, Mr. Sinaga, the head of P.P.A., spoke about my work to the head of a small Dutch foundation, which sent me nine hundred dollars simply on Mr. Sinaga's recommendation.

We received the letter from the Leakey Foundation shortly after moving into our new wooden house at Camp Leakey. The new house cost not three hundred dollars but fifteen hundred. Construction of the simple fifteen-by-twenty-four-foot wooden building took many months and two sets of carpenters. For me, it was the height of comfort. The house seemed spacious, clean, and almost elegant in its spartan simplicity. I was insulted when, a year later, a British consultant working with a U.N. agency took one look at the house and remarked, "If you're going to stay here, you must build yourself something permanent. You can't live in this small hut!"

Around the time we moved into our new house, the number of orangutans sent to me for rehabilitation began to grow. I desperately needed to expand our facilities so that I could deal with rehabilitation more systematically. This meant hiring new staff, whom we had to house, feed, and pay. We built three more structures, including a larger, more permanent wooden house, a dining hall, and a longhouse for staff. By the beginning of 1976, most of the structures found at Camp Leakey today were in place, including the tower and the six-hundred-foot walk-way over the swamp, built by the provincial government on the advice of my adoptive father, Mr. Binti.

To visitors Camp Leakey might have seemed quiet and dull, but to me it fairly bustled. In addition to Mr. Ahmad, his wife, Mrs. Bahriah, and their six surviving children, we had a second male assistant and two Indonesian biology students as well as two forestry men who had been assigned to guard the reserve. About ten ex-captive orangutans lived in or near camp, or visited on occasion.

In mid-1975, I brought four wildborn orangutans back from Jakarta. This was the first time that orangutans had been repatriated from the island of Java to their native Kalimantan. Equally important, the orangutans had belonged to two retired generals. The story appeared on the front page of newspapers all over Indonesia, and was repeatedly broadcast on the radio. Because of their own personalities, as well as their background, the generals' orangutans became instant celebrities. The adolescent females, "Siswoyo" and "Rinnie," and the subadult male, "Gundul," became important figures in my life. The other male, "Douno," returned to the wild in a week. Unwittingly, I had scored a public relations coup. The message was clear: the generals are sending their orangutans back to their home in Borneo. Orangutans are a protected species and should not be kept in captivity. The trade in endangered species is illegal, and pet owners risk having their captive animals confiscated. The message seemed to be heard at every level, from government offices in Jakarta to local villages. Indonesia's chief of police began speaking out against killing orangutans and issued a specific regulation forbidding police officers from keeping orangutans. Soon afterward, the Forestry Department of Kalimantan Tengah announced that it would begin sending wild-caught orangutans to our camp. Almost overnight, the ex-captive orangutan population nearly doubled.

With the number of ex-captives increasing, my rehabilitation program had to be reorganized. As before, the ex-captive orangutans were free to come and go as they pleased. We provided feedings of rice, milk, and fruit twice a day. In addition, we bought a relatively expensive microscope to track parasites in the orangutans' feces and strengthened the two-week quarantine for new animals with a regular deworming.

From the beginning, the ultimate purpose of my rehabilitation program was to protect the wild orangutan population and their forest habitat. This meant I had to be concerned about the ex-captive orangutans' genetic makeup and health, as well as their impact on the forest.

I didn't worry about genetic pollution, because the orangutans were from the local area. All orangutans belong to the same species, but the Bornean and Sumatran orangutans are distinct subspecies. Although they can interbreed, each has distinctive traits. I believed strongly that the integrity of the two subspecies — as well as the integrity of specific populations — should be protected. The reason is that natural selection has shaped these populations so that they are well-adapted to their particular forest. For example, an orangutan from a specific area might have an enzyme that detoxifies a plant frequently found in that area, an enzyme other orangutans lack. In mixing these populations we might be exposing them to "unnatural selection." We also might be destroying some of the genetic variability in the orangutan species. But under no circumstances did I feel that an orangutan should be denied rescue and release to the forest for genetic reasons. (Only once did I not accept an orangutan, and that was because she was Sumatran. I assumed that she would be sent home to Sumatra.)

To protect the wild orangutan population from new diseases, we tried to ensure that all orangutans returning to the wild were disease- and parasite-free. The wild orangutans, however, certainly were not disease-free, as Cara and others showed us. One adult female spent a whole day in her nest because of persistent diarrhea. I sometimes located wild orangutans on searches because they were coughing or sneezing loudly. Examination of feces revealed that many wild orangutans carried numerous parasites. Wild orangutans were not in isolation capsules as far as disease was concerned, even though their semisolitary population structure was not conducive to disease transmission.

The main threat to wild orangutans is habitat destruction: cutting down the primary rain forests, with the wild fruit trees that provide the orangutans' main food source. I worried more about food competition between wild orangutans and ex-captives than about any other issue in rehabilitation. If wild orangutans were devastated by lean fruit seasons, the addition of ex-captive orangutans might exacerbate the situation, particularly if large areas of forest were being cut down and the forests were being fragmented into isolated islands of trees. Orangutans could develop immunities to diseases; they could absorb new genetic material without changing dramatically. But ecology is the bottom line. Food is life; life begins with nourishment.

For this reason, I thought forcing orangutans abruptly to return to the wild was a mistake. Rather I favored a gradual process where the orangutan had the option of coming back to Camp Leakey for food. When the forest was full of productive fruit trees, the ex-captive orangutans could stay in the forest. But when a lean season began, perhaps it would be better for all if the ex-captives came back to camp and, thus, did not upset the delicate equilibrium of the tropical rain forest.

The loose, individualistic, and opportunistic society of orangutans, the seminomadic lifestyle of adult males, and the unpredictable fluctuations of wild fruit crops allows ex-captive orangutans to return to the wild. I suspected that some returning orangutans traveled until they encountered relatively unpopulated, ecologically attractive areas of forest where they could settle down. Others, especially females, remained in the vicinity. I respected the orangutans enough to know that when it came to evaluating forest conditions, whether in ecological or social terms, the released orangutans would be the best judge. I viewed my job as nurturing them, keeping them healthy, and providing an environment in which they could learn survival skills such as nesting and foraging. I wanted them to return to the forest on their own schedule.

Not everyone agreed with this view. A Dutch couple who had worked with orangutans in Sumatra visited Camp Leakey briefly. The Dutch researcher and his wife tried to persuade us that a sink or swim approach was mandatory. They argued that rehabilitation centers should process orangutans quickly, releasing and pushing them back into the forest almost immediately. Some would surely die, but others would survive. Perhaps such an "assembly line" operation was necessary in Sumatra where, due to tremendous deforestation, the number of captive orangutans was much greater than in Kalimantan Tengah. I listened to the Dutch couple's arguments, but I saw this approach as a last resort. To me, each orangutan needed to be treated as an individual, not routed to a depersonalized rehabilitation factory where he or she would become just another statistic in a conservation report.

The overriding issue, in my view, was keeping vast areas of primary forest intact. Forestry Department officials proposed all manner of schemes.

"Why," asked an official from Palangka Raya on a visit to camp, "couldn't we just collect all the wild orangutans in Tanjung Puting, expand Camp Leakey, and then build a fence or even a moat so that the wild orangutans would be safe and out of harm's way? If the orangutans were more confined," the official continued, "they would breed faster. After all, orangutans are an endangered species. This would be one way for them to produce more offspring."

I had just one question. "If we did this, what would happen to the forest?"

"Oh," the official replied, "we could log it."

I heard variations on the relocation theme again and again. Yet it seemed obvious that the best management plan for both orangutans and tropical rain forest conservation was to keep large areas of untouched primary rain forest and swamp intact. I stressed that we should interfere as little as possible. An environmental policy of bioregionalism — setting aside large areas of land to protect ecosystems in their entirety, rather than small patches of wilderness — would enable the orangutans to survive on their own as they have for millennia. A forest is more than a collection of trees. Replanted heavily logged areas and tree plantations would not replace the complex forest ecosystem, which had taken millions of years to evolve.

Another plan called for the construction of a fifty-foot-high observation tower and a mile-long, six-foot-high barbed wire fence. The watchtower made some sense, although I suggested that the ex-captive orangutans would eventually dismantle it. The observation tower was built, and this is exactly what happened, necessitating constant repair.

I argued vehemently against the barbed wire fence. Since orangutans are primarily arboreal, few would be kept in or out of the reserve by a six-foot-high fence, but some might be injured. Much to my relief, the local head of the Forestry Department built the barbed wire fence somewhere along the southern Tanjung Puting Reserve boundary. As far as I know, the mile-long barbed wire fence still stands rusting in the swamps, guarding the "land" approaches to Tanjung Puting. Fortunately, orangutans enter and exit the reserve along arboreal pathways.

The first returns of orangutans to the wild occurred around this time. Wildie and Subarno did not really count, as both were wild orangutans, recently captured and relatively unaffected by humans. Cempaka was the first "domesti-cated" ape, one who had lived in a house and been mothered by her human owner, to return to the wild. On the day I was to leave camp for the Wenner-Gren conference in Austria, Cempaka broke into Mr. Ahmad's hut, demol-ished some shampoo bottles, and stole some soap. Soap consists primarily of fat. Cempaka spent hours soaping her arms and licking the thick lather with her lips as if it were whipped cream. Because we only went to town once or twice a month, soap was a valuable commodity and Mr. Ahmad was annoyed.

Influenced by the Dutch couple's advice, Rod decided that it was time for Cempaka to return to the wild, like it or not. He hauled the compliant Cem-paka onto his back and informed me that he was taking her into the forest. When he told me this, I was washing my hair at the newly installed pump behind our house and in no condition to argue. Rod took Cempaka across the *ladang* to the forest. About one and a half miles from Camp Leakey he let her off his back and she climbed up into the trees. He left her sitting in a tree about thirty feet up. We never saw Cempaka again.

Did she sink or did she swim? I suspect she swam. Cempaka was one of the smartest orangutans I have ever known. I would have preferred to let Cem-paka herself choose when to return to the wild, but I feel certain she survived. A strong personality like Cempaka is clearly a survivor, whether in a cage in Palangka Raya or in the great forests of her birth.

By now Sugito, Rio, and Sobiarso had grown into big, bouncing, healthy juveniles with glossy hair. They still visited camp almost daily, but all three now nested in the trees. Rod and Sugito were still feuding. Although Sugito seemed fearful of Rod, he provoked Rod at every opportunity. For instance, Sugito would look at someone, look at Rod, bite the person, and then run away. If Rod wasn't there, Sugito wouldn't bite. Sobiarso and Rio were still together, occasionally sharing the same night nest. Sometimes they wanted to be carried, but far less often than before. Only Rio, who was both the youngest and the biggest, regularly demanded my attention and my thumb.

In 1975, on a visit to Jakarta, Rod and I met with Director General of Forestry Dr. Soedjarwo. I wanted to thank him personally for his support. Dr. Soedj-arwo was a very traditional Javanese who usually said very little but listened a great deal. I found his eyes almost hypnotic. Over and over people in Jakarta said that Dr. Soedjarwo was very powerful because he had built up the Forestry Department and the timber industry of Indonesia from scratch.

On the rare occasions when I visited Jakarta, I always tried to pay him a courtesy call. Like many traditional Indonesians, Dr. Soedjarwo woke up early for the first prayers of the day and received people shortly afterward. Sometimes I paid my courtesy calls at seven o'clock in the morning. Even then, clusters of people sat on the porch waiting to see him, with aides in attendance. I was slightly uneasy in the presence of such true power. But Dr. Soedjarwo always gave me his full attention. He seemed curious about why a young woman from California would leave her comfortable home to study apes in the humid, insect-infested swamps of Kalimantan.

Dr. Soedjarwo was sympathetic to conservation. I was told he gave a powerful speech to Forestry Department officials, saying that those who protected the forest helped to assure themselves a place in heaven. I began to understand that Dr. Soedjarwo's concern and curiosity, by themselves, helped to protect Tanjung Puting Reserve.

A year or so after we met Dr. Soedjarwo, the Forestry Department sent a team from Bogor to survey the Tanjung Puting Reserve boundaries. The team leader, Mr. Anwar, was a short man who weighed at least three hundred pounds. Merely walking seemed difficult for him. But Mr. Anwar relished fieldwork. Although a jovial man, he wore a black leather jacket that gave him a slightly menacing air.

From his tales of derring-do in various forests throughout Indonesia, it was clear that Mr. Anwar had a deep commitment to forest protection. He regaled our local assistants with long stories about his adventures and emphasized the importance of the work that they were doing, studying and protecting orangutans. Although we offered to share our home with him, Mr. Anwar preferred to stay with the assistants. Mr. Anwar lectured morning, noon, and night to the hapless local staff. It was almost a case of indoctrination. In my wooden house some distance from the staff quarters, I heard Mr. Anwar's loud voice last thing at night and first thing in the morning. During Mr. Anwar's stay, the local assistants walked around camp perpetually wide-eyed, as though they had undergone programming by some fanatic fringe cult.

As a result of Mr. Anwar's survey, the Forestry Department moved the boundary of Tanjung Puting westward, enlarging the reserve significantly. Camp Leakey no longer perched on the edge of the reserve but was now well inside it. The forestry officers evicted squatters from the area, even though some had planted coconut and rubber tree gardens.

Around the same time, the people of the Sekonyer Village voluntarily moved their settlement across the main Sekonyer River to beyond the reserve boundaries. To encourage the move, the government built a school and a mosque at the new location. The cemetery still stands where it was, inside the reserve. Moving the village had been a six-year campaign. But apparently in the end, the Sekonyer Village chief had seen which way the wind was blowing.

We now not only had more ex-captive orangutans to care for, but some of the new arrivals were older and larger than the members of my original "family." One of the generals' orangutans, Gundul, was the first wildborn subadult male ex-captive I had ever received. A subadult male orangutan doesn't look very big in a zoo, where you are separated from him by a moat or cage bars. A subadult male orangutan sitting next to you, with nothing between you, is an entirely different matter. Gundul was already the size of most adult females, but his body was more muscular and his canines were longer and sharper.

Gundul became Camp Leakey's self-appointed security guard. Late one afternoon, Gundul and I were alone at the end of the bridge when a wooden boat loaded down with about sixty local visitors from Kumai approached camp. I always attempted to provide cups of tea and a tour of camp, as well as a talk on orangutans and tropical rain forests, to local visitors. Gundul paced forward. His hair was erect, tripling his size. His eyes blazed. The transformation was amazing. He went down to the dock and hauled out of the water an enormous log which was at least twenty inches in diameter and perhaps ten feet long. Gundul heaved the log up and down, shaking it and bouncing it like a basketball. The captain of the boat, faced with a crazed, belligerent ape tossing a log in the air and uttering strange howls, turned the boat around and went straight back to Kumai.

This incident was one of many that fueled Gundul's local reputation. As I stood on the dock, wringing my hands because I could not stop Gundul, I did not realize that the incident was also enhancing my reputation. Many local people assumed that as I walked behind Gundul or other male orangutans who occasionally chased visitors, I was controlling the large red apes. Talk began to circulate in Kumai that I was a *pawong,* a person with the mystical power to call wild animals and command them.

Not long after Gundul arrived, we built a new feeding platform in the deep swamps across the Sekonyer Kanan River, some distance from camp, to encourage the older ex-captives to become more independent. We ferried food across to the platform in a dugout. One day, I went to the platform with a visitor from North America and one of the cooks. When Gundul arrived, he ate a little but seemed distracted. Suddenly Gundul grabbed the cook by the legs and wrestled her down to the platform, biting at her and pulling at her skirt. I had never seen Gundul threaten or assault a woman, although he frequently charged male assistants. The cook was screaming hysterically. I thought, "He's trying to kill her." I had a vision of Gundul tossing the cook off the platform into the shoulder-deep swamp water and drowning her.

I attacked Gundul with all my strength, trying to jam my fist down his throat. I shouted to the visitor to take the dugout back to Camp Leakey for help. My repeated blows had no effect on Gundul; but neither did he fight back very aggressively. I began to realize that Gundul did not intend to harm the cook, but had something else in mind. The cook stopped struggling. "It's all right," she murmured. She lay back in my arms, with Gundul on top of her. Gundul was very calm and deliberate. He raped the cook. As he moved rhythmically back and forth, his eyes rolled upward to the heavens. I was in shock. I felt as though this were happening to other people somewhere else, and I was watching from a distance. I have no idea how much time passed.

Gundul let the cook go, stood up, and, soundlessly, moved off the feeding platform into the trees. It was over just like that. The cook had a look of relief on her face; she seemed grateful to have survived. She assured me that she was all right. No one had come to our rescue, so we agreed that I would swim back for help. It took me more than a half hour to reach camp. The assistants and students gathered on the bridge were shocked when I appeared. The visitor who went for help did not speak Indonesian and her pantomime had convinced them that the orangutans at the feeding station were running amok. Indonesian men are not ashamed to admit fear. If I couldn't control Gundul, they had reasoned, who could? Fatalistically, they had assumed the cook and I were dead. I ordered the assistants to take a dugout to the feeding station and bring back the cook.

Although badly shaken, the cook had not been injured. Later, her husband's reaction gave me insight into Kalimantan thinking. "It was just an ape," the husband said. "Why should my wife or I be concerned? It wasn't a man." Unlike the average North American, traditional people didn't seem particularly upset by such incidents. In their view, an orangutan raping a person was no more shameful than a leopard jumping out of a tree and attacking someone — and much safer.

I thought back to my response, years earlier, when Mr. Heurybut had warned me about orangutans raping women. I had not believed him. However, he had gotten it only half right. Wild orangutans seemed to view humans as alien beings, first to avoid or threaten, and second to ignore. But Gundul had been raised by humans since infancy. His "mother" and "father" had been

Indonesians. Not surprisingly, he related sexually to women as well as to female orangutans. I believed that we could not judge orangutans by human standards. Except for the fact that he had chosen a woman, Gundul was behaving like a normal subadult orangutan male. Nonetheless, his behavior was worrisome.

The rehabilitation program was reaching a critical point. Rod and I were able to cope with the ex-captives, but for different reasons. Rod was the dominant male in camp. He inspired absolute respect, almost fear, among most of the orangutans, including Gundul. My relationship with the ex-captives continued to be warm. While I sometimes had difficulty throwing orangutans out of buildings, they did not chase or threaten me.

Unfortunately, this was not the case with the Forestry Department guards, the university students, and the local assistants. The orangutans chased the local men when they brought food out to the feeding platforms. The assistants went in pairs, armed and armored with machetes, boots, and large, brightly colored plastic garbage can covers as shields. Usually, the orangutans ignored camp visitors (although Gundul was hostile to local men). The apes seemed to know that visitors were not part of the permanent dominance hierarchy in camp and there was no percentage in trying to dominate them.

In 1975, Rod and I went back to North America together for the first time. I had visited briefly, but this was Rod's first trip home. As before, we had only a one-month exit visa. We savored going back to North America. Famished, we engaged in last-chance eating, indulging every culinary whim. We amazed hotel staff by insisting on dessert after breakfast.

We spent several days at the National Geographic Society offices in Washington, D.C., where I completed my article for the magazine and worked with the photo and caption editors. The article came out later in 1975 with a cover showing me carrying Sobiarso in one arm and Akmad standing bipedally in front of me. It eerily duplicated the cover shot of Dian Fossey taking two captive gorillas on a walk in the forest, which had appeared five years earlier. Someone at *National Geographic* commented, "After this story comes out, your lives are going to change." Rod and I were skeptical, but willing to be convinced. As it turned out, we gained our fifteen minutes of Warholian fame. We received a number of letters from friends and some from strangers saying, "We saw your article." That was the extent of our celebrity. The main change was that Rod finally got paid for his photos.

In his precise, engineer's way, Rod calculated that the payment meant that he had been working for approximately ten cents an hour all these years. Rod was good-humored about the calculation, but he mentioned it twice. We laughed. For me, the fact that someone actually paid me to write a magazine article on orangutans was a pleasant surprise. For Rod, however, working for ten cents an hour under grueling conditions wasn't altogether funny. I sensed that he felt the joke was on him.

While we were in Los Angeles, I telephoned Dave Hamburg, who, with Jane Goodall, had organized the conference on great apes in Austria. He insisted that Rod and I get full medical checkups while we were in North America and recommended a "brilliant diagnostician." The doctor was extremely thorough, running us through a battery of tests. To my surprise, he called after the test results came back and said that I was fine, but Rod might have a rare respiratory infection. The physician wanted Rod to come back for more tests. Unfortunately, the doctor called the day we were departing for Indonesia. We were due to leave for the airport in an hour.

After talking to the doctor, Rod handed me the phone with a quizzical look on his face, as if to say, "What are we going to do now?" He was puzzled. Rod felt well and he looked well, but the doctor was insistent. I talked to the doctor, then handed the phone back to Rod. Rod told him we would discuss the situation and call him back; we needed a few minutes to make a decision. Our visa expired in two days' time and we would lose one of those days crossing the international date line. The trip itself took thirty hours. If we were not on that plane, our visas would expire.

As soon as Rod put down the receiver I said, "I don't know about you, but I'm going to be on that plane to Indonesia." Rod didn't say anything. I realized that I had blurted out the words too quickly, but it was too late to retract them. Had I been the one with the mysterious malady, I would have made the same decision. "Look," I continued, "we can't hassle with the visa. You know how difficult that would be. When we arrive in Jakarta, we'll go to the best hospital. You can have your medical records sent from Los Angeles. You can check it out in Jakarta. It may not be anything."

Rod reluctantly agreed. When we called back, the doctor kept insisting that it would be best for Rod to stay in Los Angeles for a few more days. Rod assured the doctor that he would have another examination in Jakarta. He put down the phone and we raced for the airport, making the plane by only a few minutes.

At the "best" hospital in Jakarta, we found an American physician. After examining Rod, the Jakarta doctor expressed great admiration for the Los Angeles diagnostician, saying that he would not have suspected that anything was wrong. "Medicine is as much an art as a science," he stated. He prescribed some medicine, and told Rod to take it for several months and then come back for tests. When Rod was reexamined, the infection had disappeared.

"You see," I repeated to Rod. "It wasn't anything serious." But Rod was not so sanguine about the incident. After it was all over, Rod began to brood. Until then, Rod told me, he had felt invincible in the forest following wild orangutans. It was the delusion of unpained youth. Rod had been in dangerous, even life-threatening situations before, but this time he had been sick without realizing it. This was Rod's first conscious brush with mortality. It struck a chord that refused to stop reverberating, especially in the shadow of Cara and Carl's disappearance.

While we were in Los Angeles, my mother had a premonition. When I told her that Jane Goodall and Hugo van Lawick had divorced and Jane had remarried, my mother vehemently shook her head in disapproval, like the Roman Catholic she is. "Crazy. The whole world is crazy," she said. Then she leaned over to Rod and me as we sat together on the living room sofa. "Don't you dare," she said. "Don't you dare ever get a divorce," she said again, as if she saw the possibility opening up before her eyes.

My brother-in-law, Harry Franz, my sister Aldona's husband, is an inspired amateur photographer. During our visit, Harry took some photographs of Rod and me. He blew one up and presented it to my parents. The photograph was so strikingly beautiful that my mother framed it and hung it on the living room wall. It shows two people, Rod and me, our faces relaxed, smiling, very close together, very young, very innocent, looking as if we were barely out of our teens (although I was nearing thirty), and very much in love. It never occurred to me that, in terms of our marriage as in so much else, 1975 would be a watershed year.

In 1975 I began spending less time in the forest and more time in camp, transcribing my handwritten notes and organizing my data for my dissertation. Rod, Mr. Ahmad, and a junior assistant did much of the searching. When an orangutan was spotted, I dropped my paperwork and went to the forest to follow.

In March the study area, which had seemed very quiet for several months, exploded with long calls from every direction. Nick, the magnificent, even-tempered young adult male who replaced TP, had now been in the study area for almost two years without once leaving the vicinity. I knew, because we once followed Nick continuously for sixty-five days and had contacted him almost monthly since. Nick seemed to have settled in for good. I was not expecting an invasion by new adult males.

Suddenly Nick was pursuing callers left and right. Once he raced almost four miles through the swamps, the longest distance I had ever seen an orangutan travel in a single day. He barely had time to eat. For days we searched for the callers. One of the vocal males turned out to be Handless Harry, the male who had fought with TP years before. But who were the others?

On the evening of March 31, our junior assistant returned from the forest and reported that he had found a new wild adult male, one he had never seen before. I had to know who the new male was. The next day I went into the forest before dawn and sat below the unidentified adult male's night nest, waiting.

On April first, Fool's Day, just after dawn, I watched the adult male emerge from his nest. It was TP! TP had come back! More than two years had passed since he had disappeared. With the exception of Nick, TP was the most thoroughly habituated of any adult male orangutan I had ever observed and one of the few adult males who allowed me to follow him on the ground for long periods. TP's two-year absence had stretched into an eternity. I had assumed that he was gone forever; that, as with Cara and Carl, his absence had meant his death.

That morning, as I watched TP emerge from his nest high in the canopy against a whitening sky, I was ecstatic. TP's return had the force of a mystical experience. I felt wonder, and I remember saying to myself at that moment, "So there is life after death, after all."

# 17
# BINTI

A baby is God's opinion that
the world should go on.

— *Carl Sandburg*

A happy family is but an earlier heaven.

— *John Bowring*

---

**A**FTER ALMOST FIVE YEARS IN BORNEO, I became ill. I was nauseated, I lost my appetite, and I felt so tired I could hardly drag myself out of bed. I knew it couldn't be malaria, because I didn't have a pattern of chills and fever. I began combing books on tropical diseases, looking for one that matched my symptoms. I was convinced that I was dying from some obscure disease. I even sent a note to fellow researcher John MacKinnon, describing my symptoms.

Only when I missed a second period, and a third, did I realize that I was pregnant. I was going to be a mother. I could say my getting pregnant was unplanned, but that is only partly true. Rod and I had not sat down and decided, "It's time to have a baby." But other forces were at work.

The subject of pregnancy had come up long before Rod and I arrived in Indonesia. When Louis Leakey was visiting Los Angeles and staying with the Travises, Rod and I visited him daily. Normally, we would wait in the living room for him to come out. One time, however, Louis called us to his bedside; it was like being summoned by a tribal chieftain.

Having been born and raised among the Kikuyu of central Kenya, at some level, Louis *was* Kikuyu. He thought of himself as Kikuyu; he even dreamed in Kikuyu. Louis was also very earthy. Where others might hem and haw about body functions, Louis went straight to the point. It was, I assumed, the Kikuyu way.

We entered the darkened room where Louis was supposed to be napping. There were no chairs, so we stood at his bed, side by side. It was almost like being at a deathbed. Lying on his back, his hands clasped across his chest, Louis asked what Rod and I planned to do about birth control in the field. We admitted that we hadn't given it much thought, but said we would be very careful.

"That's not enough," he said, fixing me with his sharp gaze. "What if you get pregnant? You must be prepared." He was terribly concerned that if I got pregnant and had a baby the whole project would be ruined. Louis believed deeply that the study of living great apes was critical to understanding human evolution, the "missing link" in our scientific evidence. He had staked his reputation on Jane Goodall, then Dian Fossey, and now me. He had worked tirelessly to raise funds for us. He did not want to see my study of the third great ape abandoned because of pregnancy.

"You know," he continued, "the Kikuyu practice clitorectomy. Kikuyu women sometimes feel pain in the act of love. So they often abstain from sexual love and just embrace passionately. Abstinence is the Kikuyu's birth control. You can do the same," he said. "The warm embrace is what's important."

I was stunned, and so was Rod. It was not just that I was shocked or disgusted by the operation and customs he described; I knew such practices still existed. But until then I don't think I had realized just how African Louis was. Rod and I looked at each other, then told him we would investigate other methods of birth control.

I later read that when Kenya's future president, Jomo Kenyatta, was studying at the London School of Economics, Leakey heard that Kenyatta was going to discuss clitorectomy at one of Professor Malinowski's anthropology seminars, and sat in. Leakey and Kenyatta got into a heated argument. No one in the class knew how the debate ended, because they switched to Kikuyu. But the story is that Kenyatta opposed clitorectomy, and Louis approved. Louis was a more traditional African in some ways than was Kenya's founder president, the man known as "Papa Kenya."

Louis sat up on the bed and waved us closer. He put his arms around us to give us his blessing. I can't remember his exact words, but he talked of his love for us and our love for each other. He said that he would always be with us and he hoped that our purpose would endure. He wasn't speaking as a scientist any more, or even as a friend. It was as if he were a bishop delivering a benediction or a shaman casting a protective spell. To enhance this feeling of warmth and magic, he called Joan Travis and included her in the circle. The four of us hugged as he swore to support me until I received my Ph.D. I remember feeling slightly awed and mildly embarrassed at the same time; I wasn't used to hugging circles.

As we left the room, I said to Rod, "I feel like I just married you again." Rod said, "I know what you mean."

Before we left Los Angeles I went to a doctor and got birth control pills. The doctor told me to be sure to take one every day. But getting to our first stop in Africa took weeks and, with so much else to think about, I suppose I forgot to take an occasional pill. When we got to Africa I started bleeding and bled for two weeks straight. After that, I threw the pills away.

Like most traditional people, Indonesians see children as a blessing from God. When a couple does not have children it is viewed as a failure, perhaps a sign that God is punishing them. Childless couples may even go into mourning. Some Indonesians consider childlessness a legitimate reason for a man to take a second wife.

After Rod and I had been in Indonesia a few years, the whispers about our childless state became audible. When people learned that we had been married for almost eight years they would sigh and offer condolences. Like many young couples in the 1960s, Rod and I thought the world was already overpopulated. We decided that the rational, moral route to parenthood was to adopt. After all, the world was crowded with orphans and children whose parents couldn't provide for them. Holding Sugito in my arms had caused me to waver. If I loved my orangutan "child" so much, wouldn't I love my own child even more? Nonetheless, I held to my conviction that Rod and I would adopt rather than have biological children of our own. However, we couldn't convince Indonesians that we were happy as we were.

Mr. Binti appeared at Camp Leakey one day, unannounced. If Louis Leakey was my Western mentor, Mr. Binti was his Indonesian counterpart. In some ways they even looked alike. Like Leakey, Mr. Binti was short and somewhat rotund, with a benign expression and eyes that sparkled, as if he found people and life in general endlessly amusing. Where Leakey had a snow-white mane, Mr. Binti's hair was a lustrous black that caught the sunlight when he moved. Like Leakey, there were sides of his character that were not accessible to Western logic; he, too, had a bit of the shaman in him. He believed in a reality that was separate from mundane, everyday life.

Mr. Binti had come on a mission. He waited until Rod went into the forest to collect firewood. I was sitting on a wooden bench with my typewriter balanced precariously on my lap and a baby orangutan around my neck. Mr. Binti pulled up a rattan chair and began to speak.

"My wife and I have discussed this at length. We want to talk to you about the fact that Mrs. Binti had her last child when she was thirty years old. She had eight children in ten years, but after thirty no more children would come. You are now twenty-nine years old. We are worried that when you turn thirty you will not be able to have children."

He spoke in a measured, formal way, as if he and his wife had prepared this speech and rehearsed it. I listened quietly as he continued.

"We know how busy you are and how hard you work. But since you are our adopted daughter, we feel it is our duty to help you have children. If you have a child, my wife and I will be happy to raise the baby for you. But you must become pregnant before it is too late."

I wasn't totally surprised, because I knew how much importance Indonesians attach to having children. I also knew that he and his wife were raising one of their grandchildren, a three-year-old. This was not unusual; in Indonesia, children are members of an extended family and frequently live with relatives other than their parents. As heads of the extended family, grandparents have a right to expect grandchildren and a duty to help rear them. Mr. Binti was treating me like family, and I felt honored. He continued, "I wanted to talk to you alone first, and I want you to tell Rod, to discuss it with him and say what I have told you."

His mission completed, Mr. Binti never brought up the subject again.

After Mr. Binti left, Rod and I talked. I was moved because Mr. Binti was so sincere in his concern. But parenthood wasn't part of our plans right then. I was in the process of negotiating a four-year extension of my government research permit, on top of the previous two-year extension. Rod and I let the matter drop.

But Mr. Binti's mission succeeded. Within two months I was pregnant.

When I wrote to my family, friends, and professors in North America with the good news, I expected congratulations. Instead I received a barrage of hysterical telegrams and letters ordering me to return to North America immediately! How could I even consider having a baby thousands of miles from home, "in the middle of nowhere," hours by boat from the nearest doctor. Dr. Birdsell, the head of my doctoral committee, wrote to me about another graduate student who had taken his two-year-old on a field study in Nepal; the child died of meningitis. My parents sent desperate telegrams, begging me to come home and offering to pay for everything, from the plane ticket to the hospital.

I declined. After all, parts of Indonesia have the highest population densities in the world. Dayak parents have been giving birth to Dayak babies for generations. Having a baby there couldn't be all that dangerous. If I took the necessary precautions, the baby and I would be fine. Rod agreed. The jungles of Borneo seemed far more threatening long-distance than they did firsthand.

Besides, I didn't want to leave my work. I was following the life histories of particular, individual orangutans. It was a constant, ever-moving stream; you never knew when something important might happen. It wasn't like a buried archaeological site, where you could leave, come back years later, and find everything exactly as you had left it. The orangutans would carry on with their lives whether or not I was there to observe them. We decided to stay in Indonesia.

Still, I was worried. I had never been pregnant before, and the flood of warnings affected me. I went to the doctors in the nearest town, Pangkalan Bun, but the experience was not reassuring. The operating and delivery room was splattered with blood; the one light didn't have a plug, just live wires stuck into the socket; the x-ray machine wasn't working; and the doctors had run out of alcohol to sterilize instruments. I decided to have the baby in Jakarta.

The months crawled by. I grew huge, but I continued my research, wading into the swamps and following orangutans. Like many pregnant women I felt as if my body had been taken over and no longer belonged to me. Carrying on with my work, no matter how burdened I felt physically, helped me to feel that I was still myself, still capable of doing what I intended. Equally important, it helped to pass the time. The pregnancy seemed to go on forever.

I didn't have anyone, especially an older woman such as my mother, to talk to about how I felt or what to expect. In the beginning, I didn't have any baby books, either. Rod did not become the doting father-to-be, hovering over me and catering to my every whim. To the contrary, he saw pregnancy as a challenge — my challenge. Rod refused to accept the tyranny of his body. He tried not to let hunger, pain, or exhaustion influence his behavior. He felt that I should have my body under control, and that I should not allow pregnancy to interfere with my usual activities. Like many Western men, Rod was delighted at the prospect of a baby in the abstract, but not very interested in the details. We never talked about how our lives might change after the baby was born.

We were getting international news magazines now, and I read about Libyan president Omar Qaddafi's lecturing a group of Egyptian and Libyan women — including the wife of then Egyptian president Anwar Sadat — on their biological inferiority. The proof? Women who were eight months pregnant did not make good paratroopers! I was eight months pregnant. Around this time Rod and I were coming back to camp in our longboat late one night in the pitch dark. The river was blockaded with an island of weeds, and we had to push the boat over this mass of floating vegetation to continue. Rod was slumped in the back of the boat, so sick with malaria he could hardly move. Our two local assistants tried to free the boat, but they were getting nowhere. So I knotted my muumuu over my thighs, hoisted my huge belly out of the boat, climbed into the water barefoot, and started pushing the boat, despite the assistants' loud protests. Finally we broke through. I remember wishing Qaddafi could see me now.

A few weeks before the baby was due we flew to Jakarta. We stayed in a reasonably comfortable hotel, but we could not afford restaurant meals and so lived on fruits, vegetables, and snacks from street stalls and vendors who carried their stoves on their backs. I remember stumbling into the blazing hot sun, my ankles so swollen and my belly so heavy that I could barely walk. Lying on the bed in our room I felt like a beached whale. Then the contractions started.

We took a taxi to the hospital, and I was sent directly to the delivery room. Rod wasn't allowed to come with me. The waiting room for fathers was bare, stifling, and swarming with bloodthirsty mosquitoes. I urged Rod to leave and get some rest.

I thought giving birth would be a passive, relatively painless experience. I had been present when Mrs. Bahriah gave birth at Camp Leakey. It was her ninth child, and an older man, a part-time shaman, acted as her midwife. He must have given her traditional medicines, because she was unconscious the whole time. I remember her waking briefly, asking me the time, then falling back into a stupor. The women who were assisting massaged her stomach, pushing for her. Eventually we heard a squeal as the baby was born.

No one told me that in Indonesian hospitals, most doctors practice natural childbirth, with no painkillers whatsoever. When I asked my doctor why the hospital insisted on natural childbirth, he said because it was safer. I later learned that Muslims see childbirth as the female equivalent of warfare for men. Islam teaches that just as men who die in a holy war go directly to heaven, so do women who die in childbirth. It is seen as a form of holy martyrdom. There had been times, when I had malaria or dengue fever, that the pain was so bad that I thought it could not get worse. I was wrong. The night that I gave birth for the first time, the word "pain" took on new meaning.

My baby was born in the early morning hours. No one phoned Rod. He arrived at around seven, after a few hours of sleep, to find that he had a son. We named him Binti, for our adopted Indonesian father. In the Dayak language Mr. and Mrs. Binti spoke, *binti* means a small bird that flies very high.

We left the hospital some days later. A close friend, Nina Sulaiman, insisted that we stay at her home in Jakarta. Nina was the vice rector of the *Universitas Nasional,* where she also taught English. Dutch by birth, Nina had married an Indonesian who was studying in Holland after the war. Nina was tall, blond, and pale, with blue eyes, a straight nose, and a long face. She looked every inch a European. But Nina was Indonesian to the core. She had lived in Jakarta for more than twenty years, become an Indonesian citizen, and even converted to Islam. She and her husband presided over a typical upper-middle-class Jakarta household. Their home centered on an open courtyard that was the scene of constant coming and going — teenage nieces and nephews jostling; country relatives seeking favors; servants at work; an old grandfather, stooped from years of planting; and students and colleagues from the university.

In her many years in Jakarta, Nina had acquired the Indonesian gift of gab. She would talk to anyone about anything, any time, often long into the night, without saying anything that was controversial or revealing. Dispensing advice and favors was part of her role as the wife of a successful businessman from an old and respected Sundanese family (the Sundanese being the main ethnic group of West Java). Far from being overwhelmed, Nina seemed to thrive on the endless stream of visitors.

On my first night in the Sulaiman household I discovered that Binti had colic. He cried steadily from nine in the evening until eight the next morning; the only thing that relieved his distress was being walked. And so I paced, night after night. At dawn I would fall exhausted onto the bed, only to be awoken when he cried out lustily to be fed. It wasn't so much the lack of sleep that bothered me, but Binti's pain; I wanted so badly to comfort him. Nina once said that each night I aged ten years. I replied that fortunately, it wasn't cumulative.

Soon after Binti's birth, Rod returned to Kalimantan. He didn't feel he was needed in Jakarta and was restless. He wanted to get back to Camp Leakey. But I felt Binti was still too small to travel. Many Indonesians believe that a baby should not be allowed to touch the ground for forty days; parents do not take the infant out of the house during that time. I decided to observe this Eastern custom. For forty sleepless nights and days I became part of the bustling Sulaiman household.

Being a surrogate mother to infant orangutans had not prepared me for being a mother to my own infant. Orangutan infants and human babies are quite different in their demands and their capabilities. An orangutan infant is born to cling; that is his or her job. Cleaving to the mother's body, the infant suckles whenever he or she is hungry. To some degree, the infant orangutan takes care of him- or herself. This leaves the mother free to go about her normal activities. A human baby lies there, helpless. The mother has to cradle, nurse, burp, diaper, bathe, and perform countless other tasks for her infant. Many traditional people, including most rural Indonesians, approximate the primordial primate pattern by carrying their infants on their bodies at all times in a sling. The size and weight of a human infant, who weighs six to nine pounds at birth, makes this more difficult than carrying an infant orangutan, who weighs only about two pounds at birth. But despite their smaller size, orangutans are physically more mature at birth than are human infants. As many anthropologists have pointed out, human babies at birth are still essentially embryos. Their bones haven't ossified, their muscle coordination is poor, their eyes aren't focused, and most important, their brains are still developing. Not until nine or ten months does a human infant catch up to an orangutan infant at birth.

I soon realized that if I wanted to resume my work even part time when I returned to Camp Leakey, I would need help with Binti. In Indonesia, people often borrow a young relative or servant to help with small children, rather than hiring a baby-sitter or nanny. "Borrow" is the word they use in Indonesian, and it means that the person temporarily becomes a member of your household.

Yuni was a seventeen-year-old high school student who was helping Nina care for her youngest child. Slim and dark compared to the Sulaiman children, Yuni had the long tapering fingers and graceful carriage of a Javanese court dancer. She was a natural, unaffected beauty. Nina once commented that Yuni probably would marry a European, especially given the number of Europeans and North Americans who visited the Sulaiman household. At the time it seemed an idle comment.

Yuni was the only member of the Sulaiman household who was not a relative but ate at the family table (which did not endear her to less favored nieces and nephews). The youngest of nine children, she came from a traditional family that lived in one of the old capitals in Central Java, Yogyakarta. Nina had known Yuni's family for a long time, and treated her like an adopted daughter. Yuni had been living in Jakarta, where she went to high school, for several years.

When I asked if I could "borrow" Yuni for a few months to help care for Binti, Nina at first was reluctant. She did not like the idea of Yuni interrupting her senior year of high school and leaving the modern capital of Indonesia for the jungles of Borneo. I suggested that it would be an opportunity for Yuni to see a part of Indonesia she might never see otherwise and that she could write up the experience for her senior project. Yuni seemed willing and Nina finally acquiesced, with one special request. Teaching English was Nina's passion. She asked me to promise that Yuni would be proficient in English when she returned. I readily agreed.

When the time came, Binti, Yuni, and I flew from Jakarta to Pangkalan Bun. Rod met us at the airport, flanked by two of my Indonesian students. Dusk was approaching and we went directly to the German pastor's spacious storage shed, which he allowed us to use whenever we were in town. Rod and the students cleared a place for our mattresses and began to string up mosquito nets while I brewed coffee. We would all sleep in the one room, Indonesian style.

One by one Rod and the students fell asleep; only Yuni stayed by my side while I waited for the night's vigil to begin. Binti dozed off just before dusk. For the first time in his life he slept straight through the night. This was also his first night in Kalimantan. I realized that Binti's colic was due to urban stress. Although the Sulaimans lived in a fine old Dutch house in an affluent neighborhood, they were next to one of Jakarta's main roads. All night long we could hear the unmuffled roar of motorcycles and cars hurtling by. The silence of the Borneo night, broken only by the hum of insects, calmed Binti. Kalimantan has the same soothing affect on many people, especially Western urbanites who are constantly assaulted by noise and pollution. (Indonesians, on the other hand, often complain about the quiet and lack of people!)

The next day we left for Camp Leakey. In keeping with her traditional Javanese upbringing, Yuni immediately put herself in charge of Binti's wellbeing. She carried him, bathed him, fed him, cuddled him. I never had to tell her what to do or remind her of her responsibilities. It was almost as if Binti were her birth child as well as mine. Yuni simply adored babies. She once told me that the mere sight of an infant caused her to shudder in joy, and she had to cuddle the baby. Many Indonesian women feel this way. I've often thought the love lavished on babies explains why Indonesians are such happy, smiling people as adults.

Soon after our return to Camp Leakey, Yuni and I developed a routine. She would go to breakfast, eat very quickly, and come back to care for Binti so that I could have my breakfast, give my assistants their tasks for the day, and talk to my Indonesian students. If I had gone to the dining hall first, Yuni would have had to eat alone, after my assistants and I had finished. In Indonesia, no one eats alone. If one person is eating then everyone present has to be offered food. Even in Jakarta, in a restaurant, if one person sitting alone is served, he or she will turn to the people at the other tables and say, "*Mari,*" meaning "Come, let us eat together." The other people will demur, saying "Oh no, you go ahead." Only then will the person begin to eat. Asking Yuni to eat alone would have been rude.

After breakfast, I would play with Binti and give him a bath before I began working. Yuni cared for Binti during the day, returning him to me in the afternoon or early evening. I always put Binti to bed myself. My main work now was analyzing my data and writing my Ph.D. dissertation, so most days I would retreat to my study. But I often went into the forest.

Whatever I was doing, I always spent at least part of the day with Binti, and insisted that Rod do likewise. As Binti grew older, both Rod and I frequently carried him on our backs in a cloth and metal baby carrier. Binti loved peering over our shoulders, whether we were in camp or in the forest. We didn't carry him very far into the forest, though, because we were afraid of the insects and the diseases they carried. Binti was a spunky, active, determined baby, slightly small for a Western child his age but large for an Indonesian child. I have delightful memories of us playing with Binti, and Rod tossing Binti as a small toddler into the air and Binti squealing with delight.

On the days I spent in the forest, I did not have to worry about Binti's welfare. When I returned, Yuni would see me coming, open the door, and welcome me back, often with Binti in her arms. Her easy smile, thoughtfulness, and serene manner made Yuni very likeable. Her devotion to Binti was obvious. She quickly secured a place for herself in our nuclear family; her presence seemed natural and right, as if she had always been there.

With Binti, my dissertation, and orangutan observations, my days and evenings were full. How could I find time to teach Yuni English? Rod was a born teacher. He had taught Indonesian to a North American zoo keeper who visited camp, and also coached my Indonesian students in English, simply because he liked to teach. I told him about my promise to Nina and asked if he would teach Yuni. Rod said, "Sure, I'd be glad to." That afternoon, while I was playing with Binti, he walked Yuni back to the house where she stayed. He was gone five hours. When he returned he told me Yuni was a bright, eager student; he thought she would benefit from daily lessons. Without a second thought, I agreed; I wanted to keep my promise to Nina.

Around this time, I realized that Rod and I had begun arguing. In the past, if I woke Rod at four-thirty in the morning and said I was feeling too sick or too tired to go into the forest, he was happy to help out. Follow a wild male orangutan through the swamps, by himself, up to his waist in water, with only a compass and a machete, on a moment's notice? Sure. But now, if I asked him merely to sterilize a bottle we got into an argument. The fights — always about child care — were becoming more and more frequent and increasingly bitter.

Looking back, I see that Binti's birth precipitated a crisis for Rod. To me, becoming a mother was a natural expression of being a woman. It came easily, perhaps because my mother had seemed so comfortable in the role. For Rod, fatherhood symbolized a giant step, a new stage in life, a test of his manhood, not a confirmation. After Binti was born he commented several times that now he was responsible for another human being. To some degree, Rod viewed fatherhood in financial terms. It didn't matter how much time he spent cuddling Binti and playing with him, or how much love he felt for him. If he couldn't support his child, he was a failure as a father. I suspect that many Western men feel the same way: A good father is a good provider. But in Rod's case the self-doubt and self-questioning were magnified. He had no real means of support in the Western sense. For some time we had been living off my research grants. He felt like he had no life of his own and no credentials. He was just a man in the jungle with a baby and some photographs of orangutans.

Rod was also approaching thirty. I recall his once saying that he felt like a displaced housewife. He had devoted his adult life to helping his spouse further her own career. In those days, Rod was dedicated wholeheartedly to protecting the orangutans and their rain forest habitat. But it was, after all, my study and I was in charge.

Binti's presence was a constant reminder of what Rod was not. Rod didn't resent Binti; he adored him. But he was ambivalent about the role of father, and this came out as hostility toward me. He resented me for putting him in this position, as if I had gotten pregnant by myself. He was angry that becoming a father had forced him to take a closer look at himself and reevaluate what he had — or had not — accomplished. I realize now that for Rod, Yuni was an escape from feelings of self-doubt. In her young eyes he was a full-fledged adult, a man of stature, a Westerner, a teacher.

I remember walking down the causeway to the river one evening, just the four of us. Rod was on one side, I was on the other, and Yuni walked between us carrying Binti. Suddenly I imagined how this scene would look to an Indonesian. Indonesia is a predominantly Muslim country, and Muslim men are allowed up to four wives, although this is rarely practiced today. But an Indonesian watching us together would have assumed that I was the older first wife and Yuni was the younger second wife who had replaced me in my husband's affections. Whether an official wife or not, the second woman is a familiar figure in Indonesian life. Indonesians even have a name for her, the *madu*, which means "honey."

Laughing to myself, I dismissed the thought almost as soon as it appeared. "How absurd." But fleeting thoughts have a way of crystalizing events that have yet to happen, changes that have not quite begun. As Westerners, we tend to dismiss these flashes of clairvoyance as silly or meaningless.

I realized that Yuni was spending more time with Rod, sitting next to him in the dining hall, walking and laughing with him as she carried Binti. Certainly, her English was improving. I was aware that Rod seemed to be less interested in chatting with me. I told myself the reason was that I was tired all the time; Rod was being thoughtful in leaving me alone. Maybe I was preoccupied with my baby and my work, maybe I just didn't want to recognize what I sensed subconsciously.

This self-deception blew apart the morning before Yuni was due to return to Jakarta. Rod and Yuni had gone ahead to the dining hall where all the camp personnel ate meals together; there were about twelve people in camp then. I sat holding Binti, playing with him, and waiting. Usually Yuni came in about fifteen minutes. A half hour went by, maybe more. I could hear peals of laughter from the dining hall and went outside, but the mosquitoes were so numerous I went right back in. Another half hour rolled by, and another. I paced, growing angrier by the minute.

It wasn't just that I wanted my morning coffee. Meals have a special importance in Indonesia. Because people tend to be thin, they cannot afford to skip meals. This physical necessity is embodied in the cultural mandate that everyone eat together. Missing a meal is considered the leading cause of bad tempers. In forcing me to wait almost an hour and a half, Yuni was delivering a direct insult. It was almost as rude as if she had spit in my face.

For some reason, I felt paralyzed. I could have picked Binti up, braved the mosquitoes, and walked into the dining hall. But I couldn't force myself to do it. When Yuni finally came back I exploded.

"Why are you so angry?" Yuni pleaded. "I have worked for Aunt Sulaiman for many years now and I have never seen her angry like this."

Without thinking I shot back, "Of course you haven't, because you've never tried to take Mr. Sulaiman away from her! You never tried to steal her husband!"

Yuni looked stunned. She stared at me for a moment, and then she began screaming hysterically. I tried to calm her but she was unreachable. Then suddenly she fainted, dropping into a deep, comalike sleep. I moved her onto a mattress, where she slept for several hours. When she woke up she was calm and composed. I suspect that her falling unconscious was a powerful defense mechanism to protect the mind from forbidden thoughts and overwhelming emotions. These "spells" seem to be distinctively Eastern.

During the commotion Rod came running to the house. I told him exactly what happened. Rod sat down slowly on a trunk. He looked weary, like a man defeated. Finally he spoke.

"I could never give this up, living in the forest, with the orangutans. . . . You don't have to worry."

Yuni left for Jakarta the next day. Before she left, she pleaded with me not to tell Mrs. Sulaiman what had happened. I said of course I wouldn't, as it was strictly between us. And so we parted.

Rod and I were alone again with Binti, but the equation had changed.

When Binti was born, I had been at Camp Leakey for five years. All that time, I had been immersed in the world of orangutans. Orangutans were everywhere: ambling along the paths in camp, lounging on the steps of our house, napping in the rafters, hanging on my body, crowding my thoughts. The distinction between humans and orangutans had begun to blur in my mind. I could rattle off a list of the differences. But I had lost that gut feeling of separation, which is an integral part of Western intellectual consciousness. When orangutans are a natural part of the landscape, and your daily companions, it is difficult not to think of them as equals. Orangutans and humans share a particular way of interpreting the world. Even if you have never met orangutans before, their actions are predictable and comprehensible, simply from the fact of your being human. This familiarity comes from orangutans and humans sharing a long evolutionary history. We are, in this sense, kin.

Binti's birth was an awakening. My own species' evolutionary journey suddenly took on a new reality. Binti's development underscored that no matter how similar orangutans are to humans, humans are still very different. You can't get away from the similarities, or from the differences.

I had to distance myself from the ex-captive orangutans in camp, physically and psychologically. Orangutans already had been banned from all camp buildings. But now I began enforcing this more strictly. We started keeping the doors locked at all times and chasing orangutans out when they came in. Humans can pick up diseases from orangutans (and vice versa), and I worried about Binti's health to the point of paranoia. Although normally gentle, orangutans sometimes play rough, like growing boys who do not know their own strength. I also was concerned about "sibling rivalry." I did not want the orphan orangutans who viewed me as their surrogate mother to envy Binti and perhaps act out their resentment; nor did I want Binti to feel that he had to compete with orangutans for my affections.

If we had been in North America, I'm sure that we would have given Binti his own room decorated with teddy-bear wallpaper, blue curtains, a mobile, and heaps of toys. We couldn't do that in Borneo. But even in our small house, we put Binti's crib, with its own little mosquito net, in the front room, not our bedroom. To do otherwise would have been unthinkable: Western culture places a high value on individuality; even babies are believed to have an inherent right to privacy. No Indonesian mother would dream of leaving a baby alone and crying in the night. Some Western baby manuals of that time taught that letting babies cry themselves to sleep was not merely acceptable, but beyond a certain age, mandatory. The underlying philosophy seemed to be that training for independence should begin at once: Solitude builds character. As first-time parents we clung to our Western cultural upbringing, with Rod taking the lead. We even had a stroller! Like allowing Binti to sleep in our bed, carrying him all the time would "spoil" him. Just where we would stroll was questionable. After a tropical deluge, which came at least once a day, the paths in camp were running streams. There was no playground where I could sit and chat with other mothers while Binti played in the sandbox. But babies were supposed to have strollers, and we did not want Binti to be deprived.

Try as we might, it was impossible to isolate Binti from the multiprimate community we had created at Camp Leakey. Binti's very first friend was "Yally," a young, silvery gray female gibbon with a black face and hands. Gibbons are classified as "lesser apes" because of their relatively small size. Thin and wiry, gibbons normally spend their lives high in the forest canopy. Although they are only distant relatives in an evolutionary sense, in some ways gibbons look very human. When they come down to the ground, they stand upright like little soldiers, with their heads precisely balanced on their spinal cords. Their faces are flat like ours, not protruding like a monkey's or a dog's, and their expression bears an uncanny resemblance to a wizened old man.

The exiled orangutans peered through the window screens of our house and lolled about the door, looking for an opening. But orangutans are relatively large and slow; it was fairly easy to keep them out of the house. Yally was simply too fast. If we opened the door just a crack, in she flew, swinging onto the rafters in a flash. Trying to catch her was like chasing moving shadows. She seemed to be everywhere at once. When we gave up, she would wait a while, then steal over to Binti's crib. Yally was fascinated by Binti, perhaps because there were no other gibbons in camp at that time and he was the only other individual her size. (She weighed only three or four pounds.) She loved to sit on his chest and gaze into his face. We would pull her away immediately, of course, but we felt a little mean about doing so. Binti loved her attentions.

When Binti was old enough to crawl, he followed Yally around the house, trying to leap like her and imitate her birdlike calls. When she ran up a wall and swung onto the rafters, he shrieked with laughter. When she grew tired of the game and took off out the door and into the forest, he wailed in frustration. By the time Binti was a toddler, Yally was older and not as interested in childish play, although she remained tolerant of Binti. When he saw her, Binti would run toward her, trying to renew their friendship. But a human earthling, especially a toddler, is no match for an airborne gibbon.

Once Binti was able to sit up on his own and crawl, we allowed him to play with baby orangutans — but only after the orangutans had a bath with strong soap and boiled water. Binti often climbed into the plastic washtub with the orangutan. It was hot and humid, and baths were a treat. Usually the infant orangutan enclosed Binti in a wet, furry hug or tried to climb onto his back or even his head. The orangutan was only doing what came naturally. A wild infant orangutan spends all of his or her time clinging to the mother at this age. Binti usually tolerated their soggy embraces.

By the time Binti was a year old, orangutans his own age were not his favorite playmates. Infant orangutans are not very active or curious, but rather spend most of their time staring blankly at the world and clinging for all they are worth to whoever is handy. When year-old orangutans attempt to crawl on the ground (which virtually never happens in the wild), their movements are awkward and ungainly; they get tangled up in their own limbs. In contrast, Binti, who had taken his first steps at ten months, was always on the move and into everything. The very young infant orangutans would sit passively by, ignoring his antics, like glassy-eyed dolls on a shelf. Almost the only way Binti could entice them to play was to offer them bits of food, which he did regularly. One of our biggest problems was getting him to put his own food into his own mouth and not into an orangutan's.

By a year and a half, Binti was seeking orangutan playmates who, though older than he was chronologically, were his developmental peers. Three- and four-year-old orangutans who could climb and swing, tug and bite, were more his emotional and intellectual equals. We never allowed Binti to be alone with a juvenile orangutan, but we never saw one try to hurt him either. Soon Binti, like his playmates, was climbing trees (until we retrieved him), swinging from branches, playing tug of war, and — on occasion — biting.

Around this time an orphaned orangutan we named "Princess" arrived in camp. A mischievous three-year-old who delighted in ripping open pillows and splattering milk over the walls, Princess quickly became Binti's best friend. Binti and Princess would crawl on the floor together, paw each other, embrace, play handsies (and footsies), push and tug at each other, and play-bite. One memorable afternoon, Princess and Binti, along with a juvenile male named "Pola," found a sack of flour in the dining hall before the cook or I discovered them. I looked up and flour was everywhere. All three were rolling on the floor, throwing handfuls of flour at each other. Totally coated in flour, they looked like powdery ghosts. The image I carry with me was how much at ease Binti and the young orangutans were with each other, and how much fun they were having. At play, the line between the infant Binti and the young apes virtually disappeared.

The orangutans most curious about Binti were the older juveniles and adolescents, ages six to ten. Studies show that the first question we humans ask about a newborn baby of our own species is, "Is it a boy or a girl?" People are uncomfortable with an "it." Orangutans are the same way. When a new baby orangutan was brought to camp, the first thing the other orangutans did was to turn the infant upside down and inspect his or her genitals. Likewise with Binti, the first thing adolescent orangutans would do was attempt to remove his diapers.

When Binti began spending more time outdoors around these older orangutans, we had to be on constant guard. Suddenly a long, hairy arm would reach out, grab Binti, and flip him upside down. The orangutans would jab, poke, and pull him gently, as if trying to see how far they could go before he would break. Although Binti seemed to enjoy being an orangutan's toy, we never let these investigations go on for very long. If an orangutan clutched Binti to her side, or hoisted him onto her shoulder, and started to walk off, we retrieved him instantly. Older ex-captive orangutans sometimes adopted smaller ones for a few hours, days, or even years. The adoptive parent (usually a female) would carry the little one everywhere, including up into the treetops to feed or nest. Obviously we couldn't allow this with Binti. The problem was that Binti was learning to climb and trying to follow his orange friends up into the trees. At this age, he was remarkable in his climbing ability. Binti rarely cried when the orangutans toyed with him, but he howled when we pulled him from a tree and brought him back to earth. True to his name, Binti was not a hundred percent happy being terrestrial.

Binti demonstrated his uncanny climbing ability in Jakarta when he was just two years old. We were staying with the Sulaimans. I was sitting and talking with Nina in the Sulaiman's outdoor courtyard when I realized that Binti had disappeared. I could not imagine where he had gone, since the courtyard was enclosed on all four sides by the house. I had visions of Binti toddling out a half-open door into the street and being hit by a car. Frantic with worry, I called his name. Then I heard Binti's giggle. I looked up and saw him twenty feet in the air, on top of the metal water tower that ascended from the court-yard. I still don't know how he got there. I realized that if I screamed and yelled for him to come down, he might panic. I knew that just as he had climbed up, he could climb down. As calmly as I could, I said, "Binti, would you mind coming down, please?" I spoke quietly, hoping that my great trepidation would not show. Binti looked at me and, after a few seconds, climbed right down, as though it were the most natural thing in the world.

This lack of physical fear was typical of Binti. He was dauntless. Just as other children learn the games and attitudes of their culture from their friends, so Binti, whose primary playmates were orangutans and Indonesian men, learned from his friends. When Yuni was working on her high school paper or taking English lessons with Rod, the male Indonesian students and assistants in camp would take over Binti's care. They loved to carry him around and show him what they were doing. In Indonesia, it is considered manly to show affection for children. These young men in their twenties had the strength, agility, and fearlessness that we associate with professional athletes. Their ease with their bodies and physical courage influenced Binti. Rod, who is one of the most fearless, totally courageous people I have ever known, reinforced Binti's daring. In this, Binti was Rod's child.

In contrast to the infant and juvenile orangutans, the adult orangutans in camp — ex-captives like Akmad and Siswoyo, who had become mothers themselves — were totally blasé. When Binti toddled up to them and tried to engage their attention, they gently pushed him away without a second glance. When he tried to climb onto their backs or pull their hair, at most they would move away. This is precisely the way mother orangutans treat other orangutans' babies. They might inspect an infant while the mother is holding him or her, but they rarely carried or played with another female's baby. I took this "in-difference" as a compliment, another sign that they had admitted me — and my offspring — into their universe. Just as Akmad trusted me to gently touch her newborn, so I trusted these old friends, my orangutan "sisters" and "daughters."

Jane Goodall once told me that observing chimpanzee mothers taught her lessons about mothering. For instance, chimpanzee mothers do not punish their offspring when they are misbehaving, but rather use distraction. I, too, learned from orangutans. Orangutan mothers are extremely patient. When the infant is small, the mother allows her offspring anything. Of course, orangutans are individuals and some are more attentive, more sensitive, and generally bet-ter mothers than others. But I have never seen a mother orangutan hit, bite, or otherwise chastise her infant or juvenile (before weaning). If the young orangutan seems headed for trouble, the mother calmly retrieves him or her; if the youngster is annoying, the mother simply moves away. However, wean-ing can be abrupt and harsh. Once weaning has taken place, an orangutan mother may seem capriciously cruel to her growing offspring, particularly her sons. In fact, the mother is promoting the independence her son will need for the solitary life of an adult male orangutan. Patience plus autonomy are lessons I try to follow, though being human sometimes makes this difficult.

The setting, his primate playmates, and the fact that there were no other hu-man children his age in Camp Leakey at this time clearly had an impact on Binti. In his early, "gibbon stage," Binti leaped and whooped like his first companion, Yally. In his "orangutan stage," Binti scrambled on all fours after his furry friend Princess. By age two he could do a perfect imitation of almost the entire repertoire of juvenile orangutan facial expressions and sounds, from blank stares and peeled-lips play-grins to kiss-squeaks of annoyance. Seeing orangutan mothers carry their babies nearly all the time, Binti insisted on being carried, too. Like a good Western mother, I tried to resist, but often gave in, especially if a baby orangutan was draped somewhere on my body. When I did pick him up, Binti often clung to me with his legs and let his arms dangle loose, orangutan-style. Several times he even bit people, an orangutan's way of saying "Stop!" or "Pay attention!"

The intensity of Binti's identification with his orangutan playmates and the accuracy of his imitations were amazing, but also alarming. I wanted Binti to get along with other primates, but I didn't want him to become one! Fortunately, his orangutan stage, too, passed, particularly after he started to talk. Then Binti began orienting more to the local assistants and cooks. This is the place in evolution where humans and pongids may have parted ways. Spoken language almost surely marked one of the turning points in human evolution.

As I watched Binti grow and change against a backdrop of orangutans, I began to see both species in a new light. I had learned that orangutans are much closer to humans than I ever imagined when I gazed at their photographs in books and magazines.

Orangutans seem to express a range of emotions very similar to our own. I will never forget little Sobiarso sitting on the floor of our hut, playing with a piece of wood. She was lost in herself, tossing the object into the air and catching it, throwing it from one hand to the other, vigorously rubbing it on the floor, and twirling it. She was so absorbed in what she was doing that she was totally oblivious to my staring at her. Suddenly she looked up and saw me watching her. Instantly she stopped playing, visibly shrank, and then quarter-turned away from me and hunched her back, peeking at me over her shoulder. Had she been human, I would have said that she was embarrassed at being caught having so much fun. After a while, I turned away and started writing again. Within a minute she resumed playing. This time I pretended to keep writing, but watched her out of the corner of my eye. Up to that time I had never seen an orangutan so immersed in playing with an object. I was stunned by how much Sobiarso resembled a human child.

Orangutans at Camp Leakey used tools and liked to take things apart as if to see how they worked (though putting them back together was our problem). They loved to try on shirts, socks, panties, and other bits of clothing — especially hats (we had to guard our laundry line). They even love junk food. Ex-captive orangutans binge on candies raided from humans. Given a choice between a juicy, sun-ripened, golden pineapple and a gooey, fat-laden milk chocolate bar or a Tootsie Pop, I have never known an ex-captive orangutan to choose the former.

Orangutans and other apes had crossed the last Rubicon separating humans and apes: language. Although apes do not have vocal chords, which would enable them to speak, experiments have shown that they can learn to communicate symbolically, to some degree, with hand signs or computers, and are capable of some abstract reasoning. Indeed, graduate student Gary Shapiro had recently joined us at Camp Leakey and was holding lessons for orangutans in Ameslan (American Sign Language). One of his brightest pupils was Princess.

But everything "human" orangutans did, Binti did sooner, faster, and better. The contrast between Binti and Princess, who was only a little older, was dramatic. For instance, although no one actually taught Binti signs, he learned not only the signs that Princess knew, but also signs that Gary was trying to teach to Princess but which Princess refused to learn. Naturally and effortlessly, Binti between age two and three learned more signs than Princess at age five or six learned through rigorously structured, formal lessons.

At two years of age, Princess had been totally preoccupied with food. The only objects that interested her were edible. At the same age, two years, Binti was fascinated with tools and utensils — dippers, sticks, cups, hammers, screwdrivers, whatever he could find. Whenever Rod and I were working — or an older orangutan was carrying out some operation or experiment of his or her own — Binti would watch, spellbound. To Binti, objects existed to be examined, manipulated, tested. Unless he was very hungry, eating held little interest for him. He would give his food away, to orangutans in camp or to dogs and cats in local villages, and I often had to make sure he ate something himself. Sharing food seemed to give him great pleasure. In contrast, Princess, like any orangutan, would beg, steal, and gobble food at every opportunity. Sharing food was not part of her orangutan nature at that age.

Whereas Princess still wobbled on all fours, Binti was walking upright, even running. And whereas Princess was silent except for occasional squeals when she felt abandoned by her caretaker, Binti was babbling away and clearly on the verge of talking.

Even before his first birthday Binti showed signs of the cluster of traits we consider distinctively human: bipedal locomotion, speech, tool use, and food sharing. Orangutans are capable of all of these behaviors, but only at a later age, and they never develop them as fully as humans. Abilities that emerged easily and naturally in Binti appeared slowly and laboriously in orangutans, and sometimes, as in tool use, primarily through imitation, or in sign language, through extensive coaching. An ex-captive orangutan like Sugito might frustrate us with his ability to disembowel the camp's only electric generator. But aside from Cara and others brandishing sticks and pushing over snags in aggressive displays, or using branches and foliage for nests and shelters, only rarely did we observe anything resembling tool use, as traditionally defined, among wild orangutans.

It took my own child at play to remind me of the deep evolutionary differences between humans and orangutans, even though we are so strikingly similar. To be sure, there were echoes of our common primate ancestors in Binti's behavior, but even as an infant surrounded by orangutans and their tropical rain forest habitat, he was, as all children are, indubitably a human primate.

And so Binti took his place — in our human family, in our finishing school for ex-captive orangutans, and in our island in the forest. It was one of the happiest times in my life. For me, motherhood was the culmination, the fulfillment of one aspect of my destiny. Rod, Binti, and I were living in the untouched Eden of the forest, at peace with the wild orangutans. Several years had passed since Cara's apparent death, and my pain and grief at her disappearance were less intense. I still thought about Cara, but I no longer brooded about her fate. The adult male TP had come back, as if from the dead. I was constantly making discoveries and, I hoped, pushing the boundaries of knowledge forward. Years later I asked Rod if he ever thought about that period. "Those were the golden days," I mused. Rod's reply was immediate. "Maybe they were golden days for you," he said darkly. "They weren't for me."

# 18
# ROD

Women have served all these centuries as
looking-glasses possessing the magic
and delicious power of reflecting the
figure of man at twice its natural size.

— *Virginia Woolf*

The thing to be astonished by, every single
second, is not that love can be tarnished
but that times can ever be golden.

— *Georgia Harbison*

---

ANALYZING ONE'S DATA and writing the Ph.D. dissertation is all-consuming. People who have not gone through the experience themselves have difficulty understanding the obsession. It is the ultimate academic rite of passage. One's whole life revolves around it. One's spouse becomes peripheral. Friends are temporarily cast aside. Dian Fossey wrote saying this was her last letter until she finished her dissertation. One shuts oneself up for fourteen hours at a time in gloomy university libraries, staring at the wall, listening to the muffled whispers and quiet echoes of shuffling footsteps along the endless corridors of book stacks. One memorizes the smell of paper. One's whole universe is reduced to black print, crawling like tiny spiders on yellowing paper.

When I started writing my Ph.D. dissertation in earnest in 1975, Rod, Binti, and I spent several months in Los Angeles on an extended exit visa. We stayed with my parents, whose home I considered my own. Rod leaped to my aid. He learned how to work the computer and spent endless hours putting my data into the large mainframe computer at UCLA. Sometimes I would leave campus long before he did to spend time with Binti. Rod would arrive home past midnight, fall into bed exhausted, but then be out the door at dawn on his way back to the computer room while Binti and I were still half asleep.

Rod had wanted to be a helicopter pilot in his youth. Now computers replaced helicopters. Something about them galvanized him. When I asked why, Rod explained, "It's their rational perfection. If you're having a problem, you know it's your own imperfection or lack of logic, not the computer. Unlike human beings, computers are infallible. I enjoy pitting my mind against that infallibility. I enjoy their total lack of emotion, their cold perfection." He was passionate about their lack of passion.

On our return to Indonesia, Rod went directly to Camp Leakey. I spent several weeks in Jakarta, staying with the Sulaimans. When I returned to Camp Leakey I brought Yuni to help care for Binti. I had tried to find someone else, but Yuni wanted to come and Binti liked her. I was still working on my dissertation, and urgently needed help with Binti. We arrived at Camp Leakey during the early afternoon in the drizzling rain. The day was dull; a harsh white glaring light permeated the rain and drained everything of color. It was an uncomfortable light that eroded the afternoon and cast sharp angles and harsh shadows.

Rod was deep in the trackless forest, outside the study area, following a wild orangutan. Mr. Ahmad didn't think Rod would be back until the next day. I was disappointed; I longed to hear news of camp and the orangutans.

I began settling in. While I unpacked, Yuni held Binti. About an hour later, the front door swung open. I looked up and saw Rod standing shirtless in the rain. He had lost the male orangutan he was following. The cold downpour made him look pale and gaunt. His almost shoulder length hair was plastered to his skull, and his body was lean and muscular. His camera case and binocular straps crisscrossed his bare chest. Unsmiling, he looked wild and untamable. Yuni stood up with Binti in her arms. No one spoke. Rod and Yuni looked at each other. A sharp, knowing look passed between them. Rod continued to scrutinize the scene for a few moments before he stepped up into the room and said hello.

I should have known then that something was going on between them. Only my obsession with the Ph.D. can explain my blindness. Yuni seemed much more adult than before, less virginal and less little-girl innocent. But she still was wonderful with Binti and that was all that mattered to me. She did not stay very long this time, but while she was there I noticed that she and Rod didn't sit together in the dining room, as before, and rarely talked in public. In fact, Rod was almost curt with Yuni. He seemed preoccupied, almost melancholic. Sometimes he didn't come to bed until one or two in the morning. He would tell me that he had been talking to the biology students from *Universitas Nasional*. I took him at his word. Yuni was helping me with Binti and Rod was helping me with the research. I couldn't ask for more.

Rod was in his element talking to the students. Indonesians love to talk, and so did he. The students were in awe of his forest prowess and jungle courage. Rod thought nothing of spending the night curled up under his rain cape on the forest floor. He charged back at a wild adult male orangutan who was charging him. His feats rounding up illegal loggers had acquired almost mythical status. Rod enjoyed the students' company and he enjoyed their admiration. The late-night sessions had never been so frequent or so long, but it never occurred to me to check on him. I assumed Rod did not lie. He was the type who gritted his teeth and told the truth.

Over the years, the Indonesian biology students had assumed a major role in our lives. Every six months or so, another pair arrived to collect data for their *sarjana* (equivalent to our bachelor of science or arts degree) honors thesis. During their time in camp, the students from UNAS became our closest friends and confidants. In the social vacuum of Camp Leakey, the raw power of proximity was overwhelming. Just having regular daily conversations (in Indonesian) transformed strangers into friends. Often the students looked alien and homely when they first arrived, a crooked nose here, a blemish there, a too loud voice or a raspy laugh. But they always seemed engagingly intelligent and charming when they left six months later. It was always painful to say goodbye to them. While the students were at Camp Leakey, they were our entire human social world. I found it relatively easy to communicate with these urban, intellectually somewhat Western young men, with whom I shared a background in biology. The very traditional local assistants were not accustomed to discussing ideas and exchanging opinions, especially with their boss.

But the orangutans were the main inhabitants of this universe. Although they came and went into the forest, they were the baseline. I got to know each and every one so well. It was very satisfying and comfortable to always deal with a small, stable group of individuals, orangutans and humans, whose faces and idiosyncracies were as well known as one's own. For me, this was the basic power of Camp Leakey. There were no crowds, no strangers. I suspect that this is how human beings evolved, living in small groups that did not change composition except for birth, death, and marriage. Life was so familiar and at the same time so intense. With Binti's birth, my world seemed complete.

But Rod had changed. Before, if I needed Rod to go photograph orangutans or vegetation in the forest, all I had to do was ask. Now I had to write him official memos. Rod had bought a fancy programmable calculator, and disappeared for hours at a time devising ever more complex programs. Once he was missing for six hours. I was concerned enough to ask the camp staff if they knew where he was. Shamefaced, they didn't answer. In the true Indonesian fashion of avoiding conflict or tension, the staff didn't dare tell me, just in case Rod found out who had told me and became angry at them. I later discovered that Rod was in the generator shed playing with his calculator, hiding from the "crowds" at Camp Leakey.

I was annoyed, and a little amused, that Rod, the hero of the jungle, was hiding his new persona in the shed like a teenager sneaking a cigarette behind the garage. But I was too preoccupied with my Ph.D. to stop and analyze what these changes meant. I was still oblivious, like an underwater sleepwalker. The camp staff was not. Mr. Ahmad's former daughter-in-law worked for us as a cook. Her name was Ernah, and she was devilishly attractive and spunky. With fewer than a dozen people in Camp Leakey, gossip traveled quickly. Someone told me that when a Jakarta student propositioned Ernah, she replied, "It's the bearded one I want," meaning Rod. I was shocked at Ernah's audacity, but then shrugged it off. Young women pine over married movie stars and rock singers; why couldn't a cook have a crush on Rod?

Socially sensitive, the Indonesian staff could see that Rod was "available." The signals were everywhere, but I ignored them. Maybe Rod and I were not spending as much time talking or being as loving as before, but Binti and my Ph.D. came first. If there were problems, not that I really thought there were, but if by chance there were, then we would sort them out after I got my Ph.D. Rod could wait. After all, we had been together a dozen years. Another year or two working on my Ph.D. wouldn't make much difference.

The next year, 1978, Rod, Binti, and I returned to Los Angeles. My mother hired almost the entire Filipino family next door as baby-sitters. I was totally immersed in my work. What little free time I had I spent with Binti. As before, Rod worked hard putting my data into the UCLA computer. But this year he insisted on going back ahead of me. Camp needed him, he said. I reluctantly agreed, though I would have liked his moral support in Los Angeles.

The corridors of Haines Hall, which housed the Department of Anthropology, were haunted by the ghosts of doctoral candidates who never made it. For a thesis to be accepted, each member of the doctoral committee must sign his or her approval. Fellow graduate students repeated tales of last-minute betrayal by junior faculty members. I was fortunate because the members of my doctoral committee were almost all supportive and fair.

I got my Ph.D. with split-second timing. One committee member kept repeating that my thesis had to be better than anyone else's because "at least five hundred people will read your thesis." He emphasized five hundred, as though it were an enormous number. In fact, most dissertations are read only by a few dozen people. With this potentially vast audience, he probably felt his career was at stake. At his insistence, I wrote draft after draft. The situation did not improve when I was sitting in his office one day and the phone rang. When the professor answered the phone, a pained expression came over his face, and he thrust the receiver at me, saying, "It's the *National Enquirer!*"

A reporter had tracked me down to my professor's office to ask, "Is it true you share your house with six orangutans?" There certainly were no orangutans in my parents' pleasant, pink stucco home in Los Angeles, with the fruit trees my uncle nurtured in the back yard. "Absolutely not," I replied. "I don't have any orangutans in my house." Only after I firmly put down the receiver did I realize that the reporter was asking me about my hut in Borneo. Yes, I did have as many as six orangutans living with me there. But I had given the "right answer." Any other response would have convinced this junior member of my committee that putting his signature on my thesis would catapult him into headlines in the *National Enquirer,* ruining his academic reputation.

But he signed. They all signed, and I had my approved thesis in hand. Because I was leaving for Indonesia the next day, the department had waived the usual oral defense. If I didn't make that flight to Jakarta, my entry visa into Indonesia would expire. But I still had to file with the university archivist, the last step in getting my Ph.D. I glanced at my watch. It was four-fifteen P.M. I knew that the archivist closed her office at three. I was walking with Dr. Rainer Berger, a senior member of my committee and the professor who had been instrumental in my meeting Louis Leakey. He was ebullient; I was near despair.

"Dr. Berger," I said woefully, "I won't be able to file my thesis. The archivist's office is closed, and my plane leaves early tomorrow morning."

"Let's try," Dr. Berger said. "Nothing is lost by trying."

We entered the Renaissance-inspired red-brick library building with its graceful arches soaring overhead at the heart of the UCLA campus, and walked to the archivist's office. The office hours posted on the door listed the closing time as three o'clock. By now it was four-thirty. The door was closed, the hall was still. Dr. Berger put his hand on the door handle, turned it, and pushed. The door swung open. Inside, the archivist was on a small ladder fitting books into shelves.

"We came to file a Ph.D. thesis," said Dr. Berger. "We hope we're not too late. We thought the office might be closed."

The archivist, normally taciturn, smiled broadly. "Oh, no, not at all," she said and stepped down to accept the thesis. "Congratulations," she said to me, smiling even more beautifully. I kept thinking that Dr. Berger and I had blundered into the wrong place. Every other time I had gone to her office she had frowned steadily, making me feel like a nuisance. Now she couldn't have been friendlier. Surprised, I replied, "Thank you." Dr. Berger and I left, both pleased with ourselves. As we entered the central courtyard and walked diagonally across to Haines Hall, Dr. Berger seemed thoughtful.

"You know," he said, "Louis Leakey's spirit was looking after you today. She always closes at three. Let's go to the faculty club and celebrate."

⚭

After Rod returned to Indonesia, he had made a trip to Jakarta to attend a forestry conference. He called me in Los Angeles from Jakarta. Rod's main news was that he had removed Sugito from camp and released him on the lefthand branch of the Sekonyer River, far from Camp Leakey. Rod was certain that Sugito would never come back. Sugito was at least nine years old now, about the age at which Carl first left his mother. In my absence, Rod unilaterally decided it was time for Sugito to go.

When Rod told me he had removed Sugito, a hush fell over my heart. I was literally speechless. Couldn't he have waited at least until I returned to Kalimantan? Didn't Rod know what Sugito meant to me? Or perhaps he did.

The vendetta between Rod and Sugito, pursued all these years, had gotten out of hand. As Sugito grew up, he and Rod disliked each other more and more intensely. Sugito expressed his dislike by specializing in the demolition of Rod's equipment. Whatever Rod maintained or managed, such as our new electric generator, Sugito seemed to take special pleasure in dismantling. This wasn't mere curiosity; Sugito was not practicing reverse engineering. It was personal animosity toward Rod. The feud had started when Sugito was still an infant, with Sugito attempting to co-opt Rod's ear for "immoral" purposes and snapping at Rod every time Rod approached me. Sugito had been shoved from the nest, not by me but by Rod. When Rod was away from camp, I still allowed Sugito to sleep in our small wooden house. Sugito insisted on it.

Without Cara's fangs, I couldn't enforce a total separation. Nor did I want to. Sugito was spending most of his time in the forest; I saw no immediate reason to force him away.

When Rod told me over the phone that he had thrown Sugito into the forest, I felt betrayed. No doubt, this move prevented future problems. Not only was Sugito destructive, but he also viewed human males as competitors and sometimes bit them. I understood that. But Sugito was not the worst offender. Among subadult males Gundul was the biggest problem, and Rod had not removed him. Whatever Sugito's misdemeanors, I felt strongly that I should have been consulted, even by phone. Rod was not Sugito's "father" but I was, in my own way, Sugito's "mother." Sugito was the first orangutan orphan whom I had adopted. For that reason alone, Sugito had a special place in my heart. I should have been allowed to say goodbye.

During the months that Binti and I were alone in Los Angeles, I hadn't written to Rod once. "He can wait until I get my Ph.D.," I told myself. "My work comes first." But now I was eager to get back to Camp Leakey and share my triumph with my husband.

When I arrived in the Sulaiman household, I sought Yuni. She was in her small room, lying on her bed in a white slip. The room was so small that standing in the doorway I was inches from her. She half rose to greet me, but hesitated as if she couldn't stand up and face me. She seemed less gay, less welcoming than before.

In the Sulaiman household, one of the staff usually brought in the mail and the afternoon papers. The mail was put on the corner of a long chest in the large sitting room, and the newspapers were put on the coffee table for members of the household to peruse.

As I walked into the sitting room, a familiar script caught my eye. On top of today's pile of mail was a letter from Rod. I was touched. Perhaps I could forgive him for exiling Sugito after all. I picked up Rod's letter. I was about to open it when I realized that the letter wasn't addressed to me. It was addressed to Yuni. A chill swept my bones. It was just a letter. But it should have been for me, not Yuni. Something was wrong. But I still didn't get it; I still didn't understand.

When Binti and I returned to Camp Leakey, with my Ph.D. in hand, Rod met us halfway up the two-hundred-yard ironwood causeway that serves as a marker to small planes flying over Kalimantan. To the astonishment of a watching graduate student and two visiting scientists from North America, Rod and I merely shook hands. It didn't surprise me; Rod was not the most demonstrative person. Later, I was told that the three Westerners discussed this meeting for a long time that night. "A very businesslike, professional relationship" was the verdict. No one suspected that anything was wrong. In Indonesia husbands and wives usually do not engage in public displays of affection. We were, the visitors decided, respecting local customs.

Several weeks passed before I finally understood. Rod and I still shared the same bed and still occasionally talked like husband and wife, but relations between us had distinctly cooled. One night, without knowing why I was so emboldened, I asked Rod if he had ever kissed Yuni. To my shock, he said, "Yes." I had worried that he would get angry at me for even posing the question. Instead, the floodgates opened. Rod was in love, he wanted to marry Yuni; he was only waiting for her to finish high school to sweep her away to North America. Rod wanted a divorce.

There I was, in bed with my husband whom I dearly loved, and he was telling me that he was going to leave me and marry another woman. I hadn't seen it coming. Or perhaps I didn't want to see it, because then I would have had to deal with it. I knew vaguely that something was wrong, but didn't actually believe my husband would leave me for a younger woman. I had been raised as a Roman Catholic. At that time, divorce simply was not part of my vocabulary. I never considered the possibility.

Yet, strange to say, I felt relief. I knew that the relationship between Rod and me was no longer fresh and young. Rod's dissatisfaction had not escaped me totally. I was relieved that it was "nothing personal." Rod said he didn't hate me. He hated Camp Leakey, Kalimantan, following orangutans in the forest, the life we were leading. When he told me he was in love with another woman, his recent coldness and even hostility made sense. At least I had an explanation. I hugged Rod and went to sleep.

The reaction came later. My relief was soon transformed to feelings of bitterness and betrayal. Sometimes Rod could be overwhelmingly compassionate, but at other times he was archly sarcastic. We pretended that nothing was wrong and that Rod was leaving only to return to university. In Indonesia, appearances are important. You don't burden other people with your problems. I told no one. Rod and I continued living and working together, but it was a charade. At times Rod was too weary to even be polite.

Worst of all, Binti was two and his parents were splitting up. Rod made it clear that he had given serious thought to Binti's future. One of the two things that propelled him home to North America was Binti.

Rod would soon turn thirty-one. Binti would soon be three. Binti was North American. Rod was concerned about his lack of human playmates, his speaking Indonesian and even the Kumai dialect better than English, and his need to go to school. Rod's decision to leave Kalimantan, go home to North America, return to school, and divorce me and marry Yuni was not entirely an emotional one. It was also a practical one.

"Binti," he insisted, "will soon need to go to nursery school. He has to come home to North America."

The prospect of Binti leaving was heart-wrenching. Yet I had to agree. Indonesia was not an immigrant society but a traditional one; Binti would have had a difficult time fitting in. I also believed that a boy should be with his father. Had our child been a daughter, I would have insisted that she stay with me. But I knew this was the right thing for Binti. Besides, he wouldn't be leaving right away; I still had a little time.

Rod needed a mother for Binti when father and son returned to North America.

"I don't want to be a welfare father," Rod said. "I need Yuni in Canada to help me take care of Binti so I can work and go to school," he explained. "I need Yuni both for myself and for Binti."

I was not surprised that he chose Yuni. She was sweet, gentle, considerate, and passionate. She was also very pretty. And she had just turned eighteen. Yuni loved Rod. I loved Rod and I also loved the orangutans. Rod told me that he could not accept second place to a bunch of apes, no matter how important they were in the overall scheme of things.

"I've done nothing but serve the orangutans for seven and a half years," Rod emphasized. "Now it's time for me." He continued. "You have a Ph.D. now. You can do it on your own. You don't need me anymore." He explained that he had been waiting for me to finish my Ph.D. Basically honorable, Rod had not wanted to upset me while I was working on my degree. But now that I had my doctorate, I could manage on my own. He had made the decision years before but waited until the right moment.

"Every year," he said, "it got harder and harder to come back to Kalimantan. I never want to return to Kalimantan as long as I live. Never!"

Rod told me over and over how difficult it had been for him. He hated the disease and malnutrition. He hated the fact that someone else, me, made all the important decisions in his life. He hated being so short of money that he occasionally had to cross the street in Pangkalan Bun to avoid creditors.

He also hated the fact that he had no credentials.

"The Indonesian biology students look up to me," he said. "We discuss their data collection techniques and their methodology. I give them advice. We discuss theory, but I feel like a sham. They have finished their course work and are a thesis short of their bachelor's degree, but I haven't even completed my second year of university. They then go back to Jakarta and finish their degrees. I have nothing," Rod said repeatedly. "I don't have a car, a bank account, not even a mortgage. I don't have a job. Nothing."

I asked Rod if he had ever considered asking me to return to North America with him. "No," he replied, "I couldn't do that to you. You might agree, but it would be against your will. Your heart is here in Kalimantan with the orangutans."

Something else bothered Rod. I had gained thirty pounds while I was pregnant with Binti. I never considered my weight an issue, but Rod mentioned it several times. When I was completing my Ph.D. and spending all my days in the UCLA library, the pounds stayed on. Rod viewed it as an insult and a rebuke. Yuni weighed ninety pounds; I weighed close to twice that. He could pick her up with one hand; he could barely lift me off the floor. Now Rod wanted a career and a young, slim, adoring wife.

The 1970s marked the beginning of the "divorce revolution" in North America. Although Rod and I were half a world away, living in the jungle, we were going through the same experiences as our contemporaries back in North America. Far more than we realized, we were products of our times. In many ways, Rod followed the classic route for males of our generation. When I met him, he had dropped out of high school to travel the world. With his long hair, leather jacket, and motorcycle, he was the archetypal teenage rebel. Going to Borneo was in keeping with this countercultural image. I remember giving a talk on one of our return trips to North America. An old acquaintance of Rod's attended. He told us he had spent the last three years in Katmandu, "smoking dope." One day he woke up, decided that it was time to get on with his life, and returned to North America. Now Rod was waking up.

I, too, was a child of my generation, but in different ways. With my hair down to my waist, dressed in jeans and miniskirts, I may have looked like a "flower child," but I wasn't part of the countercultural scene. I remember stopping, on my way to a tedious, three-hour bone lab, to listen to a soapbox speaker. I think it was Jerry Rubin. He was talking about liberation in the broad sense. "Open the school windows, knock down the walls, and let real life come in," he urged. I didn't agree with everything he said, but his message and his passionate conviction were very seductive. I stood there listening to him for an hour. That was the extent of my participation in the cultural revolution. But my personal decisions to get my Ph.D., to go to Southeast Asia, to spend my life studying and rescuing orangutans, and to postpone having children were all part of a wave of the future. I didn't think of myself as a rebel, but neither did I ever consider becoming a full-time housewife. Men and women both changed in the 1970s, but these changes often pulled them apart.

Our divorce was as much a reflection of our culture and of the different ways Western men and women view the world, as a matter of personality conflict. The archetypal Western male, Rod went to Borneo in search of adventure. He liked testing himself, pushing himself to the limit . . . and then a little more. He was the Marlboro Man with a mission, saving the forest and the orangutans. But when you have the same adventure day after day, the exhilaration and the feeling of triumph fade. After seven and a half years, Rod felt that the laws protecting orangutans were being enforced and the reserve boundaries were secure. The job was done and it was time to move on, time to go back to "real life." I went to Indonesia for so-called "female" reasons: I wanted to help. If I had to take risks, I did. But I wasn't interested in adventure for adventure's sake. My triumph came from feeling at one with the orangutans and the forest; I exulted in the peace and the quiet. Because I wasn't looking for thrills, I never got bored. The more I knew about orangutans, the more I would be able to learn. After seven and a half years I felt even more committed than when I arrived.

After Rod told me he was leaving, I threw myself back into fieldwork. Observing orangutans and taking notes was an escape. The swamps were deep. It was the rainy season. The monsoon was with us. Beth was consorting. The rigors of daily fieldwork in the depths of the swamps caused the pounds to vaporize. Rod noticed my rapidly decreasing profile. He said, "It's a pity you lost weight now. A year ago it would have made a difference; now it doesn't. I'm still going to leave."

I remembered how Barbara Harrisson had accepted with grace and dignity the fact that her husband was leaving her. Ironically, instead of hating Rod for leaving me for another woman, my respect for certain of his qualities had grown. He taught me by example, hard, physical courage. He taught me to think big. And he taught me, by his departure, that I couldn't take anyone or anything for granted. He taught me that even honorable people need a way out sometimes. I was fortunate to have had Rod for so many years; we had made a wonderful team.

Only after Rod announced he was leaving did I realize how much I had resented the fact that it always had seemed so *easy* for him. I whimpered, I suffered, I gritted my teeth. I hated the fire ants that always invaded at three in the morning, their stings like fiery pitchfork jabs by miniature devils. I hated the oval lizard turds in my coffee and the rat droppings and bits of stone in our rice. I hated not having family and friends to talk to and books to read. I disliked not knowing what was going on in the rest of the world. Most of all, I hated the heat and the humidity. Now I discovered that Rod had hated it even more than I did. Never saying anything, never complaining, was part of his Western maleness, his "strong and silent" image.

I had grown weary, but never enough to consider leaving. For me, studying and rescuing orangutans wasn't a project or a job, but a mission. I have heard dancers and musicians say that they never consciously decided to practice their art, they simply *had* to dance, they *had* to play. So it was with me. Before I left for Kalimantan, even before I met Louis Leakey, I knew that this would be my life's work. I have always been very single-minded, very focused. I realize that some people may see this kind of determination as stubbornness. But once I began studying wild orangutans, once I realized how perilous their existence was, there was no turning back. To some degree, Rod had merely come along for the ride.

And then there was Cara. In the end, after Rod left, I realized that I had lost Rod not just to Yuni; I had also lost Rod to Cara. For Rod, Borneo in the early years had been an adventure, full of dangerous escapades and daring exploits. Cara's death brought the adventure to an end. It wasn't a game any more; now it was life and death. On some level, Rod took responsibility for not protecting Cara from her fate. It almost seemed as if he felt that in allowing Cara to die, he had failed her. Family researchers tell us that a child's death frequently leads the parents to divorce. The marriage is a constant, painful reminder of their loss. Cara's death cast the same shadow on our marriage. Had Cara not died, our fate might have been different. But on that cosmic cat's cradle being played out, somewhere far away, it was fated that Rod would leave and I would stay.

Our decision to separate was finalized during a visit to Jakarta. We hadn't told anyone we were getting divorced. But having revealed himself to me, Rod felt his secret was out in the open. When we arrived at the Sulaiman household where we usually stayed, Rod and Yuni started going out together in public for the first time. They sat together in the courtyard; they talked and they laughed. They were courting. By now I had accepted Rod's decision, but their behavior made me uncomfortable. I asked Rod to be more discreet; after all, this was Indonesia, not North America. But he didn't listen. One evening Rod, Binti, and I went out. After the three of us returned, Binti and I went to bed. Then Rod and Yuni went out.

Yuni was already somewhat resented in the household. Most household members ate in the kitchen. Only Yuni sat at the table in the dining hall with the immediate family. Her behavior with Rod did not increase her popularity with other Sulaiman relatives and the staff. Nina Sulaiman watched the situation developing. She felt loyal to Yuni, who was almost her adopted daughter, but Nina was also my friend. Not wanting to take sides, she did nothing. Mr. Sulaiman, very urbane but also traditional, was a devout Muslim who worked all day as an insurance company vice president. His evenings were filled with social events. He was oblivious. I said nothing to Yuni, who avoided my gaze.

One evening the situation exploded as it can only in Indonesia. Mr. Sulaiman knocked on my door and asked me to come to the living room. When I arrived, he demanded, "Do you know anything about this? What's going on?" Yuni began shrieking hysterically. Mr. Sulaiman's eyes were wide in shock. The rest of the household was ominously silent. Mr. Sulaiman told me that he had ordered Yuni to leave the household. Yuni's sister and brother-in-law were coming to pick her up, and Rod was leaving with them. In the midst of all this, Yuni fainted, as she had in my house at Camp Leakey. Then I learned the rest of the story.

Mr. Sulaiman had been abruptly informed of the situation by the servants — who had all gone on strike to protest the public immorality of Rod and Yuni's behavior! Indonesia is still a very traditional society, in which people place a high value on propriety and decorum. The staff were offended by Yuni spending time in public alone with another woman's husband. The strike had been organized by the more-than-sixty-year-old cook, *Ibu* Pipa, who had been in the household for years. Short, with a plain, round face and dark, intelligent eyes, always wearing the traditional Sundanese dress of West Java, a sarong and tight bodice, her thin wisps of hair tied in a bun at the back of her head, *Ibu* Pipa was very soft spoken and seemed very mild. Yet she ruled the kitchen with an iron hand in a velvet glove. If you wanted to eat, you had to get along with *Ibu* Pipa.

*Ibu* Pipa resented Yuni, because Yuni was honored above an older niece, also in the household, who was a *Bupati*'s granddaughter. Why should a *Bupati*'s granddaughter eat in the kitchen when a younger interloper from Central Java, who was not even Sundanese, sat at the table with the Sulaimans? That, by itself, was not enough to cause a palace revolution. However, Rod and Yuni flirting openly in front of the whole household, flaunting their relationship, was.

Led by *Ibu* Pipa, the servants presented Mr. Sulaiman with an ultimatum. They refused to work until Yuni left. The horrified look on Mr. Sulaiman's face that night suggested that he, too, was outraged. After Yuni came out of her fainting spell, she and Rod left.

The next morning *Ibu* Pipa, champion of West Javanese Muslim morality, looked extremely pleased. Forever after, when I came to the Sulaiman household, *Ibu* Pipa always had a big smile and warm handshake for me, as did the other older women in the household. But they held no grudges. After Rod and Yuni later married in the United States, they, too, were welcomed whenever they returned to Jakarta.

But the matter wasn't finished. Mr. Sulaiman, as head of the household, organized and moderated a meeting in his living room several days later. In keeping with the Indonesian tradition of achieving consensus, all involved parties were present. Yuni's parents came from Central Java, the first time they had been in Jakarta in fifteen years. Traditionally attired, they sat very still, very close to one another, like two small, stiff, fragile birds, at one end of the couch. One of Yuni's sisters was there, as was one of her brothers-in-law, who was Dutch but had one Indonesian grandparent. The dark Dutch brother-in-law sat next to Rod, advising him. Yuni sat next to her parents. I sat on one side of Mr. Sulaiman, and Nina sat on the other side.

The meeting had been called to restore harmony. I didn't like it. For the first and only time, I felt hostility toward Yuni. I knew that she wasn't the instigator. But now I felt exposed, naked, publicly humiliated. It was one thing to learn that my husband was leaving me for another woman; it was quite another to discuss it with people whom I had never met before. Such public discussion of private matters was foreign to me.

The outcome of the meeting was as expected. Rod and I agreed to get a divorce (which we did later in California). Rod announced his plans to marry Yuni and take her to North America. At the end of the meeting, I shook hands stiffly with everyone. I never saw Yuni's parents again, although Binti later spoke of them as one set of grandparents.

Rod left Pangkalan Bun as he had come. When he stepped on the plane for Java, he had on his back the same green backpack that he had carried seven and a half years earlier on his arrival. Rod's legs festered with lingering tropical ulcers. He was too weak to check out with the local police as required for all foreigners, or even make the customary rounds of his friends and acquaintances in Pangkalan Bun to say goodbye. He hobbled onto the plane and was gone. "Two years," I told people over and over. "He's gone to school for two years to finish his university degree."

Six months after Rod left, I took Binti to North America to enter nursery school. It was the most difficult decision I ever made. But I felt strongly that Binti should be educated in North America and that a boy should live with his father. I had been appointed to a permanent, part-time faculty position in the Department of Archaeology at Simon Fraser University, in Burnaby, British Columbia, which meant that Binti and I would have at least several months a year together in North America. During this trip Rod and I finalized our divorce. Now Rod could marry Yuni, and Binti would have a stepmother who knew and loved him. Whatever flashes of resentment I might have felt toward Yuni, I knew that I could trust her with Binti's welfare.

⁊

As one chapter of my life closed, another opened. During this turbulent time, I paid a courtesy call on the U.S. ambassador in Jakarta. At the end of my visit, Ambassador Ed Masters said, "You know, I'm certain my wife and daughter would enjoy meeting you. Let me invite you to lunch." It was the beginning of a friendship that continues today.

Ed Masters is a tall, warm, open man with a twinkle in his eye, an easy manner, and a kind demeanor. He clearly was an excellent Ambassador, but he wasn't stuffy about it. His wife, Allene, has robin's-egg blue eyes, very white skin, and fine, patrician bones that seemed to be made of porcelain. One was taken aback at how sharp she was and how quickly she read a situation.

Allene and her daughter, Julie, visited Camp Leakey, unofficially. At first, local officials refused to believe that Allene, who went into the forest with me to follow wild orangutans through the swamps and helped type observation notes late into the evening, was actually the U.S. ambassador's wife. I explained that volunteerism is a grand old American tradition. Back in Jakarta, Allene started raising money singlehandedly for Camp Leakey. For a while we became what Ambassador Masters called "my wife's favorite charity."

Allene formally introduced me to Indonesian culture. It may seem strange that I needed such an introduction after almost eight years in Indonesia, after being "adopted" by Indonesian parents, meeting with governors and ministers, and participating in numerous ceremonies, rituals, and community events. But I did. I had read virtually nothing about Indonesia because at that time books simply were not available in English. Furthermore, I had spent most of my time in the forest with the orangutans. Intuitively I knew a lot about Indonesian culture, but it wasn't fully conscious or codified. Whenever I was in Jakarta, Allene invited me to stay with her. A new world opened. She took me to *wayang kulit,* plays with magnificently colored leather puppets, which are a staple of traditional Javanese culture, and *orang wayang* plays, in which human actors play the puppets. Many of these Javanese plays were based on the great Hindu epic, the *Mahabharata,* whose characters are so familiar that to traditional Javanese they are as alive as next door neighbors. Many of the moral lessons from the *Mahabharata* had permeated Javanese culture and thus, to some extent, Indonesian culture. Allene invited me to dinner parties and concerts, introducing me to Jakarta's cultural elite.

My understanding of Indonesia doubled rapidly. Traditionally, Indonesians have prized harmony and order above all else. For them the flip side of harmony is chaos. There is nothing in between. Nothing. Terrified of the chaos that will erupt if order breaks down, Indonesians spend much of their time and energy maintaining harmony, often through endless discussion. Equally important, Indonesians believe in fate. One can't escape one's fate. In the tropics, death seems to come out of nowhere and can strike anyone at any time. If it is your turn to die, you die. Indonesians are not passive. But underneath their laughing, joyous faces is a stoic certainty that informs their lives. Fate can not be evaded. At most, it might be postponed, but ultimately, it can only be accepted.

Living in the same environment, amid tropical uncertainties, among people who embrace life and death with equanimity, I had absorbed some of these beliefs without realizing it. Cara's, Tony's, and Barbara's deaths, Binti's birth, Rod's departure, watching the wild orangutans, and living in the forest had all changed me. Following orangutans day in, day out, I had become more patient; I had become more accepting of fate's vicissitudes; I had grown more tolerant of delays and ambiguities; I had learned to live in the present and not worry so much about tomorrow. I had grown accustomed to the formalities and endless discussions that typify Indonesia. Ten years earlier, a divorce would have been unimaginable. Now it seemed inevitable.

I, in some essential way, had changed. Rod, in some essential way, had remained Western. For Rod, problems existed to be solved. He believed that rationality and logic would prevail. There was little room in Rod's universe for uncertainty and unpredictability. In his new life, once he returned to North America, he finished his degree and became a computer systems analyst. Putting the adventures and hardships of the rain forest behind him, Rod exchanged tattered blue jeans for a suit.

Even though, at the time he left, Rod spoke Indonesian better than I did and had many Indonesian friends, I was at home in Kalimantan in a way that Rod had never been. I realized this with a start many years after Rod left, when I came into Kumai. I had always preferred Pangkalan Bun to Kumai. Kumai was a staunchly Muslim Melayu town, inhabited by people still in traditional dress. Until recently, the only outsiders were Bugis and seafaring Sumatrans who blended in seamlessly. I disliked leaving the silences and cool, muted colors of the forest for the bustle, noise, and dusty heat of a tropical port town. I disliked the way little children and adolescent boys stared at me. I disliked the logistical difficulties of getting to Pangkalan Bun along a track that turned to mud in the rainy season. But, one day as my boat came out of the nipa-lined Sekonyer River into the mouth of the Kumai River, I glimpsed Kumai in the distance, shimmering like a mirage in the heat of the equatorial sun, and suddenly realized that I liked Kumai. With its coconut palms swaying gracefully in the wind, the thatch of its houses on stilts overlooking the water, the gleaming silver domes of mosques dominating the landscape, its elegant Bugis sailing ships lining the waterfront, Kumai reminded me of what Kalimantan must have been like in the nineteenth century. I wondered whether I had changed or Kumai had changed. The answer was, both.

Over the two decades I had spent in Kalimantan, the advent of electricity and television, and the arrival of settlers from Java and elsewhere, had changed Kumai. This sleepy port was becoming part of the modern world. But I had changed as well. Over the years, I had internalized much of Kalimantan reality — the timelessness, the vagaries, the unpredictability. In Kalimantan, life and death are a lottery. Sometimes, despite all of one's efforts, life-altering decisions are out of one's hands. Part of the reason that Rod left Kalimantan was that he wasn't in control. To live in Kalimantan means letting go. If a swimmer who is caught in a rip tide struggles, he or she is likely to become exhausted and be pulled out to sea or drowned. The best strategy is to swim with the current, gradually edging one's way back to shore. Only when I learned to swim with the current was I able to appreciate Kumai.

Journal articles and monographs on fieldwork talk about theory, techniques, and results. Popular books focus on the animals or on the adventure. One rarely hears how fieldwork changes people's lives. The living conditions, the funding difficulties, the practical problems, the highs of discovery, the false starts and dead ends, the drudgery of scientific record-keeping, the learning how to get along with people and societies initially very foreign to you, the learning how to get along without people, places, and things you once took for granted, the feeling of suspension in time as the world spins on without you — all have an impact. Fieldwork forces you not only to confront situations you could never have anticipated, but also to confront elements of your own character you might never have known. Every trip into the field is also a trip into yourself. Rod and I both changed, but we changed in different directions. This is why I stayed and Rod chose to go.

After we divorced, my mother bitterly took down from the living room wall the photograph of Rod and me that she had liked so much. She felt it was an embarrassing and shameful reminder of a failed marriage, the first divorce in the history of my devout Catholic parents' families. On my next visit to Los Angeles, I put the picture up again. "A marriage is not a failure just because it ends," I told my unconvinced mother. "It is a failure only if it doesn't end when its time is over."

# 19
# MAUD

---

**M**ANY YEARS AFTER Rod left Kalimantan, he was interviewed for a television documentary about my work with orangutans. "When we went to Borneo," he said, "Biruté didn't tell me she wasn't coming back." Like most people in their mid-twenties, I didn't have a detailed life plan. All I knew was that I wanted to learn as much about orangutans as I could.

When I went into the field, orangutans were strangers to Western science. Nobody knew how old wild orangutans were when they were weaned, when they first left their mothers, when they first mated and had their first offspring. Nobody knew when wild males developed cheekpads or even if all wild males did. No one knew the birth interval between successive offspring of wild orangutan mothers. Most scientists assumed that orangutans gave birth every three years. One even invented a computer model that showed that a population of orangutans would go extinct within fifty years if the birth interval were much longer. This seemed reasonable. In zoos, orangutan females gave birth every two or three years. But when I went into the field, I saw that some of the wild orangutan mothers were still nursing infants and juveniles who were much older than three.

Nor did anyone know how long orangutans live in the wild. Two orangutans had survived for more than forty years in a zoo, but no one knew precisely how old they were. When that zoo acquired the two orangutans, from a private collection in Cuba, they looked fully adult, so the zoo keepers arbitrarily decided they were about ten years old. The usual guess was that orangutans lived about thirty years in the wild.

But these were all guesses. I was determined to find out. My principal goal was to document individual life histories of as many wild orangutans as possible. I wanted to understand the forces that shape male and female life histories, respectively. I wanted to understand how different life histories shape different individuals.

My early observations of Beth, Cara, Georgina, Priscilla, and other females had shown me that daily lives of orangutans were slower-paced but also more complex than scientists had ever suspected. I had observed infants, juveniles, adolescents, and subadults. I had witnessed copulation, consortships, mothers with newborn infants, weaning, play, male combat, and orangutans (particularly males) traveling and foraging on the ground. I could describe individual orangutans and different behaviors, but to *explain* orangutans I had to observe the same individuals as they grew from dependency to maturity, compare data on many individuals, and then step back to analyze those data. Just as a photographer may not see everything the camera captured until he or she prints the negative, so a field researcher may not see patterns until he or she sits back to review reams of notes representing thousands of hours of observation.

When I began my study, I thought I would be able to describe the basic structure of the orangutan's world after five or ten years. But many observations I made in the first decade of my study only began to make sense in the second decade, when I began observing the next generation.

From the beginning, one of my main goals was to catalog the wild orangutan's diet. For many years, all of my assistants were Melayu. Although familiar with the forest, the Melayu lacked one essential skill: tree climbing. To obtain botanical samples of the foods orangutans were eating, I had to scrounge on the ground for scraps. The personnel at the herbarium in Bogor were dismayed at the poor quality of the samples I sent. When they asked how I obtained them, I explained, "from the orangutans." They laughed, but it was true. I needed someone who could collect food samples more efficiently.

After some inquiries, I hired a man who had worked for the German priest in Pangkalan Bun, a Dayak from the interior who had blue crosses prominently tattooed on his forearms. Like most traditional Dayaks, this man could climb high into the canopy and knew the forest intimately. In the week he spent at Camp Leakey, he collected more food samples than I could scavenge in several months. I asked people where I could find more Dayak men. They told me of a little village near Pangkalan Bun which had been translocated from the interior more than 150 years earlier. The village, Pasir Panjung, was famous because its Dayak residents had not melded with the coastal Melayu, but retained their customs, traditions, and forest skills.

I went to Pasir Panjung to hire one assistant. The village chief told me that one or even two would not come alone, so I hired three. Tougher and more individualistic than my original assistants, the Dayaks effectively took over. Within a year and a half, the Melayu assistants, including Mr. Ahmad and his wife, Mrs. Bahriah, all left.

Some of the Dayak assistants, especially those who had followed the aboriginal lifestyle, hunting with blowguns and poison darts, were superb searchers and trackers. Reading the forest was their native language. Having come to the tropical rain forest as a young adult, I would always speak this language with a foreign accent, even though my accent would diminish over the years. But that slight foreign accent informed my attitude toward the forest. The Dayaks never found much wonder in the forest as such. Although they understood it, they were never in awe of it. They took the forest for granted.

For me, the great forest was a sacred place. I recognized it as a relic of Eden, something to be cherished. I found its shadows and shade soothing. The young Dayak men were most at home on the forest edges and the riverbanks. Preferring open ground, they carried their savannas with them and re-created them even in the depths of the rain forest. They built their temporary shelters on ground they had first cleared of vegetation. It was as if they needed to see the sun to be one with their human natures. In contrast, I abhorred using a machete and would barely bend a piece of vegetation with my hand to mark the way. Like Hansel and Gretel, I would have preferred leaving a trail of biodegradable bread crumbs in what I considered sacred, though leech-infested, ground. For me, every day in the forest was full of discovery. I was learning for the first time what my Dayak assistants had known all their lives.

With the combination of my innocent reverence for the forest, the Dayaks' intimate knowledge and skills, and my scientific training, my orangutan study leaped forward.

❦

To learn what the "average" orangutan's life was like, I had to be able to compare a number of individuals. In the early days, I did almost all of the searching for wild orangutans myself. When I found one, I followed him or her for as long as possible because I did not know when I would locate another. It wasn't like studying a baboon troop, where I could alternate between observing different individuals while following the same group. During the early years, I spent more time searching for wild orangutans than observing them. But with several Dayak assistants in camp, I no longer had to depend on myself to find orangutans.

Now I could collect data on a number of individuals in different parts of the study area, and observe these individuals more systematically and regularly. If I didn't see Beth or Georgina for a month or more, my assistants and I would search specifically for her. It might take two or three weeks of concerted effort to find her. The reason was not that females wandered long distances; we always found them near where we left them. But if they wanted to disappear, they could, in the forest canopy. It was a little like *Where's Waldo?*

Unlike the wild female orangutans in the Tanjung Puting area, adult males did not settle down. They came and went. If an adult male cheekpadder was in the study area, you usually knew it. His long calls advertised his presence. The adult males' comings and goings were almost impossible to ignore. But attempting to monitor individual subadult males was futile, for they were always on the move. They were also difficult to identify. The subadult males looked so alike that sometimes I couldn't tell them apart even when they were in the same tree. Also, their appearance changed so much as they matured into cheekpadders that it was difficult to recognize them later. I rarely named wild subadult males unless I could positively identify them.

The orangutans' own lifestyles dictated that females and their offspring would become one baseline of my study. One of my main "informants" was Maud, Cara's nemesis, whom I had first observed when she was a young adolescent still traveling with her mother, Martha.

Maud was a "sleeper." She was one of the easiest females to locate. We found her with relatively little effort, once in only five days. I didn't know whether this was because Maud's home range was smaller than those of other females, because she was noisier than other orangutans, or because she was more self-confident after Cara's disappearance and didn't attempt to hide. Certainly, the reason was not that Maud was more habituated than other females. To the contrary, she rarely looked at me, vocalized loudly when I appeared, and moved quickly when I followed her. She seemed to particularly dislike being stared at or having a camera pointed at her. Every month or two, I dutifully recorded observations of Maud simply because she was there. I didn't have any particular affection for her. I thought of her as a supporting actor, not as a lead player. But, as sometimes happens in the movies, the supporting actor ends up being the star.

Only many years later, when I leaned back in my chair and pored over my notes and my hand-drawn maps of orangutan day-ranges did I understand why I encountered Maud so often. Perhaps Cara had reason to dislike Maud; perhaps Cara knew what she was doing when she repeatedly attacked the younger female. As I watched Maud grow to adulthood and, in relatively rapid succession, bear three offspring over the next fifteen yeas, the other adult females who had shared parts of Cara's range during her lifetime (Fran, Martha, and Ellen) gradually moved away. The process was not instantaneous. The females did not suddenly pick up and leave, as adult male orangutans do. But day by day, tree by tree, the other wild female orangutans moved. Imperceptibly, almost as if by unstated conspiracy, Maud and her offspring inherited Cara's home range. Priscilla was the only adult female who stayed where she was. Thus, the orangutan who benefited most from Cara's death was Maud.

I wondered if Cara had anticipated what I recognized only in hindsight, that Maud was a potential competitor. When Cara entered a fruit tree and surveyed the litter of broken branches, fruit skins, and stems on the ground below, she may have known that one of the orangutans who had been there just hours before, eating *her* fruit, was Maud. Who knows what an orangutan can read from the cracked remains of branches? I had learned that an adult male cracks a branch differently from an adult female, who is half his size; I could differentiate between a tree denuded of its bark by an adult male and a tree where a female had foraged. Orangutans may recognize individual signatures that I cannot perceive. Maud's pungent smell may have been her calling card. Even half an hour after Akmad left my hut, I could still smell her distinctive deep, slightly sweet, musky odor, the odor I called *Rawa* (or swamp) No. 5. Wild orangutans have a strong but not unpleasant odor. Perhaps each female orangutan had her own distinctive perfume.

When I realized that Cara had been guarding her fruit trees, her interactions with other females made more sense. Cara fought with Priscilla, the only adult female who consistently shared part of her home range. Cara was wary of adult females Fran and Martha, both of whom had large adolescent daughters who were in the process of setting up their own ranges. But Cara attacked Maud more than any other orangutan. Had she lived, Cara might have been in direct competition with these females and their offspring. Beth did not seem to threaten Cara, perhaps in part because her son, Bert, would not remain in the area when he reached maturity but would wander as all male orangutans do. In retrospect, Cara's likes and dislikes were not capricious.

I would never know the full history of Cara's relationships with other adult females, and whether her associations were based on biological relatedness or on choice. As Beth and Priscilla grew older, they began to look like virtual twins of Alice when I first met her. As often happens, age brought out resemblances. In middle age, Beth and Priscilla looked so alike that on several occasions I almost mistook one for the other. Noisy, a female I first encountered when she was an adolescent, began to resemble this trio when she reached maturity. I once saw Noisy's infant cross a tree to play with Beth. Since wild orangutan infants ordinarily do not play with strange females, this suggested that Beth was Noisy's mother or aunt. Judging from appearances, Cara was not part of this family. But I couldn't be sure.

The next generation — Georgina, Maud, Fern, and Evonne — would provide answers. I first observed Maud, Fern, and Evonne when they were still traveling with their mothers, and thus I knew they were not siblings. Although I didn't know who Georgina's mother was, Martha and Fran were unlikely candidates. Georgina was too close in age to Maud and Fern to be either one's sister. Ellen was a possible candidate, but Ellen's home range was in the wrong place. As she and Georgina gradually shifted after Cara's death, Ellen moved north and Georgina south, until their ranges barely touched. Meanwhile, Maud made herself at home in Cara's former range.

At about age twelve, Maud still spent much of her time with her mother, Martha, and her younger brother, Merv. Martha's exceptionally black face was now deeply lined. Although not as unsteady and fragile as the aged Alice, Martha seemed old. She moved very slowly, resting more than she traveled. Adult female orangutans typically move in a stop-and-go pattern. Martha's pattern was stop, stop, go, stop, stop. When Martha and her daughter, Maud, were together, Maud frequently initiated travel and Martha followed.

When Carl had reached adolescence, his mother, Cara, had literally pushed him away, frequently attacking him. Martha's relationship with adolescent Maud was quite different. I never saw Martha attack Maud, or Maud cringe in the presence of her mother. Relations between mother and daughter were respectful and cordial. Martha and Maud frequently sat next to each other on branches, once or twice so close that they almost touched. At the same time, I never saw Martha and Maud play with or groom each other. Mothers and daughters apparently do not need to test each other through play or to reassure one another by grooming, though this behavior occurs between mothers and sons or adult females and unrelated female adolescents. Mother-daughter acceptance is so strong, it borders on passivity. Since mother and daughter ordinarily share the same range for the rest of their lives, this prim and proper relationship clearly is adaptive.

I've experienced this relationship myself, with my first orangutan "daughter," Akmad. A visitor to Camp Leakey who saw Akmad come and sit five feet away from me, barely glancing at me, would conclude that nothing was happening. If I had raised Akmad, the visitor would assume, surely we would hug and play. But Akmad treats me exactly the way wild orangutan daughters treat their mothers. She doesn't impose on me, and I don't intrude on her. This combination of acceptance and distance allows us (or allows wild orangutan mothers and daughters) to inhabit the same range without coming to blows. Akmad leaning against me was, in orangutan terms, an extraordinary display of affection, as if she were pouring out her heart: "I love you, Mommy. I missed you, Mommy." But such displays are extremely rare.

For orangutans, the deepest relationship is to be able to occupy the same space and not interact. To some degree, the same is true for humans. With most people, in most situations, we find silence awkward and fill the void with chitchat. Only with people to whom we are extremely close, whom we deeply trust, are we able to be together and not talk, because there is no void to fill.

Cara and Carl's relationship seemed to typify the pattern for mothers and their growing sons. Even the large adolescent Andy, with his thick coat of orange hair, seemed frightened of the frail Alice, who, had she been human, would have belonged in a wheelchair or even a nursing home. Andy occasionally squealed or cringed and ran away from his mother for no discernible reason, just like Carl. I have never seen wild adult females threaten or attack their daughters the way they do their sons.

Relations between adult females and unrelated adolescent females are more varied and volatile. For example, I once saw Maud traveling peacefully with adult Ellen, playing with Ellen's large infant, Eve. The next day, with no warning and no apparent provocation, Ellen charged at Maud and drove her squealing out of her tree. Had I not known Ellen and Maud were unrelated I might have assumed this was a replay of Cara and Carl, a mother pushing her daughter toward independence. But it was just an adult female shooing away a pesky adolescent.

Maud now seemed as wary of Georgina as Georgina once had been of Cara. When Maud met Georgina and her infant daughter, "Gale," late one afternoon, Maud vocalized loudly for almost twenty minutes before she entered Georgina's tree. When Georgina moved past her, Maud curled out of Georgina's way, making herself seem smaller as Georgina moved past. An hour later Maud squealed and ran when Georgina approached her. But Maud nested near Georgina that night. The next morning Georgina went beyond warnings, and attacked. Squealing like a fire siren, Maud leaped out of the branches and descended the tree rapidly. I saw a wet spot on Maud's shoulder, where Georgina probably had bitten her. Maud stopped about thirty feet above the ground. Indignation seemed to replace fright. Now she stared at Georgina and issued a vigorous kiss-squeak, followed by a long hoot, a sign of extreme annoyance. Then Maud moved into an adjacent tree, where she ate young leaves for more than half an hour. Maud seemed to be asserting her rights, but at a safe distance.

Once sweet and playful, Georgina was becoming grouchy and antagonistic. In my mind's eye I could still see the adolescent Georgina playing handsies gently with her friends, squeaking delicately like a baby doll, and sitting demurely alongside adult males. But adult Georgina was ornery. This seeming personality change turned out to be a common developmental pattern, although the degree of change varied from individual to individual. Almost overnight, a gregarious female adolescent became a standoffish adult with a chip on her shoulder. If another adult or near-adult female did not observe the proper decorum, adult females could be quite disagreeable. Maud was learning which adult females in the area were mild-tempered and which irritable, as well as what they would and would not tolerate.

With Maud, I was able to observe adolescence from the beginning. Maud often traveled with subadult males, but seemed to prefer the company of females her own age, especially Fern. Although Fern was a year or two older, she was only slightly larger than Maud. But Fern's size was accentuated by a thick coat of fluffy hair, whereas Maud had shorter, coarser-looking hair. Maud's hair was so sparse that her genitals and a few patches of skin were visible, while Fern was totally blanketed in thick, shiny hair. Maud also was slightly bug-eyed.

Whereas subadult males rarely stay together for more than a few hours if no female is present, adolescent females often team up for days or even weeks.

I once saw Maud and Fern travel together for twenty-one days. The two young females often sat on branches side by side, touching. Sometimes as they sat, they briefly touched or even held hands. One might hang upside down from an overhead branch and seem to play patty-cake with the other who sat on a lower branch. Both of their faces would be scrunched up in the orangutan version of shy smiles. Maud and Fern's play was so sweet and timid, I felt as if I were watching two Akmads up in the forest canopy. Once they even sat together briefly in Fern's day nest, behavior I had rarely seen. There was little doubt that Maud and Fern liked each other. Had they been teenage girls, they would have spent their time trying on each other's clothes, doing each other's hair, going to the mall, and gossiping about boys.

At one point, Maud and Fern were joined by another adolescent female, Evonne. Fern greeted Evonne gently. Then, to my surprise, Fern began inspecting the younger female's genitals with her lips. Evonne squealed and moved away. But about twenty minutes later Fern again approached Evonne, grasped both of Evonne's feet in her hands, and tugged at her. Evonne squeaked and squirmed as Fern again put her lips to Evonne's bottom. Fern began vocalizing low raspberry sounds and lip-popping as though she were angry that Evonne wasn't cooperating. Then Fern pressed her genitals against Evonne's genitals and began thrusting. I stared in disbelief. When Evonne escaped, Fern approached Maud. To my astonishment, Evonne moved back to watch, as if she knew it was now Maud's turn. Maud escaped Fern's grasp, and the three moved into another tree and resumed eating as though nothing had happened.

I puzzled over this scene a long while. I saw nothing malicious in Fern's behavior. I don't think she was trying to dominate Evonne; Evonne didn't seem afraid of Fern, she just didn't like what Fern was doing. Nor do I think Fern was sexually excited. She didn't stare off into space as male orangutans do when they are copulating. It was just an adolescent game. Fern was imitating what subadult males did to her, just to see what it was like. Fern's mimicry was so perfect that I wondered if I had mistakenly identified Fern as a female. I spent the next several hours trying to get a clear view of her genitalia. Finally I got an unobstructed look and there was no doubt. Fern was definitely female. Although I never saw this behavior repeated, it fit the pattern of experimental adolescent sexuality.

By age thirteen, Maud was almost always accompanied by one or more subadult males. These young males did not appear to view one another as competitors, and often spent more time playing with each other than courting Maud. Mating was not yet a grim, "for keeps" contest, as it would be when they became cheekpadders. But the magnet that drew them together was a pubescent female, Maud, and their play was a way of testing one another's strength and will for the time when male competition for females would become serious.

Maud's attitude toward subadult males was unpredictable. She was just beginning to learn what attracted males, what they wanted, and how to handle them. If Maud had been a member of a social species, such as chimpanzees, she would have had numerous opportunities to observe mating. But until now, she had spent her whole life with her mother. She may have seen subadult males buzzing around her mother, and probably witnessed her mother engage in at least one consortship with a mature cheekpadder, but little more. Obviously her mother couldn't tell her the facts of life. Maud had to learn about sex for herself.

At this age, Maud seemed to be drawn to mature cheekpadders but wary of them at the same time. After all, she had even less experience with adult males than with subadults. Adult males were so big and so blasé, they probably were more difficult for Maud to figure out. Cheekpadders do not play.

I was following Maud when an adult male orangutan appeared on the ground. Although he passed within a few feet of me, he didn't seem to notice me sitting on the forest floor. His eyes turned upward, and he climbed into the tree where Maud was foraging. He was a magnificent cheekpadder with a long flowing beard. I later named him "Ulysses," because he came and went, never staying in the study area long. Maud approached him and they sat close together, motionless, for twenty minutes. Maud finally moved off. Ulysses started to follow her, but then saw me and went berserk vocalizing and kiss-squeaking.

Ulysses stayed near Maud on and off for several days. Once Maud made a day nest, which, for her, seemed to be an invitation to copulate. She spent an hour in the nest, fidgeting and occasionally peering over the rim. Eventually Ulysses moved toward the nest and sat gazing at Maud for a time, but then moved away, leaving Maud behind. Later Maud encountered one of her subadult male friends. Like magic, Ulysses materialized on the ground below her. Again, he passed within a few feet of me, seemingly oblivious of my presence. I was grateful he didn't walk right over me. Orangutans do not have hooves or claws to give them away. Barefoot, with their padded hands, they sneak up on you. I was getting jumpy; I never knew when Ulysses or some other male would appear on the ground. I didn't want an angry adult male to tear me apart on his way to a confrontation with another male.

But I was learning that the competitive energy of an adult male orangutan is focused. It isn't generalized fury, like that of adult male chimpanzees who grab anyone within reach — including stray infants and, once, Jane Goodall's then husband, photographer Hugo van Lawick — in their charges at other chimpanzees. Chimpanzee rage is indiscriminate. Male orangutans are selective and deliberate. This may explain why female orangutans frequently continued to eat in the trees as though nothing were going on in the presence of males who were chasing each other or even fighting. There seemed to be a code of chivalry among the adult male orangutans, at least in the forest.

At Ulysses' appearance, the subadult male fled. Ulysses stayed close to Maud for the rest of the day, but made no attempt to copulate with her. He behaved more like a chaperon than a suitor, nesting close by that evening. The next morning Ulysses was gone, but he would reappear in Maud's life. Perhaps he was waiting for her to grow up.

The week Maud spent carousing with Andy and her other subadult male "pals" seemed the essence of orangutan adolescence. For Maud, Andy was the boy next door. They had grown up in the same vicinity and clearly recognized each other. Maud was about fourteen now, and Andy only eleven or twelve, but he was already larger than she was.

The morning Andy appeared, Maud was traveling with a large subadult male. Andy and the other male immediately started wrestling and biting one another. The two males roughhoused for more than twenty minutes, totally absorbed in their game. Then they entered an old nest and played some more. Maud sat watching intently. The scene reminded me of preteen parties where the boys get into food fights on one side of the room, while the girls titter about who likes who on the other side.

Finally, Maud moved on. Andy immediately left the nest and followed her. As if asserting his rights, the subadult male caught up with Maud and copulated with her for twenty minutes. But later that afternoon, when the subadult male approached Maud and tried to copulate with her again, she refused. The three orangutans stayed close together the whole afternoon and nested in the same tall tree that night. How different these young males were from the solemn, mature cheekpadders, who did not tolerate another adult male's presence for a minute and jealously guarded their consort.

The next several days were filled with play-fighting and nest-building. Andy grappled with the subadult male, once hitting him with a dead stick he had broken off a tree. He also wrestled with Maud. All three orangutans were making tight-lipped grins with both their upper and lower teeth showing. Late one afternoon, when the subadult male wandered off, Andy approached Maud, spread her legs, and inspected her genitals with his mouth, then positioned her. Maud sparred with him, in token resistance. They copulated for four minutes. The whole time, Maud wore a classic play-face. It was just a game!

When the subadult male reappeared, Maud kiss-squeaked and hooted at him, as if she were telling him something. The three orangutans continued on their way, helter-skelter. Two days later another subadult male appeared and immediately copulated with Maud while the first subadult male and Andy played nearby. Maud did not welcome the new subadult male's attentions; as he thrust, she squealed sharply and tried to twist loose. Nevertheless, when the copulation was over the four orangutans moved off together with Maud in the lead, the new subadult male following her so closely that he was touching her, the other subadult male about one foot behind him, and Andy bringing up the rear. They reminded me of a toy choo-choo train, with Andy as caboose. When Maud made her nest for the night, the three males nested close by.

The following morning, the four adventurers encountered Andy's mother, Alice, sitting quietly in a tree. Andy immediately went up to her and held her hand. Had he been a human son and she a human mom, the scene could not have been more tender. Because Alice never gave birth to another offspring, she did not reject Andy in the harsh manner that Cara had rejected Carl. Even when Andy was twelve or thirteen, he and his mother remained close. Nonetheless, he was cautious around Alice. Touching her hand was unusual.

Amazingly, the two subadult males approached Alice, too. One subadult male took her other hand and the second male took her foot. I didn't know whether they were simply following Andy's lead, or whether they had their own relationships with Alice. They reminded me of well-mannered young men politely greeting an elderly lady, but that was a human interpretation. Male orangutans, like male chimpanzees, seem to prefer older females to young ones. Alice still consorted with adult males, but she never gave birth again. Perhaps these subadult males found the ancient Alice attractive.

Maud did not greet Alice, but remained sitting about fifteen feet away.

Alice let go of Andy's hand, apparently signaling that the audience was over. Andy and the subadult males immediately left her tree, but hovered nearby. When Maud moved away, however, all three males jumped to follow her. I wonder what Alice was thinking as Andy disappeared. Did she recognize that Maud's reproductive career was just beginning, while hers was ending? All four orangutans, Maud, Andy, and the two subadult males, nested in the same tree again that night.

And then the party was over. A very large, rough-looking subadult male, almost the size of a cheekpadder, appeared. He reminded me of Beast, the near-adult male who had forcibly copulated with Georgina years before. By now Andy had wandered off to rejoin Alice. Although the new "Beast" did not fight the subadult males, he demonstrated possession by staying within ten feet of Maud, a difficult task considering the complex, three-dimensional nature of orangutan locomotion. The next few days Maud and Beast were alone together. After waiting more or less patiently for three days, Beast copulated with Maud on their fourth day together and again on the fifth.

By this time our food and fuel supplies at camp were almost exhausted, and I was having medical problems and urgently needed to go to town. With great reluctance, I had to leave Maud and Beast. This is part of the untold story of field studies. Ideally, all decisions in the field should be made for scientific reasons. In reality, decisions on when to observe, or who to observe, or even how to observe are often dictated by necessity. I desperately wanted to watch Maud and Beast's relationships unfold, but it was impossible. Camp logistics and sheer survival came first.

A year later, I saw Maud and Ulysses together again, and the subadult males were gone. Although I couldn't be sure, I had the clear impression that Ulysses and Maud were consorting and that he had driven other suitors away. This seems to be the female pattern. Besieged by subadult males and somewhat promiscuous in adolescence, in young adulthood a female chooses or is chosen by a cheekpadder she encountered in her youth. Usually, this cheekpadder is the father of her first and perhaps her second offspring. Six months after I saw Maud with Ulysses, she exhibited the swollen, white genitalia that are the telltale sign of orangutan pregnancy. By now Ulysses was long gone. But like the Greek hero for whom he was named, he would return.

To me, what is remarkable about orangutans is not that they are so solitary, but that they maintain relationships over long periods despite the fact that they do not interact or even see one another for months, often years, at a time.

Maud was carrying a newborn infant, a son I named "Mel," the next time I found her. I estimated that Maud was sixteen years old when she gave birth. In the pattern typical of adult female orangutans, she was now almost always alone. Her one occasional female companion was Fern. Although Maud and Fern no longer met frequently or traveled together for weeks at a time, and no longer played as they had in adolescence, nonetheless their "friendship" was evident in the way they coordinated their travel and sat next to one another.

Maud encountered Georgina now and then, but Georgina was belligerent and Maud generally stayed away from her. Georgina's personality as an adult was a replay of Cara's. Maud and Fern seemed much more like the benign Beth. They avoided conflict and did not impose themselves on other orangutans.

During the next six months I observed Maud monthly for as long as a week at a time. The transformation from gregarious adolescent to solitary adult seemed complete. But Maud's solitude was accentuated by the fact that there were few adult females in the range she inherited from Cara. By the time Mel was born, Martha had disappeared. I don't know whether she died or moved away, but I never saw her interact with Maud as an adult. Although I still followed Fern's mother, Fran, I didn't see Fern and Fran traveling together often, either. But ten years later I saw this mother and daughter meet in the top of a tree and embrace. The only adult female who shared part of Cara's, now Maud's, range was Priscilla. They occasionally passed each other, but I did not see them interact directly.

Maud's son, Mel, was a healthy infant who passed all the developmental milestones at the normal age. He started moving off Maud's body for very short distances well before his first birthday. By the age of two he was regularly moving away from Maud when she stopped, tasting food and foraging near her, as well as taking food from his mother's mouth. Maud was an indulgent mother who usually shared. After he turned four, Mel began traveling on his own behind his mother from tree to tree. When she stopped, he frequently came up to her and suckled. Mel's infancy was as normal as it could be.

Then, suddenly, Mel began squealing incessantly. I had never heard an orangutan that young squealing as much as he did. Mel was throwing Carl-like tantrums, although he was only about five years old. I was puzzled. I couldn't understand what was going on. Mel's tantrums got progressively worse. Occasionally I saw him hanging upside down from the end of a branch, screaming with all his might and pounding the air with his fists in frustration.

Sometimes the human brain does not comprehend the obvious. I had noticed that subadult males now occasionally appeared near Maud. Then the majestic adult male, Ulysses, with his flowing beard reappeared after a five-year absence. Only then did I realize that Maud was consorting again, and Mel was being weaned.

Carl's frustration during his weaning was mild compared to Mel's hysterics. But Mel was two years younger. Maud began weaning him as soon as he started traveling on his own, the earliest weaning I had seen among wild orangutans. I rarely saw Maud with males other than Ulysses during this period. When subadult males attempted to copulate with her, Maud resisted vigorously. This is part of what confused me. Typically, a receptive female who has weaned her current offspring does not put up much resistance to subadult suitors. Maud did. After he consorted with Maud, Ulysses the "traveling man" vanished. Maud was alone again.

At approximately twenty-two years of age, Maud gave birth to her second infant, whom I later named "Michelle." When Michelle was born, Mel was totally weaned. His temper tantrums had stopped. Mel seemed to accept the fact that he had to share his mother with an infant. Except that he never attempted to suckle, Mel traveled with his mother almost as if he were her sole offspring, and sometimes shared her night nest. Mel and Michelle played, just as Carl and Cindy had. Usually Michelle initiated the play by tottering over and tugging his hand. Mel was sweet and gentle with his baby sister.

Especially after Michelle was born, Maud was unusually vocal. At first I thought she was annoyed by the human observers who haunted her. Later I realized that Maud was vocalizing to Mel. When Mel wandered more than a hundred feet away, Maud would stop whatever she was doing and kiss-squeak vehemently, looking in Mel's direction until he returned to her. I had never seen another orangutan so obviously use kiss-squeaks as a summons. Maud still treated Mel as a dependent. Only when Mel was about nine — the age at which most orangutan mothers begin driving their sons away — did Maud's kiss-squeaking stop. Mel already was semi-independent; Maud didn't need to chase him away.

At age eleven, Mel was traveling and nesting on his own, away from Maud. He was an exceptionally calm orangutan. Perhaps Maud did him a favor. She forced him off her body in one sharp break, but maintained the emotional relationship and continued looking after him for some years. Mel seemed highly self-confident, even around humans. But he had grown up staring down at humans, almost from the day he was born. We were part of his world. He didn't even display much curiosity as he looked down at us. Like Carl before him, the adolescent Mel was alone most of the time and went about his business seemingly without a worry or a care. At age thirteen, Mel wandered away from his mother's home range and out of the study area.

Michelle was more a chip off her mother's block. She stared at us intently and constantly. When she began to leave her mother's body at about age four, to travel from tree to tree behind her mother, Michelle did something that very few wild orangutans do. She started coming down trees closer and closer, to get a better look at the humans who were so much a part of her life. Sometimes, Michelle came within thirty feet of us, directly overhead. Often she threw branches and vocalized, as if experimenting with us, to see what our reactions would be.

Michelle was over seven years of age when Maud, now almost thirty years old, gave birth to a third offspring. This time Ulysses had not come back; I do not know who the father is. That third infant is still unnamed as I write this in 1994. Maud keeps the infant on her side most of the time, and I have not yet been able to determine the infant's gender with absolute certainty. At age ten, Michelle still travels with Maud and occasionally shares a nest with her. As I have learned, mothers do not aggressively chase their daughters away. But any day now, I expect Michelle to begin spending less time with her mother and more with her adolescent peers. I know that as long as the forests of Tanjung Puting stand, I will continue to encounter Maud and Michelle. If all goes well, Michelle probably will die within a mile or two of where her mother, Maud, was born.

I haven't seen Mel for several years. I know Mel well enough to recognize him if I see him again, but his life as a male may carry him far away. Increasingly, the forests around Tanjung Puting are being cut down. Depending on how far Mel has traveled, gaps in the forest may make it difficult for him to return.

Maud, in her ordinary way, is everyorangutan. In most ways, her life has been unexceptional. But she was given one major advantage. During Maud's adolescence, an entire orangutan unit — Cara, Carl, and Cindy — disappeared, leaving their range wide open. In human terms, Maud was an heiress; she inherited a small fortune in fruit trees from Cara. Perhaps this windfall allowed Maud to wean Mel and give birth to Michelle in less than six years. This birth interval was exceptionally short. Fern, for instance, did not give birth to a second infant until ten years after "Feb's" birth. But Fern shared her home range with her mother and dependent siblings, although they rarely encountered one another.

Maud grew from a slightly straggly, coarse-haired adolescent to a full-bodied adult female with a long, splendid, glossy coat and three healthy, vigorous offspring. Fortunately for Maud and her offspring, these years were uneventful. The ideal life of an adult female orangutan is serene and predictable; to a human being, it would be unbearably dull. Nearly all the females an adult female encounters will be individuals she has always known. Her life consists of traveling and eating. Her young grow up and, with a little push, become independent.

Once in a great while, the orangutan female enters into a consortship with a mature, cheekpadded male and is pursued by lustful, ever-hopeful subadult males. The same male may father one or two of her offspring, as I believe was the case with Maud and Ulysses. But the same males are not present for a female orangutan's entire reproductive life. Males come and go. After an orangutan female leaves adolescence, sexual adventures are a peripheral part of her existence. Meanwhile, day after day, she travels leisurely through the canopy, feeding. For an orangutan female, food is life and life is food.

Twenty-three years after I began my study in Borneo, I still observe some of the wild orangutan females I first met more than two decades ago. Maud is now in her early thirties. She does not look old, although she clearly is no longer an adolescent. Only the tiniest bit of white remains on her face. Beth is solidly middle-aged, almost matronly. Priscilla looks even more bedraggled now than when I first met her. Alice died at least a decade ago; Martha probably died, too. But Fran has two grandchildren. Priscilla is a grandmother as well. Even Georgina, once the sweet-faced adolescent, has a grandchild.

Years ago, when Louis Leakey sent me John MacKinnon's monograph about the migratory orangutans of North Borneo, I read and wept. Not literally, of course, but figuratively. If orangutans were migratory, a long-term study of life histories would be impossible. John probably was right about the orangutans he studied. In the rugged highlands, the orangutans have to follow the fruit up and down the mountainsides. But in the swamps, where I have worked, the females generally stay in or near their mothers' home ranges for their entire lives. Only the males wander.

In my twenty-three years, whole new sets of young adult males have taken command of the forest, one at a time. Several years after TP miraculously reappeared, he again vanished, never to reappear. Nick and Handless Harry, whom I last saw in the seventies, were replaced by Ralph. "Sam," "One-Eye," and Ulysses, first seen in the seventies, all went their ways in the eighties. Following the life history of a wild male orangutan is virtually impossible. One can only infer male histories from cross-sectional data, looking at different individuals at different stages of their life and putting these observations together to form composite pictures.

Whereas the life of a female orangutan is serene and predictable, a male's life is more complicated. For an adult cheekpadded male, every other adult male is the foe. He has to compete not only for food, but also for access to mates. He may die young, as many male mammals do. Until he retires from the fray, food and combat dominate his life.

Sarah Blaffer Hrdy, a leading American sociobiologist, studied hanuman langurs, the usually gentle, semisacred monkeys of the Indian subcontinent, in the early 1970s. Hrdy found that hanuman langurs, like many Old World monkeys, live in troops composed of related females. Periodically, these troops are invaded by new males. The new males drive out the resident male, and one of the newcomers eventually drives off his own allies, so that only he remains. In the troops Hrdy studied, the male frequently committed mass infanticide, killing all the nursing infants of the females in his troop. By killing infants, the male brings the females into estrus immediately, instead of waiting two or more years for the females to wean their current offspring. Then he mates with the females. All of the new infants will carry his genes. For a few years, he is king of the castle. But eventually he will be chased out of the troop by another male or males, to wander evermore alone.

Sarah told me that one of the memories that will always haunt her is looking into the eyes of an adult male hanuman langur. The female hanuman langurs, with their buttery-chocolate eyes, always had a gentle gaze. It was easy to look into their eyes. But the male hanumans were aloof. It was virtually impossible to catch their gaze. One day, almost by accident, a male hanuman langur turned his head and his eyes locked with Sarah's. For a second, Sarah stared into the male's unflinching eyes. She said it was like looking into "the soul of a shark." The eyes reflected a creature who was utterly alone.

Superficially, the lifestyle of a male orangutan is similar to that of the male hanuman langur. If anything, male orangutans are even more isolated. After they leave their mothers, experiment and associate with others in adolescence, and then become cheekpadders, they are alone except when they consort with a female or combat other males. But an adult male orangutan is not a fearsome, solitary predator. Wild orangutan males do not kill infants. They generally do not kill each other. Looking into the eyes of an adult male orangutan, one sees self-containment and power. Despite the fierce battles that will determine the male's reproductive fate, an adult male orangutan is not the most belligerent of creatures. Male combats are rare occurrences. In twenty-three years, I have witnessed less than a dozen.

Wild orangutan males spend most of their time waiting for the big chance: the opportunity to consort. They rest their mental and physical faculties, preparing for the rare battles that will allow them to defend their consorts. Males cannot waste themselves or fritter their energy away. Rather, they are almost meditative in their calm. In this way, male orangutans are similar to sumo wrestlers. A sumo wrestler lives to prepare himself for the few seconds or minutes in a short series of contests that will determine who, ultimately, will be grand champion. Like sumo wrestlers, adult male orangutans eat to gain weight and strength, and "exercise" (for instance, by hanging by one or two fingers from tree branches while they eat). But probably the most important thing that adult male orangutans can do is to keep their minds clear for the battles ahead, the few championship bouts that will determine whether their genetic identity will live or die. Most of the time, the adult male orangutan seems reflective and serene. Only in combat with other adult males does he become dangerous, unpredictable, and even wantonly savage.

Looking into the eyes of an adult male orangutan is like looking into pools of deep, dark water, like the water of the Sekonyer River, and seeing oneself reflected back — not one's actual self, but the individual one might aspire to be, the tranquil, serene, strong, independent individual who, with no allies but the resources of his mind, body, and soul, pits himself against all others, one on one, until he can endure no more. That is why we find the adult male orangutan so compelling. In his eyes we see a precarious balance of ruthless strength and brutality on the one hand, and gentleness and serenity on the other. The eyes of the male orangutan remind us of the awkward combination of angel and beast that characterizes the human soul.

# 20
# GARA

---

WHEN FACED with an angry, three-hundred-pound wild adult male orangutan, with an arm span of perhaps eight feet, I try not to react. I force myself to do nothing. Even if the people with me turn and flee, I remain where I am, silent, immobile, expressionless. The orangutan must make a split-second decision: engage me in combat and risk injury, or withdraw into his meditative state and save himself for the real battle. I know that to a wild male orangutan, I am basically irrelevant. Testing my strength would be a waste of his energy. Sometimes facing a wild orangutan male is not altogether different from facing the human forces aligned against him.

On a trip to Palangka Raya, I was approached by a young man at the airport. Indonesians are outgoing people and frequently strike up conversations with strangers. As part of the usual pleasantries, the young man asked me what I was doing in Indonesia. When I told him that I studied orangutans, his face brightened. "Oh," he exclaimed, "I know where there is an orangutan. Do you want me to take you there?" I said sure, and we made arrangements for him to pick me up early that evening at Mr. and Mrs. Binti's home.

The young man arrived on his motorcycle shortly after five. Motorcycles are the mass transportation of Kalimantan; often three or four family members or teenage friends climb aboard. But Mr. Binti thought it unseemly for me to ride on a motorcycle with a complete stranger, and offered to drive me in his car to the home where the orangutan was kept.

We followed the young man to a section of Palangka Raya near the waterfront where the houses were cramped so closely they had no yards. The orangutan owner's house seemed to spill over into her neighbor's, so that one could stare from her windows right into her neighbor's rooms. It was not the best part of town. When we arrived, the owner, who worked the evening shift as a cleaner at the local hospital, was not at home.

The orangutan "pet" was a dark-haired, active female, a small juvenile. Asking permission first, I took the orangutan out of her cage and sat in an armchair with the juvenile on my lap. After some polite chitchat and the invariable glasses of sweet, steaming tea, I told the owner's husband, as courteously as I could, that keeping an orangutan pet was illegal. He seemed incredulous. I suggested that now that he knew the law, he and his wife would want to do the right thing and immediately turn over the orangutan to the proper Forestry Department officials so that the orangutan could be released into the forest. I volunteered to go with him and suggested that we leave immediately.

Half a dozen people had gathered around the man. A younger relative was dispatched to the hospital to summon his wife. I continued to explain, quietly and politely, why the orangutan should be returned to the forest. By the time the wife arrived, out of breath, the living room was crowded with neighbors. The woman clearly did not want to give up her orangutan. The juvenile orangutan, however, seemed to have no particular attachment to the owner. The orangutan appeared more interested in the crush of humanity surrounding us.

We reached an impasse. The crowd of people in and around the house was growing. Every window was packed with curious spectators. The air was charged with anger; a spark and the room would have exploded. I tried to smile pleasantly and speak meekly, as if I regretted delivering this bad news. I didn't get angry or upset. I continued talking. As long as the talk continued, all was well. It was the Indonesian way.

Mr. Binti had been standing near me silently all this time. I was surprised that as a high-ranking government official, he had not spoken. His face was impassive; his usual smile gone. Now, he leaned over and said quietly, "The hour is late. We should leave." I said that I wanted to stay until the orangutan was handed over. Mr. Binti shrugged and said, "I am tired. I am going home now. Do you wish to come back with me?" When I replied, "No," he left quietly without excusing himself to the orangutan owner or her husband.

By now at least a hundred people had gathered. It was so crowded that the windows were blocked and no air circulated inside the house. The owner and her husband had lapsed into silence. An off-duty police sergeant, a neighbor, detached himself from the crowd and began speaking harshly. He said that I didn't know what I was talking about. I replied that as a police officer, he should know the law. This only made him angrier. An older man took his place, and then another.

It was ten o'clock. The crowd had become a mob. The air of menace was pervasive. I finally agreed to come back for the orangutan in the morning. I expected a sigh of relief. Instead the crowd seemed to be gloating, congratulating themselves. Where before there had been a certain respect in their anger, now they didn't bother to hide their sneers and snickers. I realized that the crowd thought I had capitulated. They had won and I had lost. I knew the orangutan would not be there the next morning. The men's eyes gleamed in the triumph of betrayal. My Western credulity had led me into a trap.

"No," I told them. "We will take the orangutan to the Forestry Department tonight. The law must be obeyed. If I did not help the owner obey the law, then I would be remiss." The contempt shifted instantaneously to naked hostility. All pretense of civility disappeared. The men's faces turned hard. I realized that the women and children had silently vanished. The crowd consisted entirely of grown men. I thought to myself, "I'm going to be lynched." But I held my ground; I had no choice. If I capitulated now, the orangutan would be lost and my credibility weakened.

Another older man in a plaid sarong glided into the room. Someone slipped off a chair to give him a place to sit. He introduced himself as the "R.T.," the administrative head of a neighborhood unit consisting of ten families. I repeated my position yet another time. A hush fell over the crowd. The R.T. did not answer immediately, but sat looking at me. I stiffened in anticipation, as if expecting blows. But his face remained benign as he looked at me thoughtfully.

Finally, the older man said, "She's right! Orangutans are forbidden." The R.T verified the law; I was not deceiving or tricking the owners. The tension drained out of the room. Almost as an afterthought, the R.T. said, "I saw it on television when I was in Java." At the time, there was no television in Kalimantan Tengah. Yet the Indonesian mass media had brought this orangutan her freedom — and perhaps saved me. I wondered if the R.T. had seen the news when I brought the generals' four orangutans home from Java.

Although by now it was eleven o'clock, eight or nine motorcycles roared out of the darkness. I rode behind the young man; the owners and a dozen of their friends accompanied us. This strange procession took the orangutan to the P.P.A. office. The local head of P.P.A., whose residence was next door, seemed reluctant to answer the door. Recently arrived from Java, where I first met him, he probably thought he was under siege by a local motorcycle gang. Cautiously, he opened his door a crack. When he saw me standing there, he threw the door open. "I didn't know you were in Palangka Raya!" he exclaimed. I apologized for waking him and explained the situation. The young man, who was holding the orangutan, handed her to the P.P.A. officer and then drove me back to the Binti household on his motorcycle.

When we arrived, I thanked the young man for his help. All evening, his face had been expressionless. Now he was wide-eyed and animated. "I had no idea that you were going to take the orangutan. Absolutely no idea!" He seemed shaken. The next morning Mr. and Mrs. Binti made no comments. They voiced neither approval nor disapproval. But their silent support became clear when Mr. Binti proudly drove me to the P.P.A. office to visit the orangutan. The P.P.A. official complained in a good-natured way, "I couldn't get rid of those people last night. You were wise to leave. I hardly got any sleep. They wanted me to pay them for their orangutan and I refused. We argued half the night."

Mr. Binti looked amused at this outpouring. "You're helping him do his job," he said when we left the Forestry Department office. "He shouldn't complain; he should be very grateful."

Like all Indonesians, Mr. Binti disliked discord. Open conflict made him uncomfortable. Like a cautious wild male orangutan, or like the seasoned politician he was, Mr. Binti did not use his power unless absolutely necessary. Although Mr. Binti found the scene the night before extremely unpleasant, he believed that I would be able to handle whatever developed. He was relieved that all had ended well, and seemed proud of his adopted daughter.

I named the orangutan "Gara" after the new governor of Kalimantan Tengah, Mr. W. Gara. Mr. Binti and Mr. Gara had met when they were eight years old. Both had been sent away from their small Dayak villages to attend missionary boarding schools in the "big city," Banjarmasin, the capital of South Borneo. This mutual experience bonded them. They were very much kindred spirits, similar in their short, robust frames, their energy, rationality, and love of laughter.

Rescuing Gara was a harrowing experience. I've rarely felt as alone in the forest as I felt in that crowded, angry room. But it was worth the risk. Few orangutans survive beyond their juvenile years in captivity. By bringing Gara back to Tanjung Puting, I was saving her life.

༃

Years earlier, when I pried Sugito from a filthy crate in Kumai, when we confiscated Akmad from the loggers, when I persuaded Sobiarso's owners, and when I was given Rio, I had simply wanted to save the young orangutans. There were no instruction books on rehabilitation at that time, no guidelines. I had no idea whether these infant orangutans would resume their natural lives in the forest. Few people had attempted to rehabilitate great apes before. Returning animals to the wild is a notoriously risky undertaking; even the most sophisticated, carefully planned rehabilitation programs often fail. I relied on common sense and my knowledge of individual orangutans. After all, a species consists of individuals. Akmad's six-month disappearance was the first sign that my improvised strategies were working.

In the early years, when I received only a few ex-captive orangutans each year, adopting the infants myself made sense. Now, less than a decade later, I had received dozens of ex-captive orangutans. I sometimes found myself with one infant on each side, a smaller infant wrapped around my neck, another infant sitting on my foot, and a gibbon attached to my other ankle. This was not the portrait of an effective professional. Sometimes my biggest achievement of the day was to waddle successfully to the outdoor toilet or to the river to take a bath.

The rehabilitation program had to become more systematic. It was impossible for me to be "mother" to all the orangutans in camp. Instead, I tried to put infants together in small groups so that they would climb, forage, and spend time together, under my watchful eyes or those of the local assistants. If they were too small or unwilling to nest, we put them in cages for the night. During the day, we spent hours encouraging the young orangutans to play and explore in the trees. I made lists of tasks to be accomplished daily and even started jotting notes for an informal training manual for the local assistants.

Older ex-captives sometimes participated in rehabilitation by adopting a new infant. Not all new infants were adopted, but many were. Most of the orangutan adopters were adolescent females, on the verge of biological motherhood, but adolescent males also took part. In some cases, the infant initiated the adoption by attaching him- or herself to an older orangutan, as Carey had done with Akmad. In other cases, an older ex-captive "kidnapped" a reluctant infant. But whoever chose whom, once the connection was made, the infant bonded as tightly to the adoptive orangutan parent as Sugito had to me. The infant usually stayed with the parent until she gave birth, in the case of females, or he began to wander, in the case of males.

I would like to take credit for the orangutan adoptions, but I can't. Although I occasionally tried to put a younger and an older orangutan together and encouraged them to bond, most of the adoptions were initiated and carried out by the orangutans themselves. Perhaps Akmad and others got the idea from watching me play "mother" to orphaned infants of their species; perhaps they learned from each other. Whatever the origin of this practice, the adoptions continued, as if handed down from one generation of ex-captive orangutans to the next.

As with humans, the smaller the infant, the greater the chances he or she would be adopted. But Gara was about five or six years old when she arrived and weighed at least fifteen pounds. Nobody adopted Gara. Fortunately, we had several large female infants in camp at that time. After two weeks in quarantine, she was free to interact with the other orangutans.

Gara was a self-sufficient infant who played with Princess, "Hani," and "Claudia," but was best pals with "Kuspati." Gara and Kuspati became inseparable. In the cage, they would huddle together at night. When they nested, they did so in the same nest. Secure with each other, Gara and Kuspati were somewhat standoffish with humans. Their main link with humans was the food and milk we provided twice daily to the ex-captives. I virtually never held either Gara or Kuspati. In fact, most of the time I was shooing them up into the trees.

Gara and Kuspati were among the most "trouble-free" of the ex-captive orangutans. Neither squealed very much, and when they did, it was because they were separated. They did not get sick; they did not raid camp. They did not use human implements or artifacts as tools. Neither Gara nor Kuspati ever came into the buildings. Rarely did their long arms and fingers attempt to reach through the wire screening into a camp building. Gara and Kuspati differed very little from wild orangutans.

At first glance, Gara and Princess, with her advanced cognitive skills and her affinity for humans, seemed to be opposites. Princess had been adopted by a human, then-graduate student Gary Shapiro. For two years Gary carried Princess, as his adopted "daughter," and taught her sign language. Treating her like the good, middle-class ape she was, he even let her sleep in her own room with a hammock slung in the corner. Cempaka would have been envious.

When Princess was a young infant, her "best friend" was my son Binti. Binti nicknamed Gary "Mr. Cookie," because he always carried cookies in his pockets to use as rewards in his signing research. "Mr. Cookie" was Princess's parent. The result of this upbringing was an orangutan who actively liked humans (or at least the people she encountered at Camp Leakey). She even occasionally offered bits of her food to Gary, just as Binti had offered bits of his food to her. But Princess also interacted with the other orangutans in camp and often accompanied them on foraging sessions in the forests and swamps nearby or went on her own.

If different species carried passports, Princess would claim dual citizenship, in both the world of humans and the world of orangutans. Princess is "bicultural." She is an easygoing ape with a quick interest in what humans are doing, but she also is able to live on her own in the forest. Sometimes she disappears for weeks at a time. But Gary's two solid years of parenting clearly affected her. Princess's tool-using skills, cognitive abilities, and imitative capacities are remarkable.

Princess once "categorized" sticks by length, neatly ordering them from shortest to longest as she played with them on the ground. Researchers working with captive chimpanzees have concluded that the great apes show intelligence roughly equal to three-and-a-half-year-old children. But in Jean Piaget's theory of human cognitive development, seriation is a milestone in reasoning and may not be mastered by children until age seven or eight. Whatever her developmental level, Princess is smart in ways that humans recognize.

Princess has used dugout canoes as portable bridges over swamps and streams. She became adept at unlocking and locking doors of camp buildings with keys. She used combs and brushes to groom her own and her offspring's hair. Princess even took a child's toy machine gun and held it so correctly that it looked as though she were ready to fire. Unlike a human, she did not use two hands to hold the gun in place, but rather a hand and a foot. Even so, the action was natural and perfect. She pointed the toy gun at me, but did not pull the trigger. No one trained Princess. She learned all these human activities on her own, by watching, imitating, and practicing, because she likes human beings and sees herself as an equal. In Camp Leakey, that is how she is treated.

Over the years, Princess became a self-appointed ambassador for the orangutan species to the world of humans. She sits at the interface between our two worlds and bridges the space that separates us. Even today, Princess often waits with "Peta," her second offspring, to greet visitors at the end of the ironwood

causeway that links Camp Leakey to the Sekonyer Kanan River and the outside world.

Gara, in contrast, stayed almost entirely in the orangutan world. For some
years, she spent most of her time in the forest with Kuspati. Just as wild female
orangutans drift away from their mothers in adolescence, so Gara eventually
left Kuspati to travel alone or with other ex-captive orangutans in the great
forest. One day, seven years after she arrived, I was walking in the swamps
some distance from camp when I noticed an orangutan in the trees. I stopped
to get a better look and she started moving eagerly toward me, descending
from the canopy. It was Gara. As if delighted to see me, she made a play-face
and, hanging upside down from a vine, took my hands in hers and began
playing. This was the first time that Gara had ever greeted me this way. I felt
like Sally Field who said, in open, honest joy at the Academy Awards, "You
like me! You like me!" It was a revelation. Gara liked me! She actually liked
me! I was an old acquaintance, who had known her as a small juvenile, possibly
an auntlike figure in her life.

Both Gara and Kuspati first gave birth when they were about fifteen years
old, about the same age as the wild orangutan females. Princess, however, gave
birth when she was only about twelve. In order to give birth, a female, whether
human or orangutan, must achieve a certain percentage of fat on her body.
Because Princess had regular access to camp food, she probably was fatter than
the lean Gara, who had the figure of a wild orangutan. Like immigrants to
America who grow faster and taller in the second generation, Princess developed ahead of her wild orangutan peers. Her second passport, the human one,
gave her access to the agricultural revolution of the Neolithic, an event wild
orangutans, who stayed in the rain forest, bypassed.

Just as Maud was the wild everyorangutan, so Gara turned out to be the
quintessential ex-captive orangutan. Neither aggressive nor timid, Gara minds
her own business, foraging for food in the forest alone or sometimes with
Kuspati. She is now in her early twenties and has two infants, separated by a
respectable wild orangutan birth interval of almost seven years. Gara's older
offspring, "Gina," still travels closely with her mother. Her second, "Gary,"
rides on her side. As an adult, Gara is now a slightly wary, standoffish female
who stays in the trees. Sometimes, but not always, she descends when she sees
me, and sometimes she attends feedings. But the average visitor to Camp Leakey most likely will not notice Gara, who rarely interacts with strangers. Most
often she will be glimpsed at the top of a tree staring down.

Princess is the orangutan who captures visitors' attention with her friendliness, her intelligence, and her uncanny imitations of human activities. Princess is the orangutan who will take your hand and peer into your eyes, as if seeking your soul. She understands humans and human culture, just as she understands orangutans and the adaptations and protoculture of her own species. She slips easily from one world to the other and back again. Princess shows us how close humans and orangutans really are, despite the ten million years of evolution that separate us.

Without question, Princess is a "star." Stars are important to rehabilitation and the conservation process. Stars capture the spotlight and highlight an issue. Gregarious creatures, human beings need an individual with whom they can identify such as the character Smokey the Bear, who personifies the animal kingdom's vulnerability to forest fires that destroy animal habitat. At Camp Leakey, Princess's persona captures the visitors' attention and delight. Many visitors find themselves enchanted with Princess and, almost in spite of themselves, involved with her as a person, even though she does not speak. She doesn't need to. It is Princess's "personhood," her vibrant personality and sense of her own identity, that the visitors will carry back with them, sometimes to stay in their minds forever.

But, in another less obvious way, the real success stories and stars of the rehabilitation process are the ex-captives like Gara, who return to their orangutan world apparently without effort or much coaching and melt almost imperceptibly into the forest. Gara and Princess are not opposites, but twins. Both are wildborn orangutans who were captured in their infancy but rescued and released at Camp Leakey. Gara chose to live her life in the forest. Except for her occasional forays into Camp Leakey for feedings, she gives little evidence that she ever had contact with humans. Princess chooses to spend much of her time in Camp Leakey and to interact directly with people. But she is neither a pet nor a performer. Like Gara, Princess grew into a competent orangutan mother. Each has borne and raised two healthy offspring. (This contrasts with orangutans in zoos, who sometimes neglect or abandon their infants, which is why the infants are occasionally taken from them.) Both Gara and Princess are fulfilling their orangutan destinies.

In their different lifestyles, Gara and Princess illustrate a mystery that has long puzzled primatologists. Captive and ex-captive orangutans, released at rehabilitation stations, are as sophisticated in their use of tools as their chimpanzee cousins. Indeed they have been taught to flake stone tools, much as our early hominid ancestors did. Orangutans score as high or higher than chimpanzees on intelligence tests in laboratories, and demonstrate an equal capacity for sign language. Yet wild orangutans have rarely been observed making tools. Rarely have they been seen hunting, sharing food with other adults, joining "war" parties, or engaging in other kinds of protohuman behavior — behavior we expect from a close relative, and behavior that has been documented (although infrequently) in chimpanzees and bonobos.

The contrast between ex-captive and wild orangutans, between what orangutans can do and what they naturally do, is vividly apparent at Camp Leakey. Princess and other ex-captive orangutans "wash" clothes at the end of the dock along with the camp assistants. The orangutans may be washing rags, but they scrub as intently and seemingly with as much pride as any human. They may use sticks, hoes, shovels, hammers, and other tools to dig and pry. They have "helped" to paint walls, siphoned fuel from large drums with hoses, and positioned pots and pans on remnants of kitchen fires.

A few ex-captive orangutans have even tried to make fire. Cempaka took burning sticks out of fires and tried to torch camp buildings. Another ex-captive uncapped a container of kerosene, scooped some into a cup, then plunged a burnt-out stick into the cup. Next she touched a burning stick to the first, now fuel-soaked, stick. When the sticks did not flare, she fanned them with a lid. Although the orangutan did not succeed in making a fire, she clearly understood the process. She knew that you need fuel, a burning stick, and fanning. But lacking practice, she didn't use the precise sequence. I once saw the same orangutan holding two burning sticks in her hand like a fire-eater in a circus.

But these are not circus acts. Nobody trained the orangutans to wash clothes; certainly, we did not encourage them to make fire. Rather the orangutans imitated people they saw at Camp Leakey. Just as Binti learned sign language merely by watching Gary Shapiro attempting to teach ex-captive orangutans Ameslan, so the ex-captive orangutans imitated humans as well as other orangutans. But in the forest these "camp" skills were of little use, and the orangutans rarely performed them. I have seen only a few certifiable examples of tool use by wild orangutans, such as Carl waving a broken branch to shoo away wasps.

If orangutans are highly intelligent, why don't they use these cognitive abilities more in the wild? Only after many years observing wild orangutans and rehabilitating ex-captives did I realize that the answer was obvious. The orangutans' deceptively simple lifestyle requires keen intelligence. Wild orangutans

appear lackadaisical in part because they carry so much information in their
heads.

Orangutans are among the most brilliant botanists on the planet. Their knowledge of plant life is staggering to the mere human scientist, who depends on
notebooks, libraries, microscopes, and computers. Confronted with the abundant and diverse plant species in the tropical rain forest, orangutans must know
which are edible, nutritious, and nontoxic. A wild orangutan's diet is a highly
diversified mix of fruit, leaves, bark, sap, insects, shoots and stems, honey, and
funguses. At Tanjung Puting, wild orangutans eat more than four hundred
different food types. Documenting the unprecedented variety of the orangutan
diet was one of the major achievements of my research.

Ordinarily, wild orangutans do not taste an item before deciding whether
to eat it. Rather they inspect the food object visually or handle and sniff it.
Rarely do wild orangutans sample new foods. Once when I was following a
wild adolescent male, I pulled a banana out of my pack and ate it. I noticed
that the young male was watching me intently. The banana was an enticing
bright yellow, a color that frequently signifies ripe fruit in the forest. I took
out another banana, peeled it, and ate it as ostentatiously as I could. Then I
took out a third banana, placed it in the fork of a small tree, and moved away.
The adolescent immediately came down, took the unpeeled banana, sniffed it
intently for about ten seconds, then dropped it. There are no wild bananas at
Tanjung Puting. Because it was not familiar, the young male rejected it. Thus
orangutans choose what to eat on the basis of stored information, not trial
and error.

I learned the role imitation plays in food selection when I was following
"Paris," a large, cheekpadded wild adult male. Paris had seen me take bananas
and other food out of my backpack numerous times, but paid no attention. I
was observing Paris sitting in the canopy one day, when an ex-captive female
named "Rani" appeared. As soon as I took out my lunch, a container of rice,
she came and sat next to me, put her face close to mine in a classic primate
begging gesture, and squealed. Not wanting a commotion, I took some ripe
bananas out of my backpack and gave them to her. Rani immediately climbed
into the trees and gobbled up the bananas with obvious relish.

I looked up and saw Paris's eyes fixed on Rani's face and hands. Rani
dropped the banana peels to the forest floor. Later, as Paris traveled through
the canopy, he kept glancing down in my direction. After a few hours, Paris
circled around and came back to the exact spot where Rani had dropped the

banana peels. Paris descended to the forest floor and gingerly picked up the peels with his thumb and two fingers. He looked at the peels, sniffed them, looked at me thoughtfully, and then looked back at the peels. His inspection of the banana peels took at least one minute.

Weeks later, one of my Dayak assistants came back to camp with an amazing story after a day in the forest observing Paris. The cheekpadder had been sitting motionless in the canopy for some time when the assistant left his backpack on the ground and walked away to defecate. When the assistant came back a few minutes later, his backpack had vanished. Perplexed, the assistant searched around the tree but couldn't find the backpack. Then he glanced up. To his amazement, Paris was sitting in the tree gingerly holding the backpack by one hand as though he thought it might explode. When the assistant banged on the tree trunk, Paris dropped the backpack. This was one of the very rare times that a wild orangutan ever showed interest in a human artifact. I am certain that Paris was thinking about the bananas when he stole the assistant's backpack. Indeed, I later saw Paris take bananas from Rani. This remarkable scene involved a complex chain of thoughts: Paris learned that bananas were food by watching Rani, figured out that my backpack was the source of this new food, and applied this knowledge to another person carrying another backpack at a later date. Obviously, the bananas made an impression on Paris.

As well as knowing what to eat, a wild orangutan must know where to find food. In the temperate forests of the Northern Hemisphere, plants of the same species often are found in clusters or groves, and flower and fruit according to regular yearly cycles. This is why migratory birds and mammals return to the same place, around the same time each year. In the tropical rain forest, however, members of the same plant species are scattered with no obvious pattern. Each tree species seems to have its own cycle of flowering and fruiting, apparently triggered by highly specific microclimatic conditions. The cycle may be as short as a few months or as long as seven or eight years. Furthermore, species that bear fruit at about the same time may vary considerably in the amount of fruit they produce. Even among members of the same species, during a given season some trees may be barren, some laden with fruit, while others yield an "empty harvest" (fruit does not ripen, quickly rots, or proves inedible for another reason).

As John MacKinnon observed during his study in North Borneo, wild orangutans do not wander aimlessly about their home range, taking pot luck. Their movements are deliberate and purposeful. Orangutans seem to operate according to detailed cognitive maps of their surroundings, which include not only the location of food sources, but also quantitative information on distances. Orangutans know that when one tree of a particular species is fruiting, other members of that species probably will be, too. For instance, an orangutan may spend an hour or so eating in a particular species of tree, leave that tree, and move rapidly toward an unseen goal, arriving at another member of the same tree species. Along the way the orangutan may stop to inspect the leaves, fruit, or bark of other species of trees, but leave without eating. Apparently, the orangutan is checking the condition of the food (much as you check on a roast or a cake in the oven). If the fruit is not yet ripe or the leaves are too mature and therefore toxic, the orangutan seems to file this information away, and returns to the tree sometime later when the fruit is ripe or a new flush of young leaves has bloomed. I once saw Cara leave her home range and head directly to two wild durian trees, which happened not to be fruiting. In one thousand hours of observing Cara, I never saw her visit those trees before or after, but I had no doubt she knew where she was going. For wild orangutans, out of sight is not out of mind.

Many animals (grazers, carnivores, scavengers) eat what they find as they find it. While some of the forest products orangutans exploit are ready-to-eat, other orangutan foods are encased in hard shells, covered with burrs, wrapped in husks, or attached to toxic material. Before these foods can be eaten, they have to be processed. Ripe wild durian, for example, weighs up to two and a half pounds, is covered with spikes, and looks more like a weapon than a meal. Orangutans get to the flesh inside by tearing open the thick husk with their powerful teeth and jaws.

The marvel is that orangutans recognize these hidden, often heavily armored plant ovaries (which is what fruits and nuts are) as food, and know techniques for getting past the plant's physical and chemical defenses to the edible nutrients within. The orangutans' ability to process embedded foods greatly expands their food supply and enables them to eat foods that are not accessible to animals that are smaller, weaker, or less handy. Wild pigs probably can digest anything wild orangutans can and more, but they have to wait for dinner to be served, when the fruits or nuts fall to the ground. Climbing high into the trees, orangutans benefit from the principle of first come, first served.

Many primates are "opportunistic foragers," altering their feeding habits according to what is available. Orangutans have developed this feeding strategy to a fine art. But they pay a price for remaining in the rain forest. Because orangutans are large and slow, and food supplies in the forest are irregular and dispersed, living in gregarious communities like chimpanzees or even in families like gorillas would be impractical. Too little food is available at the same time and place to regularly support a group of mature orangutans. I have watched single orangutans spend more than eight hours in individual trees, eating until the tree was totally stripped of ripe fruit. If, for example, two adult orangutan sisters foraged together, they would finish the fruit in a tree twice as fast as if they were alone, and perhaps would have to travel twice as far to find the same amount of fruit. Eating alone is more efficient.

I have heard people say, "All orangutans do is eat," as if this were evidence that orangutans are slow-witted. But to know what, when, where, and how to eat in the tropical rain forest takes brains. The reason orangutan foraging looks simple is that orangutans know so much that they do not have to waste time exploring and experimenting. This knowledge is not innate. Wild orangutans spend eight or more years with their mother before they graduate to "master-forager."

The orangutans' semisolitary lifestyle is as deceptive as their apparently casual foraging. Other nonhuman primates spend hours every day with members of their species, traveling, feeding, grooming, playing, fighting, mating, and sleeping in close proximity. They develop relationships that often last a lifetime and may even span generations. Monkeys and apes follow complex rules of interaction depending on kinship, age, sex, and personal histories. They are able not only to predict how others will behave in a given situation, but also to manipulate others for personal benefit. Such "Machiavellian intelligence" entails recognizing that other individuals have different information and different goals, and manipulating what another individual *thinks,* not simply what that individual does. The ability to bluff and deceive is critical. Like humans, monkeys and apes are political animals.

Some primatologists have regarded orangutans as socially retarded, the wall-flowers of the great ape family. I have never accepted this view. Although orangutans are solitary much of the time, they do not live in a social vacuum. Indeed, their relationships with one another are far more structured and orderly than one would expect, given their infrequent interactions.

Of all orangutans, adult males are the most solitary. Outside consortships, they spend 98 percent of their time alone. Female and subadult orangutans largely avoid them. Adult males are totally intolerant of one another. If two wild adult males should meet, there basically are only two possible outcomes: one male flees (especially if they are alone) or they fight (especially if a receptive female is nearby). But such confrontations are rare; rather, adult males use the long call to maintain order and distance.

During the first four years of my study, Throatpouch, Nick, and Harry sometimes occupied at least partly overlapping ranges within the main study area. I gradually realized that the three mature males were able to coexist because they had established a dominance hierarchy, even though they virtually never met. The one time I saw TP meet Harry was in combat. Even so, Nick clearly was dominant over TP and Harry, and TP was dominant over Harry. Significantly, on days when the three males were in the same area (about an eight-hundred-yard radius), Nick called frequently, but TP was quieter than usual, and Harry, almost silent. Responses to other males' calls also reflected this hierarchy. During the first years of my study, I never saw Nick move away from another adult male, no matter how close the other male was when he called. When Nick called from close by, however, both TP and Harry fled. Harry was so intimidated by Nick that once, on hearing Nick call, he sat up in his nest and urinated. Orangutans rarely soil their nests; I could only assume that Harry was terrified. I also saw Harry run when TP called, but TP never ran from Harry (whom he had overpowered in a battle over Priscilla).

What was most remarkable was that TP, Nick, and Harry maintained a dominance hierarchy without interacting very often (indeed, only once that I observed), or even seeing one another. This means that the males recognized the individual's call, were able to form a mental representation of the caller in the absence of visual contact, and acted according to the other male's rank in the hierarchy. Male chimpanzees must constantly prove their rank with vigorous physical displays, such as branch-waving and charging. For the most part, male orangutans display vocally at unseen male peers. The difference is almost as great as the difference between playing football and playing chess in your head.

Adult female orangutans have both friends and enemies, as Cara and others showed me. Orangutan friendships are not very demonstrative, in human or even chimpanzee terms. Adult females generally do not embrace, groom one another, or inspect each other's infants. All the human observer sees is two orangutans who travel and rest together for days at a time and eat in the same tree without coming to blows. But these patterns are stable and enduring. Two adult females may go months, perhaps years, without contact, and yet remember one another well. Relationships evolve as females age and have off-spring. But I have never seen a female orangutan suddenly turn on an adult friend; nor have I seen one befriend an adult orangutan female she had previously ignored or chased.

Infrequent social interaction is sometimes cited as a reason why orangutans have no need to develop social intelligence. To the contrary, I see this as evidence of the orangutan's amazing social memory. As humans we have all had the experience of bumping into someone we knew way back when, recognizing the person but not being able to recall when or where we knew them, much less their name. As far as I can tell, orangutans rarely fumble this way.

The mating behavior of orangutans is an intricate game of skill and chance. Because orangutans do not live in groups, female orangutans are dispersed over wide areas. The average birth span for orangutan females, I discovered, is eight years. Receptive females are rare in the forest. Moreover, unlike many other female primates, female orangutans do not develop sexual swellings to advertise their fertility. Silent and arboreal, constantly moving through the dense forest where visibility is limited, receptive females are difficult to locate. Adult males advertise their presence with booming long calls. But in long-calling, wild adult males run the risk of attracting potentially aggressive male competitors, as well as willing females. How often a male calls and how often he mates depend in part on whether other, dominant males are nearby. No doubt some physically fit but smaller or timid males rarely father offspring.

Locating a receptive female is only the beginning. Unlike the semiterrestrial male gorilla, who herds his females, or the chimpanzee, who takes a female on safari away from other male chimpanzees, a male orangutan cannot control a female's movement through the trees, despite his much greater size. Rather he must attract and hold her attention through his social finesse. At the same time, he must keep adult and subadult male competitors at bay.

Thus, a wild orangutan's social life is far from simple. During their long period of dependency on their mother, orangutans learn a complex system of proper pongid etiquette. They witness their mother traveling alone and with other adult females and their juveniles, fending off some subadult males and feeding peacefully with others. Encounters with adult males are probably rare. But orangutan mothers do not complete weaning their offspring until they are pregnant again, which means the young have at least one opportunity to study a male-female consortship. The young stay with their mothers for at least a year after their new sibling is born, and so are also exposed to an infant. An older female offspring may spend years with her mother after the birth of a new sibling.

Just how much social learning orangutans require becomes painfully apparent when ex-captive orangutans make their debuts into wild orangutan society. Deprived of a natural upbringing and a social network developed by their mothers and kin, ex-captives commit numerous social gaffes. For instance, when one of the generals' orangutans, subadult male Gundul, first arrived, he tried to enter the nest of a wild cheekpadder male. The adult male bit him seriously all over his back and arms. From then on, Gundul was extremely wary of adult males. It was a one-trial learning experience. An ex-captive adolescent female once blundered too close to a grouchy wild adult female who promptly bit the ex-captive, leaving a gaping hole in her back. Learning by watching others is far safer.

Imitation is often thought of as a lesser form of learning that requires little intelligence. Indeed, we often refer to imitation as "aping" what others do. In fact, imitation requires a relatively high degree of cognitive sophistication. We humans imitate so intuitively, often unconsciously, that we take such social learning for granted. Imitation is a thoughtful form of learning that goes beyond trial and error. The imitator must observe the model, form a mental image of what the model is doing, then re-create that action with his or her own body.

I recently saw a video of an afternoon at one of the feeding stations in the Tanjung Puting forest. The camera was on me when it started to rain. A juvenile ex-captive orangutan sitting on my lap reached back and handed me my umbrella. Only after I had opened the umbrella and several other ex-captive juveniles gathered around me did I realize the significance of what the young orangutan had done. Certainly, I had never tried to teach him to "fetch" my umbrella when it rained. In fact, I had relatively little contact with this orangutan orphan. Nor had I made any attempt to teach him or any other orangutan the uses of umbrellas. But clearly he had seen humans open umbrellas in a downpour, learned what the object was for, and "asked" me to put the umbrella to use. Had he been a wild orangutan, he might have plucked a leafy branch and handed it to his mother, assuming she would provide him with cover.

Imitation is rarely an exact duplicate or copy. The trained ballet dancer cannot immediately re-create a sequence demonstrated by the choreographer.

Rather he or she performs successive approximations that come closer and closer to the choreographer's vision, but never fully overlap. Similarly, Elvis impersonators can never be Elvis. But copying errors reveal the genius of imitation. Imitation is not a mechanical performance, but a creative one.

Human beings are mimics par excellence. Often we pick up phrases, gestures, and ideas from others unconsciously. This is why human societies need patent, copyright, and even reverse engineering laws. Entire careers are based on copying the paintings of the old masters or forging checks, while other careers are devoted to exposing these imitations. Orangutans are also skilled imitators. One of the main reasons that visitors to Camp Leakey feel such close kinship with the ex-captive orangutans is not so much that orangutan imitations mirror our own behavior, but that the *process* of imitation is so familiar and natural to us.

Some scientists are puzzled by the idea that orangutans, who are so solitary compared to other primates, are so adept at imitation. I believe the explanation is obvious. Aside from their mother, growing orangutans have relatively few opportunities to observe other members of their species. An infant orangutan may see a cheekpadded male adult only a few times per year, whereas a chimpanzee or a gorilla (or a human) sees adult males every day. The orangutan has to learn from one lecture, one snapshot, what a chimpanzee, gorilla, or human may learn from a full school year. Orangutans' semisolitary existence forces them to be quick studies and to attend to circumstances or situations that may be important.

Imitation is social behavior. Wild orangutans virtually never imitate human beings, because they do not interact or form relationships with us. When Paris stole the assistant's backpack, he was imitating Rani (with embellishments), not me or the assistant. Rather, wild orangutans imitate their mothers, and perhaps their elder siblings and the males that are attracted to their mothers. But lacking orangutan mothers of their own, ex-captive orangutans pay attention to humans. Like humans, orangutans imitate the individuals, whether human or orangutan, with whom they have the most intense relationships. They rarely imitate (human) strangers at camp. In this orangutans are very social. They look to social partners or parent figures for cues and single out significant others as models.

My relationships with the orangutans I have raised and orangutans I have become friends with are among the most intense relationships I have ever had. The social bonds are fierce. This makes sense if orangutans depend on a few key individuals to learn about the world and how to deal with it. Despite the fact that orangutans live alone (or with dependent offspring) in the rain forest, their dependence on imitation in the context of close social relationships is similar to our own. With an important difference. The orangutans' solitary lifestyle and self-sufficiency make them strong in a way humans can barely imagine. I felt great satisfaction in knowing that as my "foster children" adopted wild orangutan lifestyles and established important ties with other orangutans, their imitation of humans, even of me, correspondingly declined until it was virtually nil.

During the past twenty-three years I have returned more than a hundred ex-captive orangutans to life in the wild. These orangutans represent one hundred individuals who would have lived short, miserable lives, with virtually no op-portunity to exercise their bodies or their minds. One hundred individuals deprived of the serene solitude and self-sufficiency that are so much part of an orangutan's nature. One hundred great apes deprived of the opportunity to fulfill their reproductive destiny. I do not say this boastfully, for I believe this high success rate is due largely to the orangutans' innate intelligence. I could never presume to teach an orangutan all he or she has to learn to survive in the wild. I can only provide orphaned orangutans with the opportunity to develop at their own pace, in their own way.

Each rehabilitation is an individual success story. In general, the males re-turn to the forest almost automatically on their own. They don't stay in camp. Once they reach the age of nine or ten, the male hormones kick in and they begin to wander. Sometimes they briefly come back; most often they don't. Of the dozens of males whom I have released over the years, only two appear at Camp Leakey more or less regularly.

Rio, for example, never visits. After he grew into adolescence, he at-tempted to carry a woman into the trees with him and succeeded in lifting her several feet off the ground! He was very gentle with her but, understandably, the woman was alarmed. After this incident we moved him a mile or so down-river. Rio, the jolly red giant, never came back to camp. However, some of my former assistants encountered him repeatedly many miles from camp. Rio was now a cheekpadder.

The female rehabilitation pattern is somewhat different from the male pat-tern. Some females go, but many stay, especially the ones who identify Camp Leakey with "mother." Only a few visitors to Camp Leakey are treated to the magnificent, awe-inspiring sight of an adult male orangutan. But even the ca-sual visitor may encounter female orangutans and their offspring.

Sobiarso left camp while she was an adolescent. During a heavy fruiting season, virtually all the ex-captive orangutans stayed in the forests and swamps. I had left to visit North America just as the fruit season started. After a few months, the orangutans gradually began drifting back, one by one, to the feeding platforms. But a small number, including some females, never came back. One of them was Sobiarso. She vanished while I was away.

But Akmad, who is thoroughly adapted to the wild, still visits from time to time. She is carrying a new infant, and Aldona follows behind. Gara, with little Gary and Gina, stays in the vicinity but keeps her distance. Princess commutes between the forest and Camp Leakey, according to her own schedule.

When I began the rehabilitation program at Camp Leakey, I had one overriding goal. That was to create a refuge. If Indonesian officials were to enforce the laws against capturing orangutans, they would have to confiscate orangutans held as pets or crated for shipment abroad. But if there were no place to take the orangutans, there was no point in confiscating them. In creating a refuge, I hoped not only to save the lives of innocent victims of the ape trade, but also to save wild orangutans from further poaching.

I never saw the rehabilitation program at Camp Leakey as "the Solution" to the orangutan problem. Rather I saw my program as a palliative, as a way to temporarily ease the pain and suffering until a cure was found. I saw myself as holding down the fort until the cavalry arrived. When I went to Borneo in 1971, I never imagined the wholesale, massive destruction of tropical rain forest and the slaughter of thousands of orangutans that would occur over the next two decades in other areas of Borneo and Sumatra.

I believed that humans had deprived wildborn captive orangutans of their natural rights, and so humans had an obligation to rescue and protect them — but not at the expense of the wild orangutan population. At the time, the number of orangutans I was reintroducing to the wild was small and the forests were vast. Overcrowding did not seem a problem. I provided daily feedings because I did not subscribe to the sink or swim theory of rehabilitation. I believed then, as I do now, that ex-captive orangutans, who under natural conditions would spend at least eight years in their mothers' care, should be allowed to return to the forest at their own pace.

Over time, however, the number of ex-captive orangutans brought to Camp Leakey for rehabilitation increased, while the chain saws and chipping machines moved ever closer to the borders of Tanjung Puting, grinding up the orangutans' natural habitat. I continued the feedings because I was concerned about both the wild and ex-captive populations. In times of abundance, there might be enough food for all in the forest. But during lean times I did not want the wild orangutan population to be subjected to unnatural levels of competition, or the ex-captives to die because their survival skills were not on a par with those of wild orangutans. Some people view the feedings at Camp Leakey as cheating, as evidence that rehabilitation does not work. I cannot understand this purism in the face of habitat destruction, slaughter, and imminent extinction. Human beings cheated the ex-captives of a normal upbringing by an orangutan mother in the forest canopy. Human beings are also consuming the orangutans' natural habitat at an alarming rate. At the very least, we owe them some rice and bananas.

Over time, I also began to see the unanticipated benefits of a rehabilitation program. Local people, both Melayu and Dayak, who have worked at and visited Camp Leakey see the park and the orangutans as a source of regional pride. The trickle of tourists, beginning in the mid-1980s, underscored this feeling. Kalimantan Tengah had something that people would travel halfway around the world to see. Despite conflicts over logging and boundaries, local people are among Camp Leakey's strongest supporters.

Outsiders do not come to Tanjung Puting to enjoy the weather (which is almost always hot, humid, and rainy), the scenery (except on the rivers, visibility is poor), or the accommodations (which are simple to primitive by Western standards). They come to see the orangutans. Orangutans are what conservationists call "charismatic megafauna": large, extremely appealing animals. Frogs, bats, and beetles — all threatened with extinction — are just as important in the overall scheme of life on this planet. But these creatures do not capture the average person's heart. Orangutans do. Unlike many of the great animals of East Africa who live on the open savanna and are relatively easy to see, wild orangutans are hidden high in the forest canopy. The presence of habituated orangutans, who do not automatically flee at the sight of human beings, enables visitors to Camp Leakey to meet members of this branch of the hominoid family in their natural habitat. It is one of the only places on earth where humans and great apes are equals. Few people who visit Camp Leakey remain indifferent to the orangutans' plight. Orangutans are their own best public relations agents.

By their very existence, ex-captive orangutans help to protect the primary rain forest. The plight of the Penan of northern Borneo and other peoples who have been evicted from their forest homes is tragic. But on some level we know that, if worse comes to worst, people can find other places to live and other ways to live. Geographic and cultural relocation is neither easy nor desirable in most cases, but it is possible for humans. Orangutans, however, live and die with the forest. Without intact, untouched tropical rain forest there can be no wild orangutans. Princess, Gara, and many other orangutans depend for their lives on the continued existence of Tanjung Puting and its great forest.

# 21
# KIN

In my end is my beginning.

— *T. S. Eliot*

---

N OT ALL OF THE ex-captive orangutans who passed through Camp Leakey were as easygoing as Gara and Princess. Cempaka was a good-natured "troublemaker," who seemed to view human possessions as playthings. Sugito, whom I dearly loved, had a mean streak. We once saw him with a drowned kitten. This may have been an experiment on his part, but we also suspected that Sugito was responsible for the drowning of one and possibly two infant orangutans.

Gundul was by far the most difficult ex-captive I ever received. His sexual assault on the cook was one of numerous incidents. Gundul was afraid of Rod and gentle with me, but he terrorized the local assistants, the Indonesian university students, and, to a lesser degree, local visitors. He stalked a young American female Ph.D. from MIT for weeks. Gundul had been raised from infancy by humans. His owner, a general, had treated him like a shaggy orange prince. It did not surprise me that Gundul was sexually attracted to human females and viewed most local men, men without uniforms, as servants. He had all the appetites and emotions of an orangutan, but he also understood human vulnerabilities. We desperately needed someone who could control Gundul.

Before Rod and I separated, I was away from camp for a time. When I returned, Rod told me that he had hired another Dayak from the village of Pasir Panjang. And Gundul was afraid of this man! The new assistant had no problems going alone to the feeding platforms across the river; the ex-captive orangutans instinctively feared him. I asked Rod, "How is he different from the other assistants?" Rod took time to consider before answering me. Finally he said, "He's old."

A vision of a gaunt, sinewy, weather-beaten man in his fifties went through my head. But then I had the strangest thought. "He probably doesn't have a tooth in his head, but I bet he is still attractive," I said to myself. The orangutans seemed particularly intimidated by virile-looking men and men in military uniforms. They seemed to recognize characteristics that we associate with powerful males.

"What is his name?" I asked Rod. "*Pak* Bohap," Rod replied, using the Indonesian term of respect for older men.

I did not meet *Pak* Bohap immediately. Most of the Dayak assistants were farmers. Their lives revolved around the rhythms of their dry-rice fields. Typically, the Dayaks would come to camp and work for a month or two when their fields did not require attention, and then leave. When *Pak* Bohap left to return to his village, Rod had urged him to come back.

Some months later, on our way back from Pangkalan Bun, we stopped in Pasir Panjang to pick up assistants. We now owned a jeep, which we left in Kumai when we began the long boat trip to camp. I was driving, and Rod was sitting next to me in the passenger's seat.

When we got to the village, Rod got out to greet a small crowd that had gathered. I stayed in the jeep. The back door opened and one man climbed in; another stood by the side of the jeep. I turned and saw a lithe, well-muscled man with black hair down to his shoulders. He was wearing a red shirt. I saw his face in profile. There was something written into his face that made it like stone. He had a sternness and a strength that could not be fabricated. I knew instantly that this must be *Pak* Bohap, the man whom Gundul feared. But *Pak* Bohap was not in his fifties. I later discovered that he was twenty-four. When I asked Rod why he had described him as old, Rod said, "*Pak* Bohap is like a Dayak from a hundred years ago. He is not a counterfeit Dayak like so many of the others."

Like the hero of a medieval epic, *Pak* Bohap was known and described before he actually appeared in person. As I drove the jeep, I kept looking in the rearview mirror to see him. I had been in Indonesia many years, but, with the possible exception of Dr. Soedjarwo, who had recently become Minister of Forestry, *Pak* Bohap was the first Indonesian who puzzled me. Rod's comment was true. Although *Pak* Bohap was only twenty-four, something about his face was ageless. He was also strikingly handsome. Suddenly Rod grabbed the steering wheel, shouting at me, "What are you doing? You almost drove us into the ditch." I stopped pondering the new assistant and put my mind back to driving.

When we arrived in camp, it became clear that Rod was right about *Pak* Bohap's effect on the orangutans. Rod's assessments usually were very good. Even so, I was surprised at the respect the orangutans showed *Pak* Bohap. Though he never did anything to intimidate them, the orangutans deferred to him. What distinguished him in their minds?

I decided that one reason *Pak* Bohap impressed the orangutans was his voice. He had a deep, resonant voice, once described as a "natural radio voice." When male orangutans listened to long calls in the distance, they seemed to be evaluating the caller. Probably both male and female orangutans were highly attuned to judging the strength, health, and stamina of an adult male orangutan from the sound of his voice. I suspect that the rich, low tones and projection of *Pak* Bohap's voice signaled to the orangutans that here was a powerful male. Even I felt somewhat intimidated. Although *Pak* Bohap worked for Camp Leakey and I paid his salary, I never felt like I was his boss.

As a child, *Pak* Bohap had grown up in the traditional Dayak lifestyle. A hunter, he had killed many pigs and deer with his blowgun, as well as virtually every other animal or bird in the forest that could be eaten. I later discovered that in his youth, *Pak* Bohap had eaten orangutans. He was the only assistant from Pasir Panjang who admitted doing so. *Pak* Bohap was honest about who he was.

In the late 1970s and early 1980s, after Rod left, I became involved in a Forestry Department survey of the reserve. In those days, there were almost no roads in Kalimantan; the only means of transportation were walking, dugout canoes, and *kelotoks*. To get to the other side of Tanjung Puting, we had to hike thirty miles through the swamps, a punishing trek that took two days out and two days back. On these forced marches through the trackless swamps and forests, I was surprised to discover that over long distances I outwalked all the men. Except *Pak* Bohap. No sweat fell from his cheerful face. No complaint issued from his mouth. He was at ease in the forest as only one born to it can be. It was on these dreary, exhausting marches that *Pak* Bohap and I were drawn together. We fell in love.

Not long afterward, *Pak* Bohap and I were married. Marrying *Pak* Bohap was like coming home to a place I had known before. Although he was younger than I, his wisdom was ageless and profound. His humor and exuberant good nature brought me laughter, joy, and passion. He was a Dayak horticulturalist with a grade six education. I was now a young college professor with a recent Ph.D. No doubt some of my Western colleagues were puzzled by my marrying a "native." But since I had come to see the forest as my home, and the study and conservation of orangutans as my life's work, it was only natural that I would fall in love with someone born of the forest. Like two pieces of a puzzle, the knowledge I had acquired through formal education and painstaking scientific observation fit with the deeper understanding of Kalimantan, the forest and its creatures, that *Pak* Bohap had gained through his Dayak culture and his traditional upbringing. We were perfectly matched.

Love at first sight is a recognition of something long known by the heart; it feels like a second encounter. Being adopted by Mr. and Mrs. Binti had introduced me to elements of Dayak culture, Dayak thinking, and Dayak pride. At the time some people saw Dayaks as backward, much as some North Americans perhaps see Native Americans. Mr. Binti was very proud of being Dayak. He wanted others to understand that Dayaks were just as Indonesian as anyone else and ready to take their place in the modern world and the global economy. He was determined that Dayaks would not be left behind. As my traditional but forward-looking adoptive Dayak parents, Mr. and Mrs. Binti prepared me for recognizing and marrying *Pak* Bohap.

*Pak* Bohap's and my first child was Frederick; a few years later we had our second child, Jane. Fred and Jane have grown up in the small Dayak village of Pasir Panjang, where many of our neighbors are relatives. Both Fred and Jane have benefited from the universal love of children that permeates Indonesian society. Fred and Jane frequently come to Camp Leakey and are at ease with the ex-captive orangutans. Like children everywhere, they spend most of their time attending school and playing with their friends. Fred and Jane almost always come with me on trips to North America, and have attended school there as well.

Both strong individualists, Fred and Jane synthesize their dual Dayak and North American heritage in their own ways. Fred enjoys working in the rice fields with his father and other Dayak men. At age eleven, he is in love with baseball. With his baseball cap glued to his head (backward) and extra-baggy jeans, whether in North America or Kalimantan, Fred seems to embody the international youth culture. Jane, now age nine, is developing traditionally feminine interests by cooking, gardening, and collecting clothes for her Barbie dolls. At the moment, Jane plans to become a baker — after she gets her Ph.D. Inquisitive, quick-witted, and disarmingly candid, Jane often surprises adults with her poise and her casually delivered, penetrating observations.

Both children fit so easily into their two native cultures that I sometimes forget that their reality is not a carbon copy of my own. Fred once asked me, matter-of-factly, why the ancestors stay in Kalimantan. Dayaks believe that the ancestors pull children's hair when the children misbehave. Fred explained that the ancestors never pulled his hair in North America. "Why do we have to take vitamins when we're just going to die eventually anyway?" Jane asked one morning, echoing the Dayak view that life is an interruption of death. I suggested that even though we all will die some day, we need to take care of our bodies while we're alive. Jane said simply, "Okay," and went back to what she was doing.

Binti is North American to the core. When his father and stepmother emigrated to Australia, he chose to stay in Canada and finish high school with his friends. Binti is now seventeen, and his dry sense of humor and rebellious streak remind me of the qualities I admired in Rod when he was the same age. Fred and Jane very much look up to big brother Binti.

The logistics of maintaining a family on two continents can be overwhelming. My happiest times are evenings in Kalimantan with Binti, Fred, and Jane, listening to *Pak* Bohap strum his *gambus,* a stringed instrument related to the mandolin, as he sings traditional Dayak songs or, in North America, our weekly ritual of watching "Saturday Night Live" together. Like most children, Binti, Fred, and Jane take my work for granted, reeling off "Mom studies orangutans" as automatically as they might repeat "Mom is a doctor" or "Mom keeps house."

When I married *Pak* Bohap, he told me that he was marrying me the woman, not the Western scientist or the crusader for orangutans. He respected my work. As my husband, he would help me in my fieldwork and stand by me in my battles. But he was a Dayak farmer when I met him and would remain so after we married. He expected me to put our children (including Binti, whom he had known as a toddler) first. Under no circumstances would he allow orangutans into our house.

We have lived by this agreement. *Pak* Bohap does not come with me when I lecture or teach in North America or even in Jakarta. He does not speak English and has never left Indonesia. We live in a large house he built for us in his native village of Pasir Panjang. As *Pak* Bohap's wife I am part of an extended

Dayak family, I attend Dayak ceremonies and rituals, and I run an Indonesian household. I try to keep my private and public lives separate. My work takes me away from home far more than I would like, but that is my only regret. Cross-cultural marriages often become strained. Because *Pak* Bohap and I take equal delight in our children and our roles as parents, and because we have retained our individual identities, our marriage endures.

*Pak* Bohap's maternal grandfather was one of the last Dayak rulers under the Sultan of Kotawaringan. Before the Dutch colonial government was over-thrown, the sultan ruled through seven Dayak "kings" who held sway over seven regions. *Pak* Bohap's long-dead grandfather was one of the seven. One night shortly after *Pak* Bohap and I were married, we sat on the floor of my wooden house at Camp Leakey talking by the light of a candle. The talk turned to *kris*es.

*Pak* Bohap told me how sorry he was that his mother had sold the family *pusaka,* a *kris* his mother had inherited from her father. *Pak* Bohap regretted that he no longer had a *kris* to pass on to his children. Thinking of the *kris* I had acquired many years earlier, I immediately brightened. I told *Pak* Bohap that I was sorry I could not return the original *kris* to his family, but I would like to give him a *kris* that I had bought. I went into my storeroom and brought out the magnificent dagger. I handed the *kris* to *Pak* Bohap. As he carefully examined the dagger by the light of the candle, *Pak* Bohap fell silent. He looked at the *kris* and then looked at me several times before putting the *kris* aside. He didn't say thank you.

Soon afterward, *Pak* Bohap went to Pasir Panjang while I stayed at Camp Leakey. He took the *kris* with him. Several days later I arrived in Pasir Panjang myself. *Pak* Bohap uncharacteristically greeted me in front of other people with a kiss. He took my hand gently and squeezed it, saying very warmly and forcefully, "Thank you for returning my *kris* to my family." His mother had verified what he had immediately suspected at Camp Leakey when I presented him with the *kris* — that the *kris* was actually his.

A Westerner would say that my buying *Pak* Bohap's *kris* years before I met and then married him was sheer coincidence. But an Indonesian would say that the *pusaka* always returns to its rightful owner. It is a law of nature. When *Pak* Bohap told me that the *kris* was his, a shiver went up my spine. I knew that, in some unfathomable Kalimantan way, the destiny that I had chosen for myself had been decided long before.

❧

I was on a plane, leaning against the window and gazing at the clouds, when I was overcome by sadness. It was all I could do to keep from weeping. This wasn't the first time. I had had these sudden, unpredictable, unexplained spells of melancholy several times before. As I stared blindly through the airplane window, I realized that I was thinking about Dian.

Dian Fossey was murdered in her cabin at the Karisoke Research Centre in the Virunga Volcanoes on December 27, 1985. I was horrified by the violence of her death, but not surprised. Even before I learned of her death, I knew Dian would be killed, I knew this was her destiny.

When Dian died, I lost a sister. Dian and I worked on different continents, studying different apes. We corresponded from time to time, attended some of the same scientific meetings, and with Jane Goodall went on a lecture tour together in the United States in the early 1980s. When we got together we sometimes stayed up half the night talking. But I wouldn't have described us as best friends. Dian, Jane Goodall, and I were family. Louis Leakey had recognized us as kindred souls and become our spiritual father. Our individual experiences alone in the forest with great apes created a bond much deeper than friendship. As with biological sisters, whether we liked each other or shared similar tastes was irrelevant. We had been places other people had not. In terms of our mission to understand and protect the great apes, we understood each other in ways other people could not fathom.

As I gazed into the clouds, I knew that Dian would be misunderstood in death, as she had been misunderstood in life. The attacks on her character in the latter years of her life had been just as savage, in their way, as the machete blows that had killed her. The scientific community, as well as conservationists, had abandoned Dian long before. For years the rumor mill had been grinding out stories of her bizarre behavior. Students (some of whom stayed only a few days) and visitors to Karisoke competed in a game of one-upmanship with tales of outrageous goings on. Dian, they said, is taking the law into her own hands. Dian is her own worst enemy. Dian has lost it. I knew that her murder would only embellish her image as the mad woman of the mountains. I could hear fellow anthropologists saying, in triumph or in pity, "I knew it" and "She had it coming."

All at once I understood how terribly alone Dian had been. I realized how few people understood Dian's dilemma. It was one that many field researchers face, but one that most turn away from. When you study members of another species, when you habituate them in the wild, when you begin to understand the intimate details of their private lives, and then you learn that that population or whole species is sliding toward extinction, what do you do? In good conscience, you must defend them, but the effort may be all-consuming.

When Jane, Dian, and I went into the field, none of us anticipated that we would be pushed to the forefront of the environmental movement; that our lives would be threatened at the same time that others called us "angels" and "heroes for the earth"; that we would be caught up in global political, economic, and even spiritual crises. In those early days of innocence, we were motivated simply by curiosity and the desire to better understand our non-human kin. People thought we were crazy to go into the forest alone and unarmed. What we did was dangerous, but not because the apes we were studying threatened to harm us. Danger wears a human face.

Jane paved the way for all of us. When she went to Gombe in 1960, no one had conducted a long-term, close-up observational study of a great ape in the wild. People said it couldn't be done, certainly not by a lone young woman with no scientific training. Even today, few people understand just how revolutionary Jane's approach was.

Science in the 1960s rested on a set of assumptions. The goal of science was to develop universal rules and principles that would ultimately enable human beings to understand and thus control nature. The scientist was a detached observer, who never let personal feelings get in the way of objectivity. Animals were interesting, not in themselves but as models or stand-ins for human beings. The primatologist Robert Yerkes referred to the apes he studied as "servants of science." The idea that animals might have thoughts, emotions, and personalities was considered a projection of human traits. Differences between individuals were dismissed as messy details that spoiled the data, as background noise to be whited out.

A scientific outsider, Jane ignored these dictums. Her idea of science was not to dominate, but to discover nature. In the words of Roger Fouts, a pioneer in teaching apes sign language, "Jane's is a humble science. She asks the animals to tell her about themselves." It is a science of collaboration, not control.

Jane had no fixed plan when she went into the field and no theoretical ax to grind. She followed her intuition, adapting her behavior to that of the Gombe chimpanzees. At that time, conventional scientific wisdom held that the way to study animals in the wild was to build a blind and observe the animals surreptitiously (a leftover from the days when naturalists were gentleman hunters, collecting specimens rather than studying behavior). Jane did the opposite, climbing in the predawn hours to an open peak where the chimpanzees could easily see her as they moved through the surrounding slopes and valleys. Then she sat and waited. She reasoned that if the chimps saw her in the same place day after day they would learn that she was harmless.

Jane violated a scientific taboo by naming the chimpanzees she recognized rather than assigning them numbers. Part of the reason Jane did this was practical: names are easier to remember. But she also felt that just as assigning numbers to prison inmates obliterates their humanity, so numbering chimpanzees robbed them of their individuality. Further, she believed that looking at individuals as models or archetypes for "*the* male," "*the* female," and "*the* juvenile" blinded observers to the differences among them. The first paper she sent to the scientific journal *Annals of the New York Academy of Science* was sent back. The editors had crossed out the personal pronouns Jane used to refer to chimpanzees, substituting "it" for "he" and "she" and changing "who" to "which." They insisted that she substitute numbers for names. Jane stood her ground, and the article was published.

Jane held that the social structure of a community of chimpanzees could only be understood in light of the different temperaments and personal histories of a particular group of individuals. But this point was lost on scientists accustomed to dealing with anonymous animals and generalizations. From the beginning, Jane was accused of anthropomorphizing the chimpanzees of Gombe, treating them like family members or pets. The not-so-hidden message was that Jane was a typically sentimental female.

Jane blithely went her own way. She made two of her most important discoveries in her first six months at Gombe: chimpanzees hunt and eat meat, and chimpanzees use tools. Because of Jane, two of the reigning definitions of humankind, Man the Hunter and Man the Toolmaker, would have to be revised. In 1965, she was awarded a Ph.D. from Cambridge University. Publicly, colleagues congratulated Jane and commended her work, but privately, some still muttered that she was a storyteller, not a serious scientist. Part of Jane's strength was that she didn't give a hoot what they thought. Or in the chimpanzee lexicon, a pant-hoot.

Today Jane is probably the best-known living scientist in the world. In recent years, she has become a leading spokesperson in the campaign to save the dwindling number of chimpanzees in the wild from extinction and to provide humane conditions for those in captivity. Jane now spends only part of her time at Gombe, because she knows that ultimately the fate of the African chimpanzees will be decided elsewhere in the world. She is resigned to the probability that the chimpanzee community at Gombe will not survive long into the twenty-first century.

Yet even as Jane is showered with well-deserved awards, many scientists still quietly question the value of in-depth, close-up, long-term studies. A few of our associates wince when she or I refer to the apes we have studied by name. Certain colleagues think that in crusading for chimpanzees, Jane has "retired," and that my work rehabilitating wildborn ex-captive orangutans is just a sideline to the "real work," which is science.

Jane has always given the impression that she is guided by an inner light that never wavers; that her desire to understand chimpanzees is a calling, akin to a religious vocation. Over the years Jane has had more than her share of criticism, threats, and tragedy, but she never went public with her personal pain and struggles. Jane always took the Buckingham Palace approach. "Ignore your critics," she once said to me. "I always do. Never dignify them with a response." British to the core, Jane always seemed to emerge unscathed and unflappable.

If Jane is like Dorothy in the *Wizard of Oz,* following a yellow brick road with animal companions, Dian was more like the talented but tormented actress who played Dorothy in the film, Judy Garland. Dian's journey into the world of mountain gorillas went along twisting, slippery paths, like the elephants' trails she followed in the mountains of central Africa. Jane fit easily into the role of the British gentlewoman who goes out to Africa to seek her destiny. The country where she worked, Tanzania, is one of the most stable in all Africa. Dian had no experience living in Africa; she had never even lived in a tent. As an American in former Belgian colonies, Dian had no post-colonial support system. Unknowingly, she walked into political chaos.

Just six months after Dian began her study in what was then the Congo, civil war broke out. Soldiers marched Dian to a nearby town, where she was held for weeks, displayed in a cage, and from what she told me, raped. Starting over took raw courage and teeth-grinding determination. Dian had both. She set up another camp on the Rwandan side of the Virungas, at the place she named Karisoke and would call home for the rest of her life. She often said she felt as though the first part of her life had been led by someone else.

Prophetically, on her first day at Karisoke, Dian watched laughing Watutsi drive a herd of cattle through the meadow below her tents. Later, two Batwa hunters with bows and arrows came into camp and volunteered to lead her to a group of gorillas they had startled in their pursuit of antelopes. As I discovered in my early days at Tanjung Puting, Dian found that the Parc National des Volcans was a reserve in name only. Herders and hunters openly moved in and out of the protected area. Gorillas were not killed for meat in Rwanda, but they were murdered for *sumu*, "black magic," and gorilla heads and hands were sold in local markets as grisly souvenirs. Understandably, the gorillas in the area were shy.

Ten months passed before Dian cabled Louis Leakey: I'VE FINALLY BEEN ACCEPTED BY A GORILLA. This was the cable Louis carried in his pocket on a tour of America, and which he patted proudly the day I met him. I remember wondering how she did it, what it felt like, what sounds or smells told her gorillas were nearby. The films of Jane and Dian in the field, released some years later, made studying great apes in the wild look easy, almost glamorous. But from my reading and conversations with other fieldworkers, I was beginning to learn about the untold story of frustrations, complications, illness and injury, drudgery and disappointments behind the beguiling photos in glossy magazines.

One of Dian's greatest moments was captured on film some years later. She and photographer Bob Campbell were observing Group Four, a stable gorilla family led by the magnificent silverback "Uncle Bert." A young male, "Digit," had always shown a special interest in Dian, perhaps, she speculated, because he had no peers in his family group. As usual, Dian settled in the grass and busied herself with gorillalike activities. Suddenly, after a few nervous chest-beats, Digit plopped down beside her, less than a foot away. With Campbell's camera rolling, Digit picked up one of Dian's gloves and examined it with a delicacy that belied his size. As Dian watched enraptured, Digit flipped the pages of her notebook and tasted her pen, gently returning each item after he inspected it. Digit's shy curiosity and gentle respect rivaled Dian's. As the scene unfolded, it was difficult to tell who was the observer and who was being observed. The two roles merged, and the millions of years that separate the human and gorilla species seemed to melt away. Then Digit paid Dian the ultimate pongid compliment: he turned his back, flopped over, and went to sleep.

I know how Dian felt. Ordinarily, I do not make physical contact with wild orangutans. I couldn't climb with them into the forest canopy even if I wanted to. But I have looked into the eyes of a wild orangutan and seen that orangutan looking back at me. The experience is almost indescribable. We tend to think that the other creatures who share our planet inhabit the same reality as we do, especially if they resemble us, as monkeys and apes do, or live with us, as pets. But their senses, their needs, their perceptions are not the same as ours. Communing with a wild animal of another species means glimpsing another reality. Perhaps the closest analogy would be visiting the parallel universe of the Dayaks, or experiencing ecstasy in the classic, medieval religious sense. A psychologist I met, Dr. Tony Rose, compared the impact of interspecies communication to near-death experiences in intensity. One is never the same again.

The scene with Dian and Digit became the centerpiece of a *National Geographic* television special that made them both stars. The public was enthralled by the easy rapport between the lanky American woman and the ever-so-gentle giant. In a few moments, the gorilla's King Kong image as a ferocious killer was relegated to the trash bin of celluloid history. Introducing the public to gorillas was one of Dian's major accomplishments. But Dian's scientific peers were not so impressed. A scientist's job was to be a passive observer, not a playmate. Many saw Dian as a primatologist who had "gone native."

Indeed, I've been quoted as saying that Dian "became a gorilla." I meant this metaphorically. Dian never thought that she *was* a gorilla. But to some degree she did learn to think like a gorilla, and she sometimes behaved like a gorilla. Her empathy with her subjects went beyond expertise. In time, she became accepted almost as a family member in gorilla groups. Even her harshest critics admitted that nobody understood gorillas like Dian. Certainly, Dian's relationship with Digit was unique.

Dian's triumph was mixed with tragedy. About a year and a half after she settled at Karisoke, Dian rescued two infant gorillas from park officials who had arranged to sell them to the Cologne Zoo. "Coco" and "Pucker" were close to death when Dian received them. She knew that perhaps a half dozen adult gorillas had died in the capture of the infants. Virtually every member of a gorilla family will give his or her life to save an infant.

Dian nursed the two infant gorillas back to health. She launched a letter campaign to conservationists and wildlife funds, pleading to be allowed to return the captives to the wild. No one came to the orphan gorillas' aid. At the time, it was accepted practice to acquire wildborn animals for zoos (and other purposes). Dian had begun to introduce Coco and Pucker to the forest when the park conservator suddenly appeared and demanded custody of the infant gorillas. Dian argued and pleaded, but gave in when he threatened to acquire two more wild infants. It was "Sophie's Choice": if she hid Coco and Pucker, she might save them, but she would be condemning other gorilla infants and their families to death.

I have long felt that Coco and Pucker's fate probably affected Dian much more than anyone realized. Dian's anguish and guilt at not being able to protect her "children" were combined with the knowledge that all gorillas were imperiled and that she was fighting alone. In a sense, Coco and Pucker were Dian's "first Digit." Their future was decided by European zoo directors thousands of miles away. The local poachers who set traps to ensnare gorillas were themselves ensnared by an economic system designed and controlled by Westerners. If Europeans had not been willing to pay for live baby gorillas and gorilla trophies, there would have been little incentive for local people to hunt them. For the first time, Dian realized that she and the gorillas were caught in the same trap. She had gone to the Virungas as a peacemaker, a liaison between the human and gorilla species. Now that peace was shattered.

I know how the deaths of infant orangutans Barbara and Tony haunted me. As if by unspoken agreement, Dian and I rarely discussed her loss or mine; it was too painful. Now as then, there are some who would say we were just sentimental.

I have no doubt that some field researchers remain aloof and detached from their subjects; I've met them. But most people who study a single species or a single population for any length of time end up falling for their subjects. This is particularly true when the research involves primates, who are so much like ourselves. Even researchers who study animals who are neither majestic and imposing, nor cute and cuddly — such as snakes or spiders — become passionate observers. Once they are hooked, it is only a matter of time before they confront "Dian's dilemma."

Should you allow yourself to identify with your subjects, or should you remain uninvolved? If a population or species is threatened, should you continue to study them or attempt to save them? Should you act now, on your own, or wait for others to go through official channels?

This is a classic catch-22 situation. If you don't immerse yourself in your subjects' world, you only gather facts and figures, a computerized image; if you do become involved, you're accused of being unscientific. If you continue to study from a safe scientific distance subjects who are endangered, your time runs out. Your last paper would read "The operation was a success but the patient died." If you do try to save them, you have little time for research and even less for writing and publishing; your main sources of support may abandon you, forcing you to squander your time and energy on fund-raising. If you act directly, at the ground level, you're accused of going too far; if you don't, you suffer the guilt of not having done enough.

Certainly, there are practical problems in trying to combine research and conservation. When you try to do both, you may end up not doing either very well. You have to choose one or the other or alternate between the two. The knowledge that a species is headed for extinction leaves no moral choice.

If you are studying an animal, or a people, or even a language that is struggling for survival, how can you *not* interfere? To turn your back on your subject is to turn your back on your Western Judeo-Christian heritage, on what it means to be human. The essence of being human is the capacity for *disinterested* compassion. When you protect your family, your friends, or even your dog, you are being compassionate. But it is a self-interested compassion, because your relationship with them is reciprocal. Disinterested compassion is helping the helpless, with no expectation of reward. For all his size and strength, the massive mountain gorilla is as defenseless as a small kitten in the face of human predation and encroachment.

Overinvolvement in her subjects was only one of Dian's alleged offenses. Even before the current civil war, Rwanda was one of the poorest countries on earth. Dian was criticized for putting the survival of the gorillas ahead of the desperate neediness of local people. She was accused of being a foreign meddler who took the law into her own hands. Many of us who are concerned with protecting apes in the wild face the same criticisms.

The idea that the needs of human beings and the needs of wildlife are opposed, that helping one hurts the other, is a common misconception. In most places where wildlife survive on this planet, the habitat is exceedingly fragile. As a scientist, Dian knew that mountain forests function as a catchment area, which slowly releases water to irrigate the crops below. If the forests were cut down and the mountainsides cultivated, the fields soon would become dry and barren. Gorillas contribute to the maintenance of this environment by breaking saplings, promoting the growth of secondary forest and allowing for the development of a mosaic of habitats. Neither the mountain forests nor the gorillas were "luxuries" a poor country cannot afford. They were and are a backup system Rwandans cannot afford to lose.

The poachers who operated in the Parc des Volcans were not breaking "Dian's laws," they were breaking the laws of Rwanda. For park officials to dabble in the ape trade, and for park guards to routinely accept bribes from poachers and "private" fees from tourists, created an atmosphere of lawlessness. Dian believed, as I do, that the person who illegally kills or tortures an animal today might tomorrow do the same to a human.

On a deeper level, Dian did not accept the view that humankind has dominion over the earth and all its creatures. Dian felt that the line between humans and great apes, humans and other animals, which gives all rights to humans and none to other animals, is artificial. Gorillas are a kindred species, fellow citizens of the planet Earth. Having promoted ourselves to masters of the earth, we owe them respect and protection. This is what Dian believed. This is what many of us who work day in, day out with the great apes believe.

By the time she earned her Ph.D. (like Jane, from Cambridge University), Dian was convinced that science would not save the gorillas. She knew that the mountain gorillas, who numbered only four hundred or so at the time, were in immediate peril. They couldn't wait for plans to encourage tourism (and thus make gorillas profitable), glossy brochures and calendars, and diplomatic niceties. Publicly, Dian called such abstract, big-budget schemes "theoretical conservation." Privately, Dian called this "comic book conservation": given the constant, daily threat to the gorillas and their habitat, theoretical conservation was a joke.

Dian saw the alternative as "active conservation": trekking deep into the forest, cutting traps, confiscating weapons, freeing trapped animals, and imposing stiff penalties on poachers and traders in illegal animals and animal products — *now*, not later. Theoretical conservationists plan a bright tomorrow; active conservationists face a grim today.

Dian made her choice. Saving the mountain gorillas was more important than studying them. Not waiting for approval from funding agencies or the scientific community, Dian began organizing her own patrols, offering a bounty for poachers, threatening hunters and herders, and pursuing poachers into their villages, demanding their arrest. Career conservationists thought she was moving too soon, too fast, too aggressively. Dian would later blame herself for acting too late, too slowly, too passively.

On January 1, 1978, Dian's beloved Digit was killed. Alerted by Rwandan trackers, Ian Redmond, a young British biologist who spent two years at Karisoke, found Digit's mutilated body lying in a pool of blood. Digit died defending his family from poachers, sustaining five spear wounds and killing one of the poachers' dogs before he died. As an afterthought, the poachers had hacked off his head and hands to sell as trophies.

Porters carried Digit's body back to Karisoke, to be buried near Dian's cabin in what became a gorilla graveyard. Dian was unnaturally calm, as if she were beyond grief. "There are times when one cannot accept facts for fear of shattering one's being," she later wrote in her book. "From that moment on, I came to live within an insulated part of myself." Almost surely, it was then that Dian the scientist turned activist became Dian the avenging angel.

Single-minded and uncompromising, Dian launched a one-woman war in defense of the gorillas. Inventing her own forms of "magic," she embellished her image as *Nyiramachabelli*. Dian liked her African nickname and asked that it be inscribed on her tombstone. As if ruefully embracing her solitude and isolation, she bragged that *Nyiramachabelli* meant "the woman who lives alone on the mountain." Some say that the name came to mean simply "Dian."

Rumors about Dian's terrorist tactics spread. Dian's harshest critics were not Rwandans (except for those who would profit by her leaving), but Western students who were neophytes to Africa, starry-eyed, romantic, and uninitiated. Dian knew that working through official channels was futile; often park rangers and poachers were relatives. She had no patience with students who put their own research goals ahead of the welfare of the gorillas and refused to devote much of their time to patrols. Unrealistically, she expected them to be as totally dedicated as she was. These young people, in turn, were aghast at the way Dian harangued her staff. No doubt she was dictatorial; as a lone foreign woman in a land where might often makes right, she had to be.

Much of the problem, I believe, was that visitors to Karisoke did not understand how African Dian had become. She was born and raised in the United States. She looked American. Culture is more than skin deep. At Karisoke, Dian was Western in appearance only. When an African, or for that matter a European, behaves in ways we don't understand, we attribute it to his or her foreignness. When one of our own, a fellow North American, behaves strangely, we question that person's sanity.

Students and researchers who go into the field for a year or two, or during their summer breaks, remain outsiders in the host culture. Typically, they go home with amusing stories about strange local customs, along with masks, carvings, batiks, and other cultural trophies. They may devise theories to explain their hosts' beliefs and practices in Western terms. They may even see themselves as experts and spokespersons for the culture they visited. But they remain outsiders. They remain wrapped in the cocoon of their own culture.

Dian had undergone a metamorphosis, one that requires long periods of immersion in another culture. The difference is the difference between learning to speak another language and dreaming in that language. It's not a conscious choice. It just happens. Suddenly you find that people who once looked alien appear familiar and comforting. Ideas you once had to translate now make perfect sense. Personally, you may not believe in spirits or spells, but when everyone around you does, you grow to accept this as normal and natural. It no longer requires explanation. You may not realize how much you have changed until you see another Western face and are shocked at how pale, round-eyed, and beak-nosed the person looks — forgetting that that's how you look.

Traveling between cultures is manageable, but attempting to operate in two cultures simultaneously can be treacherous. Incidents or comments that make perfect sense in one culture may mean something entirely different in the other. A witticism may be taken as a serious pronouncement; personal animosity may be reported as "public opinion," in the researcher's host or home country. You make a joke and no one laughs.

I never visited Karisoke, so I do not know what Dian did or did not do. But as a lone woman in a remote place, Dian had to learn to play by African rules. The few Rwandans with whom I've spoken in North America say local people saw her as one of their own and that even her enemies respected her. Reportedly, she was on good terms with Rwanda's then president. But Rwandans are conspicuously missing from the lists of people interviewed for biographies of Dian. The full story may never be known.

In 1980, at the urging of friends and colleagues, Dian reluctantly agreed to take a sabbatical. While she was teaching at Cornell University, I visited her for several days at her apartment in Ithaca, New York. She was extremely gracious, showering me with gifts and advice. For Dian, gift giving was routine; I have more gifts from her than from most of my closest friends, except those in Indonesia. I suspect that in Rwanda, as in Indonesia and Japan, gift giving is culturally mandated. When I casually mentioned that my shoes hurt, Dian disappeared for a short time, then returned with a new pair of the most comfortable shoes I have ever owned. Where she got them, and how she knew my size, I never learned. She pampered me like a favorite younger sister.

While Dian was in North America, she, Jane, and I went on a lecture tour. Dian, as well as Jane, charmed our audiences. But I sensed that Dian was preoccupied, even melancholic. She constantly talked about returning to Africa. I last saw her in New York City in 1983. She said she was returning to Rwanda and told me not to expect her back.

Dian's murder was brutal and savage. Yet in the end, she won. Because of Dian, the mountain gorillas secured a place in public consciousness. In the Virungas, the mountain gorillas not only survived, but increased in number during the years following her death. In 1990, researchers estimated that there were 600 to 650. Gorilla tourism became a major source of foreign currency for Rwanda. When the civil war in Burundi in the early 1990s spread to the Virungas, researchers had to flee. But both the rebels and the government forces agreed to protect the gorillas out of respect for their country. Their current fate is unknown. But if gorillas had a saint, her name would be *Nyiramachabelli*. In years to come, the words "mountain gorilla" will be inseparable from the name "Dian."

After Dian's death, I knew the battle to save the orangutans was not over. It was only beginning.

At the heart of Dian's dilemma is the inescapable truth that the battle to save endangered species and their habitats never ends. On the front lines of conservation there are no time-outs, no shortcuts, and few final victories. Writing international laws to prohibit the traffic in wild animals, creating and policing parks and reserves, boycotting to save the whale and the dolphin, joining with celebrities who pose nude rather than wear fur — all help fight the battle for the survival of animal species. But sadly, many conservation "success stories" are Pyrrhic victories, which may lull us into complacency and blind us to the truth of what is actually happening to animal populations and ecosystems in far-off corners of the globe. Or even close to home.

As I sat on the plane, trying to hold back the tears, I realized that I wasn't weeping just for Dian or for the mountain gorillas. I was also weeping for chimpanzees, for orangutans, and for a world that is rapidly disappearing.

Once wild orangutans numbered in the hundreds of thousands and roamed throughout Asia. Now fewer than thirty thousand remain in the rapidly disappearing tropical rain forests of Borneo and northern Sumatra. In the last decade alone, the wild orangutan population has declined by at least 30 percent, and perhaps 50 percent. Equally disturbing, only about ten thousand to fifteen thousand of the orangutans still in the wild are in protected tropical rain forest reserves or parks. One of these protected areas is in northern Sumatra. All the others are in Borneo, but some may not be suitable orangutan habitat.

Tanjung Puting, where I have worked for two decades, is far more important than size alone would indicate. It is one of the few parks in Southeast Asia where large areas of tropical peat swamp forest and tropical heath forest are protected. Tanjung Puting is prime orangutan habitat with stable primate populations. It is one place on earth where wild orangutans and their habitat have been protected for the last twenty years, which is why protecting Tanjung Puting is so important.

Orangutans face extinction because the tropical rain forests where they live are being cut down for timber, plantations, roads, and permanent agriculture. Every day, between forty thousand and one hundred thousand acres of rain forest are destroyed around the world. The murder of orangutan mothers and capture of orangutan infants for the pet trade is a direct consequence of habitat destruction. Once forest is destroyed, once orangutans become "homeless," their death warrants are signed.

Along with other endangered species, orangutans are the innocent victims of human population growth, of development schemes and power struggles, of an insatiable global economy that creates greed but not satisfaction, desire but not happiness. The same global forces that ensnare the mountain gorilla have cost tens of thousands of orangutans their lives.

With the other great apes, orangutans are among our closest living relatives. More than other species, great apes remind us of our unity with nature. Because we are so closely related to the great apes, scientists often use them as stand-ins for humans in experiments. But we ignore the "natural experiment" taking place in tropical forests right now. As we watch the great apes slip toward extinction, we are witnessing our own future on an increasingly inhospitable planet. If we take action to save our nearest relatives and their tropical habitats, we are taking the first step toward saving ourselves.

I have always believed that destiny is something you achieve, not something you are given. Yet I can't help thinking that the private dreams and separate motives that drew Jane to the chimpanzees, Dian to the mountain gorillas, and me to the orangutans were part of a larger plan, one of the patterns on the cosmic cat's cradle. We cannot understand ourselves until we understand where we come from and what sets us apart from our closest kin. Such understanding requires passionate observation as well as hard data, empathy as well as empiricism.

In my years in Borneo, I have learned much about orangutans and much about human nature. Humans and orangutans inhabit the same planet. But we experience different universes. Orangutans are not human; they move in a different realm. Orangutans are self-contained and self-sufficient. Because this is so unlike us, it took me years to understand. What I saw as rejection was in fact the deepest form of acceptance. Orangutans do not need to give, because they do not need to receive.

In modern, Western societies we yearn to be like orangutans. In their serene self-sufficiency, orangutans embody much of what we seek in today's frantic, frenetic world. Westerners place a high value on independence. Some of our wealthiest celebrities (Howard Hughes, Greta Garbo, Michael Jackson) have been recluses. We long for "blissful solitude." We admire the self-made man or woman. Many of us live alone or in fragmented families.

Orangutans led me to reevaluate these cultural trends and assumptions. By being themselves, orangutans forced me to come to terms with my own human nature, with the "weakness" of simply being human. *Homo sapiens* is a sociable species. We need mates, children, loved ones, friends, acquaintances, even pets. Without intimate relationships, without communities, we are stranded. Perhaps, without respect for the other inhabitants of the earth, without communion with nature, we also lose something of ourselves. Learning to accept orangutans for who they are, respecting our similarities and differences, has made my own family, my extended family of Louis, Jane, and Dian, and the human family at large more precious to me.

Orangutans teach us that the important differences between human beings and our close kin are not the differences we think they are. A friend of mine overheard a conversation between a zoo director and a colleague. The colleague was describing the Great Ape Project, an attempt to bring certain civil rights (life, liberty, and freedom from torture) to great apes.

"Will you sign the petition?" the colleague wanted to know. The zoo director threw back his head and laughed.

"Yes" he replied, "I will, but only when an orangutan phones and asks me to!"

I'm certain that we could teach an orangutan to dial the correct number on the phone and kiss-squeak into the receiver. But I agree that the day is far away when an orangutan, without prompting, will manufacture and communicate via phone. For orangutans, the long call will suffice.

Technology, or tool use and manufacture, is probably the greatest difference between humans and orangutans — today. Orangutans do not manufacture or use computers, cars, lightbulbs, or even digging sticks and hand axes. They do not have access to any of the technology that has freed human beings from dependence on what nature provides.

Our earliest hominid ancestors, the ones who first diverged from the pongid path to find their own separate destiny, did not manufacture telephones either. What separated them from our cousins, the great apes, was not technology. Chimpanzees make and use tools in the wild. It is doubtful that our own first ancestors were much more sophisticated in tool use than chimpanzees are today. Nor was the first major change our large brain (three times the size of an orangutan brain, after correcting for body size). The relative brain size of the earliest hominids was not much greater than that of contemporary apes.

Rather, the hallmark of human evolution lies in our hips, knees, and toes. The most significant difference between the earliest humans and the great apes was bipedalism, walking upright on two feet. Orangutans are specifically adapted for traveling in the treetops. Even the African apes, who have special adaptations for knuckle-walking, are only semiterrestrial. Many anthropologists hold that bipedalism was important because it freed our hands to use tools and carry food. After years of watching orangutans, who have four hands, I think the emancipation-of-the-hands hypothesis is only part of the story. Orangutans are extremely "handy," but also slow. Bipedalism was important because it enabled our ancestors to cover long distances at a relatively fast pace. A human can easily outrun an orangutan on a flat surface. I remember once not wanting to share food with an adult male orangutan. Nine months pregnant, in a cotton muumuu and slippers, I outran him on an even, flat surface. (He would have outrun me, however, on the uneven, obstacle-ridden terrain of the forest floor.)

The second way that the ancestral hominids differed from the great apes was social organization. As we know from the slaughter of orangutans in places where the forests have been cut down, a slow, semisolitary ape would have been an easy mark for predators on the open savanna. The australopithecines, who were probably the first hominids, undoubtedly lived in groups. Although we will never know for certain what form their groups took, there are strong reasons to believe that the division of labor by sex was a crucial element in this emerging adaptation. To be sure, males and females play different roles in great-ape social groups. Typically, females nurture the young and males guard the females or the range. Chimpanzees have been observed sharing food, not only with their offspring but also with other adults. But this is rare. By and large, great apes are solitary feeders. Even when eating in the same tree, each individual picks food only for him- or herself and eats or discards everything picked.

Among modern hunters and gatherers, men and women usually go separate ways, the men to hunt, the women to gather. Although women sometimes hunt and men sometimes gather, the basic division remains. Then the men and women meet to share what they've collected or killed. This division of labor gave hominids a distinct advantage. Because women are usually pregnant or carrying infants, they are not very efficient hunters, especially of large game. But motherhood does not interfere with gathering fruits, nuts, and roots. Free from pregnancy and nursing, men are better hunters. But hunting or even scavenging is always a gamble, especially for a relatively puny hominid competing with "hunting machines" like the great cats. Hunting does not provide a steady, reliable source of food. However, *combining* hunting and gathering was a revolutionary development, one that enabled the early hominids to take full advantage of their mobility and invade new habitats.

There is a catch, however. If men go one way and women another, yet they depend on one another, they need some reliable way to arrange rendez-vous. This is where speech comes in. Speech might have evolved because it made it easier for our distant ancestors to coordinate their activities. Once speech evolved, it probably developed its own momentum. Not only could men and women coordinate today's activities, they could communicate their individual experiences and use the past to plan for the future, and over time develop a collective information bank, or what we call "culture."

Almost certainly, speech was one dividing line between our hominid ancestors and the great apes. But one must distinguish between speech and language. The great difference between pongids and humans is *spoken* language. The great apes are incapable of speech; they lack the vocal apparatus that speech requires. But great apes can be taught a simple language, as the chimpanzee Washoe, the gorilla "Koko," and the lesser known orangutan Princess will attest. Great apes can learn that gestures or other symbols stand for individuals, objects, actions, emotions, even categories, and that the order of symbols can change the meaning (syntax). They not only learn to recognize and produce symbols, but combine them in novel ways. The great puzzle is why, if the great apes have latent linguistic abilities, they never developed this asset.

Again, orangutans gave me an answer. When Gary Shapiro left camp in the early 1980s, his prize pupil, Princess, had learned more than thirty signs. But as I watched Gary ride a graduate student's roller-coaster highs and lows — highs because Princess and his other orangutan subjects could sign with the best of them, and lows because the orangutans mainly wanted to sign about food and contact — I realized why orangutans don't have spoken language. They don't need phonemes, words, and sentences. Quite simply, they have nothing to say to one another that can't easily be communicated through facial expressions, gestures, movements, and vocalizations. Why build a rocket ship when you only want to move from one tree to another?

A fourth distinction between pongids and ourselves is our birth intervals. Perhaps my most important single discovery is that orangutans are one of the slowest breeding mammals on this planet. Certainly, orangutans are the slowest breeding primate. At Tanjung Puting, orangutan females give birth, on average, only once in eight years. The birth interval varies from as few as five years to almost ten and a half years. So far, the greatest number of offspring I have seen a wild female orangutan produce is four. But the average adult female bears three offspring or fewer in her lifetime. Maud, with three offspring at age thirty, is already leading in the evolutionary sweepstakes.

At the same time, wild orangutan mortality rates are low. In all my years at Tanjung Puting, only one orangutan unit — Cara, Carl, and Cindy — died of disease, probably facilitated by nutritional stress. Other orangutans died of old age. But infant mortality and predation are virtually nil. This contrasts with a troop of wild crab-eating macaques who occasionally appear at the end of the camp bridge. During casual observation of these small gray monkeys we saw, on three separate occasions, individual macaques fatally attacked by predators, including a crocodile and a large python. But these monkeys can "afford" the high mortality rate because female macaques give birth every two years.

An orangutan female is doing well if she bears three or four offspring in her lifetime. A chimpanzee female may produce one offspring every six years, and a gorilla female, one every four. But in many traditional societies, women have six, eight, or ten children (not counting infant deaths). Monkeys are also fast reproducers, bearing offspring every year or two. But humans outmonkey the monkeys in fertility. In terms of reproductive strategies, great apes, especially orangutans, took the slow but safe route. Monkeys took the fast but risky route. Humans took the fast route but made it safe through the division of labor and, later, food production and technology. Perhaps this is why humans colonized the planet, leaving their pongid cousins behind. Certainly, this is why orangutans are so vulnerable to extinction, while humans are overpopulating the planet.

The question of when and why our hominid ancestors diverged from the great apes is still controversial. For many years, paleoanthropologists believed that a fossil hominoid called *Ramapithecus* was the first member of the human family, the "missing link." Ramapithecines were found in India, Pakistan, Greece, and East Africa and estimated to be at least fourteen million years old. In the early 1980s, however, the ramapithecines were shown conclusively to be ancestral orangutans. I have seen the casts of fossils, and their dishlike faces and jaws clearly seem related to modern orangutans.

The "unmasking" of *Ramapithecus* as an ancestral orangutan supported Darwin's belief that the origins of humankind were in Africa, and Africa alone. But the growing number of fossil discoveries in East Africa, combined with the persistence of chimpanzees and gorillas on the same continent, raised more questions than were answered. Richard Leakey's discoveries in northern Kenya and Don Johanson's finds in Ethiopia deepened the mystery. Recently, the distinguished French paleoanthropologist Yves Coppens reviewed the fossil evidence. He realized that all of the australopithecines were found east of the Rift Valley, the great gash that divides the African continent for over a thousand miles. All of the ancestors and surviving members of the *Pan* family (chimpanzees, our closest kin) were west of the Rift Valley.

Coppens concluded that human evolution was an "East Side Story." About eight million years ago, in a tectonic crisis, one plate of the earth's surface sank, creating the Rift Valley. This, in turn, pushed up mountains to the west, including the Virungas, where Dian Fossey studied the mountain gorillas. Coppens hypothesizes that this tectonic crisis created a breach and barrier between related chimp-human ancestors, as well as two distinct climates. The west retained its humid forests, and the east evolved into open, drier savanna. Forced out of the Garden of Eden by climatic change, the eastern branch of the human-chimp family diversified, leaving behind fossilized variations on the australopithecine theme. Eventually, one branch of this family — fully bipedal, with a division of labor, the rudiments of speech, and a higher birth rate because of a shorter birth interval — prevailed.

Not all paleoanthropologists agree. There is some evidence that the climate in East Africa changed before the opening of the Great Rift Valley; perhaps the first hominids moved out onto the savanna by choice. But whatever the cause, the result was the same. Some three million years ago, on the African savanna, the hominid family split in two. Whereas one branch developed robust jaws and teeth and a highly specialized vegetarian diet, the second branch widened its diet, developed a large brain, and started depending on tools for survival. The first branch, the robust australopithecines, eventually went extinct. The second branch, our branch, emerged from Africa, eventually spread around the globe, and developed the largest (in relation to body size) and most complex brain of all the creatures on the planet.

This large brain, with its convoluted cerebral cortex, gives us the ability to contemplate the past and the future. We can sit back, gaze at the stars, and reflect on our origins in the dim past. We can reflect on events in the story of creation of our Judeo-Christian culture, a powerful tale of the expulsion of our ancestors from Eden and of Cain killing his brother, Abel a story already known to Hebrew pastoralists thousands of years ago. We can also ponder in modern scientific times the massive tectonic event that may have separated us from our pongid kin and propelled us out of the tropical rain forest. We can think about how our line of hominids, *Homo,* outcompeted, and thus killed, a sibling hominid line. The first fossil hominid ever found at Olduvai Gorge, the one which catapulted Louis and Mary Leakey into fame, was the superrobust australopithecine *Zinjanthropus.* Later investigation revealed that Zinj had been left as garbage on a probable *Homo* living room floor, perhaps even the remains of dinner.

The ancestors of today's orangutans, who remained in the tropical rain forest, retreating with the forests to Asia ten million to fourteen million years ago, escaped this fate. When I look at orangutans I am reminded that we are only human. Our appearance on the earth was relatively recent; orangutans are far older, as a species, than we are. I wonder, when *Homo erectus* strode into Asia: were orangutans watching from the trees? It is a humbling thought.

Our departure from Eden allows us reflection — reflection on our origins and our relations to other creatures, reflection on good and evil, and, ultimately, reflection on the possibility that we are engineering our own extinction. Never having left Eden, our innocent pongid kin are not burdened with this knowledge and the responsibility it entails. Looking into the calm, unblinking eyes of an orangutan we see, as through a series of mirrors, not only the image of our own creation but also a reflection of our own souls and an Eden that once was ours. And on occasion, fleetingly, just for a nanosecond, but with an intensity that is shocking in its profoundness, we recognize that there is no separation between ourselves and nature. We are allowed to see the eyes of God.

For more information on how to
help the orangutans, please contact:

Orangutan Foundation International
822 South Wellesley Avenue
Los Angeles, CA 90046

1-800-ORANGUTAN

# ACKNOWLEDGMENTS

The long-term orangutan research and conservation efforts described in this book were made possible by the help and support of many people to whom I would like to express my appreciation.

The late L. S. B. Leakey's support was crucial. It was an enormous privilege to know Louis Leakey. Even now his memory is an inspiration. I will always be grateful to him for helping make my dream of a long-term orangutan study a reality.

My orangutan work would not have been possible without the support of the government of the Republic of Indonesia. I thank H. E. President Soeharto for truly caring about conservation and the environment, and for allowing me and other academics access to Indonesia's great forests and magnificent orangutans. In December 1991 President Soeharto opened the Second International Great Apes Conference at the National Palace in Jakarta, and received the Most Distinguished Honor Award for Conservation jointly presented by the Orangutan Foundation International and the Jane Goodall Institute. I thank President Soeharto for his government's support and for his wisdom and kindness. In its legislation and its policies to protect tropical rain forests, the Republic of Indonesia is a world leader.

I owe an eternal debt of gratitude to Minister Soesilo Soedarman for his extraordinary vision, his strength, and his support. Minister Soesilo's help was essential in enabling me to continue my orangutan work. Likewise, I am profoundly grateful to Minister Joop Avé for his many kindnesses and vital support. I also thank Minister Djamaludin Suryohadikusumo and Mrs. Djamaludin, who encouraged and nurtured me at critical times. In addition, I thank Minister Ali Alatas for his encouragement.

My deep appreciation to Dr. Soedjarwo for establishing Tanjung Puting National Park in 1982 and for his wise stewardship of Indonesia's forests while he was Minister of Forestry. I also thank Dr. and Mrs. Soedjarwo for their warm friendship and, on many occasions, their generous and gracious hospitality. They are truly my "adoptive" parents in Jakarta and my children and I will always be grateful to them. I thank Professor Emil Salim for his efforts on my behalf. Professor Salim is universally respected for his work as Indonesia's first Minister of Environment. I also thank Professor Sumitro Djojohadikusumo for his vital support, brilliant advice, and friendship. Professor Sumitro helped to establish the Orangutan Foundation Indonesia and became its first chairperson.

I thank U.S. Vice President Al Gore, a visionary conservationist, for his support and encouragement. I thank former U.S. Ambassador to Indonesia Edward Masters and Mrs. Allene Masters for their help, concern, and friendship. I am also very grateful to Ambassador Robert Barry and to Mr. Sidney Smith.

My sincere thanks to the government of Canada for its support, particularly Ambassador Ingrid Hall, Ambassador Bill (and Julie) Montgomery, Ambassador Lawrence T. Dickenson, M. P. Svend Robinson, and Consul Michel Dupuis.

I would like to recognize the generous support provided by the Indonesian Embassy in Washington, D.C., represented by former Ambassador Abdul Rachman Ramly and Ambassador Arifin Siregar. I also thank the Indonesian consulates in the United States, particularly in Los Angeles and New York, and Consul Generals Sudkono Haridadji, Djunaedi Sutisnawinata, and Arkelaus Pantow, Consuls Sunten Z. Manurang and Haru Kandou, and Mr. Ariono Suriawinata, as well as Malaysian Consul General Wan Yusof Embong.

I thank the former governors of Kalimantan Tengah Governors R. Sylvanus, Gatot Amrih, Soepramanto, and especially Governor W. Gara. Words are insufficient to express my gratitude to the late Mr. and Mrs. G. T. Binti, who became my "adoptive" parents in Kalimantan and after whom Rod and I named our son. I thank the late *Bupati* Mien Rafii and *Bupati* Dharman for their commitment to protecting the forests of Tanjung Puting. I thank Mr. Musti Rinda for his help, and also General and Mrs. Maulani, and Sekanye village chief *Ta'ib*.

My sincere gratitude to the former heads of Indonesian Nature Conservation and Forest Protection (PHPA), including the late Mr. Walman Sinaga, the late Mr. Prijono Hardjosento, Mr. Lukito Daryadi, Mr. Wartono Kadri, and Dr. Rubini Atmawidjaja. Special thanks go to the local heads of Forestry in Pangkalan Bun, including Mr. and Mrs. Rombe, who were especially gracious and hospitable during my first years in Kalimantan, Mr. Bahrun Harun, Mr. Berigin, and Mr. Sujut. I also thank Mr. Widajat Eddypranoto as well as Mr. and Mrs. Siswojo Sarodja, Mr. Goenari, Mr. Toga Siallagan, and Mr. Soegito Tirtomihardjo for their help and friendship. I also thank Mr. Somoedhadi, Mr. Heurybut, Mr. Aep, and Mr. Yusuran. A deep note of thanks goes to Mr. Hadi Rohadi, former head of PHPA in Palangka Raya, and Mr. Jumidi, former "rayon" head in Kumai for their devoted work in the field. I also thank the former head of Tanjung Puting National Park, Mr. Kusasi, for his ceaseless and heroic commitment to the park, and the current head, Mr. Herry Soesilo, for his dedication to protecting and upgrading the park.

I thank the park personnel in Kumai, including Mr. Yayat, Mr. Sabri, Mr. Sadi, Mr. Helmie, Mr. Dollah, Mr. Pampang, Mr. Budiman, Mr. Arsat, Mr. Usman, Mr. Asep, Mr. Mursiman, Mr. Yanto, and the late Mr. Idrus. In addition, I thank Mr. Effendy Sumardja and Mr. Widodo Ramono as well as Dr. Djuwantoko and Mr. Kuswanto for their help and kindness. I also thank Dr. Kunkun, Mr. Darsono, and Mr. Harijaka.

I am very grateful to the Indonesian Institute for Sciences (L.I.P.I.) and thank Professor Samaun Samadikun, Dr. Setijati Sustrapradja, Mrs. Moertini Atmowidjojo, Mr. J. Bima, and Mr. Napitupulu as well as former head Dr. Bachtiar Rifai, Ms. Sjamsiah Achman, and the late Mr. Hainold. The support of the late Professor Sutan Takdir Alisjahbana, Ms. Nina Sulaiman, and Mr. Ismo Sutano Suwelo from the Universitas Nasional was invaluable. In particular, I thank the late Nina Sulaiman and her husband for their wonderful hospitality.

I also thank (retired) Generals Hoegeng and Rachman Masjhur for trusting us with their orangutans. I owe special thanks to the late Sultan Hamengkubuwono IX, the former Vice President of the Republic of Indonesia, for extending his moral support to my orangutan conservation efforts.

I am extremely grateful to the foundations, organizations, and individuals who provided funds over the years. Just as Louis Leakey was instrumental in enabling me to begin my study, so the Leakey Foundation was crucial in providing initial funding. My gratitude is boundless. I thank Mr. and Mrs. Larry Barker, Mrs. Tita Caldwell, Mrs. Olive Kemp, Mr. and Mrs. Rex Allen, Mr. Jeff Short, Mrs. H. S. Lokey, Mr. and Mrs. D. J. Postma, the late Mr. Farley O'Brien and Mrs. E. O'Brien, Mr. and Mrs. S. Bruce, Mrs. Kay Jamison, Ms. Barbara Newson Pelosi, Ms. Nancy Pelosi, Ms. Kay Woods, Mr. G. Jagels, Dr. Ned Munger, and Dr. Clark Howell for their support. Words cannot express my profound gratitude to Mr. Arnold and Mrs. Joan Travis. I am very grateful to Mrs. Ann Getty and Mr. Gordon Getty for their support and friendship. I thank Dr. Gayle Gittins for her tremendous support as well as Mrs. Sandy Johnson (who was one of the first to visit Camp Leakey).

My deepest gratitude goes to the Jane and Justin Dart Foundation, the National Geographic Society, the Herz Foundation, the New York Zoological Society, and the Van Tienhoven Foundation of Holland, who funded my early work. My deepest thanks go to the late Mr. Justin Dart and Mrs. Jane Dart, the late Dr. Leonard Carmichael, the late Dr. Melvin Payne, Dr. Edwin Snider, Mrs. Mary G. Smith, Ms. Joanne Hess, and Mrs. Neva Folk as well as Mrs. Gilbert Gosvenor and Dr. Barry Bishop. I am also indebted to the late Dr. Westermann, Mr. Wayne King, Dr. Barbara Harrisson, Mr. Dennis Kane, Mrs. M. Moomey, Ms. Sue Byrnes, and Mrs. Alice Hall as well as Mr. Robert Gilka.

A special profound thank you goes to the late Mr. Leighton Wilkie and especially to Mr. Robert Wilkie. Not only did the Wilkie Brothers Foundation provide me with my first grant, but Mr. Robert Wilkie continued to fund me for twenty-three years, first through the Leakey Foundation and later through the Orangutan Foundation International. My gratitude to Mr. Robert Wilkie is boundless.

I thank the World Wildlife Fund, P. T. Georgia Pacific Indonesia, the Chicago Zoological Society, Huffco Indonesia, the Weyerhaeuser Foundation, and the John Simon Guggenheim Memorial Foundation. I thank Mr. Bill Franklin of Weyerhaeuser Asia for his support. I also thank the gracious people of the British Women's Association Jakarta for providing funding at a critical time, especially Mrs. Shelagh Hilton.

In particular, I owe a heavy debt of gratitude to Earthwatch, especially Mr. Brian Rosborough and Mr. James Burnes, Mrs. Linda Knight, Dr. Andrew Mitchell, Mrs. Dee Robbins, Ms. Susanne Yin, Ms. Laurie Rothste, Mrs. Betty Parfenuk, Ms. Wendy Sisson, and Mrs. Mary Blue Magruder. My gratitude to the wonderful volunteers, the "Earthwatchers" who came and helped, is immeasurable. I thank them all from the bottom of my heart: Marilyn

Abers, Elizabeth Abrams, Glenda Adams, Donna Albert, Eleanor Allen, Gabrielle Allen, William Alley, Anna Alvisi, Dr. Richard Ambrose, Suzanne M. Amodio, Sheila Amos, Carol Anderson, Paula Anderson, Debbie Antonienko, Linda Apsitis, Bruce Arboit, Carol Arboit, *Ralph Arbus,* Eldon Archer, Portia Arutunian, Alison Asche, Rosemarie Atencio, Willette Austin, Joyce Axton, Irene Baier, Margaret Baisley, James Balcer, Paul Barr, David and Camilla Barry, Anita Bartlett, Diane Mary Batson, Ava Baum, Diane Beck, Joanna Becker, Maxine Becker, David and Donna Beddell, Melanie Bedell, Robert Bender, Steve Benjamon, Robert Benke, Betty Benson, Judith Berger, Dorothy Berke, Jill Berlin, Thomas Berner, Alan Bernstein, Larraine Best, Richard Beye, Barbara Biebush, Jay Birnbauer, John Blas, Gary Blond, Francis Bomer, David Bond, Share Bond, Arden Bowers, Beth Boyer, Charles Keith Boyle, Gail Bradley, John Brand, Alice Bray, Bill Breilmeyer, Alberto Brenes, Dr. Christina Brewer, June Bristow, Rick Brocato, Joan Brock, Brenda Brockelsby, Lila Brown, the late Robert Brownlee, Robert Buchanan, Margaret Buckland, Elizabeth Buckner, Victor Buehler, Brooke Bullinger, Kevin Buncman, Lee Burbeck, Alan Buxton, Shari Caldwell, Mike Callahan, Bryan Callen, Kathleeen Callen, John and Wendy Calmette, Mary Kay Calvert, Dr. Bill Calvert, Jay Cammermeyer, Dennis Campbell, Peter Carlson, Barbara Carse, Lisa Carse, Linda Cary, Patricia Cashmore, Charlie Casselman, Alejandro Castro, Joycelyn Cerul, Carolyn Chambers, Barbara Champlin, Michael Charters, Branden Chattmen, Barbara Chen, Dee Christian, Carol Christiansen, Christopher Clark, Dr. Crawford Clark, Patrick and Theresa Clark, Dr. Susanne Clark, Mary Clausen, Courtney Cline, Tia Coble, Dillon Cohen, Ed Cohen, Martha and Philip Cole, Ronald Coleman, Linda Colucci, Phyllis Conner, Louis Connick, M. Considine, Doris Cook, Margaret Cook, Stuart Corliss, Rita Costick, Barry Court, Lisa Couturier, Joseph Covino, Elizabeth Craft, Peter Crayson, Jeanne Cummings, Cheryl D'Amato, Jan Davies, Gordon Kennedy Davis, Kathryn Davis, Roy Davis, Robert Day, Eva Dayan, Renée De La Haye, James Delara, Joyce de Lorenzo, Fernando DePiero, Lisa Remington Dietel, Ralph DiGaetano, *Linda Di Sante,* Colonel Bill Disher, Catherine Disher, Maria DiStefanio, LaVon C. Doner Hall, Maryanna Dotson, Karen Dotter, Charlene Dougherty, Donald Dowbenko, Kenneth Dubuque, Maryke Dusoswa-Kehlenbrink, Harolynn Dyer, Mary Dyyert, Sarah Easterbrook, Doris Eckstrom, Sharon Edelman, Graham Edwards, Kathleen Edwards, Ann Ellenboyen, Elizabeth Elliot, George Elliot, Mimi Ellis-Locke, Elizabeth Ann English, Kay Erwin, Catherine Evans, Chris Evans, Susan Evans, Archie Falardeau, Carol Feld, Robert Fenley, Earl Ferguson, Carrick Ferini, Jean Fernman, Marion Fiero, Laura Finlayson, Andrew Fisher, Ann Fisher, Donna Fisher, Louann Folkman, Joyce Forest, Carol Forsyth, Douglas Foss, Sarah Fox, Diana Francis, Marcia Frank, Thomas Freeman, Sherrie Frieling, Joan Friend, Nicolas Froelicher, Chris Fryer, Desley Fryer, Roy Fuller, Ann Furr, Shannon Furr, Catherine Gaither, Coleen Gannon, Ruth Ganter, Dr. Serge Gasparini, Ann Gates, Monica Gawthorne, Katrina Gazdzik, Carol Gee, Wynn Geiger, Louise Geist, Jean Gelato, Doris Gerald, Charles Germain, Pam Gerould, Mary Gershanoff, Laura Gerwitz, Amy Gheres, Cynthia Gibat, Dr. Gayle Giottins, Linda Kim Girey, Elizabeth Glover, Carolyn Goettsch, Ellen Goff, Herb and Ellen Goldstein, Arlene Golenfrienski, Edward Gomez-Angel, *Andria Goodkin,* Alicia Goranson, Gail Gordon, Dr. Jan Taylor Gordon and Dr. Ken Gordon, Karen Gordon, Nancy Gormezano, Kay Gottesman, Kathy Graham, Jane Gray, Robyn Gray, Timothy Graybill, Leslie Greenbaum, Daniel Greenberg, Sheila Greenberg, LaVonne Grimes, Lucy L. Grimm, Mullie Groendyke, Anne Grosshans, Jeremy Grosvenor, Elisabeth Grout, David Grove, Beverly Gubbins, *Ralph Gut,* Stephen Guthrie, Pat Hackley, Anne Hademan, *Bonnie Hall,* Cynthia Hall, Theresa Hallinan, Joan Hampson, Liz Hampton, Thomas Hanley, Anne Hansen, Nancy Hanson, Julie Harding, Dorothy Hardy, Richard Harlow, Robert Harper, Louise Harrell, Larry Harrigan, James Harris, Phyllis Harrison, Valerie Hart, Joseph Hassett, Connie Hastert, Kathleen Hawley, Betty Hays, Constance Hefferan, Carla Heiland, Barbara Henderson, Janet Herbruck, Jason Herrick, Dorothy Heslop, Valarie Hetherington, Lucy Hibberd, Dr. Albert and Marka Hibbs, Helen Hiscocks, Bill Hobbs, Jerry Hobbs, Barbara Hobbs Withey, Yvonne Hoefer, David Hogg, JunAnn Holmes, Heidi Hoop, Paulette Hopke, Glen Hori, David Houghton, Muriel Houghton, Sheri Houser, Marian Howard, Barbara Hughes, Debra Hull, Susan Humpert, Gary Huntsman, Lindsay Huppe, Suzanne Husband, Gordon Hutchinson, Lilia Illes, Sylvia Ann Illes, Richard Ingraham, *Ann Inversen,* Kathy Irwin, Barbara Isaacman, Alice Jacklet, Jon Jacobsen, Geri Jacobson, Vivian Jamieson, Arlene Jastrzembowski, Joel Jeral, Jill Johnson, Paul David Johnson, Carol Jolley, Ellen Jolley, Elizabeth Jones, John Karl Jones, Burt Kahn, Priscilla Kane, Gurson and Sue Kantor, Steven Karbank, Eleanor and George Karl, Donatus, Jennifer, Fiona, and Emma Katauskas, Deborah Keever, Sharon Keith, Margaret Keller, Denise Kelley, Marie Kenny, Nigel Kerby, Ellen Kern, Lynn Killan, Mary King, Penelope King, David Kirkham, Alex Kiviary, David Kleeman, Leslie Klein, Delores Knopfelmacher, Christopher Kogan, Ellen Kohner, Diane Koosed, Patricia Korn, Lee Kottke, Martha Kronholm, Jan Krupnick, Ted Krystosek, Brooke Kurzon, Dr. Jill Kusba, Rita Kusinitz, Gerald Kutzman, Pamela Labadie, *Gladys Lacey,* Yvonne LaChapelle, Coloriss Lackey, Linda Laddin, *Peggy Lambert,* Rosalie Lambis, Dr. Eric and Lori Lander, Nancy Lange, Jill Langman, *David Lappen,* Patricia Lawless, Leonora Lawrence, David Lee, Charles Leeming, Ashley Leiman, Dianne Leiter, Susan Leith, Anne Leonard, Suzi Leonard, Becki Levine, Harry LeVine, Jan Levine, Phillippa LeVine, Margaret Lewis, Nedra Lexow, Carol Liebmann, Jennifer Lindert, Larry Little, Jane Lohmar, Dennis Londergan, Abigail Lubliner, Donna Lukshides, Jennifer Luna, Hank Luria, Lois Lyndon, Katherine Macarthur, L. Macaulay, Margaret MacInnes, Jack MacKenzie, Jay Mackie, Pat Mackie, David MacLeod, Phyllis MacLeod, Jane Maczuzak, Kris Maine, Maureen Malloy, Janice Mangels, Cathy Manjunath, Judy Mansfield, Marcus Manson, Ruth Marshall, Denise Martin, Marcia Martini, Walter Marzinkos, Kathy Masters, Chrys Matterson, Hill Maury, Robyn Mayes, Joy Mayfield Rowe, Ann McAllister, Sarah McCandless,

Allyson McCauley, Georgia McClelland, Amanda McConnoughy, Dorothy McCormick, Helen McCormick, Lisa McCowan, Susan McCree, Susan McDiven, Meleisa McDonnell, Barbara McGinley, Douglas McGregor, Kimball McKechan, Kirk McKelvey, Louise McLoughlin, Cynthia McMillan, Clare McNamara, Mary McNelly, Dale McRaven, Carol Means, Dorothy Mebane, Debra Lou Melahn, Charlotte Meloney, Carole Meltzer, Margaret Menell, Christel Mertens, Audry Mertz, Mary Merwin, Kirk Mettam, Ruth Meyer, Harold Michlewitz, Jean Mickey, Alison Middleton, *Lisa Miekle,* Christine Mielock, Carole Mikelson, Esther and Mark Millea, the late Glenn Miller, Julia Mills, Virginia Minick, Larry Mitchell, *Soren Mitchell,* Mark Monaco, John Montgomery, Hasty Moore, Joan Moran, Sys Morch, Marcene Mork, Bonnie Morrison, Sandra Moura, Margaret Muat, Robert Muat, Victoria Mudford, *Dr. Pat Mueller,* Kris Mulder, Brian Muller, James Murphy, Thomas Murphy, Holly Myers, Karen Myers, Patricia Nave, Lisa Naylor, Fergus Neilson, Helene Nelkin, Bea Nemlaha, Connie Ness, Diana Ness, Lone Nielsen, Karen Norvig, Patrician Noud Zucker, Susan Novick, Anouk Novy, Dr. Frank Ochberg, John O'Hara, Pamela Okano, Claudia Olejniczak, Beth Oliver, Naomi Oliver, Dr. Warren Osborne, Margot Paddock, Mary Lee Paoletti, Audrey Patterson, Nancy Patton, Kay Paull, Liselotte Paulson, Richard Pearce, John Pearson, *Carole Peccorini,* Dr. Carl Pelazzolo, Airi Peltonen, Elaine Penwell, Judy Perkins, Wesley Perkins, Julianne Perron, Jana Perry, Janice Pfenninger, Marilyn Piccatto, Carol Piligian, Ellen Piligian, Janice Pole, Herschel Day Post, Betty Power, Joni Lynn Praded, Geraldine and James Pratt, Donald Preston, Melissa Probst, Harriet Provine, Susan Raisin, Christine Ranck, David and Georganna Ranglack, Herbert Rau, Eric Raymond, Karen Reed, May Inga Reed, Tim Reed, James Reeve, Colleen Reid, Sieglinde Reynolds, Ann Riall, Ione Rice, Philata Riley, Amy Rinaldi, Carol Ritchie, David Roby, Conrad Roelli, Scott and Theresa Rogers, Susan Rose, David and Kathy Rosenberg-Wohl, *Dr. Mark Rosenthal,* Dr. Norm Rosenthal, Barbara Russell, Shirley Russo, Nancy Sabat, Susan Sabor, Peter Sadori, Nili Sahlev, Dr. Irving Salan, Barbara Sallee, Dr. Patsy Sampson, Jean Savage, Pauline Scarrott, *Sharon Schembs,* Terri Scheuneman, Karen Schmidt, Nancy Schmidt, Debbie Schober, Pauline Schorman, Rothe Schubot, Zipora Schulz, Judith Schwartz, Martha and Miles Scofield, Dema Scott, Thomas Scripps, Elizabeth Sears, Jane Seegal, Laurie Seidler, Kathleen Sestrich, Miriam Shapiro, Darrin Sharp, Julia Shaw, Sarah Shellow, Linda Shifman, Alice Shirakawa, Carol Sidell, Diane and Fred Sidon, Judith Silver, Janet Silvers, Julia Silzer, Isabella Simmons, June Simpson, Dr. Patrick Skelly, Tom Slone, Jeff Slonim, Caren Smeltzer, Helen Smith, *Nancy Smith,* Ellis Snare, Phyllis Snyder, Elide Solomon, Debra Sonnen, Jenny Spaeth, Michael Spector, Paul Spencer, Sally Spencer, Matt Starr, Edith Statons, James Stephens, Gail Stockwell, Graeme Stride, Pauline Stride, Rodney Sturdivant, Gerald Sugarman, Robert Sullivan, Weona Sutton, Arland Swanson, Sally Symonds, Steve Dale Szurvas, Rachel Tarses, Val Tartaylino, Sumi Tatsui, Karen Taubner, Dr. Beverley Taylor, Carlene Taylor, Elizabeth Taylor, Leonard Taylor, Robert Taylor, Tanya Taylor, Velvet Tetrault, Ingrid Thew, Betty Thomas, Harrison Thornell, Maryann Thorpe, Joan Thuebel, Joanne Tilghman, Carol Tilton, Edith Timken, Vicki Timmermaus, Pat Traub, Dr. Jill Trip, William Troetel, Tina Tselentis, Patricia Tunney, Rundall Turner, the late Karen Ugalde, Elizabeth Ujluiki, Dr. Virginia Valadka, Linda Veale, Robert Veale, Claudia Vicas, Shirley Voellinger, Hagen Vonburchard, Pam Voorhees, Janis Waggener, Christina Walker, Harold Walker, Margery Walker, Ernest and Janice Warrick, Catherine Watson, Kristina Watts, Meredith Webster, Sue Weigall, Dr. Judy Weinstein, Marcia Weinstein, Claudette Weiss, Richard Weiss, Dorothy West, Tara Wethington, Gerald Wetta, the late Bobby White, Sheila Wickouski, Cynthia Wilford, Edmund Wilford, Warren Williams, Sue Wilson, Kate Withey, Dr. Oliver and Helen Wolcott, Anne Wolff, Kimberly Wood, Susan Wood, Wilfred Wood, G. Woodley-Page, Scott Wyse, Sharon Yanish, *John Yondorf,* Dr. Bryant York, Jerree Young, Caryl Zaar, Mitch Ziontz, and Starr Zuckerman.

I am also grateful to the OFI service teams who visited the field: Marlan Stocking, Maxine Bruhns, David Lunato, Vincent Lunato, Joanne Altman, Brenda Pangen, Michelle Deselles, Karen Dinev, Henry Linden, Doris Hedman, Jean Gleason, Jeanne Carter, Al Russell, Bob Wong, Elaine Shusterman, Dolores Stromberg, Sally Smith, Carol Ritchie, Cynthia Wilford, John Borja, Darin Klein, Lynn Branecky, Dr. Anthony Rose, Dr. Michael Sachs, Nancy Katz, and Keny Bowman.

My deepest gratitude belongs to the generous, dedicated people who established the Orangutan Foundation International and made it the vigorous institution it is today. My first thanks go to the founding board: John Beal, Gordon Getty, Norman (and Mrs. Lyn) Lear, Dr. Gary Shapiro, Suzy Dorr, *Pak* Bohap, Blanche Whittey, and David Churchman, as well as later board members Caroline Gabel, Dr. Nancy Briggs, and Judy Twentyman, who supplied tremendous grace and vigor. My mother, Filomena Galdikas, is our outstanding volunteer and office manager. I cannot thank her enough. My special thanks also go to Blanche Whittey who sustained us in the early days, as well as Dr. Lillian Rachlin, Michael Charters, Gerry Sugarman, Noel Rowe, Andrew Fisher, Judith Brown, Carla Heiland, Paul and Barbara Spencer, Dr. Jill Kusba, Dr. Maylene Wong, Dr. Ed Sleeper, Susan Raisin, Patti Ragan, Judy Perkins, Evelyn Gallardo and David Root, Katherine Rust, John and Joanna Pearson, Glenn Hori, Suzy Leonard, Sue Wilson, Kay Harrigan Woods, Dr. Gayle Gittins, Mark Monaco, Betty White Ludden, Bill Raffin, Dorothy Hardy, Amory B. and Mrs. L. Hunter Lovins, Lucy Grimm, Liselotte Paulson, Graham Edwards, and to Julie Harding, Maurine Taubman, Lisa Couturier, Charles Schwartz and Nancy Drosd, Hatsy Kniffin, Joyce Axton, Gail Gordon, Peggy Lambert, Dr. Patsy Sampson, Sally Spencer, Ellen and Herb Goldstein, Eric Raymond, Cynthia Wilford-Borja, Drs. Jan and Ken Gordon, Betty Thomas, Linda Lyon, Les Greenbaum, Ellen Jolley-Dotson, Ann Tompkins, Charlotte Ross, Karen Friedman, Peter Carlson, Sally Robinson, Barbara Chen, Tina Holmes, Lynn Killam, Dr. William Doyle, Sari Jane Koshetz, Rosemary Olszewski, John Paul Jones

DeJoria, Earl Holliman, Tippi Hedren, Ronald Ornstein, Rob and Holly Laidlow, Dr. Terry Maple, Lori Perkins, Melanie Bond, Nick Rutgers, John Pearson, Linda Lyon, Susan Raisin, Neal Weissman, Dr. Vincent Sutlive, George and Sally Bell, Kristy Anderson, and Alan Altchech who provided funds, photographs, and drawings, allowed the use of their homes, organized fund-raisers and lectures, wrote books and articles, and volunteered long hours. I also want to thank Lloyd Yoshira, Gordon Granger, Tom Gause, Christine Stevens, and particularly, Larry Williams and Stephen Mills of the Sierra Club and Ken Wherry of the Eddie Bauer Foundation. I am indebted to Mark Starowicz, Susan Bloomstone, Thomas Sennatt, Jay Branagan, Robin Moyer, Donny Metri, and Charles Lindsay for their concern.

My gratitude to the hardworking, dedicated people who established OFI chapters in Canada (Mrs. Karen Lind, Ms. Elizabeth Crocker, Mrs. Ingrid Nystrom, Mrs. Noreen McDonald, Mr. Garnet Hardy, Mrs. Gillian Boothroyd, Mr. David Braide), the United Kingdom (Mrs. Ashley Leiman), Taiwan (Mr. Marcus Phipps, Dr. Lee, Dr. Ling Ling Lee, Ms. Sunny Ho), and Australia (Mrs. Denise Martin, Ms. Lisa Naylor, Mrs. Jennifer Katauskas).

At UCLA I was guided by Dr. Joseph Birdsell, Dr. Bernard Campbell, and Dr. Rainer Berger, as well as Dr. D. Lindburg, Dr. D. Simmons, Dr. Y. P. Chen, Dr. J. L. Kavanau, and Dr. P. Miller. I also thank Dr. C. Meighan, Dr. J. Sackett, Dr. S. Robbins, Dr. B. J. Williams, Dr. J. Hill, and Dr. Nicholson. I wish to express my deep gratitude to friends who sent packages to the field in the early days, including Mare Tiido, Maie Liiv, Judy Rassen, Dr. Jeff Jones, and Patrick Finnerty. I thank Tan, Fay, and Romeo Fabros for helping me with Binti when he was small.

The unfailing support of my friends and colleagues at Simon Fraser University has been invaluable. In particular, I thank past president Dr. Bill Saywell, current president Dr. John Stubbs, past Dean of Arts Dr. Bob Brown, Dr. Richard Shutler, Dr. Roy Carlson, Dr. Jack Nance, Professor Phil Hobler, Dr. Jon Driver, Dr. Dave Burley, Dr. Erle Nelson, Dr. Herb Alexander, Dr. Mark Skinner, Dr. Knut Fladmark, Dr. Brian Hayden, Dr. Alan McKillan, Dr. Charles Crawford, Dr. Stan Copp, Dr. Andy Beckenbacks, Dr. Martin Smith, Denise Kask, Ann Sullivan, Linda Bannister, Lynda Przubula, Andrew Barton, Jacqueline Duffy, Dr. Olga Klimko, Eldon Yellowhorn, and Cam Muir.

For their collegiality, advice, and support I especially thank Dr. Jane Goodall and the late Dr. Dian Fossey, Dr. Jeff Froelich, Dr. Alison Jolly (and her gracious husband, Richard), Dr. Ann Zeller, Dr. Ann Russon, Dr. Geza Teleki, Dr. Suzanne Chevalier-Skolnikoff, as well as former students Rosemary Power, Lyn Prestash, Howard Passell, Dr. Kim Bard, Dr. Nora Gillis, Dr. Ruth Hamilton, Juliet Craig, Jane Fitchen, and Wendy Hoole, and volunteers Dr. Clive Barrett, David Augeri, Luba Madjarow, Anna Mike, Patti Jones, Alexandria Denham, Lona and Martina Bertilsson. I am deeply grateful to Chancellor Tien, Dr. Yuan Lee, and Dr. Glenn Seaborg of the University of California at Berkeley.

I thank my former students from UNAS whose dedication and hard work in the field was extraordinary: Mr. Suharto Djojosudarmo, Mr. Jaumat Dulhaja, Mr. Jito Sugardjito, Mr. Endang Soekara, Dr. Barita Manulang, Dr. Yatna Supriatna, Mr. Dwi Sutano, Mr. Benny Djaya, Mr. Natusudraduat, Mr. Mahfudz Markaya, Mr. Dadang Kusmana, Mr. Richard Pattan, Mr. Pepen Abdullah, Mr. Benny Ismunadji, Mr. Toto Susilarto, Mr. Coke Gede Parthasuniya, Mr. Mudjiono, Mr. Mohammed Boang, Mr. Djoharly Debok, Mr. Undang Halim, Mr. Heru, Mr. Edy Hendras, Mr. Dayat, Mr. Yan Suriyana, Mr. Maulana, and Mr. Ichalas al Zackie. I am indebted to my local staff, both former and current: Mr. Hemat, Mr. Tumin, Mr. Dollah, Mr. Sehat, Mr. Achmad, Mrs. Bahriah, Mrs. Waliyati, Mr. Inu, Mrs. Ijun, Mrs. Rasi, Mr. Achyar, Mr. Atak, Mr. Uil, Mrs. Juni, Mrs. Naming, the late Mrs. Karmi and the late Mrs. Ernah, Mr. Tempelaku, Mr. Manis, Mr. Idai Laju, and Mr. Bagus Ardianraharjo. I also thank Dr. John Rideout, Dr. Giedraitis, Dr. W. S. Cheung, Dr. Chang, and my friend Mrs. Audrey Buell. I wish to express my deepest gratitude to Mr. Rod and Mrs. Yuni Brindamour. I thank Mr. Hartani Mukti, Mr. Aju and Mrs. Mardiana Chandra, and other friends in Pangkalan Bun. I thank Alex Pacheco and Jeanne Roush of PETA.

I thank my parents, Filomena and Antanas Galdikas, my sister Aldona, brother-in-law Harry Franz, and brothers Tony and Al for their tremendous support over the years. I thank Dr. Gary and Mrs. Inggriani Hartanto Shapiro and Lori Jenkins for their warm friendship and for their devotion to science and conservation, as I do Dr. Nancy and Rod, Eric and Nicole Briggs. Words are insufficient to express my appreciation. I am deeply grateful to Charlotte Lowell Grimm and Andrea Gorzitze for their wonderful friendship and dedication to protection of orangutans and forests. My thanks to them and to Pak Uil and Dr. Dale. I also thank dedicated volunteers Michelle Dujomovic (and her parents) and Alex Ebert for their strong and selfless support.

I thank my publisher Fredrica Friedman for her patience and belief in this book and my agent, Mike Hamilburg, for his strong friendship and support, as well as Stacy Holmes for being a gracious host and friend. I especially thank my editor, Ann Levine, for her guidance, inspiration, advice, sharp editorial pen, true friendship, and mutual love of orangutans. Finally, I thank my husband, Pak Bohap, and my children, Binti, Fred, and Jane for putting up with my long hours writing and for giving me the loving support I needed to write this book.

Biruté M. F. Galdikas
Pasir Panjang, September 1994